# Ways & Means

## THE ESPERTI PETERSON INSTITUTE CONTRIBUTORY SERIES

Eileen R. Sacco, Managing Editor

*Generations: Planning Your Legacy*
*Legacy: Plan, Protect, and Preserve Your Estate*
*Ways and Means: Maximize the Value of Your Retirement Savings*
*Wealth Enhancement and Preservation*, 2d ed.

# Ways & Means

## Maximize the Value of Your Retirement Savings

*Practical Answers
from America's Foremost
Retirement Planning Attorneys
and Financial Advisors*

— *A Special Edition* —

RICHARD L. RANDALL    SCOT W. OVERDORF

RICHARD L. OVERDORF

BRET A. OVERDORF

The editors and contributors are not engaged in rendering legal, tax, accounting, financial planning, investment or similar professional services. Examples in this text are used for illustrative purposes only and do not represent recommendations or actual results. While legal, tax, accounting, financial planning and investment issues covered in this book have been checked with sources believed to be reliable, some material may be affected by changes in the laws or in the interpretations of such laws since the manuscript for this book was completed. For that reason the accuracy and completeness of such information and the opinions based thereon are not guaranteed. In addition, state or local tax laws or procedural rules may have a material impact on the general recommendations made by the contributing authors, and the strategies outlined in this book may not be suitable for every individual.

Copyright © 1999 by Esperti Peterson Institute Incorporated. All rights reserved. No part of this book may be reproduced or used in any form or by any means, electronic or mechanical, including photocopy, recording, or by any information or retrieval system, without the prior written permission of the Institute.

ISBN 0-922943-07-9
Library of Congress Catalog Number 98-074337

Managing editor: Eileen Sacco

Project manager: Christy Allbee

Marketing services: Brian Budman, George Chamberlin, Reneé Garcia, Eric Johnson, Ling Lam, Lydia Monchak

Jacket designer: Richard Adelson

Composition, design, & editing services: C+S Gottfried, http://www.lookoutnow.com/dtp

Printed and bound in Canada by Quebecor Printing

**Esperti Peterson Institute Incorporated**
410 17th Street, Suite 1260
Denver, CO 80202

# Contents

| | | |
|---|---|---:|
| *Preface* | | *ix* |
| *Introduction* | | *xiii* |
| **CHAPTER 1** | RETIREMENT PLANNING GOALS | 1 |
| | The Importance of Retirement Planning | 2 |
| | When to Start Planning for Retirement | 4 |
| | Starting to Save for Retirement | 6 |
| | Beginning the Planning Process | 11 |
| | Approaching Retirement | 24 |
| | Working with Advisors | 31 |
| | Income Analysis | 43 |
| **Chapter 2** | EMPLOYER-SPONSORED RETIREMENT PLANS | 61 |
| | Types of Employer-Sponsored Plans | 62 |
| | Qualified Plans | 63 |
| | Nonqualified Plans | 93 |
| | Tax-Sheltered Annuities | 112 |
| **Chapter 3** | INDIVIDUAL RETIREMENT ACCOUNTS | 115 |
| | Types of IRAs | 116 |
| | Features of IRAs | 118 |

| | | |
|---|---|---|
| Deductible IRAs | | 130 |
| Roth IRAs | | 134 |
| Rollovers to Roth IRAs | | 137 |
| Education IRAs | | 140 |
| **Chapter 4** | INVESTING FOR RETIREMENT | 143 |
| Investment Principles | | 144 |
| Investment Vehicles | | 167 |
| Investment Strategies | | 188 |
| Investing with Existing Retirement Plans | | 241 |
| **Chapter 5** | ANNUITIES | 247 |
| Annuities in General | | 248 |
| Types of Annuities | | 257 |
| Multiple Annuities | | 270 |
| Exchanges or Rollovers | | 271 |
| Surrendering Annuities | | 273 |
| Tax Aspects of Annuities | | 274 |
| Tax Planning | | 278 |
| Gifts of Annuities | | 281 |
| Qualified Annuities | | 284 |
| **Chapter 6** | DISTRIBUTIONS FROM RETIREMENT PLANS | 289 |
| Early-Distribution Rules | | 291 |
| Minimum Distribution Rules | | 312 |
| Death before the Required Beginning Date | | 335 |
| Calculating RMD | | 338 |
| Death after the Required Beginning Date | | 353 |
| Beneficiaries | | 366 |
| **Chapter 7** | ESTATE PLANNING AND RETIREMENT PLANS | 373 |
| Coordinating Retirement Planning and Estate Planning | | 374 |

| | | |
|---|---|---|
| The Family Trust | | 389 |
| Planning for Spouses | | 393 |
| Income Taxes | | 402 |
| Estate Taxes | | 404 |
| Charitable Planning with Retirement Funds | | 417 |

**appendix A** *The Contributory Book Series*
*and Protocol for Ways and Means* ........................ 443

History of the Contributory Book Series ........................ 443

Protocol ........................ 445

**appendix B** *Contributing Authors* ........................ 451

*Index* ........................ 467

# Preface

*Ways and Means* is the product of a unique collaboration between financial advisors and attorneys. This interdisciplinary approach makes perfect sense for a book on retirement planning because the topic spans income and investment planning, long the domain of financial planners, and estate tax and distribution, traditionally the realm of attorneys. Thus, by drawing on both specialized fields, *Ways and Means* is able to present a truly comprehensive view of retirement planning and its related topics.

The fifty-four authors who contributed to Ways and Means are affiliated with one another through their participation in organizations founded by Robert A. Esperti and Renno L. Peterson. Every attorney contributor is a member of the National Network of Estate Planning Attorneys, and some are participants or graduates of the Esperti Peterson Institute's Masters Program for Wealth Strategies Planning. Many of the financial advisor contributors are participants in the Institute's Financial Masters Program. All the financial advisors work closely with National Network attorneys in a team setting to best serve their mutual clients.

The National Network and Esperti Peterson Institute are recognized as cutting-edge institutions that have significantly enhanced the quality of estate and wealth planning in the United States. Both organizations encourage professionals to work together for the benefit of their mutual clients in order to offer the best and most effective planning possible. They believe that when professionals work together to combine their respective talents and skills—rather than compete with one another—clients and professionals alike are the winners. As a demonstration of this principle, the Institute has published *Ways and Means*—its first contributory book containing input from both attorneys and financial professionals.

*Ways and Means* is not an annotated reference book intended to cover everything about retirement planning in great detail. All of our contributing authors were challenged with a single goal: to provide the reader with the best possible answers to the questions they are most frequently asked by their clients.

The consistency of the questions provided by the contributors reinforced our belief that most families have similar concerns regardless of differences in their cultures, economics, and geography. This consistency has been the highlight of every Institute contributory book project.

The responses of our contributing authors reflected their differing professional views, feelings, and emotions with regard to virtually every retirement planning issue. As editors, we have attempted to blend these differences into an overall perspective that will provide the reader with the best overview and understanding possible. At times, we have included similar questions with differing responses in order to present a variety of good approaches and allow the reader to decide which one he or she would be most comfortable with.

Readers will find a subtle repetitiveness in the text. Rather than referring readers back and forth among several sections or chapters of the book, we have attempted, whenever possible, to include some of the same information in different sections. Our goal was to ensure that readers can turn to virtually any section and find complete information. If you read *Ways and Means* from cover to cover, you will doubtless encounter repetition. If you skip around, reading specific sections, you'll have all the background information necessary to understand each topic.

*Ways and Means* contains the most current information available on retirement planning. Many statistics relevant to this topic are indexed for inflation, however, and not yet available for 1998. For this reason, our contributing authors have had to use 1997 figures in some of their explanations. In all cases, the theories and strategies behind the figures are completely up to date and incorporate the latest legislation affecting retirement planning.

As with all general reference works, the reader should be careful not to treat the information in *Ways and Means* as a recommendation for any particular course of action in individual circumstances. No other concept came through to us more clearly as editors than the diversity of successful strategies available to individuals, as well as the damage that can result from inappropriately implementing the wrong strategy. We specifically recommend that in planning for your retirement you seek advice from competent professionals in each relevant discipline. We hope this book will motivate you to do just that.

We are proud of the efforts of our contributing authors in bringing you such practical information and strategies to effectively implement retirement planning. We especially wish to thank Richard L. Overdorf and Bret A. Overdorf for their contributions to *Ways and Means* and are honored to dedicate this special edition to them.

Richard L. Randall
Scot W. Overdorf
October 1998

# Introduction

*Richard L. Overdorf*
*Bret A. Overdorf*

We are grateful for the opportunity to participate in *Ways and Means*. Contributing to the material in this book has been an exciting experience. You will find that the question-and-answer format gets to the heart of matters much more quickly than the usual, continuous-text approach. Our contribution comes from many years of face-to-face planning, involving all phases of our clients' personal and business lives.

Regardless of people's ages, retirement planning is a common denominator in our country today. Because so much information exists on the topic of retirement planning, it could take you a significant amount of time to identify the essential aspects that affect you. We sincerely hope the information provided in *Ways and Means* will help you to quickly and easily understand some of the complexities surrounding various retirement issues.

The Overdorf organization has 36 years of experience working with individuals and businesses in all areas of financial services. It specializes in retirement, insurance, estate, investment, income tax, and business succession planning. As an association of advisors, the organization consists of financial professionals from independent corporations who work together within their areas of expertise to develop solutions tailored to each client's unique circumstances. Overdorf Financial Services, Inc., is a solution-oriented firm with a tradition of kind, friendly, courteous service provided with integrity.

We believe the key to learning in today's multifaceted financial environment is repetition. As we implement multilevel solutions for clients, we help the clients expand their knowledge of complex planning concepts and we show how those concepts relate to their specific financial circumstances. To accomplish this, we meet with each client at least annually, using a checklist to review all aspects of his or her financial plan. The discussion involves education, review, and proposed solutions unique to the client's personality, needs, and goals.

We have truly been blessed and find our practice growing through client referral. It is very rewarding to see our clients grow and mature both personally and financially. Many of our clients have expanded their business structure to include multiple entities to accomplish their financial dreams and desires.

**Acknowledgments**
We would like to thank God for providing several individuals who have helped us develop and expand the Overdorf organization over the years. Without their help we would not be able to provide the quality products and services that our loyal clients so richly deserve. Special thanks goes to Scot Overdorf for his encouragement and guidance in this book and for the contributions he and Tanya Overdorf have made to the estate planning process. We are indebted to our associates, Monte Lively and Bruce Cain, for their loyalty to us and for the countless hours they have spent assisting us on this book. Also, thanks go to Dawn Dempsey for technical research and help in many areas. We truly have been blessed with an excellent supportive staff and appreciate their help in this endeavor.

Last, and most of all, our thanks and gratitude go to our families. From Richard: To Rita, who has been there from the beginning and helped structure the organization. Thanks for being you. From Bret: To my family, for being my reason to balance time at home with time at work. Special thanks to my wife Carol, for her godly, loving support, and to my dear children, Jordan and Rachael. With you I am well pleased.

Richard L. Overdorf has specialized in estate tax, fringe benefit, investment, and insurance planning for more than 36 years. He has extensive experience participating in seminars given for associations, societies, and groups. Mr. Overdorf is the owner of Overdorf Financial Services, Inc., a Registered Investment Advisor and Registered Securities Representative. He earned his Chartered Life Underwriter (CLU) designation in 1970.

Bret A. Overdorf devotes his practice to income, estate, and financial planning. He is responsible for the entity structure and continued planning for more than 600 farm, business, and professional clients. Mr. Overdorf has practiced as a certified public accountant (CPA) for 12 years and has earned his Certified Financial Planner (CFP) designation.

# chapter 1

## Retirement Planning Goals

This chapter is a "potpourri" of essential information for creating an effective retirement plan. Our contributing authors have provided "big-picture" questions and answers covering material that serves as the foundation for the rest of the text. One of the most striking results of our research is how important our authors believe the psychological factors are in formulating a successful retirement planning strategy.

In this chapter you will find answers to why, when, and how you should plan for retirement, as well as useful observations on the psychological barriers to successful planning. The importance of building an interdisciplinary retirement planning team is also discussed. Our contributors share what to look for in an advisor from each discipline, as well as what role to assign to each of the professionals on the team.

Finally, in this chapter we begin the important task of determining how much money you'll need to comfortably retire. The importance of setting measurable, specific goals, and the need to carefully and accurately quantify what you'll need to do to develop a retirement plan that will ensure the accomplishment of those goals, is, for most people, both sobering and motivating.

## THE IMPORTANCE
## OF RETIREMENT PLANNING

*I keep hearing about the dangers of dwindling Social Security and employer-provided retirement benefits. Should I plan for these shortfalls in my retirement funds?*

The retirement planning system in the United States is a three-legged stool. The three legs represent federal benefits, employer benefits, and individual (or employee) contributions. In the current economic condition, the strongest leg—the largest part of the retirement plan—should be individual contributions.

A great deal has been said about the low savings rate in the United States. This lack of wealth accumulation for retirement planning stems in part from our society's traditional dependency on Social Security. However, given the baby boomers' pending economic strain on the Social Security system, together with the reduction in employer benefits brought on by increasingly complex retirement planning tax laws, there has never been a more critical time for individuals to assume more responsibility for their own retirement planning funds.

*Should I count on Social Security's being available to me?*

We know that Social Security has a rather large unfunded liability. Estimates vary, but all seem to indicate that the program, as it is, will be broke within a number of years.

Art Laffer, economist, author, and University of Chicago pro-

# Chap. 1: Retirement Planning Goals

fessor, recently said that if the age for retiring and beginning to collect Social Security is extended to 71, we can eliminate the program's unfunded liability completely. He feels that this is a reasonable solution since people are tending to live and work longer. An alternative scenario of this type could be included in your planning model.

### Why should I plan for retirement?

Fewer and fewer workers are supporting a larger contingent of elderly dependents within the Social Security system. Although our government continues to state that Social Security is "sacred," many people have already realized that they cannot rely solely on Social Security benefits at retirement—benefits may not be available to certain income classes of retirees, or they may not provide sufficient income—and that they may have to work longer before they retire.

In addition, Medicare costs are continuing to "spiral out of control," and politicians have been focusing on curbing Medicare spending. With continual cutbacks in Medicare payments, physicians are being forced to decide whether or not certain services can be provided to patients. This is a perplexing issue and one which affects all citizens wanting and needing health services.

What all this means is that you, as an individual, are responsible for taking care of your "golden years" of retirement—hopefully, in a way that enables you to retire with dignity and without having to supplement your retirement income needs by working at minimum-wage jobs.

### How long can I expect to be retired?

Longer than you think! Retirement is a relatively new concept. Around the turn of the century, a 61-year-old was expected to live another 1.2 years—a life expectancy of 62.2 years. People worked and then died. Over the past 60 years, life expectancies have steadily increased: today the life expectancy of a 61-year-old is another 20 years, and the fear of dying prematurely is being replaced by the fear of outliving one's money. Life expectancies are expected to continue increasing.

If you work until age 55 and then live to age 90, it is quite possible that you will be retired longer than you worked. This is one of the main reasons the Social Security system is in trouble, and it is why you need to make certain that you have enough financial resources to sustain yourself for a long time.

*Is planning for retirement more important for a single-income family than for a two-income family?*

No. Planning for retirement is equally important for both types of families. In two-income families, however, it's particularly important that the spouses discuss how they're going to retire and agree on what they're going to do. There are additional psychological issues with married participants when both are working and generating income—one may be psychologically ready to retire while the other may want to continue working. When does each plan to retire? What will the retired spouse do if the other is still working? These issues need to be addressed—and prepared for—in the retirement planning process.

## WHEN TO START PLANNING FOR RETIREMENT

*When should I start planning to retire?*

Retirement can seem like a foreboding, mysterious, scary event somewhere off in the future, an event that we don't like to define. Thinking about it necessitates our dealing with how long we will work and how long we will live to enjoy the fruits of our labors. That's why postponing retirement planning is easy to do. As we get into our fifties and sixties, without having planned for retire-

## CHAP. 1: RETIREMENT PLANNING GOALS

ment, we have the critical problem of how to maintain a comfortable lifestyle when earned income stops.

For this reason, the best time to address retirement is *today.* Time is the most valuable commodity in retirement planning. Most people are unaware of the impact a small investment made each year can have toward achieving their retirement objectives. It's impossible to make up even 1 year that you wait to start saving—so start now, even if you save a smaller amount than you would like.

*I'm a long way from retirement—why do I need to know anything about retirement planning now?*

Too often people don't learn about retirement planning and the decisions they must make until they attend a retirement seminar a few years, months, or even weeks before their retirement. At that time, they are under a great deal of stress about their upcoming retirement and are often unable to cope with all the decisions that must be made. Therefore, they frequently make decisions which do not reflect their real goals, needs, objectives, and values and which often inadequately protect them, their assets, and their loved ones.

The younger you are and the sooner you start planning, the easier it will be to accomplish your goals. If people would learn the value of retirement planning and the power of compounding at an early age, there would be many more 40-year-old millionaires and 50-year-old retirees.

*I'm only 25 years old. Why should I start investing for retirement now?*

There are three reasons why: time, time, and more time. The compounding of returns can be staggering over a 45-year period as opposed to only 15 or 20 years, especially in a tax-deferred account. For example, if you begin a tax-deferred IRA at age 20, invest $2000 after-tax per year, and earn 10 percent per annum, you will have $1,437,810 in the account by the time you turn 65. If you invest the same after-tax $2000 per year in the same investments but pay the income tax on the earnings on those investments at the combined federal and state bracket of 30 percent, you will have only $571,491 at age 65.

Using the same assumptions but beginning at age 30, you will have $542,049 at age 65 in your tax-deferred IRA but only $276,474 with a non-tax-deferred investment.

An early start, even a modest early start, can guarantee a comfortable retirement for nearly everyone, provided the funds are invested wisely.

*I have a small family business, and I can use any money the business earns for my needs. Why should I even think about having a retirement plan now when there are more important things I can do with my business earnings?*

There may never be a time when there are no "more important" things to do. For many small-business owners, the business is the largest asset owned. Owners should consider the result of having 100 percent of their investments tied into the family business. Some businesses go out of business, while others may not be marketable at retirement time—and there may be nothing else to fall back on. It is often recommended that a retirement program be put into place for diversification and as a safety net. Before dismissing the idea of using a tax-qualified retirement plan, you should seek the advice of a financial professional who can help integrate your current and future needs into one package. In this way, your business can support all your needs.

## STARTING TO SAVE
## FOR RETIREMENT

*Why is systematic saving for retirement so important?*

The greatest financial security most individuals achieve results

## Chap. 1: Retirement Planning Goals

from putting aside money on a regular, automatic basis before they ever see or even consider it as "spendable." Such saving can be done through pension plans, 401(k) plans, salary saving plans, employer-sponsored plans, and individual investments. This "forgotten" money compounds year after year, so when you need money for retirement, it is there. This approach also establishes the habit of simply saving money, which is critical if you are to retire someday and no longer have an earned income.

### ⋺ *Why do most of us not plan for retirement?*

There are numerous reasons, but studies show that the following are the major contributing factors:

- *Procrastination:* In the early years, our desire to consume, the expenses of our growing families, and education costs delay retirement savings. Paying off debt also seems to outrank the need to save for retirement.

- *Inability to focus on retirement years:* People believe that somehow retirement income will "happen." But company plans and Social Security provide only a portion of the income necessary.

- *Failure to define retirement objectives:* Most people have only a vague idea of what it will take to have adequate retirement income. Without a clear picture, an effective plan can't be developed.

- *Ignorance about the use of money and how to get the most from it:* With the busy schedules we have today, managing work and family, there is little time left for people to educate themselves about all their retirement planning options.

- *Failure to understand tax laws:* Tax deductibility, deferral, and leveraging are not well understood by the public.

### ⋺ *It's really hard for me to stick with any kind of a savings plan. Any suggestions?*

Many people find it difficult to make a commitment to something and carry it out. Commitment, however, is the critical aspect of retirement planning. One way to become committed to saving is to have a retirement plan in conjunction with your employment. In many companies, an employee can make a voluntary contribution that the employer puts in trust for the employee. In some instances, the employer will even match the employee's contribution to some extent. The funds in trust are normally not accessible without penalties until the employee reaches age 59½, so there is a natural deterrent to taking the money out early. Also, if you participate in such a plan and your employer is making a contribution equal to all or part of what you are contributing, there is more incentive for you to save because you know you will lose the "free dollars" matched by your employer if you do not contribute. With such a strong inducement, you might find it easier to focus on the long term.

*Save for retirement? Where am I going to get the money to save?*

Although the media have drawn much attention to the importance of planning for retirement, the reality of saving money can be difficult with the financial demands of everyday life. Most financial experts recommend that a person save a minimum of 10 percent of his or her income to prepare for a comfortable retirement—a time which, for some people, could be longer than the time they spent working. Unfortunately, the average savings rate in the United States is the lowest of the industrial countries— 4.5 percent of income earned.

*Why do Americans have such poor saving habits?*

Most Americans don't have the time or the money to save for what they want. With so much credit available, they just use their credit cards indiscriminately and say "Charge it." The result, unfortunately, is that most Americans have a tendency to focus on their short-term needs and lose sight of their long-term goals,

CHAP. 1: RETIREMENT PLANNING GOALS 9

such as retirement. Collectively, our greatest challenge is halting this overall trend and becoming a nation of savers rather than one of spenders.

*Retirement is really important to me, but I seem to spend all the money I have. I don't know how I'll ever save for retirement! What can I do?*

As they near retirement, people often have too much debt and seem to overspend instead of getting ready for their retirement years. There's no easy answer to this dilemma, but discipline is necessary to reorder and realign one's life today to get ready for tomorrow.

This realignment may include some pretty difficult decisions, like selling highly mortgaged real estate and changing spending patterns in order to start saving even small amounts of money today rather than postponing saving. Working into our sixties and seventies with the same interest, strength, and conviction we had in our thirties and forties is not easy, so reducing debt is a must for most of us.

*I know I need to save, but I don't know where to get started. Any suggestions?*

It's good that you recognize the need to save. Saving is a very personal matter, and it requires that you establish priorities: Are you willing to spend less today in order to have a financially comfortable future? Once you make saving for retirement a priority, you need to actively work toward your goal: Is there something you can do to remind yourself to take actions that promote good financial habits?

Here are several steps that will help you start planning for your financial future:

1. *Review your monthly expenditures.* Divide your expenses into fixed expenses—those that recur on a regular basis and must

be covered (mortgages, car payments, necessary costs of daily life, etc.)—and variable expenses—those that occur sporadically and often can be eliminated (the costs of luxury items, a vacation, movie tickets, etc.).

    **2.** *Calculate your monthly net income.* If you are spending more than you are taking in, you must get a handle on your expenses. Look for variable expenses that can be eliminated to ensure that your income is greater than your expenditures.

    **3.** *Budget your living expenses.* Allocate your funds so that you are capable of building a reserve for emergencies. If you have high consumer debt, consolidate and "surf." Surfing the credit card world is pretty easy today. You may be able to consolidate your cards and accounts into one account with a very low first-year introductory rate. Keep paying at the same level as before, and you will rapidly pay down the debt. The important point is to develop a lifestyle that prevents excessive use of credit in the future; your goal is to eventually eliminate your debt and use your cash reserves only in emergencies. Don't forget to lower your budgeted expenses after your debt is fully retired.

*All this is well and good, but I'm totally broke. How could setting up a retirement plan possibly be useful to me?*

Even if you have to finance a retirement plan by borrowing money in the short run—and particularly if the interest you pay is tax-deductible—you will actually be better off in the long run with a retirement program. Even the after-tax IRA will prove to be beneficial for people with modest financial means (more so for people in higher brackets). Remember, the government has created strong inducements to lead people away from their reliance on Social Security and Medicare for their retirement income. These inducements are available to everyone, not just the rich.

# BEGINNING
## THE PLANNING PROCESS

*I have no idea what I want to do at retirement or even when I want to retire. How can I plan with no clear goals in mind?*

You can't! Remember the adage, "If you don't know where you're going, you'll probably end up somewhere else." However, even if you haven't made any specific decisions about your retirement, you can still put together a flexible retirement plan that will be of benefit no matter what you decide later on.

*What are some of the things my spouse and I should consider as we formulate our retirement goals?*

Retirement can be one of the most fulfilling parts of life, or it can be dull and empty. How it turns out for you depends in large part upon how you *and* your spouse view retirement. Each of you should ask, *"What does a fulfilling retirement mean to me?"* To help elaborate in answering this fundamental question, you and your spouse should ask yourselves the following questions and discuss your answers with each other:

- What am I doing now that I'd like to do less of?
- What would I like to learn or be doing more of?
- During the remainder of my lifetime, what is the most significant thing I would like to accomplish?
- How will I know when I have achieved financial independence?
- Where do I want the relationship with my spouse to take us?
- What do I want for my family?
- How do I want to grow spiritually?
- What lasting thing would I like to do for my church, school, and community?

12 WAYS AND MEANS

- How do I define good health now, and how will I define it at older ages?
- To what places would I like to travel?
- Would I like to live elsewhere?

This exercise does two very important things. First, it helps you better define your core values. Second, it helps you better envision your retirement. If you and your spouse have a clear vision of what your retirement should be, it is easier to plan for it and make the transition into it. That makes your retirement an attractive goal as a new phase of your life, and not just an escape hatch from your job.

*Since retirement brings up future fantasies, I need simple, concrete, meaningful steps to help keep my dream a reality. Do you have any tips that are easy to remember?*

Yes, here are a few basic tips.

Set exciting retirement goals (travel, etc.); make sure your goals are realistic, meaningful, measurable, and attainable. Put those goals in writing; prioritize your retirement goals according to which are the most important to you. Don't be afraid to set ambitious goals, and reward yourself when you progress toward your goals.

A goal is the first step toward achieving your financial objectives. Remember, only assets create wealth, and wealth is largely a result of good habits. Many years ago Henry Ford said, "Believe you can, believe you can't. Either way you're going to be right."

*Do people today generally want to work later in their lives?*

While many people today are choosing to work well past traditional retirement age, an increasing number of individuals are finding it a financial necessity more than a personal choice. It's not unusual today to see older-age individuals taking on part-time jobs or second careers or simply staying in their present work

# CHAP. 1: RETIREMENT PLANNING GOALS

situation well into their retirement years to make up for shortfalls in their retirement savings. Early retirement planning is a must to avoid facing those extra years of required work.

> *What role, if any, should my children and grandchildren play in my retirement planning process?*

They should have very little, if any, role in the planning process itself, but they should play a substantial role in the psychological aspects of retirement planning. In particular, your long-term-care needs and their impact on your children and grandchildren should be addressed—as should your need to physically relocate to be near your children and grandchildren. With loneliness being one of the major retirement problems, relocation—if necessary— to be near family members should be a primary consideration in every retirement plan. Planning for these psychological aspects of retirement not only will make your retirement years more enjoyable but also may reduce your financial dependency on your children, grandchildren, and other family members.

> *Should I do anything to assist my children, such as setting something aside for their retirement?*

You can do for them what is often difficult for young people to do for themselves. With continual economic realignment and the downsizing of corporate bureaucracies in favor of smaller and more nimble companies, it is very unlikely they will stay with one, two, or even three companies for their entire careers. Planning strategies like the stretch-out IRA, discussed later in this book, allow for astronomical continued tax-deferred growth of your retirement plan for the benefit of your loved ones long after you're gone.

> *We've been thinking about a retirement plan, but can't seem to get started. How should we begin?*

At some point action must replace thought. The finest thoughts and plans are worthless until executed. Each objective should be well-defined and clearly understood by everyone involved. Unless you really know and understand what you are trying to accomplish, you probably will not succeed.

Good retirement objectives are generally stated in quantitative terms. A comment such as "I want a safe and secure retirement income" does not provide much guidance for retirement planning. It merely expresses a wish that, although very real to you, is hard to put into effective terms and plans. Only by attaching numbers to your objectives can you measure your progress.

Each objective should have a time limit for accomplishment.

Finally, make sure you prioritize your objectives, and you are on your way!

## Financial Considerations

*Can you recommend a good book that will help me get started financially?*

There are several books that we highly recommend for laypersons. The principles shared in these books are easy to understand, financially correct, and powerful when put to the test:

- *The Richest Man from Babylon,* George Clason (Penguin, 1972)
- *The Wealthy Barber,* David Chilton (Prima, 1991)
- *The Wise Investor,* Neil E. Elmouchi, ChFC (Dunhill & West, 1997)

*How do I begin setting my financial goals?*

By using the traditional comprehensive financial planning process, you can determine your financial needs for your retirement. You can begin this yourself or seek the advice of a financial professional. The process includes the following steps:

# Chap. 1: Retirement Planning Goals

1. Gather the data that relates to your present financial situation.

2. Outline your financial goals and expectations for retirement.

3. Identify the shortfall between your needs and your resources.

4. Decide on investment, tax, and estate planning strategies.

5. Implement.

6. Review regularly.

*How do we develop our financial goals and expectations?*

You need to budget for your anticipated financial needs. Make a budget for today. What changes would need to be made to this budget if today were the first day of your retirement? Plan for a comfortable standard of living with savings for emergencies. Would your housing be the same; would you need the same clothing and personal care; would your food requirements change; how about medical expenses and transportation? You also need to have enough protection in life, health, disability, property, and liability insurance coverage. In other words, you need to reflect upon the changes that will probably occur at retirement and then use that projected budget as the basis for your financial goal planning, adjusted for cost-of-living increases. Do you want to work part-time during your retirement? or truly be retired? or have the option to decide then?

Having answered these questions, you can begin the process of determining the amount of money that you will require to support your retirement needs and where it will come from.

At what age do you want to retire? Traditionally, most companies and the U.S. government defined "normal retirement" as occurring at age 65. Today, many retirement plans define "normal retirement" as beginning at age 67 to 70. For many individuals, however, the goal is still to retire at an earlier age. You need to determine your anticipated benefits at any planned retirement age, and see if the amount meets your needs. If not, you may need to delay your anticipated date of retirement or adjust some of your other goals.

*I'm ready to make a commitment to retirement planning. What do I need to concern myself with, and what's the best way to go about it?*

There are three critical time periods in retirement planning:

1. *Contribution stage:* If possible, make contributions of money that are tax-deductible so that the money you would have paid in taxes is also compounding.

2. *Accumulation stage:* After you make contributions, it is possible to have those monies accumulate on your behalf for retirement in some way without incurring current taxable income. There are opportunities available for your earnings to grow tax-deferred or even tax-free. (This is discussed in detail in Chapter 6.)

3. *Distribution stage:* When you begin taking distributions from your retirement accounts, you will want to do so in the most tax- efficient ways possible. There are ways to structure receipt of your retirement funds to provide you with the best financial and tax advantages. (This is also discussed in detail in Chapter 6.)

*How will we know if we have enough to retire?*

It is difficult to identify the amount of cash needed to effect a change in lifestyle, which is really what retirement is. However, defining how much you will need financially to maintain your new lifestyle is vital to determining whether you are financially ready.

Think about how your time will be spent. It is usually assumed that cash needs at retirement decrease, but every situation is different. Consider the case of two retired bank presidents of the same age and health who have similar compensation structures and net worths. One enjoys the contemplative life at his fishing cabin in the North. He loves his relaxed, casual life, works a huge garden, teaches his grandchildren the lore of the woods,

CHAP. 1: RETIREMENT PLANNING GOALS    17

and has taken over most of the cooking from his wife. They visit and are visited by a close network of loving family and friends and are extremely happy at their leisure. His counterpart participates on several charity boards, plays golf almost daily, and has joined two new country clubs near his second warm-climate home. He and his wife entertain lavishly, travel extensively, and glory in the fact that they now have time to enjoy and indulge their children and grandchildren with an annual family cruise. Life is good for both couples. However, each requires completely different financial planning.

Having leisure time means making choices. If you are old enough to retire, you are old enough to know that it is very easy to drift on the whims of others unless you have thought through and defined a course for yourself.

### ⩗ *How much should I try to save for retirement?*

Good question. Today's 65-year-old has a 1-in-4 chance of living to age 90. If you stop working at age 65 and live to age 90, you'll need 25 years of retirement income! In the ideal world, your retirement nest egg should be substantial enough for you to live comfortably off the earnings. In a 28 percent tax bracket, which assumes no state taxes, in order to provide a $25,000 after-tax retirement income, an account growing at a total return of 8 percent must have a nest egg of over $434,000. If you want your retirement income to be $40,000, the account must have more than $694,400.

### ⩗ *How else can I prepare myself financially for retirement?*

Another good way to prepare for retirement is to put yourself into "practice" retirement. Set your postretirement budget and live by it on a trial basis. See how you feel about the adjustments you'll need to make.

*Why do we need to include estate planning in our financial goals?*

Your retirement plan may very well be the largest asset you own. While the person you choose to be the beneficiary of your retirement plan is purely a personal decision, the impact of that decision will have financial and tax consequences to you as the participant as well as to the beneficiaries ultimately inheriting the funds.

The tax laws governing your decision are complex; without proper advice, you may be playing Russian roulette with funds which have taken you decades to accumulate. You may sabotage your ability to structure a retirement plan to meet your needs, goals, and desires for ensuring your lifestyle, and you may also forfeit strategic planning that could increase the wealth you leave to your loved ones.

*In the past, I've been impatient in my planning. It's so hard to look 10 or 20 years into the future. Do you have some suggestions?*

Patience and discipline are critical to proper retirement planning. People who lack either the patience or the discipline to follow through on a long-range plan will end up, at the least, with a number of nonaligned objectives or ill-conceived strategies and will possibly be unable to realize their retirement dreams.

Retirement planning success depends upon:

- Setting reasonable expectations
- Being tax-efficient
- Being willing to accept and properly monitor risk
- Having discipline and patience
- Continually educating yourself or having a professional advisor who keeps up to date
- Periodically reevaluating your plan

CHAP. 1: RETIREMENT PLANNING GOALS                    19

■ Knowing when to start and when enough is enough

*How exact do I have to be in developing my financial goals when there are still 15 or 20 years before I retire?*

It's very difficult to be exact in retirement planning. There are simply too many changes that will occur between now and retirement. Investment return rates will change, future tax rates and tax laws will change, your life expectancy and the life expectancies of your family members will change, or extraordinary needs for cash, such as for college or graduate school, may occur. Nevertheless, it is critical to determine retirement targets and goals as best you can. Decide what to do and how to get there, and then begin your journey toward those goals. You will make plenty of adjustments as you go along, but it is important that you at least start now to point yourself in the right direction.

*What special concerns are there if I am self-employed?*

Since you do not have the advantage of an employer contributing to your retirement plan, you will have to structure a plan and make contributions to it on your own. This requires a great amount of discipline on your part.

*I work for a large company which has a retirement plan. How do I determine exactly what benefits I will receive so that I can decide whether I should supplement the plan with my own individual retirement plan?*

Most companies have benefit summary booklets that make it easier for participants to understand their retirement plans. If your company has one, you should carefully review the information it contains. If you can't get a summary with the current values of what you have in your plan and what your rights are under the plan, you should contact your company's human resource department and obtain a copy of the most recent information. There is probably an individual in the human resource department who can help you with your questions.

*What are the financial considerations if we want to relocate to a different region of the country?*

You need to compare the costs of living in the new region with those in your present location. Consider, for example, taxes from all sources, utility costs, vehicle licensing fees, housing costs, and expenses of daily living.

A major consideration is your health and health insurance. Is your insurance portable with full benefits? How are the hospitals in the new region? During a convalescence or an extended illness, how will you manage if there are no close relatives or adult children nearby?

Try to schedule your vacations at different times of the year and spend them in the area you are considering. This form of "practice retirement" will help you identify any possible shortcomings related to the area or differences between your anticipated lifestyle and the region's actual lifestyle—you may find that you need more or less retirement income than you anticipated.

*I've always wanted to run my own business, and I have enough money vested in my company's retirement plan to retire and open a home-based business on the Internet. What sorts of concerns should I have about this move?*

There are many considerations in forming a new business. A complete discussion of the topic is beyond the scope of this book; however, because your situation is somewhat common, a few comments are in order.

You must conduct a personal assessment to determine if you are suited to running your own business. Remember, nearly two out of every three businesses fail financially within the first 5 years. Does your business need to make money? Typically, finan-

CHAP. 1: RETIREMENT PLANNING GOALS 21

cial failure is the result of poor management and poor planning. To determine whether you have the unique personality and character traits to succeed financially at your own business, you should ask yourself a number of questions:

- Are you willing to spend 6 months to a year researching and preparing for launching your venture?

- Are you willing to use professional advisors, such as lawyers and accountants, in starting it up, or do you plan on doing this yourself? Surveys indicate that 90 percent of successful businesses used professional advisors at start-up, while 75 percent of failed businesses did not. Also, the professionals can possibly assist you in weeding out scams.

- Have you taken courses in the field of the business, and do you subscribe to the industry publications pertaining to it?

- Do you have modest expectations of income? Financial failures tend to be the businesspersons who vastly overestimate (by three times the successful start-ups, according to one recent survey) the net income they would make from their ventures.

- Do you have to start a new business, or is there an existing operation you can buy so that you can see past performance?

- Most importantly: Will your new business jeopardize either the resources necessary for your retirement or your purpose in retiring (e.g., more time with friends and family)?

Carefully consider these questions and discuss them with your loved ones and your advisors before launching into something totally new.

## Psychological Considerations

*I love what I do. Why should I retire at age 65?*

You shouldn't! Too many people are programmed by their families, society, and their work environments to believe that their productivity ends at midnight of their sixty-fifth birthday. This isn't so. If you truly love what you do, then by all means, continue to do it.

People stay young because of their contributions to society. There is indeed a "psychological adjustment period" that all retirees go through as they make the transition from being important in the workplace to being important someplace else. *What are you going to do the day you retire?* It is vitally important that you have a plan which specifies where you are going. Your mind should be excited about this new adventure, this new challenge. Don't fall into the trap of retiring *from* somewhere; instead, create the opportunity to *go* someplace else! Contributions to society are different for different people. You are valuable today—stay that way.

⊁ *What are some of the nonfinancial retirement issues for which I should be prepared?*

We spend all our lives preparing for our careers. We gain assistance from many sources, and decades are spent in our preparation and mastery of a chosen discipline. In contrast, retirement, which statistically can last longer than a typical career, gets little or no attention until we're almost upon it. As our society ages, more people are becoming acutely aware of this anomaly. The key is to plan early.

Redefining oneself and *retiring to something* are essential. Everyone experiences career withdrawal symptoms to various degrees. You will no longer be the department head, vice president in charge of finance, company president, master carpenter, or local chapter authority on "whatever." Your professional career will have ended. Your environment will change dramatically, the respect you once garnered may diminish, fewer people will come to you for assistance or advice, and, believe it or not, you can begin to feel left out. There is only so much that needs to be

## CHAP. 1: RETIREMENT PLANNING GOALS     23

done around the house and only so much fly-fishing, golf, or tennis you can play. Your children and grandchildren will be off making their own lives, and your spouse has his or her own life too.

During our careers we base a great deal of what we do and why we do it on psychological rather than financial rewards. If we are financially able to retire, money will not be the major concern; boredom, and the feeling of uselessness, can be of concern. Retiring *to* something can help replace the psychological fulfillment we leave behind with our careers and can provide a means by which we can stay connected, active, and vital.

*We want to live in a warmer climate when we retire. Are there nonfinancial issues we should consider in advance?*

There are many factors that must be considered when moving, psychological as well as financial. When you relocate, you basically cut yourself off from all the contacts and social interaction that sustained you. These include your children, service club, church, coworkers, neighbors, golf buddies, bridge club, relatives, the scenery, changes in seasons, the local newspaper, and even friendly faces at retail establishments you frequent.

Don't base your decision on just one or two visits at the same time of year. Phoenix, Arizona, in July is very different from Phoenix in January. Don't stay at a vacation resort; rather, try an extended stay in the residential area in which you will actually live. Do you want to live with only other retirees or in a demographically diverse community with young families? Talk to both retirees and nonretirees.

If you have done your homework and concluded that you still want to relocate, go for it! But remember, the key to a successful retirement in a new location is to immediately establish as many connections as you can. As with those who choose to stay put, your quality of life will depend in large part upon the quality of your relationships.

## APPROACHING RETIREMENT

*Should I consider early retirement?*

There are a number of reasons that a person might consider early retirement, including:

- Health issues
- Corporate downsizing
- A spouse's retirement
- Death of a spouse
- Physical demands of the job

However, there are potential downsides to early retirement as well. Considerations should include:

- Reduction in Social Security benefits
- Reduction in pension benefits
- Much higher medical insurance costs before being eligible for Medicare benefits
- Increased vulnerability to inflation
- Fixed liabilities with a reduction in income
- Feelings of boredom or lack of purpose in life

*Are there any special considerations I need to be concerned about as I near retirement?*

If you are close to retirement, there are three critical areas that you need to focus on right now.

YOUR ABILITY TO EARN AND SAVE DURING YOUR REMAINING WORKING YEARS What impact will the disability of you or your spouse or the death of your spouse have on your ability to continue building retirement income? Do you have sufficient insur-

CHAP. 1: RETIREMENT PLANNING GOALS                    25

ance coverage to make up the loss of this income during your remaining working years?

MEDICAL CARE   Are there options under your current employee health care plan to continue medical insurance until you are eligible for Medicare or even afterward? Is there a supplemental plan? Will it be adequate? Does it include long-term nursing care? What does it cost?

HOUSING   Will you continue to live in your present home? Will you sell your residence and move to something smaller to free up additional dollars toward your retirement, or would you prefer that your children inherit your home? On the one hand, your house might be a large, unlocked source of funds if you sell it and scale down. On the other hand, the home's sentimental value may override financial considerations and rule out a sale for retirement income needs. You need to think through your feelings on this important issue.

*I am 60 years old; my wife is 58. I'm concerned about whether we'll be okay during retirement. Do you have any advice?*

This is a concern shared by nearly everyone who is approaching retirement. It does not matter how much has been accumulated. Couples or individuals have different lifestyles, so the right amount for your needs may be different from that for your wife's needs. It is this uncertainty, combined with the change in lifestyle, that produces anxiety.

If your company or local community college has courses on planning for retirement, you should consider attending so that you are more aware of the issues you will face as you approach retirement. You should also meet with your advisors so that they can assist you in planning for a retirement income stream, taking into account inflation and income taxes, that will provide the retirement lifestyle you envision.

## Financial Considerations

> ☙ *How will my attitude toward money change during retirement?*

One of the most difficult transitions awaiting us during retirement is the change from a saving mode to more of a spending mode. Many people with adequate retirement incomes and assets feel guilty about spending and are constantly worrying about the future.

By the time you reach retirement, you will have been saving all your life and you will then start consuming the savings you worked so long and hard to accumulate. This can be a very difficult and uncomfortable thing to do. No matter how large your retirement fund is, spending the assets is tough; unless you are fully confident about your financial position, you may never feel truly comfortable doing so. Make a budget, stay within your means, and seek professional planning help, if needed, so that you can enjoy yourself without apprehension or guilt.

Getting comfortable with the fact that it is time to spend down some of the accumulated wealth can be accomplished by replacing the ingrained habit of saving with another program, such as giving. Further, it is good to remember that as we age and become frail, travel and sports will often become less attractive. Our lifestyles can become less expensive rather than more.

> ☙ *Will I be able to work, say, on a part-time basis, to supplement my retirement income during retirement?*

Absolutely. You may find that you become interested in charitable or fraternal organizations, some of which may pay you a small wage or salary for your assistance to the organization. Many of these organizations rely upon retired people, who often have excellent skills and diverse interests. They frequently have some resources to pay office staff, bookkeepers, and administrative assistants. Alternatively, you could, depending on your background, conduct part-time consulting or mediation or engage in other

# Chap. 1: Retirement Planning Goals

projects for compensation. Obviously, you will have to pay income taxes on the income you receive from these sources.

*How can I relax and enjoy an active lifestyle in my early retirement years when I'm worried that I might run out of money?*

Money worries really do hold retirees back from getting the most out of retirement. This is especially true among current retirees who had some exposure to the Great Depression. Starting retirement is much like going on an extended vacation to a distant destination with a one-way ticket, a limited amount of cash, and no credit cards. Fortunately, this problem can be solved.

First, analyze the source of your anxiety. Is it fear of catastrophic long-term medical costs? Is it wanting to leave an inheritance for the children and grandchildren? Is it inflation, the effect of market fluctuations on your assets, or the lack of a steady paycheck?

Once you have isolated the source of the anxiety, your financial advisor can help you identify options for eliminating it. If the anxiety is provoked by concerns about cash to live on today, your financial advisor can provide you with assurances or suggest a monthly income that won't deplete your savings. If you are concerned about unexpected—or even probable—expenses, perhaps long-term-care insurance could allay your fears and leave you free to spend more money in the early years.

If wanting to leave an inheritance for your children is a concern, second-to-die, or "survivorship," life insurance could provide your family with that benefit, thereby releasing you from feeling obligated to sacrifice during your "golden years" solely for their benefit.

If worries about your portfolio and the lack of a steady paycheck are a source of anxiety, discuss them with your financial advisor. He or she can show you ways to manage the risk of market fluctuations and inflation. You could also arrange for a systematic withdrawal plan that sends a check every month from your account directly to you or your bank.

Most retirees have these worries, especially during the first few years of retirement. However, most relax after taking a major trip or two, doing some expensive projects around the house, and seeing that their asset bases are holding steady. If you are obsessed with worry, either seek counseling or think very seriously about continuing to work.

## Psychological Considerations

*According to my financial planner, my retirement plan has enough money in it to continue my current lifestyle for decades without working. What sorts of things should I consider in deciding whether to retire now?*

It sounds like you and your planner have performed the mathematical calculations that need to be made, which is where some people start. Obviously, you have some interest in retirement or you would not have performed the financial analysis.

The main issue to consider now is whether you *want* to retire. For many people, work is the source not just of money but of their self-esteem, entertainment, amusement, energy, purpose, and direction. You should conduct a thorough and serious self-analysis with your loved ones and your spiritual liaisons, as well as your advisors, to determine whether you are ready for retirement.

*I'm planning to retire next year. What are the psychological pitfalls I need to watch out for as I enter this new stage of life?*

A financial planner sees people ranging from retirees who have made perfect transitions to busy, productive retirements to persons who have gone back to work on some basis because they couldn't stand being retired. We recommend that you explore your own retirement goals, and those of your spouse if you are

CHAP. 1: RETIREMENT PLANNING GOALS    29

married, to decide such things as whether you want to stay in the same residence or remain in your current locale. You and your spouse may have differences of opinion which both of you should attempt to reconcile before your retirement. Many couples fear the extra "togetherness" or the possibility that their independence will be curtailed. The more open you and your spouse are in addressing these issues now, the easier your retirement transition should be.

### ⚜ *What am I going to do with all the years ahead?*

As probably the longest-living generation in history, we are faced with the challenge of reinventing the concept of retirement. We can no longer consider life as a closed circle—birth, education, work, retirement, death. Rather, the phases of education, work, and retirement or leisure can be repeated and rearranged to add fulfillment and depth to our lives.

Between birth and our physical and mental growth to adulthood and our eventual physical decline and death lies an ever-increasing number of healthy, productive years. The options available to us become a challenge, because very few role models are available. We must each invent our own fulfillment.

Previous generations basically had enough time to get an education, work for a time, and retire to some leisure before leaving this life. Now, we can go through that cycle several times if we choose. We can master several disciplines. We can take a prolonged sabbatical to contemplate and renew our spirits. This quality of life, however, takes preparation and planning.

### ⚜ *Why am I so stressed out as I enter retirement? I thought this was supposed to be fun and exciting!*

The transition to retirement can be stressful, especially if you haven't given careful thought and planning to the issues surrounding it. You are in good company. According to a *Worth* magazine poll cited in *American Demographics* (January 1995), 41 percent of retirees say retirement was a difficult adjustment. By contrast, only 12 percent of newlyweds saw marriage as a difficult adjustment, and only 23 percent thought the adjustment to parenthood was difficult.

You've basically changed jobs. You have left the structure and relative security of working for someone else or running your own business. You are now "unemployed" in an unstructured environment, managing your free time and the income sources that support it. For better or worse, you and your spouse are together more, which can provide opportunities for conflict or for getting to know each other better.

Finally, retirement is based on the assumption that leisure is more fulfilling than work. For many people, especially those who enjoyed their careers, that assumption is false and goes against the grain of their need to be productive.

That is why it is essential to develop a vision of your retirement and the rest of your life *before* you retire. It could very well be that your idea of a fulfilling retirement is filled with work—not because you have to work but because you want to.

*I'm enjoying my career and want to work longer, but my spouse is older than I am and wants to retire now. Can a "split retirement" work?*

Split retirement is becoming a more common occurrence. Because it often ensures a steady income and medical insurance, this arrangement can relieve some of the money pressures during retirement. However, a split retirement can also create tensions in the marriage, the working spouse's job, and the nonworking spouse's retirement.

If you and your spouse have a relationship in which both of you always do things together, a split retirement can be extra challenging. This will be particularly true if your spouse's vision of a good retirement includes extensive traveling with you and doing other activities together.

On the other hand, if you and your spouse have separate

Chap. 1: Retirement Planning Goals 31

interests and have pursued them independently, split retirement could work. It can also work if your spouse absorbs some of your chores while you continue working, thus freeing up your time for doing more activities together. Above all, you and your spouse need to discuss this in advance and create a joint vision of exactly what type of retirement you want this to be.

*I dread our retirement. My spouse and I have been very independent with successful careers. How can we maintain our independence and not drive each other crazy?*

You have expressed a very common concern. Preparation for both of you will make the transition go more smoothly.

Give yourselves some time. If you and your spouse are used to having a staff and colleagues, you may both be feeling set aside and useless. If you have not nurtured interests outside your careers, you will be bored and lost and look to each other to fill the void. If at all possible, address these issues and share your feelings.

Plan to spend some of your new leisure time together going to new places and doing new things. Get involved in household projects you've been putting off for years.

Focus on the positive: Think about the possibilities for each of you; both of you can continue to be involved in independent activities. Would you like to do more community service or charity work? get a job? start a business? go back to school? This could be your opportunity!

Keep in mind that communication can cure a great deal. This would be a great time for the two of you to get reacquainted and rekindle the relationship you had before the children and the jobs consumed your time. Explore the possibilities!

## WORKING WITH ADVISORS

*I'm intimidated by the retirement planning process—the tax laws, the diversity of products and investments, and the finan-*

*cial advisors to choose from. What's the easiest way to get started?*

The easiest way to get started is to get help getting started. Select one key person to help you bring together a team of advisors that includes an attorney to draft the plan documents, a CPA who knows your personal financial and tax position, an investment and/or insurance specialist to help in the selection of the retirement planning products to be used, and a trustee who will manage your affairs in the event of your psychological or physical incapacity.

Once you have this group together, they will help you develop the retirement planning goals discussed earlier: when you want to retire, what you want your lifestyle to be at retirement, and who will be financially responsible for you and your spouse in the event of any prolonged incapacity. For married couples, it's important to address each spouse's individual retirement plans and objectives.

*Who is the best person to talk with about retirement planning?*

There may be no single, best person to talk with about retirement planning. In fact, in our experience proper retirement planning combines financial planning, investment planning, benefit planning, compensation planning, and traditional estate planning. These diverse subjects must be addressed in an integrated fashion to create the best retirement plan for you.

The team approach to retirement planning is almost always best. You do, however, need to appoint a "quarterback," or team captain, to be the lead person who will continuously focus the team on your values and goals and make sure the job gets done. The good quarterback must be open, honest, and astute enough to know when to bring in a specialist in an area where one is needed and must be able to psychologically connect with you.

*I'm a very private person. I'm not sure I want to have a group*

*of professionals know all about me—they'll probably try to sell
me something I don't need. Why can't I rely on one advisor?*

Privacy is extremely important and valuable. So is trust. It is
critical that you find a team of advisors you can trust completely
so that you know unequivocally that their primary goal is protecting your best interests.

One advisor cannot have expertise in all areas; therefore, all
the members of your advisory team must share with one another
their skills and expertise in order to coordinate their efforts and
achieve the results you seek. Once you have completed the planning process, you will feel much better knowing that your affairs
are in order.

## The Accountant

*What role does an accountant play in planning for my retire-
ment?*

Your CPA or accountant can advise you on key income tax issues
that will arise in your retirement and estate planning.

Accountants are keenly interested in minimizing their clients'
income taxes in any given year; however, they are also concerned
with increasing clients' long-term net spendable income. Someone
on your team needs to run the numbers to test various retirement
plan design strategies and make the arithmetic evaluations and
recommendations. The estate planning strategies recommended
by your attorney may also require tax planning coordination. An
accountant is uniquely qualified to provide these services.

## The Financial Planner

*What does a financial planner do?*

Most financial professionals seem to fit into one of two categories:
financial planners or investment managers. Both types are needed

to properly organize your retirement finances. Ideally, you will find one person capable of acting as both a planner and an investment manager. But if not, it would be better to have two financial professionals on your team than to have just a planner or just an investment manager.

*Financial planners* are primarily involved in what might be called the "big picture"—analysis and planning. A financial planner will review your current situation and future goals and then propose ways of getting "from here to there." This typically includes analyzing your investment mix, current insurance coverage, tax situation, and estate planning considerations and then making recommendations regarding what you should do in order to achieve the designed plan. Frequently, a formal, written financial plan document is part of this analysis.

*Investment managers* tend to be more concerned with managing investments on a day-to-day basis; they generally do not do the initial big-picture planning. Investment managers are usually specialists in stock, investment counseling, or money management and are very familiar with the investment markets.

## ﹌ *What role does the financial advisor play on my team?*

As you will see throughout this book, there are probably many things that you have not considered as you think about retirement. The role of the financial planner is to identify these major challenges and opportunities as they apply to you and then coordinate the implementation with the other experts on your team.

A good financial planner, or financial advisor, will spend considerable time learning about you, your family, your goals, and your financial situation. After taking a thorough inventory, he or she can illustrate the feasibility of achieving your retirement goals and make recommendations to help you achieve them. The planner will work closely with your tax professional, attorney, and other advisors to make certain that everything is coordinated on your behalf. If you don't have an existing relationship with other

# CHAP. 1: RETIREMENT PLANNING GOALS

specialists, your planner can refer you to qualified professionals who understand the need for teamwork.

## What is a Certified Financial Planner?

The Certified Financial Planner designation is awarded by the International Board of Standards and Practices for Certified Financial Planners (IBCFP) on a candidate's successful completion of a 2-year course of study in six interrelated financial disciplines mandated by the IBCFP. These disciplines are employee benefits, retirement, investment, tax, insurance, and estate planning. The candidate must also pass a comprehensive day-long examination and have 3 years of relevant financial planning experience. The curriculum is offered through the College for Financial Planning in Denver, Colorado, and dozens of other universities across the country. The certification also requires 30 hours of continuing education credits every 2 years.

## Will I have to tell my financial advisor about all my finances?

You should expect a professional financial advisor to ask you very detailed questions about your financial background, goals, net worth, liquid assets, expenses, risk tolerance, age, tax bracket, debt, investment experience, time horizon, expectations, and any additional information or pertinent facts related to your financial well-being. Much like a medical doctor performing a thorough diagnosis before administering any prescription drug or treatment, a responsible advisor should know you and your needs before rendering any investment advice.

Your estate planning attorney will also need accurate information about your assets. Your financial advisor can provide the attorney with this data, reducing the time the attorney has to spend compiling the same data and thus allowing your attorney to focus more on counseling you regarding your options.

36          WAYS AND MEANS

*How do I go about finding a financial planner or financial advisor?*

The best way is through referrals. You can also check the Yellow Pages and the Internet. Perhaps the easiest way to get the names of several advisors in your area is to contact one of the financial planning associations:

> Institute of Certified Financial Planners
> 800-282-7526
> www.icfp.org
>
> International Association for Financial Planning
> 800-945-4237
> www.iafp.org
>
> Society of Financial Service Professionals
>    (formerly American Society of CLU & ChFC)
> 888-243-2258
> www.financialpro.org

These organizations will send you the names and backgrounds of four or five planners in your area. They also have excellent web sites with additional information that will help you evaluate and interview a prospective financial planner.

*How are financial planners compensated?*

There are essentially three types of compensation systems: fee only, fee based, and commissioned:

- *Fee-only* financial planners charge a fee or charge an hourly rate for designing the financial plan.
- *Fee-based* planners typically charge a fee for designing your plan. On investments, they typically charge a flat annual fee (.75 to 2.5 percent of the assets managed), regardless of how many transactions occur.
- *Commissioned* advisors are compensated by the commissions

# CHAP. 1: RETIREMENT PLANNING GOALS

generated by the purchase of products to implement the suggested plan. Stockbrokers and insurance agents are usually in this category.

It is not unusual to have an advisor whose services encompass all or a combination of the above.

### ⚜ *Should I be concerned about how my financial planner gets paid?*

Good professional advisors can be found practicing under any one or a combination of the above fee structures. Whether your planner gets compensated by fees only, commissions only, or a combination of the two, it is important that you have trust in your advisor and feel comfortable that he or she is being compensated fairly for the work performed.

### ⚜ *What questions should I ask a financial advisor?*

Before engaging a financial advisor, ask these questions:

*What services do you provide?* Advisors may provide a range of services from designing your plan through selling the investments to implement your plan.

*Do you specialize in any area?* Many planners specialize in a particular area of the marketplace. For example, if the planner serves the retired market, he or she knows more about the problems and challenges of retired individuals. Some financial advisors specialize in planning for physicians or for business owners. You may feel more comfortable with a financial advisor who specializes in a particular area.

*What will you do to help me ascertain my goals?* Your financial advisor should help you analyze your needs and long-term investment objectives. This will be accomplished after a lengthy conference with the advisor, during which you will be asked a number

38 WAYS AND MEANS

of pertinent questions about your short-term and long-term financial goals.

*What are your credentials, academic background, and experience, and how long have you been a financial advisor?* You should try to find an advisor whose background indicates a high level of investment expertise and knowledge.

*Can you give me a few references?* You should be given names of some of the advisor's clients so that you can talk to them to determine their opinion of the advisor. It is important to make sure you feel that the mixture of expertise, service, and "chemistry" is right for you.

### *What else should I look for?*

In a word, service. You have worked hard to accumulate capital for retirement, and you want to know it is being managed and planned for by someone who truly cares about you and your future. Look for someone whom you can relate to and who can give you personalized service.

You should interview more than one professional. The matching of personalities becomes as important as the knowledge level of the professional. The planner you choose should be an active listener, since he or she needs to understand your objectives in order to provide you with the best service.

## The Estate Planning Attorney

### *Why do I need an estate planning attorney to advise me about retirement planning?*

There are two main reasons. First, many of the strategies you choose for your retirement plan may require use of legal documents that must be drafted by an attorney. Second, the investment plan and strategies that you design may be inefficient and unfulfilled, if not totally unattainable, without proper legal advice

# Chap. 1: Retirement Planning Goals

and a structure in place for you and your loved ones in the event of your disability or death.

With proper planning, your goals can be achieved, your wealth increased, and your taxes substantially reduced. Financial planning cannot be successfully implemented on a long-term basis without coordination with legal consultation in the areas of tax and estate planning.

### ⚜ *What should I look for when selecting an estate planning attorney?*

As with each of the advisors you pick for your team, you may wish to interview several attorneys. Estate planning is a highly technical discipline, so choose an attorney who focuses his or her practice on estate planning.

Find one whom you are comfortable talking with and who will take the time to listen to you and answer your questions in terms you can easily understand. Keep in mind that good estate planning attorneys know that their clients come to them to enhance feelings of financial security and freedom. They pride themselves on helping clients attain that security and freedom by designing estate plans that reflect the clients' values and goals.

As with a good financial advisor, personalized service should be a cornerstone of the attorney's practice. (How to find and work with a good estate planning attorney is covered in detail in *Generations: Planning Your Legacy*, published by the Esperti Peterson Institute.)

## The Investment Counselor

### ⚜ *What is an investment broker?*

An *investment broker* is an employee of a New York Stock Exchange member firm or an independent broker/dealer who has at least a National Association of Securities Dealers Series 7 license, meaning that he or she is licensed to sell registered securities.

There is no minimum education level, but most are college graduates.

*⚜ Do I need an investment counselor to complete my retirement plan?*

No. Some individuals have the willingness and capacity to structure and oversee their portfolios. However, many individuals also have the capacity to tune up their automobiles and change the oil, yet they choose to have their mechanics take care of these tasks.

There is an overload of retirement information available today. Periodicals, radio, television, and the Internet have volumes of investment ideas to share. You need both the desire to sort through this information and the time to do so. If you are not committed to devoting the time and energy that are necessary to manage your portfolio, you should recognize this and seek professional assistance to accomplish your goals.

*⚜ Should I work with a professional investment counselor or manage my retirement assets myself?*

It is fine to self-manage retirement assets. However, unless managing assets is your passion, you are seriously committed to the endeavor, and you possess the experience to do so, you are likely to be better off establishing relationships with trained professional advisors.

A qualified financial advisor with substantial experience can lighten the burden of planning for your retirement. In addition to handling transactions, an advisor can be a great resource. Good investment advice is more than achieving investment performance. It is also structuring your investments to best fit your overall plan, helping to manage your investment expectations, and reducing investment risk.

# Chap. 1: Retirement Planning Goals

41

*How do I find a good investment counselor?*

Get the names of advisors recommended by friends, business associates, your CPA, or your attorney. It is always good to talk to someone who has already had direct experience with an advisor. However, be sure to find out in what capacity the advisor is being praised. Friends may know someone who is "the best they've ever seen," but you need to determine what exactly the advisor is "the best" at. Know the particular skills you really need and find out if the advisor meets those criteria. The financial and investment business is highly segmented, and many advisors specialize in one area but not in others.

*What are some key things to consider when I meet with a prospective investment advisor?*

BACKGROUND   Keep in mind that your hard-earned money and your retirement security are involved in your choice of advisor. Thus you have every right to know relevant facts about the advisor, and asking is the only way you will find out about them. You should ask about the advisor's title and credentials, what he or she had to do to get them, and how much experience the advisor has.

UNDERSTANDING   Try to determine if the advisor is really attempting to understand you and to learn about you. Ask how the advisor gets to know his or her clients. Will he or she complete a detailed questionnaire and ask to review your tax returns and other documents? The advisor should be willing to spend considerable time talking with you to understand your attitudes, values, and concerns. A good investment counselor will not make recommendations before having a clear picture of your tax, income, and investment situation and a thorough understanding of how you feel about your money, how much risk you want to take, and so on.

You should also consider whether the counselor is attempting to help you understand what is going on. Although you will be delegating responsibility for your investments and other financial matters to this counselor and your other advisors, you still need to know what is going on with your money. A good investment counselor will make sure you understand the various investments as well as their risks and limitations. You want the advisor to be able and willing to teach you the basics of every aspect of your plan. Remember, ultimately it is your financial future at risk; you need to know enough to understand your advisor's recommendations and feel comfortable with the decisions that you make.

TRUST   Look for someone you trust. This point is extremely important, but it is also a rather abstract one. Essentially you must trust your own instincts and intuition in making the final choice.

Your investment advisor can dramatically affect your ability to get the most from your money before and during retirement. Although few people are actually ruined by someone tragically mismanaging their money, as you occasionally read about in the newspapers, many do not achieve their desired standard of living because they erroneously assumed their advisors were competent. Be selective in choosing your investment counselor.

*You mentioned that investment counselors and brokers are paid commissions on the products they sell. Is it important for me to know what those commissions are?*

It is very important for you to know both the investments an advisor can sell and the compensation he or she receives for each. Many investment advisors are licensed to sell only certain products, such as insurance or mutual funds. Others can sell many investments but may receive a larger commission for selling some products than for selling others. Some work for fees in lieu of commissions.

Ask the advisor why he or she is recommending the products and approximately how much commission the advisor will receive for them, because the commission could affect which products are recommended. One advantage of asking about commissions

CHAP. 1: RETIREMENT PLANNING GOALS

43

is that the advisor realizes you will expect justification for recommendations which involve high commissions.

*Should I choose brokers who specialize in particular stocks so that I can diversify my investments?*

Diversification can be beneficial, particularly for the larger portfolio and for the younger investor. However, diversification doesn't require numerous brokerage accounts.

Frequently, when individuals split their assets among several brokerage houses, they sacrifice higher returns and volume discounts. Further, many people believe they are diversified by having, say, five brokerage houses represent them, when, in fact, the portfolio in each brokerage house is composed of the same or similar investments.

Also, when a person works with a number of different brokers, the brokers may not always know the specifics of his or her total portfolio and estate planning objectives, so they are unable to put their full knowledge and expertise to best use for that person.

## INCOME ANALYSIS

### Income Requirements

*I've decided to begin saving for retirement. What's the first thing I need to do?*

As we discussed earlier, your goals and expectations are critical in saving for retirement. First, you need to know what it is you are trying to accomplish and how you are going to accomplish it. Then you need to compile a budget that will estimate your future retirement living expenses. What changes would have to be made if today was the first day of your retirement?

Some financial analysts say that you can retire on 60 to 75 percent of your preretirement income. Few retirees actually do, especially in the early years of retirement. Most retirement planners believe that some amount less than the final salary should provide adequate retirement income. The rationale for planning a retirement income that is less than 100 percent of final salary is based upon the following assumptions:

### Reductions in taxes

- Social Security taxes are not applicable to most retirement income.

- Standard deductions are increased.

- Some or all of a taxpayer's Social Security benefits are excluded from taxation.

- Many states exempt retirement benefits from state income taxes

### Reduced living expenses

- Work-related expenses such as clothing, communication, and meals are reduced.

- Home-ownership expenses such as mortgage, rent, and repair costs will be retired or decrease.

- Dependent children are usually not a factor.

- Educational expenditures tend to decrease with age at all income levels.

- You are no longer saving for retirement.

*Will any of my expenses increase as I get older?*

According to the Bureau of Labor Statistics' Consumer Expenditure Survey (the same data that generates the consumer price index), some changes occur gradually with aging. For instance, health care costs and household expenditures tend to increase

CHAP. 1: RETIREMENT PLANNING GOALS 45

with age at all income levels, and entertainment expenditures tend to increase with age at lower income levels.

*Are there any other factors I should consider in determining how much I'll need when I retire?*

Think of three phases of retirement when making your income-need assumptions:

- *Phase I:* This is the active phase, in which you have the health and energy to travel and do other things. This phase is usually the most expensive.

- *Phase II:* This is the passive phase, in which you still have your health but you don't have as much energy or desire to travel extensively, drive at night, and spend money on other forms of entertainment. In this more contemplative stage of life, tending the garden, walking in the neighborhood, or reading may occupy your time. This phase may well cost less than your current lifestyle does.

- *Phase III:* This is the final phase, in which health and mobility become larger issues. You may end up spending very little or a great deal, depending upon whether you have to pay for long-term-care costs or other medically related expenses.

*Taking all these factors into account and assuming I live to be 100, how do I actually calculate what percentage of my income at retirement would create a comfortable income?*

First, calculate 75 percent of your income at retirement, and increase that amount annually for inflation to age 100 (assuming an inflation rate of 3.5 percent). This will give you a reasonable estimate. Then calculate how much you will have to accumulate in your retirement nest egg to provide that income. This asset number is the investment goal or objective you are trying to achieve between now and when you plan to retire.

*⊰ As my financial planners, how would you help me determine how much money I'm going to need for retirement?*

We would start by completing a thorough cash-flow analysis for your current situation. Then we would do a projected cash-flow analysis for your retirement years based on such factors as age of retirement, taxes, inflation, debts, your family situation, and all sources of income during retirement. While it is difficult to anticipate exactly how much you will need, this is where we would start.

*⊰ What is a cash-flow analysis?*

Basically, a *cash-flow analysis* is simply a look at your monthly income from all sources, less monthly expenses and taxes, extended beyond your normal life expectancy. All monthly surpluses or shortages are either added to or subtracted from investment and savings reserves.

Over time, adjustments are made for all your goals, aspirations, and objectives that can be quantified. These might include college education for the children or grandchildren, care for an elderly parent, that super vacation you have always wanted to take, a mobile home to travel the country, or a new roof for your house.

*⊰ Why is doing this analysis so important?*

There are many reasons why the cash-flow analysis is important: The process helps you confirm your retirement goals for yourself and enables your advisors to determine your retirement financial needs.

The analysis provides a financial model that is really the beginning of your retirement planning process. The model includes annual milestones to track and compare your progress. It also lets you see which variables are important and how changes and variations may affect the results.

## Chap. 1: Retirement Planning Goals

*⍨ How do I start putting this analysis together?*

First, determine all your annual living expenses. You must be as accurate as possible because these expenses are going to be projected well into the future. You should include everything from vacations to vitamins. Next, you must estimate future expenses and expense reductions—for example, college costs, the costs of caring for an elderly parent, debt retirement, decreased expenses when children move out (perhaps 5 percent per child), and increased expenses when they move back. Do not forget items such as paying off the mortgage and any other reductions that you think might be appropriate at retirement.

Next, you need to list sources of income including your current income and future pension plan benefits.

You then make adjustments for inflation. You should now have a fairly good idea of what your living expenses are going to be over the years.

The following are additional variables that should be factored into the analysis:

- Conservative, current, and reallocated rates of return on investment portfolio

- Cost-of-living increases on Social Security and pensions

- Retirement plan assets, including the timing and amount of their mandatory distributions

- Future anticipated inheritances

- The timing and after-tax proceeds from the sale of a business

- Mortgage payoff dates

- Your joint life expectancy based on health and family history

- Income tax rates

- Inheritances you would like to leave for your heirs

- Your current health status

*⚘ What should the result of this cash flow-analysis or retirement planning report cover?*

The end result of a retirement planner's professional analysis of your circumstances should be a carefully prepared document that summarizes:

- *Analysis:* Where are you now
- *Objectives:* Where you want to be
- *Strategies:* How to get to where you want to be
- *Outcome:* Probable results from different strategies

*⚘ How often will I need to review my retirement plan to make sure I'm on track?*

Your financial plan should be reviewed at least once a year to ensure that you still have the same objectives and that you are still on the right financial track for reaching them. It's also important to verify that you have the same amount of discretionary funds to allocate to retirement. If you have more or fewer funds available, you may want or need to adjust your plan accordingly.

*⚘ What will my sources of income be for the cash-flow analysis?*

For the income side of the equation, you will need to detail income from all sources over different periods in your life. If you are still working, you will obviously include your current salary and bonuses. Include rental and investment income, as well. Retirement income will potentially come from sources such as Social Security; your pension; personal resources such as savings, IRAs, and trusts; and postretirement earned income.

## Projections
### Income
*⚘ How can I find out what my Social Security benefits will be?*

You can submit a Request for Earnings and Benefit Estimate

CHAP. 1: RETIREMENT PLANNING GOALS 49

Statement (form SSA 7004-SMOP7) to the Social Security Administration. This statement, which generally takes 4 to 6 weeks to arrive, is a review of your Social Security earnings history and estimates of your future benefits. It is important to verify your Social Security earnings from time to time in case there is a mistake in the records.

*Should I plan on working after retirement?*

A lot of people who have led active, successful careers see themselves in retirement as playing an endless string of tennis sets or golf games or doing nothing but fishing from now until forever. That may work for the rare individual, but the reality for most of us is different. The very characteristics that helped you have a career that is giving you the ability to one day retire will still be there in full bloom on the day you walk out the office door. Instead of shutting down the type of activities that have occupied over half of your waking hours for well over half of your life, you may want to actively plan for postretirement earned income. Your services may be very valuable to another, perhaps smaller company, where you could work either as a part-time employee or as a consultant. From the practical standpoint, a few more years of income, even at a reduced level, may be a very powerful addition to your financial plan. Your cash-flow analysis should be able to help you determine how much income might be required and for how long.

*What projections on earnings should I make?*

Some investment counselors will tell you that the wise investor will assume a lower-than-hoped-for rate of return on investments. Some will tell you that 8 percent per year has proved to be a moderately conservative rate of growth over the long term; others, that 10 percent is a realistic rate of return. You should experiment with rates depending on your ability to tolerate volatility in your investment savings and the type of assets you own.

It is probably best to look at the worst-case, best-case, and probable-case scenarios rather than a single set of figures. People often put undue reliance on figures that are mathematically accurate but are built on inaccurate long-range assumptions.

⨇ *What about rental income for retirement?*

This can be good, steady income if you actively manage your tenants or have a reliable service to do it for you. Be selective in your investments to avoid as many of the pitfalls of being a landlord as possible during your retirement years.

⨇ *I know I'll need additional monthly income after I retire. I'm considering accessing the equity in my principal residence, but I don't want to sell the house and move. What are my options?*

Two of the most popular options are the reverse mortgage and the sale leaseback. Both allow a retiree to continue to live in his or her home and receive a monthly income in return for assigning or mortgaging part of the home's equity.

The *reverse mortgage* is available to retirees age 62 and older through various financial institutions. Mortgage companies will allow up to 80 percent of the home's value to be considered, and there are similar programs available through the FHA. The administration, insurance, and closing costs for the reverse mortgage usually make it more costly than a sale-leaseback arrangement.

The *sale-leaseback* arrangement typically is an agreement in which a prosperous member of the family purchases the home from the retiree with the understanding that the retiree will live in and "lease back" the home. Unlike the reverse mortgage, which entails little or no tax liability for the income received, the sale-leaseback arrangement generates taxable interest income to the retiree in the form of mortgage payments received from the buyer.

⨇ *What will the financial difference be if I decide to work an additional 2 years?*

Working an additional 2 years means having 2 more years of

# CHAP. 1: RETIREMENT PLANNING GOALS                                    51

income and 2 less years of withdrawals. After taking into consideration the gains of the 2 additional years of income, interest on that money, and 2 less years of distributions, the 2 extra years of working could amount to as much as 6 additional years of retirement income. Your Social Security income would be slightly increased as well.

### Inflation

*How will inflation affect my retirement?*

Inflation will tend to devalue the purchasing power of your available dollars. Your dollars invested for retirement must keep pace with or, better yet, exceed expected and actual inflation. Inflation and taxes are the biggest threats to your retirement.

*What rate should I use for inflation, and what impact will it have on my projections? Will inflation rob me of my hard-earned savings?*

Inflation is usually measured by using the Bureau of Labor Statistics' *consumer price index* (CPI). The CPI is a measure of the average change over time in the prices paid by urban consumers for a fixed basket of consumer goods and services. While it is only an index of price change and does not reflect the changes in buying or consumption patterns, the CPI is the most common index used as a means of adjusting dollar values.

Over the 50-year period from 1945 to 1995, inflation averaged 4.36 percent per year. From 1900 to 1995 (95 years), it averaged 3.22 percent. The inflation rate for almost the entire nineteenth century—from 1802 to 1900—was minus .02 percent. While we have no way of predicting the future of inflation, it would not be prudent to ignore it for planning purposes. We generally recommend using around 4 percent over the next 40 or so years.

At 4 percent inflation, your cost of living doubles every 18 years, according to the Rule of 72. (The Rule of 72 states that 72 divided by the rate of return equals the number of years it will take to double.) Inflation *can* rob you of hard-earned savings and purchasing power. For example, if you are 42 years old and inflation is a steady 4 percent, a loaf of bread that costs $2 today will cost $4 when you are 60 years old and $8 when you are 78 years old! With 4 percent inflation, $100,000 of retirement savings will lose $50,000 of purchasing power every 18 years—a far greater and seemingly more probable risk than a major stock market crash. You should have a plan that works just as well for you when bread is $8 a loaf as it does now!

Ask your financial advisor to present two or three inflation scenarios. Be aware, however, that overly pessimistic inflation assumptions can induce you to invest more than you need to, retire later than necessary, spend less than you may wish, or take on more investment risk than necessary.

Therefore, plan for inflation, but don't overplan for it. It will come and go over the course of a 30- to 40-year retirement, just as it has over the last 40 years.

*I'm trying to determine if I have enough money to retire. Since inflation is currently only about 3 percent, is it really that important to include it in my calculations?*

Inflation is one of the more important factors in determining your income requirements throughout retirement. Many people do not significantly change their spending habits when they retire, yet their cost of living goes up. It can be a devastating mistake not to consider inflation when calculating the ability to retire. To maintain your current lifestyle, you must increase your living expenses by an inflation factor.

A simple example can show the effect of inflation on the cost of living: Let's assume that a married couple currently spend $5000 per month on living expenses; for simplicity, let's also assume that they have no mortgage payment. Even with a 3 percent inflation rate assumption, their monthly income require-

# Chap. 1: Retirement Planning Goals

ments would increase to $5796 in 5 years, to $6720 in 10 years, to $7709 in 15 years, and to $9031 in 20 years.

### Taxes

### ❧ *How should I calculate taxes for all those future years?*

Calculating taxes accurately can become a very complicated process. Given the frequency of changes to the Internal Revenue Code, there seems little point in trying to do more than estimate future taxes.

First, take your total income and subtract your normal deductions and exemptions to arrive at your adjusted gross income (AGI). Then use the following table:

|  | Tax rate | |
| --- | --- | --- |
| AGI | High-tax states | Low-tax states |
| $ 50,000 | 24% | 20% |
| 100,000 | 30 | 23 |
| 150,000 | 33 | 25 |

Using these broad rules of thumb will give you a close approximation of what your taxes might be in the future. Remember to adjust deductions downward as your mortgage is reduced.

### ❧ *Besides income taxes, are there any other taxes I should plan for?*

There are other taxes, and there may even be penalty taxes as well! If you take money out of a retirement plan before age 59½, with few exceptions, you could incur a 10 percent penalty tax. If you do not take out at least a required minimum IRS-calculated distribution after age 70½, you will incur an extra 50 percent penalty!

Do not forget federal estate taxes. If you die with an estate

54                                                    WAYS AND MEANS

larger than the applicable exclusion amount (discussed in detail in Chapter 7), your family may owe taxes ranging from 37 to 55 percent of the amount of your estate over the applicable exclusion amount. There are also income taxes that your heirs will eventually have to pay on retirement assets such as individual retirement accounts and also on the profit built up within tax-deferred annuities.

Finally, beware of generation-skipping transfer taxes if you wish to leave assets or distribute your retirement funds to your grandchildren upon your death.

### Expenses

*In my overall analysis, how should I handle my consumer debt?*

Expensive consumer debt is deadly to a retirement accumulation plan. With costs that can run as high as 22 percent per year, you may be left with very little opportunity to get ahead if dramatic action is not taken. It does little good to invest and earn good returns if those returns are being eaten up in interest payments. There are a couple of action steps that you can take.

First, work on reducing your living expenses to a point where you are capable of building a money market reserve for emergencies.

Second, consolidate your debts into one account, if possible, and try to take advantage of the low introductory rates offered by many credit companies today. Pay the same amount as you did before, and you will quickly reduce the debt.

Last, but not least, avoid excessive use of credit in the future, and use your cash reserves only in emergencies. Don't forget to reduce your expenses when your debts are paid off.

*Should I pay down my mortgage as well?*

If your mortgage is in the early stages, adding to the principal

## CHAP. I: RETIREMENT PLANNING GOALS

payment (after adequate emergency reserves are in place) can save a great deal of money.

You may want to calculate some alternatives in your cash flow such as, "What if I paid $200 per month more on my mortgage?" On a $150,000, 30-year, 8 percent mortgage, you would fully pay the mortgage in 18½ years, saving over $153,000. To make an informed decision, you would have to compare this amount saved to the amount of money you would accumulate if you contributed the $200 each month to a tax-deductible, tax-deferred IRA or 401(k).

Many people like to keep the mortgage in place because their interest payments are one of the few tax deductions they have. However, for every dollar you save in taxes, you are still spending around three to create the tax savings. Also, experience has shown that the increased sense of security that many people have when their mortgages are paid off can be worth the few percentage points in missed investment returns on this money.

### Now what?

*I've tracked my income, expenses, and taxes until age 100—now what?*

By subtracting your taxes and living expenses from your income, you will generate a surplus or a shortfall each year. A surplus represents income available for savings and investment. A shortfall draws down from the savings. Your cash-flow analysis should add those savings and subtract those shortfalls each year. Clearly, the plan has to be for your overall savings accounts to increase over time. The increases will come from both your savings and the earnings rate of those savings.

You should have at least two types of savings. One is savings that are not taxed as they accumulate, such as IRAs, 401(k) plans, tax-sheltered annuities, and profit-sharing plans. The other is savings that are not tax-deferred or tax-free.

*⇘ What do I do if my cash-flow analysis doesn't work? What if it shows that I'll run out of money too soon?*

The whole point of developing the cash-flow analysis is to have a tool that will serve you in a variety of ways over time.

First, the analysis will tell whether the plan works. With this tool, you can look out year after year and determine whether you will outlive your money or your money will outlive you. The latter is certainly more preferable.

Second, the analysis becomes a plan with milestones that you can go back and recheck every year or so. If your plan starts to get a little off track, you will have an early warning system that will allow you to look at alternatives for getting back on course. It's better to know that now rather than 10 years later.

Third, you have a tool for testing "what ifs." "What if I sell this house and move to the mountains?" "What if I retire in 5 years instead of 8 years?" "What would be the long-term consequences on our retirement plan of buying a mobile home now?" You can do what-if scenarios for a large variety of alternatives. They will assist you immensely in making good financial decisions.

Fourth, the analysis becomes a very important tool for your investment decisions. When your entire situation is accounted for and the plan is set up just the way you want it to be, the last variable is the minimum acceptable rate of return required for you to accomplish all your goals and live out your life with financial dignity. This will be the rate of return that your investment advisor will need to know to properly design your investment plan.

Finally, the plan will help you determine from which assets you should first withdraw your retirement income. For example, should you withdraw first from your taxable or from your tax-free investments?

## During Retirement

### Income

*⇘ I have money spread all over the place—my 401(k), IRAs,*

# CHAP. 1: RETIREMENT PLANNING GOALS 57

*mutual funds, deferred compensation account, banks, and a brokerage account. From which one should I start withdrawing first?*

This is a very common question, especially from those who retire before they are eligible for their pension or Social Security benefits. Every situation is unique, and that is why you should consult with your financial planner and tax advisor. Here are a few guidelines:

- Withdraw from the account that has the least flexibility first. This keeps your options open in the future. Certain deferred compensation plans and annuity contracts often fall into this category.

- Withdraw from the account that is earning the least.

- Keep your tax deferral going as long as you can. If you have large sums inside IRAs or other qualified plans or are considering converting all or part of these assets to a Roth IRA, consult with your advisors.

- If at all possible, wait until the early-withdrawal or surrender-charge periods on certain investments are over before withdrawing from them.

- If you are working closely with a particular advisor, you may wish to first withdraw from the accounts that cannot be consolidated or supervised by him or her. As time goes by, you will want more simplification in your life. It is a little more difficult for your advisor to give you good advice and service on accounts held by other advisors or institutions.

- If you are retiring midyear and are receiving accrued vacation pay or bonuses, special consideration should be given to the income tax implications on the investments you will be liquidating.

### Inflation

*I am already retired. How can I ensure that inflation won't deplete my savings and that I'll still have enough income many years from now?*

The key to staying ahead of inflation during retirement is continuing to increase your investment capital. Simply put, this means spending less than your investments earn. "Living within your means" does not just mean spending less than comes in; it entails planning for future inflation as well. You will need more income to do and buy the same things as years go by, so you'll need more investment principal to provide that higher income.

Generally, if you can increase your principal every year for the first 10 to 15 years of retirement, assuming retirement at age 65, you will be able to sustain your lifestyle no matter how long you live. Even if you have to use some principal after that time, overall spending style typically starts slowing down around age 75 to 80. As a result, you will probably use less, if any, of the principal, leaving you with sufficient resources.

### Taxes

*My husband and I have recently retired, and we'd like to move into a smaller home. How do we take advantage of the capital gain exemption so that we'll have more retirement money?*

As of August 1997, Congress significantly increased the allowed exclusion. Retroactive to May 7, 1997, married couples filing jointly can now exclude $500,000 of gain ($250,000 for individuals) from the sale of their primary residences. The new regulation enables people to "downsize" their residences and retain the remaining proceeds to help pay their retirement expenses.

There are qualifications that must be met, but they are not stringent. The home that you sell must have been your primary residence for at least 2 of the 5 years before the date of sale. It might be possible to receive partial exclusions for special circumstances if you have to sell your home because of employment, health status, or other unforeseen changes. There are no longer any age restrictions, and there is no limit to the number of times

# CHAP. 1: RETIREMENT PLANNING GOALS 59

you can use the new exclusion as long as you use it only every 2 years. The new exclusion is a tremendous boon for many people.

*I'm 62 years old. Should I take my Social Security now or wait and receive a higher amount at age 65?*

There are three rules of money that can help you make your decision:

- It's better to have it than not have it.
- More is better than less.
- It's better to have it now rather than later.

Generally, you should start taking the money as soon as you are eligible and, as long as you are not working, at an amount that exceeds the "deemable earned-income threshold." If you do not have a current need for the funds, merely reinvest them and allow them to grow until you do need them. In this way, you will create an emergency source of funds, a lump-sum payoff at death, and opportunities to earn more in good investment years.

All things considered, it is usually better to start taking Social Security as soon as you can. More control, more options, more fun!

# chapter 2

## Employer-Sponsored Retirement Plans

Mastering the vocabulary of retirement planning and understanding the options available can be very difficult tasks for a layperson. This chapter's questions and answers clarify the terminology of employer-sponsored plans and provide a concise overview of your planning options in this area.

Our contributors begin with a review of the various employer-sponsored "qualfied" plans available to investors, including the recently created SIMPLE retirement plans. The discussion covers the contribution limits and participation requirements for most types of qualified plans. Each has its advantages and disadvantages, both to the employer and the employee.

Our contributors then turn their attention to the many "non-qualified" types of plans available. Their questions and answers demonstrate how you can coordinate and supplement your employer-sponsored qualified plans with life insurance, stock options, salary continuation, and other valuable programs.

Maximizing the benefits available under the law is obviously necessary to ensure that you make the most of what you're able to contribute toward your retirement savings goals.

## TYPES OF
## EMPLOYER-SPONSORED PLANS

### ❧ *What is an employer-sponsored retirement plan?*

An *employer-sponsored retirement plan* is a type of savings vehicle which is established and maintained by employers to provide retirement benefits for their employees. There are two main categories of employer-sponsored plans—qualified plans and non-qualified plans—and several types of plans within each category.

### ❧ *What is a "qualified" plan?*

As a matter of public policy, the government wants to encourage everyone to save for retirement. To accomplish this objective, the government has created a system of special tax rules. These rules, found in Section 401 of the Internal Revenue Code, allow for the creation of various types of savings vehicles which are known as *qualified plans.* To encourage employers to establish qualified plans and employees to contribute part of their earnings to these plans, the government generally provides various income tax incentives to both employers and employees for doing so.

### ❧ *What is a "nonqualified" plan?*

A *nonqualified plan* is one which does not meet the requirements of the strict tax rules contained in Section 401 of the Internal

Revenue Code. Normally, nonqualified plans are designed to benefit a certain select group of employees, such as senior managers or highly compensated employees. Because these plans do not offer benefits to all employees, the government does not provide the same income tax incentives to the employers and employees as are allowed under qualified plans.

*As an individual, which of these should I be using?*

As a general rule, you should first take full advantage of all qualified plans available to you and then consider the nonqualified plans.

## QUALIFIED PLANS

*I work for a company that has a "defined-benefit" plan, and my wife works for a company that has a "defined-contribution" plan. What is the difference between these two plans?*

There are two principal types of qualified plans, often referred to as defined-benefit plans and defined contribution plans.

DEFINED-BENEFIT PLANS    A *defined-benefit plan* specifies the benefit amount that the employee will receive at retirement. The benefit is normally determined through a formula contained in the plan and is often based upon the employee's prior compensation and number of years of service. For example, your defined-benefit plan might provide that, upon retirement from your employer, you will receive $1200 per month for the rest of your life. Many plans contain cost-of-living benefit increases.

The amount of the contribution made to the plan by your employer will vary each year and depends upon an estimate of how much must be set aside that year in order to accumulate enough money to pay your retirement benefit. The employer assumes all the risk of financing and investing the retirement benefits because the employer is responsible for providing you with the stated benefit, even if the assets contained in the plan are insufficient.

There is one fund containing all the contributions made by your employer on behalf of all of its employees. When you are eligible to begin receiving benefits, the payments will be made from this common fund. Therefore, there is no separate account established on your behalf. At your death, payment of your benefits will usually end, and there are no remaining benefits which you can leave to your family.

Thus, under a defined-benefit plan, there is very little flexibility, and few planning opportunities are available. You generally will not have options to determine the amount, duration, or timing of the benefits or the ability to leave any benefits to your family at your death. The benefits will generally be paid during your lifetime or, sometimes, during the joint lifetime of you and your spouse. However, you should review your plan because some plans may allow you to compute the income stream of your monthly pension and then roll that amount over to your IRA.

DEFINED-CONTRIBUTION PLANS  A *defined-contribution plan* generally contributes a percentage of the employee's current salary to the plan each year.

There is no designated benefit at retirement, however. The employee normally receives a statement each year indicating the amount allocated to his or her account and the earnings during the past year. Because there is no guaranteed retirement benefit, the investment risk rests solely on the employee.

It is important to distinguish that there is no "best" plan. The best plan for each employer is based on facts and circumstances as well as the objectives of the employer.

🔖 *I have a "pension" plan at work. Is it a defined-benefit plan or a defined-contribution plan?*

It could be either one or a combination of both that is known as

## CHAP. 2: EMPLOYER-SPONSORED RETIREMENT PLANS    65

a target benefit plan. Most pension plans are defined-benefit plans.

*Is there more than one type of defined-contribution plan?*

Yes. Among the most common are:

- Corporate/business-entity profit-sharing plans
- 401(k) profit-sharing plans
- Money purchase pension plans
- Savings incentive match plans for employees (SIMPLE plans)
- Simplified employee pension (SEP) plans

Each of these is discussed in detail below.

There are various other types of defined-contribution plans as well. Some, such as stock bonus plans and employee stock ownership plans (ESOPs), enable the employee to accumulate stock rather than money.

*If my employer establishes a qualified plan, who puts the money into the plan for my benefit?*

The answer depends upon the type of qualified plan. Under a defined-benefit plan, generally only your employer would make contributions to the plan. Under a defined-contribution plan, you alone, your employer alone, or both you and your employer could make contributions.

*What are the income tax incentives with qualified plans?*

If you are an employer, your business will normally receive an income tax deduction for contributions which the business makes on behalf of your employees.

If you are an employee, the contribution made by your employer is generally not considered taxable income for you. Furthermore, if you are an employee and make contributions out of your earnings to the qualified plan, those contributions will generally not be included in your taxable income.

In addition to the income tax deduction for the employer, all growth on the plan investments accumulates on a tax-deferred basis. When the funds are distributed to the employee at his or her retirement, the funds may be eligible for favorable tax treatment but, in most cases, are subject to both federal and state income tax.

> ⚐ *I've heard people say they are "fully vested" in their company retirement plans. What does that mean?*

If you are a participant in a qualified plan, contributions have been made to the plan on your behalf. In a defined-benefit plan, you will be entitled to a stated benefit (e.g., $1200 per month for the rest of your life) that will normally be available to you when you retire. In a defined-contribution plan, an account will be established for you, and the proceeds in this account will normally be available to you when you retire.

The term "vested" generally refers to that percent of the benefit (in a defined-benefit plan) or that percent of the account (in a defined-contribution plan) of your employer's contributions that you are legally entitled to should you leave your employer before retirement. If you are *fully vested*, you are entitled to 100 percent of the benefit or account; if you are three-fourths vested, you are entitled to 75 percent of the benefit or account; and so on. You will always be 100 percent vested in the contributions you make.

The law places limits on the maximum time that can be required before you are fully vested in a qualified retirement plan.

## Corporate/Business-Entity Profit-Sharing Plans

> ⚐ *What are the features of a traditional profit-sharing plan?*

Employer contributions to a traditional profit-sharing plan are

## Chap. 2: Employer-Sponsored Retirement Plans    67

discretionary; that is, they are neither determined in advance nor required to be made in any year. Under current law, profits are not required in order to make a contribution, although this was the case in the past. Generally contributions are made as a specific percentage of an employee's pay, and this percentage must be the same for all employees.

Employer contributions are tax-deductible for the employer. The maximum annual deduction that an employer can take is 15 percent of the covered payroll. Employer contributions are not currently taxed to the employee, and growth on the contributions accumulates on a tax-deferred basis.

Distributions are generally fully taxable, but lump-sum distributions may receive favorable income tax treatment. However, many employees will roll these distributions into IRA rollovers and time the taxation of distributions throughout retirement.

It is interesting to note that the individual limit for allocation purposes is 25 percent of includable compensation, subject to a dollar limit of $30,000 per year. While contributions are normally based on a uniform percentage of pay, Social Security integration is typically built into a formula whereby individuals whose income exceeds the current Social Security wage base receive up to an additional 5.7 percent of compensation. This compensates for the fact that participants whose income exceeds the Social Security wage base do not have a government-financed benefit for the income they will need at retirement in excess of this amount. In addition, the maximum covered compensation limit individually is $160,000 of income (1998 limit, subject to indexing). All contributions are based on compensation, whether defined as W-2 wages, base salary, bonuses, overtime, and so on.

Although a profit-sharing plan does not require contributions, it will be considered terminated if contributions have not been made in a substantial and reoccurring way. Previously, the IRS rule of thumb was that contributions were to be made in at least 3 out of every 5 years or 5 out of every 10 years. The current rule of thumb is that contributions should be made in at least 1 out of every 3 to 4 years.

*I've been offered a position with a profitable company that says it will start a profit-sharing plan in which I'll be included. Will I get significant benefits from this plan?*

Your retirement benefits will be tied to the fortunes of the company and the decisions of its management. The risks you face may include any of the following:

- The company will not be profitable.
- If profitable, the company will not in fact start a profit-sharing plan.
- If it starts a plan, the company will choose not to make contributions to it.
- Assets in the plan will not be invested wisely.
- Your account under the plan will not be vested as soon as you would like.
- The company will terminate the plan before your account has accumulated to the amount you had hoped for.

If you have bargaining power at the onset of your employment, you should talk with a consultant who understands qualified plans and you should consider requesting a written employment agreement giving you direct rights against the company for equivalent benefits if the expected profit-sharing plan benefits do not accrue for you.

*I don't want my business to be obligated to make retirement plan contributions, since this could cause my business to fail during a downturn. How can I retain employees without contracting to contribute to a retirement plan for them?*

You can start a profit-sharing plan to which your company may contribute, when it is financially able, without obligating itself to make contributions. Although technical requirements must be met in forming and maintaining the plan, the plan may be dis-

Chap. 2: Employer-Sponsored Retirement Plans    69

continued. Be careful about what you communicate to employees with respect to whether you intend to make contributions to the plan. Expressions not carefully thought out can lead to claims by disappointed employees.

## 401(k) Profit-Sharing Plans

### *Features*

⚑  *What is a 401(k) plan?*

A *401(k) plan,* so named because it was created under Internal Revenue Code Section 401(k), is a plan offered through an employer for the benefit of employees and contains a cash-or-deferred arrangement. Usually you must be an employee with the company for a certain period of time, normally 1 year, before you become eligible and may begin contributing to the plan. You may elect to have your employer take pretax dollars from your paycheck or other compensation and contribute it to the plan, where it will grow tax-free until you withdraw the funds.

⚑  *What does "cash-or-deferred arrangement" mean?*

Under a *cash-or-deferred arrangement (CODA),* you, as the employee, can elect to defer a percentage of your compensation, in which event your employer will make a contribution to the plan on your behalf, or you may elect to take that percentage in cash, in which case you are not participating in the 401(k) plan.

If you choose the deferred arrangement, the money cannot be currently available to you. For instance, you can specify that it be taken directly from your paycheck, but you cannot take the money in cash and then contribute it to the plan. Also, you cannot acquire the money until a certain time, namely, retirement or termination of employment, disability, or death.

### Creation

*Can I create a 401(k) for myself if I am an owner, partner, or sole proprietor of a business?*

Yes. Under the Internal Revenue Code you are treated as an "employee" and may participate in a 401(k) plan.

*What are the advantages of a 401(k) plan?*

Any company, regardless of size, can establish a 401(k) plan. The maximum salary deferral was $10,000 for 1998. This amount is indexed annually for inflation, rounded to the nearest $500. Thus, the 1999 figure will be either $10,000 or $10,500. The plan may include:

- A vesting schedule for employer contributions
- Flexibility in matching contributions and plan design
- A profit-sharing element
- A targeted group
- Participant loans and controlled withdrawals
- Contributions to other plans

*I don't want the burdens of setting up and maintaining a profit-sharing plan. Can I set up a plan that simply lets an employee have a portion of salary go into a qualified retirement plan whose investments are directed by the employee?*

You may set up a 401(k) profit-sharing plan that allows contributions under a cash-or-deferred arrangement. Talk with your retirement consultant about how to structure the plan to achieve a balance between your objectives and your employees' objectives.

*Is it difficult or expensive to allow my employees to direct their own investments?*

The cost of providing an investment management program in a

## CHAP. 2: EMPLOYER-SPONSORED RETIREMENT PLANS 71

401(k) profit-sharing plan is nominal, and as technology becomes more prevalent, the administration involved is becoming more affordable for smaller companies. In the past, the complexity of administration was one of the major reasons why smaller companies did not allow employees to direct their own investments.

The typical cost of providing full daily valuation services with quarterly statements and 24-hour toll-free telephone access for participants for making investment changes is approximately $1250 per year, plus $24 per participant, plus 1 percent of the assets under management. These fees typically include the use of a corporate trustee, all plan participant record keeping and trust accounting, voice response, ongoing fiduciary liability management, semiannual on-site participant education and communication sessions, interactive software to help employees measure their progress toward retirement, quarterly participant statements in writing, and an annual update measuring each employee's progress toward retirement.

### Contributions

*How are contributions actually made to a 401(k) profit-sharing plan?*

If you are an employee under a 401(k) profit-sharing plan, you can have money contributed to your account in three ways:

- You can elect deferral of your salary.
- Your employer can make a matching contribution.
- Your employer can make a profit-sharing contribution.

By having three methods of making contributions, this plan is much more flexible than a traditional corporate/business-entity profit-sharing plan. In fact, a 401(k) is simply an appendage that is attached to a profit-sharing plan to create a more flexible planning environment.

In a 401(k) profit-sharing plan, it is common for the employer to induce employees to save on a pretax basis by holding out an incentive in the form of a matching contribution. Matching contribution formulas vary from employer to employer. For instance, your employer may agree to contribute a certain percentage of your *contribution* (e.g., 100 percent), a certain percentage of your *compensation* (e.g., 6 percent), or a combination of both. A typical match might equal 25 percent of your contribution up to the first 5 or 6 percent of pay. In many cases, if this is the only retirement plan, the match will be 50 percent of the employee's contribution up to 6 percent of pay. More generous contributions are allowed, and there is no cap on the amount of matching contributions other than as noted above. For example, your employer might have designed a plan in which the matching contribution is 200 percent up to the first 5 percent of pay. In this way, if you save 5 percent of your pay, you receive a matching contribution equaling 10 percent, for a total contribution of 15 percent of pay. Companies that use such a generous matching formula obviously will not experience a great deal of turnover other than at retirement.

Your elective deferrals are tax-favored, since no federal income tax is withheld on these amounts and your contributions are made via payroll deduction. In addition, in most states no state income taxes are withheld. However, all contributions which constitute your elected deferral are subject to FICA withholding. In other words, you may save federal and state taxes by contributing to a 401(k), but regular Social Security withholdings of 7.65 percent—6.2 percent for the old-age retirement fund and 1.45 percent for Medicare—are deducted from your 401(k) elective-deferral contributions.

*As an employee, how much can I contribute to my 401(k)?*

Your maximum contribution will be subject to the terms of the plan, but for 1998 the IRS allows you to contribute income tax–free up to $10,000 or 15 percent of your salary, whichever is less. Any amounts over $10,000 are considered "excess deferrals" and

CHAP. 2: EMPLOYER-SPONSORED RETIREMENT PLANS   **73**

will be included in your gross income for income tax purposes. The IRS maximum amount you can contribute increases every year to compensate for inflation. So check with your employer and put away the maximum.

*Is my employer required to match my elective contributions under my 401(k) plan?*

No. Your employer is not required by law to match any of your elective contributions. Under the terms of the plan, your employer may have voluntarily elected to match some or all of your contributions. The match will vary from employer to employer.

### Loans

*Is it a good idea to borrow money from my 401(k)?*

While a 401(k) is an easy source of money, borrowing from your plan is not a good idea for the following reasons:

- Interest on 401(k) loans is not deductible.

- Loans must be repaid within 5 years (unless used for the purchase of a residence).

- Money borrowed from the plan stops earning interest and can seriously diminish your retirement nest egg.

- If you do not pay the loan as scheduled, you may be subject to penalties and interest to the IRS.

- You will pay taxes on the loan interest twice: as nondeductible interest payments on the loan, and again when you withdraw money for retirement—the proceeds you receive and will pay tax on include the nondeductible interest which you paid to your 401(k) account.

### Distributions/withdrawals

*I've heard that I can start taking money out of my 401(k)*

*plan at age 59½ without incurring an early-withdrawal penalty and that I must start taking it out at age 70½. Is that still the case?*

Well, yes and no. Subject to the terms of the plan, you may withdraw any amount after age 59½ without the 10 percent penalty for early withdrawal.

Recent changes in the law now generally allow you to postpone withdrawals from qualified plans—including 401(k)s—beyond age 70½ if you are still working for your employer. Generally you must begin distributions by April 1 of the year following the year in which you retire. However, the ability to postpone distributions beyond age 70½ does not apply if you own more than 5 percent of your employer's business.

If you don't need your retirement dollars and you continue to work, leave the money in the plan as long as you can—you may be able to leave a more substantial inheritance for your family. This should be done through careful tax planning, as it may expose retirement assets to both income and estate taxes.

### *When can I take money out of my 401(k)?*

There are several situations in which you are allowed to withdraw funds from your 401(k) plan:

- Upon your retirement, disability, death, or termination of employment.

- If the company cancels the 401(k) and doesn't replace it with another type of plan.

- If the company sells all or substantially all of its assets to a corporation or sells or disposes of a subsidiary. If you continue to work for the company that was sold, you may take money out of the plan on the date of sale. For this method of withdrawal, the purchasing entity cannot be a partnership.

- When you reach age 59½.

# CHAP. 2: EMPLOYER-SPONSORED RETIREMENT PLANS 75

■ When you can show a hardship that requires the distribution of funds from the plan.

*⋈ What is a "hardship" in regard to taking distributions from my 401(k) plan?*

You may make a penalty-free withdrawal on the basis of hardship if you meet two requirements:

1. You must have an immediate and heavy financial need.
2. It must be necessary to use 401(k) funds to meet the need (i.e., you have no other resources or ways of satisfying the need).

The hardship may be determined by looking at the facts and circumstances of each individual situation, or the 401(k) plan may set forth certain situations that conclusively satisfy the "immediate and heavy financial need" part of the test. Some examples of needs that qualify as hardships are funeral expenses; purchase of a home; avoiding foreclosure on a home or avoiding eviction; college tuition for a child or the employee; or medical expenses for the employee and his or her immediate family.

### Investments

*⋈ Can I direct the investments of my 401(k)?*

It depends upon the terms of the plan. The ideal 401(k) plan would contain provisions that allow you to direct your retirement account from a menu of investment choices, all diversified by asset class. An independent pension and investment management consultant would screen a database of 1800 to 3000 funds and recommend the best 3 to 5 funds by asset class to the plan sponsors, trustees, and retirement committee, who would make the final decisions. Every year, the consultant would provide an update measuring the performance on a risk-adjusted basis, net of fees, so each of the choices stands against its peers. Periodically, the consultant would recommend that changes be made to the menu; when the right technology is used, these changes are transparent to the plan participants. This interactive process allows the plan participants to benefit from having experts watch over the plan investment menu and make changes as necessary.

However, in many plans, the employer may select a single mutual fund company with a variety of different funds from which to choose, including one that invests exclusively in the employer-company's stock.

## Money Purchase Pension Plans

*What is a money purchase pension plan?*

A *money purchase pension plan* is an employer-sponsored retirement plan that requires a fixed contribution which is set out in the plan document and can be changed only periodically. If an employer adopts this type of plan and arbitrarily changes the formula from year to year, the plan will be subject to IRS scrutiny and could be disqualified.

*As the owner of a company, why would I set up a money purchase pension plan?*

There are various reasons for selecting a money purchase plan. In most cases, employers who do so are reassuring their employees that, as an additional benefit, the company is interested in helping them have a secure retirement.

*How would it work in my company?*

In today's retirement planning environment, most companies that set up money purchase plans are personal service corporations or other small businesses that use them in tandem with business-entity or 401(k) profit-sharing plans.

In the professional services environment, money purchase plans typically are integrated with Social Security. Employees receive a contribution of 5.7 percent of wages to the Social Security wage base ($68,400 in 1998, as indexed), and employees whose incomes exceed this wage base receive an additional 5.7 percent of compensation up to the maximum covered compensation limit of $160,000 (in 1998, as indexed). As a result, an employer using this type of plan can enable a highly compensated employee whose income exceeds $160,000 to receive a maximum allocation of $14,341.20 (in 1998).

*Why would an employer use a money purchase pension plan when a discretionary formula in a profit-sharing plan can accomplish the same objective without the fixed requirement?*

In addition to having a money purchase plan, many companies also have a 401(k) profit-sharing plan with a matching contribution equal to a percentage of pay or of the employee deferral up to a specified cap. Typically, the most efficient design is to not use the profit-sharing formula in the 401(k) but to keep this method of contribution available as a fallback. The primary objective in implementing the matching contribution formula is to allow highly compensated employees to receive a contribution that, when added to the money purchase amount indicated above, enables them to get the maximum $30,000 allocation at the least cost in financing benefits for non-highly compensated employees. A typical match is 100 percent for up to 5 percent of pay in this plan design. As a result, an executive earning over $160,000 (1998, as indexed) can defer an amount equal to $7829.40 (in 1998) and receive an identical matching contribution, which, when added to the money purchase allocation above, equals $30,000. The executive deferral is only 4.89 percent of pay (in 1998) and should easily enable a company to meet its average deferral percentage (ADP) nondiscrimination test and average contribution percentage (ACP) nondiscrimination test without any additional qualified nonelective contributions.

In summary, a money purchase pension plan is typically used in tandem with a 401(k) profit-sharing plan to enable companies to finance a floor benefit of a fixed nature yet create a plan under which all employees can save on a pretax basis. Typically, the company can limit its cost each year to a budgetable amount equal to the money purchase formula of 5.7 percent and a discretionary match that is communicated in advance.

*What is the optimum plan when the objective is to enable highly compensated employees to receive a maximum $30,000 allocation at the least cost of financing benefits for non-highly compensated employees?*

Without looking at any of the complex formulas available in profit sharing, it is important to note that 401(k) profit-sharing plans typically will not allow a participant to receive a $30,000 allocation unless some type of formula based on age or job classification is used. As a result, many professional firms and small businesses whose objective is to finance a $30,000 allocation—the maximum deductible allocation for highly compensated employees—will use a combination arrangement of a money purchase plan integrated at 5.7 percent of adjusted compensation and a 401(k) profit-sharing plan allowing pretax deferrals and a matching contribution.

To accomplish this objective, the ideal 401(k) plan design is to have a 100 percent match of all employee contributions up to the first 4 percent of pay. Based on the covered compensation limit of $160,000 (1998, as indexed), the maximum employer obligation is 4 percent of payroll under this formula. A highly compensated employee earning more than $160,000 will then be able to defer $10,000 in 1998 (6.25 percent of pay) and receive a matching compensation equal to $6400 (4 percent of pay)—a total of $16,450. However, this plan may have difficulty passing the ADP test. In general, a maximum contribution of 4.25 percent of pay by all employees would be needed to pass this test. It is recommended that highly compensated employees defer no more than 5 percent of pay under this plan design. When coupled with the money purchase plan, this design will enable them to receive $30,000.

The ultimate plan design would be determined by the company on the basis of all facts and circumstances. In general, a tandem-plan environment with a contribution of 5.7 percent of adjusted pay in the money purchase plan and a maximum 4 percent matching contribution in the 401(k) profit-sharing plan will enable a company to finance $30,000-per-year allocation contributions to all highly compensated employees at a maximum cost of only 9.7 percent of payroll. While there are numerous methods for achieving this desired result, the experience of many pension consultants has been that the formula described above meets with the most success because it is both simple and effective.

## Savings Incentive Match Plans

### Features

⋙ *What is a savings incentive match plan?*

Created by the Small Business Job Protection Act of 1996, a *savings incentive match plan for employees,* or *SIMPLE plan,* is a retirement plan mechanism designed for small businesses. It does not require the onerous government reporting and nondiscrimination tests that are applicable to regular 401(k) profit-sharing plans.

There are two types of SIMPLE plans: SIMPLE IRAs and SIMPLE 401(k)s.

⋙ *What are the features of a SIMPLE IRA?*

The most common features of a SIMPLE IRA are the following.

**Employee eligibility** If you are an employee, you must be covered under the plan if you received $5000 or more of compensation during any 2 prior years and are expected to earn $5000 during the current year.

**Employee deferral** If you are an employee, you may defer or contribute up to 100 percent or $6000 per year of your compensation, whichever is less. In other words, whether you earn $10,000 or $20,000 per year, you can defer only $6000 into this plan; if you earn $6000 per year, you can defer 100 percent—$6000.

**Employer contributions** Your employer must make contributions under one of two methods. The first method is the matching method, which requires a 100 percent employer match up to a limit of 3 percent of your compensation. For any 2 years out of 5 your employer can elect a lower match but not less than 1 percent. Thus, if you earn $200,000 or more, the maximum employer contribution is $6000.

Furthermore, the employer cannot impose conditions on its matching contributions, such as your completion of minimum hours of service or your being employed on the last day of the year.

The second option is a mandatory contribution equal to 2 percent of your compensation up to $160,000. Thus, whether you earn $160,000 or more, the maximum employer contribution is $3200 (2 percent × $160,000). Your employer must make this 2 percent contribution for all employees whether or not the employees contribute to the plan.

**Employee vesting** All contributions made by you and your employer are 100 percent vested. Thus, if you are fired or you terminate employment, you will not forfeit any benefits under your plan.

**Reporting to employee** By January 30 of each year, your employer must provide you with a statement setting forth account balances as of December 31 of the preceding year and all activity during that year.

# CHAP. 2: EMPLOYER-SPONSORED RETIREMENT PLANS    81

**WITHDRAWALS**  Any withdrawals within the first 2 years are subject to a 25 percent penalty, plus income taxes.

**ESTABLISHMENT**  The plan must be established before the end of the tax year. If the employer wishes to elect the first matching option, the plan must be established by November 1 to give the employees 60 days' notice regarding the matching provisions.

### *What are the features of a SIMPLE 401(k)?*

The common features of a SIMPLE 401(k) are as follows.

**EMPLOYEE ELIGIBILITY**  If you are an employee, you must be covered under the plan if you have completed 1 year of service (normally at least 1000 hours) and are over 21 years of age.

**EMPLOYEE DEFERRAL**  If you are an employee, you may defer or contribute up to 100 percent or $6000 per year of your compensation, whichever is less. In other words, whether you earn $10,000 or $20,000 per year, you can defer only $6000 into this plan; if you earn $6000 per year, you can defer 100 percent— $6000.

**EMPLOYER CONTRIBUTIONS**  Your employer must make contributions under one of two methods. The first method is the matching method, which requires a 100 percent employer match up to a limit of 3 percent of your compensation up to $160,000. Thus, whether you earn $160,000 or more, the maximum employer contribution is $4800 (3 percent × $160,000). For any 2 years out of 5 your employer can elect a lower match but not less than 1 percent.

Furthermore, the employer cannot impose conditions on its matching contributions, such as your completion of minimum hours of service or your being employed on the last day of the year.

The second option is a mandatory contribution equal to 2 percent of your compensation up to $160,000. Thus, whether you earn $160,000 or more, the maximum employer contribution is $3200 (2 percent × $160,000). Your employer must make this 2 percent contribution for all employees whether or not the employees contribute to the plan.

EMPLOYEE VESTING   Contributions made by you and your employer must generally be 100 percent vested after 5 years of service. Thus, if you are fired or you terminate employment within this 5-year period, you will probably lose some or all of your benefits under the plan.

REPORTING TO EMPLOYEE   By January 30 of each year, your employer must provide you with a statement setting forth account balances as of December 31 of the preceding year and all activity during that year.

WITHDRAWALS   Any withdrawals within the first 2 years are subject to a 25 percent penalty, plus income taxes.

ESTABLISHMENT   The plan must be established during the current tax year. If the employer wishes to elect the first matching option, the plan must be established by November 1 to give the employees 60 days' notice regarding the matching provisions.

### Creation

*I own my own business. Can I establish a SIMPLE plan?*

Maybe. Both the SIMPLE IRA and the SIMPLE 401(k) are available to a sole proprietor, partnership, or corporation which has 100 or fewer employees and maintains no other tax-qualified retirement plan. Furthermore, nonprofit organizations, including government entities, are allowed to establish SIMPLE plans.

*What type of company would be an ideal candidate for a SIMPLE IRA?*

A SIMPLE IRA would generally appeal to:

# Chap. 2: Employer-Sponsored Retirement Plans    83

- Employers with 100 or fewer employees and minimal turnover

- Employers wishing to exclude employees for up to 2 years

- Business owners wishing to maximize their personal allocation (To illustrate, an owner earning $36,000 could defer $6000 and receive a $1080 match—an allocation equal to 19.6 percent of total compensation. Under traditional plans the limitation would be 15 percent or $5400.)

- Employers who want reduced fiduciary liability

- Employers wishing to reduce administration burdens, including voluminous filing and reporting requirements

*As the employer, am I responsible for administration of the SIMPLE IRA?*

There is very little administration. However, you are responsible for maintaining salary-reduction agreement forms and providing information about the plan to your employees.

*As the employer, am I going to be bogged down with paperwork from a SIMPLE IRA?*

No. The SIMPLE IRA has no discrimination testing and no form-filing requirements, and when contributions begin, they are fully vested. Employers must provide a summary plan description to newly hired employees when they become eligible and to all employees annually.

*If I have employees who don't want to participate in the SIMPLE plan, will this affect the other participants?*

It depends. Each of your employees has the right to elect not to participate in the plan. If your company has selected the 3 percent matching method and an employee signs the election form not to participate, your business is not required to make a contribution for that employee. However, if your company has selected the nonelective 2 percent method, the business is required to make a contribution for every employee, even if some of them choose not to participate in the plan.

Sixty days before the plan is officially adopted, each employee must receive the appropriate paperwork from your business, informing him or her of the plan and its provisions.

### ⚑ *When must I give my employees the right to enter into a salary-reduction agreement under a SIMPLE plan?*

You must give your employees the right to enter the plan during the 60-day period immediately preceding January 1. In addition, for the year in which an employee becomes eligible to make salary-reduction contributions, the employee must be able to begin these contributions as soon as he or she becomes eligible, regardless of whether the 60-day period has ended. During this period, your employees also have the right to modify their salary-reduction agreements without restrictions.

### ⚑ *As an employer, can I provide additional or longer election periods in my SIMPLE plan?*

Nothing precludes a SIMPLE plan from providing additional or longer periods for permitting employees to enter into salary-reduction agreements or to modify prior agreements.

### ⚑ *When is a SIMPLE plan too simple for a small business that is seeking the optimum retirement plan design?*

While the intent behind the SIMPLE IRA and SIMPLE 401(k) legislation is notable, these plans are not the solution to all retirement plan problems. With proper designing, a conventional 401(k) profit-sharing plan might be a better solution. You should seek professional help to determine which plan is best for your business.

CHAP. 2: EMPLOYER-SPONSORED RETIREMENT PLANS  85

### *Contributions*

📝 *I work for a company that has a SIMPLE IRA. What is a salary-reduction contribution?*

A *salary reduction* is the amount you elect to have deducted from your salary as your contribution to your SIMPLE IRA. As part of your election, you can specify the amount as a percentage of your annual compensation or as a specific dollar amount.

📝 *What is the annual limit on the amount of salary-reduction contributions I can make under a SIMPLE plan?*

For 1999, the maximum annual amount of salary-reduction contributions that you can make to a SIMPLE plan is $6000. This amount will be adjusted by the IRS to reflect any changes in the cost of living.

📝 *I am self-employed. How is "compensation" defined for purposes of my SIMPLE plan?*

If you are self-employed, *compensation* means net earnings from self-employment before subtracting any contributions you have made to a SIMPLE plan on your behalf.

📝 *Can I stop contributions to a SIMPLE plan during the plan year?*

Yes, at any time. However, your employer may restrict you from reentering during the same year. This will be spelled out in the summary plan description.

📝 *May I participate in a SIMPLE plan with two different employers for the same year?*

Yes. However, your salary-reduction contributions are subject to the limitations which provide an aggregate limit on the exclusion for elective deferrals for any individual.

*Can contributions made under a SIMPLE IRA plan be made to any type of IRA?*

No. Contributions under a SIMPLE IRA plan can be made only to a SIMPLE IRA sponsored by your employer, not to any other type of IRA.

*Must contributions under a SIMPLE IRA plan be nonforfeitable?*

Yes. All contributions under a SIMPLE IRA plan must be fully vested and nonforfeitable when made.

*When must my employer make salary-reduction contributions under a SIMPLE IRA plan?*

Your employer must make salary-reduction contributions to the SIMPLE IRA no later than 30 days after the end of the month in which the money is withheld from your pay.

*When must my employer make matching and mandatory contributions under a SIMPLE IRA plan?*

Matching and mandatory employer contributions must be made to the financial institution maintaining the SIMPLE IRA no later than the due date for filing the employer's income tax return, including extensions, for the taxable year that includes the last day of the calendar year for which the contributions are made.

### Loans

*Can I borrow money from my SIMPLE plan?*

It depends upon the type of SIMPLE plan. You cannot borrow

CHAP. 2: EMPLOYER-SPONSORED RETIREMENT PLANS   87

from a SIMPLE IRA, but you can borrow from a SIMPLE 401(k). The limitations on loans from the latter are similar to those on loans from a regular 401(k).

### Distributions/withdrawals

*May I withdraw funds from my SIMPLE IRA at any time?*

Yes. Your employer cannot impose any withdrawal restrictions and cannot require that you retain any portion of the contributions in your SIMPLE IRA.

*Are there any penalties for withdrawing money from a SIMPLE IRA?*

Sometimes. If you make withdrawals within 2 years of the day you first participated in the plan, the withdrawals are subject to a 25 percent early-withdrawal penalty. After the 2-year period, the penalty is 10 percent. There is no penalty for withdrawals made after you reach 59½.

*What are the income tax consequences of withdrawing money from a SIMPLE IRA?*

Normally, the amounts you withdraw will be subject to income tax in the year you make the withdrawal.

### Investments

*What kind of investments can I or my employer put in the SIMPLE IRA?*

You or your employer can choose any investments that are suitable for retirement plans: mutual funds, common stocks, certificates of deposit, government bonds, corporate bonds, and variable or fixed annuities.

*As an employee, do I have the right to select the financial institution to which my employer will make all SIMPLE IRA contributions on my behalf?*

Yes. Generally your employer must permit you to select the financial institution.

## Simplified Employee Pension Plans

### Features

*What is a simplified employee pension plan?*

A *simplified employee pension (SEP) plan,* is a retirement plan especially suited for self-employed owners or small corporations. For this reason, it has been coined by some the "self-employed person's" IRA.

*What is the major benefit of a SEP-IRA?*

The major advantage of the SEP-IRA is that you, as the employer and often the sole employee, are permitted to make tax-deductible contributions directly to your or an employee's IRA account. Furthermore, you are not limited to the $2000 cap of a regular IRA.

*What are some of the features of a SEP-IRA?*

EMPLOYEE ELIGIBILITY   To be eligible, an employee generally must be over age 21, have earned a minimum of $400 of compensation during the year, and worked for the business for 3 of the preceding 5 years. These are the maximum limits of eligibility; the employer may select less restrictive eligibility requirements.

EMPLOYER DEDUCTIBLE CONTRIBUTIONS   Employers may contribute and receive an income tax deduction for the lesser of $24,000 or 15 percent of compensation. In the case of self-employment income, the percentage cap is 13.04 percent.

CHAP. 2: EMPLOYER-SPONSORED RETIREMENT PLANS    89

EMPLOYEE VESTING    Any contribution made to a SEP vests immediately. This means it becomes the property of the employee the moment it goes into his or her IRA account.

### Creation

⋙ *Is a SEP difficult to set up or maintain?*

SEPs are no-frills retirement plans that are easy to set up and less expensive to maintain than traditional pension and profit-sharing plans. They require minimal reporting and paperwork. Many mutual fund companies and annuities have IRS-approved SEP documents ready for your use. Therefore, SEPs are ideal for small family businesses, nonprofits, partnerships, and sole proprietorships.

⋙ *I am the owner of a small business. If I establish a SEP, how much do I have to contribute for each employee?*

As the employer, you are free to determine each year what percentage of compensation you will contribute for each employee up to the lesser of 15 percent or $30,000. However, in no event can you deduct more than $24,000 for any employee. Thus for each employee earning more than $160,000, you will be limited to $24,000 in deductible contributions. Your business must contribute the same percentage for all eligible employees in a given year. For instance, if you, the employer, are going to contribute at a rate of 10 percent, you would fund each employee's SEP with 10 percent of his or her compensation.

### Contributions

⋙ *Can I make contributions to my non-Roth IRA as well as to my SEP?*

Yes. In addition to contributing to the SEP, you can make up to a $2000 contribution to your deductible-IRA account if your adjusted gross income is within the requirements for contributions to deductible IRAs. If your gross income exceeds the amount for contributions to deductible IRAs, you can make contributions (up to $2000) to a nondeductible IRA. Thus, you can have two tax-deferred retirement accounts working for you.

*I'm an employee and participate in my employer's qualified plan. I also run a small business out of my home. Can I set up a SEP and make a contribution based on my self-employment income?*

Yes. You are eligible for a SEP based on your self-employment income regardless of your participation in a qualified plan through your regular employer. However, the total annual contributions to a SEP and any other qualified plans generally cannot exceed $30,000.

### Loans

*Can I borrow money from a SEP?*

No. Borowing from SEP plans is not allowed.

### Investments

*Can I control the investments inside my SEP?*

Yes. As with any other IRA, you, as the employee, may direct the investment of the contribution into any variety of available investments—mutual funds, stocks, bonds, CDs, and so on.

## Qualified Plans and Asset Protection

*Is my 401(k) plan protected from creditors?*

Yes. Qualified plans, including 401(k) plans, are protected from attachment, garnishment, execution, and any other process from

# CHAP. 2: EMPLOYER-SPONSORED RETIREMENT PLANS  91

a creditor. The only creditor that may attach or levy against your 401(k) funds is the IRS.

*I am considering filing for bankruptcy because of bills I cannot pay. Is my 401(k) money at risk of being seized by the bankruptcy court?*

If you file a bankruptcy, the bankruptcy court cannot take your 401(k) funds to pay your creditors. All qualified plan retirement benefits are protected by the Employee Retirement Income Security Act of 1974, which requires that qualified plans prohibit the voluntary or involuntary taking of plan funds for the payment of debt.

*Is the vested portion of my 401(k) plan accessible to creditors?*

It depends. Generally, an interest in a qualified plan cannot be reached by a participant's creditors, even in bankruptcy. There are circumstances, however, where the creditor may attempt to show that the plan was set up as a sham to avoid creditors. Under many states' laws (e.g., California), the key factor is whether the plan was designed and used for retirement purposes. Any use of a plan for nonretirement purposes would tend to eliminate its creditor protection. Nonretirement purposes include substantial control over the contributions, management, administration, and use of funds, such as unsecured loans taken from the fund without payment of commercially reasonable interest and last-minute (before bankruptcy or execution of judgment) deposits of cash into the fund. When a participant takes a loan from a retirement fund, it is critical for tax as well as creditor-protection issues to ensure that a note bearing commercially reasonable interest is supplied and that regular interest payments are made on the note.

*My closely held corporation established a qualified retirement plan, and I am the sole participant. Are my benefits under this plan accessible to my personal creditors?*

It depends. Under many states' laws, a qualified retirement plan is exempt (creditor-protected), even if a closely held corporation runs the plan and even if the sole shareholder is the only participant. Under federal bankruptcy law, however, a closely held plan with no third-party employee beneficiaries is not exempt. In other words, as long as you do not file for bankruptcy, the plan will be out of your creditors' reach. But avoiding bankruptcy, particularly involuntary bankruptcy, can be difficult to accomplish in those situations where the protection is needed most.

*I'm thinking of moving to Florida when I retire, but all my debts have been incurred in my home state. Will I be limited to the exemptions allowed in my home state, or will the more liberal laws of Florida be available to me?*

Each state has exemption laws which set forth certain types and amounts of property which are beyond the reach of creditors. These laws come into play only when creditors attempt to collect on judgments, and this occurs in the jurisdiction in which the debtor lives when the attempt is made. Therefore, if you move to Florida, the exemptions which will apply are those of Florida. However, the exemption laws of your former state of residence might apply if you leave assets in that state. For this reason, if you relocate to the debtor-friendly state of Florida, you should also move all your assets into Florida.

*Can my spouse take part of my qualified plan as part of a divorce settlement?*

Yes. A judge, through a qualified domestic relations order, can transfer up to one-half of your qualified retirement plan to your spouse or former spouse for child support, spousal support, or property award. The amount of property awarded to the spouse or former spouse is generally based on the ratio of the years of marriage while you were a participant in the plan to the total years of the marriage.

## NONQUALIFIED PLANS

⅍ *What is a nonqualified plan?*

A *nonqualified plan* is a retirement plan which does not meet the Internal Revenue Code's requirements for qualified plans. Nonqualified plans are usually designed for a select group of employees, such as top management, rather than all employees. For this reason, the government does not offer the same income tax incentives for nonqualified plans as it does for qualified ones. Generally, contributions to a nonqualified plan are not deductible for income tax purposes by either the employer or the employee.

⅍ *As the owner of a business, why would I want a nonqualified plan?*

There are several reasons why you might wish to create a nonqualified plan for your business:

- To avoid discrimination requirements: You can provide benefits to yourself and/or designated key employees, rather than to all of your employees. In fact, the plan design for one employee can be different from that for another employee.

- To increase the benefits for key employees and executives to a higher level: You can be responsive to specific compensation issues or tailor an arrangement to an employee's specific circumstances, thus encouraging longer years of service.

- To provide benefits in excess of the contribution limits imposed under qualified plans.

- To shift income to later years.
- To recruit or retain certain employees.
- To provide performance incentives for specific employees.

*What are some examples of nonqualified plans?*

The most common types of nonqualified plans are:

1. Deferred-compensation plans
2. Salary continuation plans
3. Bonus plans
4. Rabbi trusts
5. Stock option plans
6. Split-dollar plans
7. Reverse split-dollar plans
8. 403(b) plans (tax-sheltered annuities)

## Deferred-Compensation Plans

*Can you briefly describe a deferred-compensation plan?*

A *deferred-compensation plan* is exactly what it sounds like. As an employee, you elect to defer some of your current compensation in order to reduce your current taxable income. The company reduces your compensation and uses the deferred funds to begin accruing benefits for the purpose of providing an income payout to you at a later date, such as at retirement.

The company receives no income tax deduction for the amount of deferred compensation set aside for you. The contribution is not currently taxable income for you because the law considers that you have a considerable risk of not being paid (called a "substantial risk of forfeiture"): The company is only making a promise to pay you in the future, and the assets are

CHAP. 2: EMPLOYER-SPONSORED RETIREMENT PLANS 95

subject to your employer's creditors. While you are still employed, the growth on the funds set aside for your future benefit will also be tax-deferred for you.

On your retirement, the company will receive an income tax deduction for the benefits it pays to you, and you will report those benefits as ordinary taxable income.

*As an employee, how would I benefit from this type of plan?*

If you are in a high income tax bracket, do not currently need the money, and expect to be in a lower income tax bracket in the future, deferring part of your income makes sense. Your benefit will be the amount you save in taxes by delaying receipt of the money.

*Do I have any risks with this type of plan?*

Yes. The company cannot protect the plan assets for your benefit. These assets must be available to the general creditors of the company. Therefore, if the company goes bankrupt or becomes insolvent, you could lose some or all of your benefits.

## Salary Continuation Plans

*How is a salary continuation plan different from a deferred-compensation plan?*

A *salary continuation plan* is a promise by the employer to continue an employee's salary, according to a given formula, after the employee's specified retirement date.

A salary continuation plan, sometimes known as a *select executive retirement plan (SERP)*, provides a benefit in addition to the employee's compensation package, rather than as a reduction in his or her current pay (deferred-compensation plan). The amount of the benefit will be equal to the annual cost of the benefit being provided.

For example, your company would enter into a written agreement with you to pay you an annual sum beginning at retirement, at a specific triggering date (such as age 59), at death, or at the onset of disability. These payments can be made for a "period certain," which ensures that the benefits will continue to your named beneficiary if you die before the end of the period, or for your lifetime, or for a combination of the two.

A SERP design allows your company to selectively choose which executives will participate and at what benefit level. The plan requires minimal IRS or Department of Labor reporting.

### *Do I have any risks with a salary continuation plan?*

Yes. As with the deferred-compensation plan, the company cannot protect the plan assets for your benefit because they must be available to the general creditors of the company. Therefore, if the company declares bankruptcy or becomes insolvent, you could lose some or all of your benefits.

### *As the owner of a closely held business, how do I make sure I can pay the benefit when the time comes?*

Your company has two options. It can pay out the benefits from earnings at some time in the future when the benefits are due, or it can set up an "informal funding" arrangement now to ensure that the benefits will be there when they are needed. Although any investment vehicle can be used, certain investments offer greater tax advantages than others. Careful consideration should be given to this area.

An investment option often used is "key-person" life insurance. In this approach, your company would purchase a policy on the executive's life, naming itself as owner, premium payer, and beneficiary of the policy. At the executive's retirement, your company could pay the benefit by using current cash flow or by withdrawing, surrendering, or borrowing funds from the policy's cash value.

CHAP. 2: EMPLOYER-SPONSORED RETIREMENT PLANS    97

The current cost is not income tax–deductible for your company and is not reportable as income to the executive. Later, as benefits are paid to the executive, they are tax-deductible for your company and are taxed as ordinary income to the executive and/or the executive's named beneficiary. One of the additional tax advantages of a properly structured life insurance policy is that the investments grow tax-deferred and the company can withdraw funds from the policy tax-free.

At the executive's death, your company could recover all its costs in the program through the receipt of the life insurance policy's death proceeds. The accrued liability incurred by your company for the promised benefits is indirectly offset by the life insurance policy values. These policy values are exempt from company-accumulated earnings calculations.

If the executive dies before retirement, your company will have the funds from the death benefit to pay to the executive's beneficiary.

## Bonus Plans

### What is a bonus plan?

A *bonus plan* is a nonqualified retirement plan in which an employer compensates an employee for services by paying the premiums of a life insurance policy that the employee owns on his or her life. The cost of the premiums paid by the employer is deductible to the employer and is included in the employee's gross income. The employer has no rights in the policy, only the promise to bonus the premiums on the employee's behalf. There are two common variations of bonus plans.

TRADITIONAL 162 BONUS PLAN    In addition to assisting you, as the employee, in acquiring life insurance coverage, a traditional bonus plan can also provide you with a vehicle for accumulating retirement funds in the form of a tax-deferred income buildup of cash value—or tax-free income if the cash value remains in the policy until your death.

Your employer pays all or part of the policy premium for a specified period—until your death or termination of employment, or for a fixed number of years. The premium payment by your employer can be paid directly to the insurance company or be paid as a bonus to you. Furthermore, your employer can "gross-up" the bonus to cover both the premium due and the income tax you will pay on the bonus.

The premium and the gross-up bonus are taxable income to you and are deductible for your employer if they constitute a necessary business expense in connection with payment of reasonable compensation for personal services actually rendered.

RESTRICTIVE BONUS PLAN   In a restrictive bonus plan, the policy contains an endorsement stating that you shall not, without your employer's consent, surrender, change the ownership of, or borrow cash values of the policy or assign or pledge the policy as collateral. The endorsement may have an expiration date tied to a fixed date, an attained age, or your retirement. The endorsement may expire upon bankruptcy or dissolution of your marriage.

A vesting schedule can be included so that if you terminate employment (for reasons other than disability or death) before the full vesting date, you must reimburse your employer for all or part of the premium payments (and gross-up).

### Rabbi trusts

⚸ *What is a "Rabbi" trust?*

A *Rabbi trust* is an innovative tool for segregating nonqualifying retirement benefits for executive-level employees. The employer creates an irrevocable grantor trust and contributes money to the trust. The employer does not get an income tax deduction when making the contribution, and the employee is not currently taxed on the contribution. Upon the employee's retirement and receipt of the benefits, the employer gets a tax deduction and the employee pays income tax.

Employees have only an unsecured right to the assets. If the employees' rights were secured in some manner, the employees would be considered to have received the funds when you put them into the trust and thus the funds would be included in the employees' taxable income. Although the Rabbi trust protects employees from a spendthrift employer who exhausts all the funds from which deferred-compensation payments could be made, it does not protect against the possible forfeiture of the payments in the event of employer insolvency or bankruptcy.

## Stock Option Plans

### *Types of stock option plans*

⅍ *What is a stock option plan?*

A *stock option plan* is an arrangement in which an employer gives employees options to buy company stock at a bargain price. There are actually three types of stock option plans:

EMPLOYEE STOCK PURCHASE PLANS These are part of the employment compensation package and are regulated by the Internal Revenue Code. Participation in a stock purchase plan must be made available to all the company's regular employees; employees who are also current owners of more than 5 percent of the business must be excluded from participation. Part-time employees can be excluded entirely, and relatively new employees can be excluded for a period of time at the discretion of the employer.

The *option price*—the price at which you can purchase your employer's stock—is determined by your employer when the plan is created. Your employer can choose to have the option price be a set dollar amount (not less than 85 percent of the stock's fair market value at the time the option is granted) or a set percentage (not less than 85 percent of the stock's fair market value at the time the option is exercised).

**INCENTIVE STOCK OPTION PLANS** These also are part of the employment compensation package and are regulated by the Internal Revenue Code. Unlike an employee stock purchase plan, however, an incentive stock option plan may be created for the benefit of a certain class of employees. This capability comes with some restrictions: The option price can be no less than the stock's fair market value at the time the option is granted, and employees who are also current owners of more than 10 percent of the business must be excluded from participation.

**NONQUALIFIED STOCK OPTION PLANS** These are any employee stock options that do not come under the rules for employee stock purchase plans or incentive stock option plans. Nonqualified stock options are not regulated by the Internal Revenue Code. Most of the details of these compensation packages can, therefore, be determined by the employer.

*Are employee stock purchase and incentive stock option plans considered qualified plans?*

No. Technically they are not qualified plans because they are not covered in Section 401 of the Internal Revenue Code.

*If my employer grants me a stock option, what effect will it have on my income taxes?*

The effect depends on the type of stock option your employer gives you. With an employee stock purchase or incentive stock option, you will recognize no income when the stock option is granted to you. Generally, receiving a nonqualified stock option will also not cause you to realize any income. However, if the nonqualified stock option has a readily ascertainable value when it is given to you, that value will be considered ordinary income to you. The good news is that it is very rare for a nonqualified stock option to have a readily ascertainable value at granting.

CHAP. 2: EMPLOYER-SPONSORED RETIREMENT PLANS 101

## Employee stock purchase
## and incentive stock option plans

*⋈ When must I exercise my stock option?*

If you have an *incentive stock option,* you will generally have 10 years from the date the option was granted to you in which to exercise it. However, your employer is allowed to shorten this period at the time the option is granted to you.

If you have an *employee stock purchase option,* you will generally have 5 years from the date the option is granted to you in which to exercise it. If the option price, however, is not restricted so that it will equal no less than 85 percent of the fair market value when the option is exercised, the time limitation is reduced to 27 months from the date the option is granted to you. Again, your employer is allowed to shorten these limitation periods at the time the option is granted to you.

If you leave your employer, you must exercise the stock option no later than 3 months from the date your employment ends; otherwise, the time limitation will depend upon which of the stock options your employer grants to you.

*⋈ If I decide to exercise my stock option, how soon can I sell the stock I've purchased?*

Once you exercise the option, you must retain the stock you receive for a specified "holding period." This period is either 2 years from the day the option was granted to you or 1 year from the day you exercised the option, whichever is longer.

The holding-period rules will not apply to your estate or any beneficiary receiving your stock option if you die before exercising the option.

*⋈ What is the income tax consequence of exercising my stock option and then selling or transferring the stock before the end of the holding period?*

Since this is a violation of the holding-period rules, it triggers immediate income taxation at ordinary-income tax rates as opposed to capital gain tax rates. If the fair market value of the stock at the time of the sale or transfer exceeds the option price at which you purchased the stock, you will realize ordinary income on the difference. For example, if you purchased the stock for the option price of $85 per share and then sold it for a fair market value of $100 per share, you would have to report $15 per share as ordinary income.

Given the major reduction in the capital gain tax rates which were passed as part of the Taxpayer Relief Act of 1997, this distinction is crucial.

*What is the income tax consequence of exercising my stock option and then selling or transfering the stock* after *the end of the holding period?*

The effect depends upon which stock option you have.

With an *incentive stock option,* if the stock's fair market value at the time of the sale exceeds the option price you paid for the stock, you will have to report the difference as capital gain. For example, if you purchased the stock for the option price of $85 per share and you sold it for a fair market value of $100 per share, you would have to report $15 per share as capital gain.

Unfortunately, the sale of stock obtained by exercising an *employee stock purchase option* is somewhat more complicated. There are two possible results. If the option price set by your employer was greater than or equal to the stock's fair market value when the option was granted to you, the tax result of selling the stock will be the same as that described above for an incentive stock option.

If, instead, the option price set by your employer was less than the stock's fair market value when the option was granted to you, you will have to report as ordinary income the lesser of:

■ The difference between the stock's fair market value when

CHAP. 2: EMPLOYER-SPONSORED RETIREMENT PLANS 103

the option was granted to you and the option price for which you purchased the stock

- The difference between the stock's fair market value when you sell it and the option price for which you purchased the stock

For example, let's assume that the stock's fair market value was $100 per share at the time your employer granted you the employee stock purchase option and that the option price was set at $90 per share. You exercised your stock option 3 years ago and sold the stock this year for $98 per share. You will have to report $8 per share as ordinary income for this year (the $98-per-share fair market value at the time of sale minus the $90-per-share option price).

If we change the example, the tax situation gets even more complicated. Let's assume the same facts as before but with one change: You sold the stock for $106 per share this year. Now you will have to report $10 per share as ordinary income (the $100-per-share fair market value at the time the option was granted to you minus the $90-per-share option price). You will also have to report the additional $6-per-share profit as capital gain (the $106-per-share sales price minus your adjusted basis in the stock of $100 per share).

*What are the income tax consequences to my estate or my beneficiary if I die before exercising my stock options?*

Assuming your stock options did not lapse at your death, as may be required by your employer, your estate or a beneficiary who has received your qualified stock options will not be subject to the holding-period requirements. Just as there would be no income tax implications to you if you had properly exercised the options during your lifetime, your estate or your beneficiary will recognize no income when the options are exercised. In addition, the income tax consequence on a subsequent sale of the stock will

104                                    WAYS AND MEANS

be the same for your estate or your beneficiary as it would have
been for you.

*⅄* *Can I transfer my stock options to another person or to a trust?*

No. Stock options cannot be transferred by you to any other
person or entity during your lifetime. You cannot even transfer
your stock options to your revocable living trust.

Your employer can specify that, upon your death, any unex-
ercised stock options owned by you will lapse and can never be
exercised. If your employer does not require that the options lapse
at your death, they can be transferred to the beneficiaries under
your will or to your heirs by intestate succession. Either way, the
probate process will probably be required to transfer the stock
options to your beneficiaries or heirs.


## Split-Dollar Plans

*⅄* *What is a "split-dollar" life insurance policy?*

There is no such thing as a split-dollar life insurance policy. *Split
dollar* is an arrangement whereby the premiums, cash values, and
death benefits of a regular life insurance policy are split by two
or more parties, usually an employer and an employee.

*⅄* *Why would I use a split-dollar arrangement for my employees?*

The primary reason for using a split-dollar arrangement is to
provide life insurance benefits to select employees at an affordable
cost.

*⅄* *What advantages does a split-dollar arrangement provide to
my company and my employees?*

Since a split-dollar plan is a nonqualified benefit, you can cover

# CHAP. 2: EMPLOYER-SPONSORED RETIREMENT PLANS 105

one employee or a number of employees and there are no limits on how much insurance coverage you can use.

A split-dollar plan is a tremendous way to help you retain key employees and give them current as well as future benefits. They receive life insurance protection at a fraction of what it would cost them to personally carry the same level of coverage and, at the same time, are able to accumulate funds for supplemental retirement income or other uses.

Split-dollar plans must meet only minimal reporting and disclosure compliance requirements, and most administrative details are handled by the insurance company.

For select owner-employees and key executives, the technique is an exciting method for providing substantial permanent coverage on a cost-effective basis.

### *How does a split-dollar arrangement work?*

Each life insurance policy (except term insurance) has a portion of the annual premium assigned to cover costs of mortality, sales administration, ongoing policy expenses, state premium taxes, and so on. The balance of the premium is invested, creating a policy account value known as *cash value.*

In a split-dollar arrangement, the respective parts of the policy premium are paid by the employer and the employee, and the separate and distinct parts of the premium are used to meet certain objectives. Typically, the employee, who is the insured, pays the portion of the premium attributable to the annual policy expense—mortality, administration, and the like. This is known as the *imputed economic benefit* or *PS-58 cost,* which is initially about 10 to 20 percent of the annual premium. The balance of the premium is paid by the employer.

In the event of the employee's death, his or her beneficiaries receive what is left of the insurance policy's death proceeds after repayment of the total amount of premiums advanced by the employer during the employee's lifetime. For example, let's assume the life insurance policy has a $500,000 death benefit and a \$5000 annual premium. Of each \$5000 premium, \$800 is paid by the employee and the balance of \$4200 is paid by the employer. Should the employee die after 2 years of premium payments, the employee's family would receive \$491,600, since the employer would first be repaid its total premium payments of \$8400.

### How is the PS-58 cost determined?

According to the Internal Revenue Service, the economic benefit is determined by using either the government's published PS-58 term rates or the issuing insurance company's standard annual renewable term rates offered to the public. In most instances, the company's annual term rates are much lower than the published PS-58 rates. Therefore, an employee and an employer will normally select the company's annual term rates in order to reduce the amount of the economic benefit that is taxable to the employee.

### Are there different types of split-dollar plans?

There are two main types: collateral-assignment split dollar and endorsement split dollar. The type of split-dollar plan an employer uses depends on the employer's goals and objectives.

### What is a collateral-assignment split dollar?

A *collateral-assignment split dollar,* also known as *equity split dollar,* is an arrangement that uses a policy owned by an employee on his or her own life. In a separate agreement, the employee assigns to the company an amount of the policy's cash value and death benefit that is normally equal to the cumulative premium payments made by the company. Furthermore, the employee assigns to the company his or her rights in the policy as collateral (security).

### ✍ *What is an endorsement split dollar?*

An *endorsement split dollar* is an arrangement that uses a policy owned by the company on the life of an employee. The company endorses part or all of the "at-risk" portion of the policy (the face value minus the cash value) to the employee for his or her personal life insurance coverage needs. The employee's rights in the policy are usually limited to the right to name the beneficiary. The company retains an interest in the policy equal to the policy's cash value, with all rights to exercise any incidents of ownership over that interest.

### ✍ *What is required to establish a split-dollar plan?*

For each form of split dollar, there needs to be a written agreement between employer and employee that represents a bona fide contract for adequate and full consideration. Certain documentation (either the assignment or an endorsement) should be recorded with the insurer, and the agreement should be properly documented in the employer's records.

### ✍ *What are the immediate income tax ramifications of split dollar?*

If your employer pays the entire premium, you have to include in your gross income for the current year the economic benefit—the PS-58 cost—of the insurance coverage. This is understandable as you are receiving a current benefit. The tax result is the same as it would be if you had simply purchased an individual term policy on your life. If you pay the PS-58 cost, there is no additional income to report.

Your employer does not take an immediate income tax deduction for its portion of the premium payments, since they will eventually be reimbursed.

*If I don't die before retirement, will a split-dollar plan provide me with any retirement benefits?*

Normally yes. Split dollar can be designed to provide both death proceeds to your family if you die before retirement and cash upon your retirement if you are still living.

When the split-dollar plan begins, your employer will maintain some type of control over the policy to guarantee that the company will be repaid its cumulative share of the premium payments in the event of your death. However, at some point in the future, generally no later than your retirement date, you will probably receive your life insurance policy free of your employer's control. This feature is known as a *roll-out option.* At the time of the roll out, the policy is distributed to you. Your employer has a right to an amount equal to its share of the premiums paid into the policy from inception. You receive the remainder of the cash value, if any. The balance of the cash value is owned and controlled entirely by you and can be accessed for retirement needs.

Your employer is repaid for the premium payments it has made. You can make the repayment by using your personal funds or by borrowing on the policy. Alternatively, your employer can give you the policy and include it as a taxable bonus to you. Amounts treated as a bonus will be taxable to you at the time of the roll out.

*Would you explain further how I access the life insurance values for retirement?*

Let's say you and your employer have a collateral-assignment split-dollar arrangement for a policy with a death benefit of $500,000. The cumulative premium payments total $100,000—$10,000 paid by you and $90,000 paid by your employer—and the current cash value is $150,000.

If your employer forgives its $90,000 of premium advances, you will have $90,000 of taxable income and will own the policy free and clear. This gives you a cost basis of $100,000 in the

# Chap. 2: Employer-Sponsored Retirement Plans  109

policy—$10,000 paid by you plus the $90,000 of ordinary income. The difference between the cash value and your cost basis ($150,000 − $100,000), or $50,000, will not be taxed to you at the time of the split-dollar termination unless you surrender the policy.

You can access the remaining cash value on a tax-free basis for retirement. One way to do this is to make partial withdrawals from the policy. Under current tax law, any withdrawals (up to your basis) are not taxable income to you. The withdrawals could end up reducing the death benefit of the policy. You can also borrow on the policy. Although interest will be due on the amount borrowed, some types of insurance policies actually pay you interest at or near the amount of interest charged. Therefore, the net cost of borrowing (the difference between the rate you pay the insurance company and the rate it credits your cash values) can be extremely low or even zero.

Finally, you can always surrender the policy and receive the net cash value. However, this cancels the policy and you will have to pay ordinary income taxes on the gain (the difference between the amount you receive and your basis in the policy). The surrender of life insurance does not qualify for capital gain treatment, so the cash-value proceeds are taxed at ordinary-income tax levels.

### ⅓ *How do I terminate a split-dollar agreement?*

Your employer's payment of premiums on your behalf must be fully repaid in order to terminate the agreement. A split-dollar arrangement between you and your employer can be terminated at any time by simply repaying, directly or indirectly, the cumulative amount of the premiums which have been paid by your employer. This gives you clear title to all policy values.

There are three typical methods of terminating the plan: "lump-sum roll out," which means repayment all at once; "crawl out," which involves repayment to your employer over a specified period of time; or forgiveness of the cumulative amount by your employer.

Before choosing the method, you should consider a variety of factors, including the income tax consequences to you and your employer, availability of cash for you and your employer, the policy cash values, and the amount of your employer's cumulative loans.

*Can an existing policy become a split-dollar policy?*

Yes. Structured properly, a split-dollar arrangement can begin at any time, whether with a newly issued policy or an existing policy that was not previously used in a split-dollar arrangement.

### Reverse split-dollar plans

*What is reverse split dollar?*

*Reverse split dollar,* like traditional split dollar, is a funding arrangement associated with a permanent life insurance policy. In a reverse split-dollar arrangement, a policy owned by an employee is used to provide "key-person" insurance to his or her employer. Key-person insurance is intended to indemnify the employer should the employee die prematurely.

Reverse split dollar simply reverses the roles and benefits of a traditional split-dollar arrangement. It grants the "pure death protection" (death benefits minus cash values) to the employer and the cash value to the employee.

*What are the practical differences between traditional split-dollar and reverse split-dollar agreements?*

Under a traditional split-dollar plan, you and your employer agree to purchase a life insurance policy and split the premium payments on it. Your employer agrees to pay a majority of the premium, while you pay the portion of the premium equal to the imputed economic benefit. The imputed economic benefit is usually the published term rate of the insurance company, which is

# CHAP. 2: EMPLOYER-SPONSORED RETIREMENT PLANS  111

lower than the government-published PS-58 cost. Therefore, you pay less of the premium. Upon your death, or at the termination of the agreement, your employer will receive a return of premiums paid, and you or your beneficiaries will receive the balance.

Under a reverse split-dollar plan, you and your employer agree to split the premium payments and death benefit on a life insurance policy purchased by you. You own the cash value. Your employer pays a portion of the premium equal to the imputed economic benefit in return for a specified death benefit. Unlike the case with traditional split dollar, the preferred cost for the imputed economic benefit with reverse split dollar is usually the higher, government-published PS-58 cost. Therefore, your employer pays more of the premium. The arrangement is terminated when you reach the age specified in the agreement. At that time, your employer has no further rights in the plan. You own the entire cash value and the entire death benefit.

With a traditional split-dollar plan, the major objective is to have the death benefit payable to your beneficiary. Your employer pays most of the costs, but you get most of the benefits.

A reverse split-dollar plan usually has equity accumulation for you as its major goal. Although your employer still pays most of the costs, it receives most of the benefits if you die during the term of the agreement. Reverse split-dollar involves your "renting" the lion's share of a life insurance policy death benefit to your employer for a limited number of years. The objectives are to have your employer pay most of the cost of funding the policy during the time the employer rents the death benefit. This result is by design because most reverse split-dollar plans call for the plan to terminate when cash premium payments are no longer required to continue the policy. At that point, you own the full policy, including substantial cash values—all paid for by your employer.

*Are there any problems with the reverse split-dollar technique?*

There is probably no type of split dollar more tax-uncertain than reverse split dollar. It is, after all, the opposite of the split-dollar arrangement envisioned in 1964 by the IRS. Many professionals recommend use of the reverse split-dollar only by those who are comfortable with more aggressive tax planning.

*Is there a way to combine a traditional arrangement with a reverse split-dollar design to meet multiple needs?*

Certainly. Let's look at an example: You, as a key executive, apply for and own a life insurance policy with \$2 million coverage. You and your employer enter into a reverse split-dollar agreement. You assign, by endorsement, \$1 million of the \$2 million death benefit to your employer for key-person indemnification purposes. Your employer pays the increasing PS-58 costs, and you pay the balance of the premium on the \$1 million portion.

You and your employer also enter into a split-dollar agreement (equity or endorsement) for the remaining \$1 million portion of the policy. You pay the published term rates for that portion and your employer pays the balance.

At your retirement, the reverse split-dollar agreement is terminated, thereby giving you full rights to the first \$1 million. The split-dollar agreement is also terminated thereby giving you full rights to the second \$1 million. (Note that the latter termination is a taxable event: deductible to your employer and reportable as income to you is the most conservative method.)

Policy equity values are owned by you, subject to any assignments or endorsements.

## TAX-SHELTERED ANNUITIES

*What is a tax-sheltered annuity?*

A *tax-sheltered annuity (TSA)* is a tax-deferred retirement program for employees of public education systems and other tax-exempt organizations. The federal government has encouraged nonprofit

CHAP. 2: EMPLOYER-SPONSORED RETIREMENT PLANS **113**

charitable institutions to set aside funds for their employees' retirements. Plans that are available to teachers employed by public school systems generally fall into this category.

Before enactment of the Employee Retirement Income Security Act (ERISA) of 1974, tax-sheltered annuities were available only by investing in an annuity contract, hence their name. Today, you can also have your contribution directed to a 403(b) mutual fund or brokerage account.

A TSA is also known as a 403(b) plan, after the Internal Revenue Code section which outlines such retirement arrangements.

### Is a 403(b) plan a qualified plan?

Technically, no. Qualified plans fall under Section 401 of the Internal Revenue Code. However, 403(b) plans have many of the same tax advantages as qualified plans have.

### Who can establish a 403(b) plan?

Two types of organizations can offer 403(b) programs:

- *Public educational organizations:* kindergarten through twelfth-grade public schools, junior and senior colleges, and universities

- *501(c)(3) organizations:* nonprofit organizations, specifically designated by the IRS through a Letter of Determination, which are organized and operated for the exclusive benefit of the general public for charitable, religious, scientific, public safety testing, literary, or educational purposes; for the promotion of national or international sports activities; or for the prevention of cruelty to children and animals.

### How does a 403(b) plan work?

The board of the organization eligible to offer TSA retirement benefits determines which investments can be designated for pretax payroll-deduction contributions. The options can be fixed annuities, variable annuities, or mutual funds. As an employee, you can then elect to contribute. You can contribute up to certain statutory limits and can make up contributions not made in previous years under certain guidelines.

Furthermore, you can periodically roll your accumulated TSA contributions into other TSA investments, but only those approved by your employer can be designated for pretax payroll-deduction contributions.

### ⚜ *What funding vehicles are available for 403(b) plans?*

Typically, annuity contracts and mutual funds having custodial arrangements with a financial institution are the primary funding vehicles for 403(b) programs. Recently some brokerage accounts have become available. Churches and church-related organizations can also establish *retirement income accounts,* which allow for a broader array of investment choices, including individual stocks and bonds.

### ⚜ *What are the income tax advantages of a 403(b) plan?*

Regardless of whether the money is actually set aside by you or by your employer, or whether the funds are contributed by you through a reduction in salary, the funds placed into a 403(b) plan can be excluded from your current taxable income. In addition, gains on the contributions are tax-deferred. As with other retirement plans, distributions are taxed as ordinary income. Although the distribution rules and penalties are similar to those of qualified plans and IRAs, there are a few subtle differences.

# chapter 3

## Individual Retirement Accounts

One of the most popular and effective changes in retirement plan law in recent years was the expansion of private retirement plans. This chapter's questions and answers focus on individual retirement account (IRA) rules and regulations. As Congress has watched the IRA expansion and its positive impact on American savings, it has continued to increase such opportunities for savings.

Our contributors explain the rules for deductibility of regular IRA contributions and the rules for the newly enacted Roth IRA and education IRA, as well as how to analyze rollover opportunities from both the tax and investment perspective.

Knowledge of the opportunities available through efficient use of IRAs is critical to building an effective retirement plan investment strategy. The questions and answers in this chapter will help you determine which of the many retirement plan options might be appropriate under your individual circumstances.

## TYPES OF IRAS

⋈ *What is an individual retirement account?*

An *individual retirement account (IRA)* is a savings plan that receives favorable income tax treatment under the Internal Revenue Code. The favorable treatment is designed to encourage taxpayers to save for retirement.

⋈ *Is an IRA the same as a qualified plan?*

Not exactly. IRAs and qualified plans are defined in different sections of the Internal Revenue Code. Qualified plans are established by employers to provide retirement benefits to employees. IRAs are established by individuals with their own money in order to provide for their own retirement.

However, the same favorable income tax treatment generally applies to both qualified plans and IRAs. Thus individuals looking for income tax advantages are attracted to both qualified plans and IRAs.

⋈ *What are these favorable income tax advantages?*

With all types of IRAs, earnings—such as interest, dividends, and capital gains on the assets inside the IRA—grow tax-deferred during the accumulation period. This can provide years of income tax–free compounding, which will result in increased retirement savings.

In addition, with *some* types of IRAs, you receive an income tax deduction, up to certain limits, when you contribute money

CHAP. 3: INDIVIDUAL RETIREMENT ACCOUNTS 117

to the IRA. Finally, with *some* types of IRAs, certain withdrawals are not subject to income tax when withdrawn.

### What are the different types of IRAs?

Historically, there have been two types of IRAs, deductible and nondeductible.

With a *deductible IRA,* you receive a current income tax deduction when you contribute money to the IRA; with a *nondeductible IRA,* you do not. Your ability to receive an income tax deduction depends primarily upon the amount of income you earn that year and whether you are participating in a qualified retirement plan at work.

With both types of IRA, the earnings inside the account accumulate tax-deferred each year, but generally the money is fully subject to ordinary income tax in the year withdrawn. With a deductible IRA, your contributions and your accumulated earnings are taxed when withdrawn; with a nondeductible IRA, only your accumulated earnings are taxed when withdrawn.

The Taxpayer Relief Act of 1997 created a new type of IRA that is known as a Roth IRA. The deductible IRA, the nondeductible IRA, and the Roth IRA each have unique features, advantages, and disadvantages.

### What is a Roth IRA?

As part of the Taxpayer Relief Act of 1997, Congress and the White House established the *Roth IRA Plus,* named for Senator William Roth, who wrote the bill. It is commonly referred to as a "Roth IRA," "dream IRA," or "super IRA." Individuals were able to make contributions to Roth IRAs beginning in the 1998 tax year.

### Could you compare a Roth IRA with a deductible and nondeductible IRA?

As with a nondeductible IRA, there is no income tax deduction for contributions to a Roth IRA. As with both a deductible IRA and a nondeductible IRA, the earnings in a Roth IRA accumulate tax-deferred.

Unlike the case with the deductible and the nondeductible IRAs, accumulated earnings in a Roth IRA can be withdrawn tax-free provided certain conditions have been met. This tax-free withdrawal of accumulated earnings is the major distinction between the Roth IRA and the other two types. In addition, for the Roth IRA, there is no requirement that mandatory distributions begin at a specific age.

## FEATURES OF IRAS

### Contributions

*How much can I contribute to an IRA?*

Generally, you can contribute to up to $2000 to an IRA—regardless of whether it is a deductible, nondeductible, or Roth IRA—provided you have earned income of at least that amount. *Earned income* includes wages, salaries, tips, and earnings from self-employment. It does not include interest, dividends, or rental income.

*What is the maximum amount I can contribute to all my IRAs each year?*

The maximum combined amount you can contribute annually to all your IRAs—including deductible, nondeductible, and Roth IRAs—is $2000, assuming you have earned income of at least that amount or do not exceed the income limits for each type of IRA.

*What are the income limits for the various types of IRAs?*

You can make contributions to a nondeductible IRA regardless of

CHAP. 3: INDIVIDUAL RETIREMENT ACCOUNTS    119

your income and regardless of whether you or your spouse is covered by a company-sponsored plan provided that you have earnings equal to your contribution (up to $2000) and that the total contributions to all your IRAs (deductible, Roth, and nondeductible) do not exceed $2000 for any given year.

The income limits for the deductible IRA and the Roth IRA are discussed later in this chapter.

*I can't afford to put $2000 in an account. Do I have to have that much to open an IRA?*

No. Just because you cannot afford the $2000 maximum is no reason to forgo an IRA. The tax-deferred benefits of an IRA are available on any amount up to $2000 and must not be overlooked.

You can open, or fund, an IRA with the minimum amount required by the financial institution or investment company. This will vary from institution to institution and fund company to fund company. Mutual fund companies often waive the normal minimum amounts for IRAs.

*I can contribute $2000 to my IRA because I have sufficient earned income. How much can my wife, who has no earned income, contribute to her IRA?*

Under the Small Business Job Protection Act (SBA) of 1996, a non-wage-earning spouse can make an annual contribution of up to $2000 to an IRA. For your wife to be eligible to make a contribution, (1) the two of you must file a joint tax return for the tax year, and (2) your wife's gross income for tax purposes must be less than your gross income. If these two requirements are satisfied, her contribution can be the combined compensation for both of you up to the maximum $2000.

Therefore, even if your spouse is not employed outside the home, the two of you can contribute up to $4000 providing your combined earned income is at least $4000 and your joint adjusted gross income is at least $4000.

*※ I'm covered under a plan at work. Can I still have an IRA?*

It is possible to have your cake and eat it too! Even though you are covered under a company-sponsored plan, you may be able to have an IRA as well. If your adjusted gross income (or combined adjusted gross income, if married) does not exceed certain limits (see Table 3-1 on page 133), you can contribute to a deductible IRA.

If you cannot contribute to a deductible IRA because your income exceeds the limits, you can still make contributions to a Roth IRA if your adjusted gross income does not exceed $110,000 if you are single or your combined adjusted gross income does not exceed $160,000 if you are married.

If your income exceeds the limits for a Roth IRA, you can always make contributions to a nondeductible IRA and still obtain the tax-free-growth benefit.

Remember, the total contributions to all of your deductible, Roth, and nondeductible IRAs in a given year cannot exceed $2000.

*※ When should I make my IRA contribution?*

The deadline for making an IRA contribution is April 15, the tax return due date without extension. However, to obtain the most from your IRA, it is best to fund up to the maximum amount as early as possible; ideally, on the first business day of the new year. Over the years, the returns you earn from funding your IRA 15 months early will add up considerably..

## Trust IRAs and Custodial IRAs

*※ I've seen advertisements referring to "trust IRAs" and "custodial IRAs." What is the difference?*

An IRA account can be either a *trust IRA,* which is a trust agreement, or a *custodial IRA,* which is a custodial account.

# Chap. 3: Individual Retirement Accounts 121

A trust IRA is an account established with a bank. A custodial IRA is an account established with a nonbank entity, usually an investment company. The Internal Revenue Code contains extensive and strict requirements for custodial accounts because they are not subject to bank regulations or FDIC insurance.

## What are the advantages and disadvantages of a trust IRA?

The primary advantage of a trust IRA stems from its nature as a trust. The laws governing trusts are well established, and practitioners are generally familiar with the rules governing trusts.

Within a trust IRA, you can establish separate trusts for the benefit of your family and others. However, you must use the bank's form, on which you can only designate the beneficiaries— you cannot include provisions controlling the distributions to them.

## Are there any advantages of a custodial IRA?

The wider range of investments available with a custodial IRA is the most recognized advantage. Typically, the investments in custodial IRAs are in mutual funds, stocks or bonds, and so on.

Another advantage of a custodial IRA comes from what may also be a weakness: It is not a trust and thus is not governed by trust laws. Therefore, rather than being limited to a bank's form, with only a beneficiary designation and little, if any, direction for distribution of the funds, you can create a separate living trust and name it as the beneficiary of the custodial account. In this trust, which must become irrevocable at your death, you can establish the terms and conditions for your death or disability and for distributions to your loved ones.

Custodial accounts are not as well understood as trust accounts, and there are few cases interpreting their application. Custodial IRA beneficiary designations have been questioned in some states where the law is unclear as to whether the designation or the owner's will controls distributions to beneficiaries.

## Self-Directed IRAs

 ⚑ *What are self-directed IRAs?*

A *self-directed IRA* is not a type of IRA as defined in the Internal Revenue Code. Financial institutions use the term to refer to an IRA for which the account owner directs the investments. In this situation, the financial institution serves as the custodian of the account and performs the services related to tax reporting of activities to fulfill the IRA's tax-deferral motives, but the IRA owner chooses the investments.

 ⚑ *Are there advantages to having a self-directed IRA?*

The primary advantage of a self-directed IRA is your freedom to choose the investments inside the account.

For a self-directed IRA, the custodian's agreement specifically provides that the financial institution will not offer investment or legal advice. Some individuals might consider it an advantage that the custodian is not routinely soliciting them to invest in custodian-owned mutual funds, annuities, or other investment products. Generally, however, financial institutions that offer self-directed IRAs seek only to provide the services related to the IRA and not the products as well.

For an IRA owner under age 59½, a planning opportunity exists: He or she is able to withdraw money from the self-directed IRA without penalty in the form of "reasonable" management fees—fees approximating what an institutional manager would charge for the same service.

 ⚑ *Am I limited in the choice of investments for my self-directed IRA?*

As specified by the tax law, you may invest in many of the investment products offered by U.S. companies, such as mutual funds, stocks and bonds, certificates of deposit, private placements or partnerships, real estate, mortgages, and private notes. Some un-

CHAP. 3: INDIVIDUAL RETIREMENT ACCOUNTS 123

usual investments also qualify, such as viatical settlements, unit trusts, and secured contracts, to name just a few. You have literally thousands of products from which to choose.

Companies that offer only self-directed IRAs generally allow you to follow the tax rules for investments. However, many companies that offer self-directed IRAs structure them so that you must invest in only their products. Thus, most bank IRAs offer only fixed-rate certificates of deposit, and investment companies offer only their own mutual fund groups. This practice effectively eliminates thousands of investment opportunities.

### *What are the disadvantages of a self-directed IRA?*

The advantage of being able to direct your own investments in a self-directed IRA could turn into a disadvantage. The custodian not only will not provide investment advice but also will not give you legal counsel as to which investments are prohibited within an IRA and what transactions are prohibited.

Some of the prohibited investments under the Code are insurance policies and certain collectibles and other tangible personal property.

Prohibited transactions under the Code are:

- Borrowing money from the IRA
- Selling, exchanging, or leasing any property between the IRA and a "party-in-interest" or "disqualified person," such as a member of your family
- Receiving "unreasonable" compensation for managing the IRA
- Using the IRA as security for a loan
- Buying property for present or future personal use with IRA funds (This means any use by which you gain any economic benefit either directly or indirectly. Therefore, you should not occupy the office owned by the IRA, or even rent it for your own business.)

*What happens if I make a prohibited investment or a prohibited transaction?*

If you make a prohibited investment or prohibited transaction in connection with your IRA, the account will not be treated as an IRA as of the first day of the year in which the prohibited investment or transaction takes place. Therefore, all the assets, with some minor exceptions, will become taxable income and reported on your income tax return for that year.

For purposes of determining the tax, the assets will be valued at their fair market value. Depending on the type of asset, a valuation by a qualified appraiser might be required to determine fair market value, adding even more expense to an already disastrous situation. But more bad news awaits: if you are under 59½, the amount that is disallowed as a deductible contribution will be treated as a premature distribution, and it is more than likely that you will have to pay a 10 percent penalty on it.

*Are there any other disadvantages of a self-directed IRA?*

Most of the custodians that provide self-directed IRAs are fee-based service providers and do not rely on the income stream generated by product sales and management fees for their incomes. Therefore, you may pay a higher fee to the custodian for a self-directed IRA than for what some call "captive IRA" custodial services. Furthermore, you will still pay the "load" fees and management fees associated with mutual funds or fees for the investment products. However, the independence and larger variety of investment options may outweigh these costs. Information available from each company will allow you to pick and choose an acceptable level of fees.

## IRA Accounts and IRA Annuities

*My financial advisor told me I can set up an IRA account or an IRA annuity. What are these?*

Generally, IRAs can be structured as either accounts or annuities.

CHAP. 3: INDIVIDUAL RETIREMENT ACCOUNTS                125

An individual establishes an *IRA account* with a bank, brokerage firm, or similar company that acts as a trustee or custodian of the account. IRA accounts can also be established by employers and employee associations. Upon the death of the owner, the beneficiary previously selected by the owner (or the default beneficiary if no one was selected) will be entitled to the balance remaining in the IRA account.

*IRA annuities* are annuity contracts or endowment contracts purchased by individuals from insurance companies or financial institutions. The annuity guarantees fixed periodic payments which begin on a preselected date and continue during the lifetime of the owner or often during the joint lifetimes of the owner and the owner's spouse. Upon the death of the owner (or deaths of the owner and his or her spouse), payments cease. Generally no further payments will be made to the owner's family.

### ⚐ *Should I set up an IRA account or an IRA annuity?*

It depends. An IRA account will provide you with the most flexibility. You can change it during your lifetime, including changing investment strategies, varying the amounts of withdrawals, and changing beneficiaries.

Once payments from an IRA annuity have begun, you generally cannot change them. However, if you prefer guaranteed fixed payments for the rest of your life, an IRA annuity might make sense.

Upon balancing the advantages and disadvantages of each, most people prefer the flexibility of an IRA account.

## Investments

### ⚐ *What types of investments are allowed for an IRA account?*

Investments that are eligible for an IRA include bank IRAs, mutual funds, brokerage accounts holding stocks and bonds, annuities, government securities, unit investment trusts (UITs), limited partnerships, and U.S. minted gold and silver coins.

*Are there limitations on these types of investments?*

Yes. Your IRA cannot be invested in debt on which you are the debtor. Furthermore, investing in most collectibles, such as stamps, precious stones, and antiques, is prohibited. Also, investing IRA assets in coins other than U.S. minted gold and silver coins is prohibited. You should seek professional advice before investing in any of these types of assets.

*Can my IRA custodian or trustee use the IRA funds to buy life insurance on my life?*

No. Doing so would be considered a prohibited investment.

*If I invest my IRA in a company that fails, will the Pension Benefit Guaranty Corporation cover my loss?*

No. Your IRA is not a pension that qualifies to be guaranteed.

*What will my IRA pay?*

It depends upon the underlying assets within the account. Your IRA may be invested in mutual funds, stocks, bonds, or CDs. What your IRA pays, or returns, will depend on how well the fund, stock, or other investment performed during the year or on the interest rate your CD or annuity yields.

## Loans

*Can I borrow from my IRA accounts?*

No. Borrowing from an IRA account is considered a prohibited transaction. You cannot borrow without having the loan treated as a taxable distribution.

CHAP. 3: INDIVIDUAL RETIREMENT ACCOUNTS 127

### ⚔ *What happens if I sell my IRA?*

You should not attempt to sell your IRA. The attempted sale would probably be treated as a withdrawal, obligating you to pay income tax on the entire IRA and, depending on your age, obligating you to pay a 10 percent excise tax. The sale might be void, giving the buyer legal remedy for your taking the buyer's money without giving the buyer anything of value.

### ⚔ *Can I give my IRA away during my lifetime?*

Just as with a sale, if you give your IRA to someone during your lifetime, the transaction will be treated as a distribution. You will pay income tax on the entire IRA and, depending on your age, might also pay a 10 percent excise tax.

## Asset Protection

### ⚔ *Are IRAs protected from creditors?*

Yes. IRAs have some federal but mostly state law exemptions from attachment by creditors. The exempt amount is usually limited to the amount "necessary" to support you (the judgment debtor), your spouse, and dependents when you retire. As long as you can show necessity, coupled with a lack of ability to make up the earnings before retirement, the IRA may be exempt under most states' creditor protection laws.

You cannot, however, overfund an IRA when you are on the threshold of bankruptcy and expect the exemption. There are a number of cases in which debtors unsuccessfully attempted to do this.

### ⚔ *If my IRA is in an annuity with periodic payments, can a judgment creditor get it?*

Yes. However, your creditor is limited, in most states, to the amount normally available to it under the wage-garnishment laws and exemptions.

*Is it easier for a creditor to get at my IRA than my 401(k)?*

Yes. To protect a qualified plan from your creditors, all that needs to be shown is that the funds will be used for general retirement purposes. To protect an IRA, you must demonstrate that the funds are actually necessary for your and your dependents' support during retirement after considering all sources of income that are likely to be available, including Social Security. This is one factor to consider when deciding whether to roll over a qualified plan into an IRA. If you realistically fear the possibility of a substantial liability, you should consider keeping the funds in the qualified plan until the potential liability is cleared.

*If I take large amounts out of my IRA, pay the income tax, and invest what's left of the withdrawal, will my state's law protect the new investment from creditors as well as it protects the IRA?*

It is very doubtful that the new investment could be inexpensively protected from creditors as well as your IRA was protected under the law of your state. You should talk with a knowledgeable lawyer about other creditor protection strategies permitted by law in your state.

*Can I take my certificate of deposit and buy an IRA with it to prevent creditors from seizing this money?*

The purchase of this type of investment would probably constitute a fraudulent transfer under the Uniform Fraudulent Conveyances Act, the Uniform Fraudulent Transfers Act, or a state law forbidding fraudulent transfers. If creditors can establish that you transferred the funds with the intent to hinder, delay or defraud your creditors, they can get a court order reversing the transac-

## Chap. 3: Individual Retirement Accounts 129

tion, thereby making the funds available for the payment of your debts.

**⚜ Is my IRA subject to the claims of my creditors in a bankruptcy proceeding?**

It depends on your state's law. IRAs are not qualified plans protected under the Employee Retirement Income Security Act (ERISA) but fall under state jurisdiction. Some state courts have ruled that IRA assets are subject to creditors claims in a bankruptcy proceeding; other courts have considered the needs of the individual before allowing some or all of the IRA assets to be subject to creditors; and still others have ruled that an IRA is exempt property under state law.

**⚜ Is my IRA subject to levy by the IRS for payment of back taxes?**

Under federal law, all assets subject to tax can be placed under lien to the U.S. Treasury for payment of taxes due. Although the IRS could take the IRA, it is very unlikely that it would do so until you take distributions from it.

**⚜ If a creditor does get access to my IRA, do I have to pay income taxes and penalties on the funds the creditor gets?**

Yes. However, you should bring this to the attention of the court which hears your exemption claim. It is typically required to set aside from the creditor sufficient funds to allow you to pay the taxes on the portion the creditor is permitted to receive.

**⚜ After my death, can my retirement funds be protected from seizure by my husband's creditors?**

You can create an *irrevocable trust* and name it as the beneficiary of your IRA. In the trust agreement, you can name your husband as the beneficiary of the trust and provide specific instructions to your trustee that no funds coming into the trust, including the retirement funds, shall be available for payment of your husband's debts.

As long as the IRA funds remain in trust for the benefit of your husband, they are safe from the claims of his creditors. Once payments are made from the trust, however, they become vulnerable to his creditors.

You should talk to an experienced asset protection attorney in your state to determine the limits of the trust protections that are available where you live, as these can vary considerably from state to state.

*Can my wife take part of my IRA as part of a divorce settlement?*

It depends upon the laws of the state where both of you lived at the time of the divorce. In almost all states, a judge can divide "marital property," including IRAs, among the parties in a divorce proceeding. Under the Internal Revenue Code, a judge, in a divorce order or marital settlement agreement, can transfer all or part of an IRA to a spouse or former spouse for child support, spousal support, or property award. The amount of property awarded to a spouse or former spouse is generally based on a ratio of the number of years married while participating in the IRA to the total number of years married. Generally the transfer of part of your IRA to your former spouse as part of a divorce settlement will not be considered a taxable distribution to you.

## DEDUCTIBLE IRAS

### Features

*Would you summarize the features of the deductible IRA?*

The main features are these:

CHAP. 3: INDIVIDUAL RETIREMENT ACCOUNTS    131

- Generally, you can contribute to up to $2000, provided you have earned income of at least that amount.

- You receive a current income tax deduction, up to certain limits, when you contribute money to the IRA.

- Earnings—such as interest, dividends, and capital gains on the assets inside the IRA—are not taxed until you withdraw the funds.

- Both your contributions and your accumulated earnings are fully subject to ordinary income tax in the year you withdraw them.

- You cannot make contributions after age 70½.


## Contributions

*What are the income limits for contributions to a deductible IRA?*

Income limits for contributions to deductible IRAs are as follows:

- If you are single and are not covered by a company-sponsored retirement plan at work, you can make a contribution to a deductible IRA of up to $2000 or the amount of your compensation, whichever is less.

- If you are married and neither you nor your spouse is covered by a company-sponsored retirement plan at work, each of you can contribute up to $2000 or the amount of your compensation, whichever is less, regardless of the amount of your income for that year. Even if one of you makes less than $2000 in a given year, both you and your spouse can still make full contributions provided that your total combined earnings were at least $4000 for that year.

- If you are married and your spouse (not you) is covered by a company-sponsored plan, the amount you can contribute to a deductible IRA begins to decrease when your and your spouse's combined adjusted gross income exceeds $150,000. You can make no contributions when the combined adjusted gross income reaches $160,000.

- If you are covered by a company-sponsored plan at work, the amount you can contribute decreases between certain income limits. Under the Taxpayer Relief Act of 1997, the income limits for contributions to deductible IRAs are as shown in Table 3-1.

*Can I continue to make contributions to my IRA after I retire?*

Before reaching age 70½, you can make IRA contributions in any year that you have earned income, provided you meet the income tests outlined earlier in this chapter. The amount may be as much as your earned income up to $2000.

Upon reaching age 70½, you can no longer make contributions to deductible IRAs.

*Our income is rent, interest, and dividends and does not include earnings from personal service. Can we contribute to a deductible IRA?*

No. A deductible IRA is available only if you have earnings within limits. If you manage rental activities, you might talk with your income tax advisor about whether you can lawfully treat some of your income as earnings from self-employment so that you can set up a deductible IRA. Having self-employment income requires that you pay self-employment tax in addition to income tax.

*If the money I use for an IRA contribution is a gift from someone else or is borrowed by me, can I still get the income tax deduction?*

Yes. As long as you meet the qualifications, the source of your

## CHAP. 3: INDIVIDUAL RETIREMENT ACCOUNTS  133

**TABLE 3-1  Income Limits for Deductible IRA**

| | Contribution | |
|---|---|---|
| | Decreases if modified AGI reaches | Eliminated if modified AGI exceeds |
| **Married filing joint tax return** | | |
| 1998 | $50,000 | $ 60,000 |
| 1999 | 51,000 | 61,000 |
| 2000 | 52,000 | 62,000 |
| 2001 | 53,000 | 63,000 |
| 2002 | 54,000 | 64,000 |
| 2003 | 60,000 | 70,000 |
| 2004 | 65,000 | 75,000 |
| 2005 | 70,000 | 80,000 |
| 2006 | 75,000 | 85,000 |
| 2007 and after | 80,000 | 100,000 |
| **Single or head of household** | | |
| 1998 | 30,000 | 40,000 |
| 1999 | 31,000 | 41,000 |
| 2000 | 32,000 | 42,000 |
| 2001 | 33,000 | 43,000 |
| 2002 | 34,000 | 44,000 |
| 2003 | 40,000 | 50,000 |
| 2004 | 45,000 | 55,000 |
| 2005 and after | 50,000 | 60,000 |

IRA contribution does not matter. However, before you borrow money to make the contribution, you might want to consider the interest you will have to pay on the borrowed money and whether that interest will be deductible.

## Distributions/Withdrawals

*How soon can I begin to take money out of my deductible IRA?*

You can take money out of your deductible IRA at any time. However, if you are under the age of 59½, you will pay income taxes on the funds you withdraw and, with a few exceptions, will also pay a 10 percent early-withdrawal penalty on those funds. (The exceptions are discussed in detail in Chapter 6.) After 59½, you will not pay the 10 percent penalty, but you will have to report and pay income tax on the funds you withdraw in the year you withdraw them.

## ROTH IRAS

## Features

*What are the primary differences between the new Roth IRA and a deductible IRA?*

A Roth IRA differs from a traditional IRA in several ways:

- Income limits for making contributions are higher for a Roth IRA.

- There is no tax deduction for your contribution to a Roth IRA.

- Since you contribute to the account with after-tax dollars, you can withdraw all contributions income tax–free.

- You can withdraw your contributions at any time without penalty.

- You can continue to make contributions after age 70½.

- As with a traditional IRA, earnings grow income tax–free.

## Chap. 3: Individual Retirement Accounts 135

- Some distributions of earnings are not subject to income tax when withdrawn.

- You are not required to make any distributions during your lifetime.

### ↜ Why would I contribute to a Roth IRA when I can't deduct the contribution?

One of the primary reasons you should make IRA contributions, whether deductible or nondeductible, is to obtain the benefit of tax deferral on earnings. This benefit allows the investment to grow to a larger amount than it would otherwise. In addition, certain "qualified" distributions of earnings after age 59½ will not be subject to income tax.

### ↜ I'm 30 years old and have a retirement plan at work. How could I benefit from a Roth IRA?

If you have an employer-sponsored retirement plan, you should consider annual, nondeductible contributions of $2000 to a Roth IRA because the earnings will accumulate tax-free. Your contributions can be withdrawn income tax–free at any time, and most withdrawals of earnings after the later of 5 years or age 59½ will also be completely income tax–free.

### ↜ My wife and I are in our early fifties. Would a Roth IRA benefit us?

A Roth IRA is an excellent supplement to other retirement planning strategies. You can continue to make contributions during your lifetime in order to take advantage of the tax-free accumulation of earnings. You can make tax-free withdrawals of earnings either after 5 years from the contribution or at age 59½, whichever is later. In addition, you are not required to make any withdrawals during your lifetime; therefore, you can leave the balance of the account to your spouse or children after your death.

⚑ *If I have a company 401(k) plan, can I also contribute to a Roth IRA?*

Yes, you can, provided you meet the income requirements.

## Contributions

⚑ *How much can I contribute to a Roth IRA?*

The exact amount depends upon your adjusted gross income (AGI) for the year in which you make the contribution, but it cannot exceed $2000.

- *If your AGI is less than $95,000 (or $150,000 for joint filers),* you can contribute up to $2000, minus any contributions you've made to other IRAs in the same year.

- *If your AGI is between $95,000 and $110,000 (or $150,000 and $160,000 for joint filers),* the phase-out rules begin to apply. To determine your contribution, subtract $95,000 (or $150,000, if married) from your adjusted gross income. Divide by 5 and round to the nearest $200. The result is the amount you can contribute to your Roth IRA that year. For example, a single taxpayer with an adjusted gross income of $101,000 could contribute $1200 to his or her Roth IRA ($101,000 − $95,000 = 6,000 ÷ 5 = $1200).

- *If your AGI is more than $110,000 (or $160,000 for joint filers),* you cannot contribute to a Roth IRA.

Your ability to contribute to a Roth IRA is determined only by these income limitations regardless of whether you or your spouse is covered by a company-sponsored plan.

CHAP. 3: INDIVIDUAL RETIREMENT ACCOUNTS 137

### ⅏ *How long can I make contributions to a Roth IRA?*

Unlike the case with deductible and nondeductible IRAs, contributions to a Roth IRA can be made every year, even after you reach age 70½, provided that you have earned income and meet the income requirements discussed above.

## Distributions/Withdrawals

### ⅏ *When can I take a distribution from my Roth IRA?*

You can take a tax-free, penalty-free distribution of your contributions at any time. You can take a tax-free, penalty-free distribution of the accumulated earnings from your Roth IRA if it is a *qualified distribution.* A distribution is considered qualified if it is made 5 years after the tax year in which you established the IRA *and* it meets one of the following requirements:

- It is made when or after you reach age 59½.
- It is made after your death to your beneficiary.
- It is made because you are disabled.
- It is made to pay for expenses directly incurred for the purchase of a principal residence, as a first-time home buyer, for you, your spouse, your or your spouse's ancestors, children, or grandchildren. The maximum distribution to cover these expenses cannot exceed the lifetime limit of $10,000, and it must be used within 120 days.

### ROLLOVERS TO ROTH IRAS

### ⅏ *Are there any provisions for rollovers to the Roth IRA?*

A married person who files separately is not allowed to roll over an existing IRA to a Roth IRA. Anyone else may roll over an existing IRA to a nondeductible Roth IRA at any time, provided he or she is single, or married and filing jointly, and has an adjusted gross income of less than $100,000 (excluding the rollover amount) in the year of the rollover. Amounts rolled over are not subject to the 10 percent early-withdrawal penalty tax.

If you do a rollover, however, the amount you roll over from a deductible IRA or qualified plan becomes nondeductible and will be treated as ordinary income to you.

The Taxpayer Relief Act of 1997 created a window of opportunity for rollovers: if a rollover was made before December 31, 1998, the taxes on the amount rolled over could be prorated over a 4-year tax period. Unfortunately, many people would not know until after that date if their adjusted gross income would be below the AGI limits, and thus they could not know if they were eligible to make a rollover. Congress wisely corrected this problem by providing, in the IRS Restructuring and Reform Act of 1998, that if people who rolled over their traditional IRAs to Roth IRAs before December 31, 1998, later found they were ineligible to make the rollovers, they could cancel their rollovers with no adverse effects.

Also, unlike the case with a "nonconverted" Roth IRA, once you have rolled over the funds from a traditional IRA to a Roth IRA, a 10 percent penalty will apply to withdrawals of the converted amount if made within 5 years of the taxable year in which you made the conversion.

*Can I convert my deductible IRA to a Roth IRA so that I won't pay any taxes on the distributions when I retire?*

Yes, you can roll over your deductible IRA to a Roth IRA. Whether you should do so depends, as with many financial planning decisions, on your circumstances.

If you have an adjusted gross income greater than $100,000 per year, you are not eligible to convert your deductible IRA funds into a Roth IRA without being assessed penalties.

In all cases, to make the transfer you must pay the income

CHAP. 3: INDIVIDUAL RETIREMENT ACCOUNTS 139

tax on the amount that you roll over. However, if you made the transfer before December 31, 1998, you can spread your tax payments over 4 years.

You should consider several factors before rolling your deductible IRA over to a Roth IRA:

*Whether you anticipate being in a lower or higher income tax bracket when you retire:* Remember, you will have to pay income tax *today* on the amount you roll over. If you do not do the rollover, you will continue to defer the income tax until the money is later withdrawn. The lower the income tax bracket you will be in at the time of withdrawal, the less benefit the rollover will have.

*Whether you can pay the income tax due from the rollover from an outside source:* If your only source of money to pay the income tax is from the IRA proceeds, you will have fewer proceeds to immediately reinvest in the Roth IRA, so the rollover will have less benefit. Making the transfer could be beneficial if you can pay the tax with money outside the IRA, thereby leaving more in the Roth IRA to grow tax-free, and have a sufficient length of time until distribution to make the transfer worthwhile.

## ☙ *Should I roll my existing IRA into a Roth IRA?*

There is no blanket answer that would be appropriate for everyone. Therefore, you should consult with your advisor, who can prepare customized calculations for you.

As a basic planning principle, it is usually better to pay taxes as late as possible in order to keep all your money growing tax-deferred. However, rolling a traditional IRA over to a Roth IRA may be a little different. A rollover might make sense if you are young, your account balance is relatively small, your taxable income is low, and you have the resources to pay the income taxes from sources outside the IRA. The longer you can leave the money in the new Roth account, the more time it has to recoup the amount of income taxes you had to pay to make the transfer.

If your emphasis is on estate planning for your heirs, a rollover may offer you benefits. Because no distributions from a Roth IRA are required during life, the participant who reaches age 70½ does not have to start taking distributions from his or her Roth IRA, as would be the case with a traditional IRA. This could provide substantial estate planning opportunities for the participant who does not need the IRA funds to live on.

The rollover may not make sense if you have a high income and are close to withdrawing the funds anyway.

*I am already taking distributions from my deductible IRA. Are there any advantages to rolling over to a Roth IRA?*

Under the traditional IRA, certain choices *must* be made before age 70½ that determine how distributions will be made to the owner during his or her life and to beneficiaries after the owner's death. These choices may *not* be changed under any circumstances after age 70½.

A Roth IRA owner has the advantage of being able to change the choices *after* age 70½ that can determine how distributions will be made after his or her death. This allows more flexibility in family wealth transfer planning. For example, converting a traditional IRA to a Roth IRA after age 70½ offers a way to "clean up" choices that were made for the traditional IRA at age 70½.

## EDUCATION IRAS

*What is an education IRA?*

The Taxpayer Relief Act of 1997 established another new nondeductible IRA called an *education IRA*. Although it is referred to as an IRA, it is generally *not* an IRA for your benefit. You can establish an education IRA to pay for higher education—room

## Chap. 3: Individual Retirement Accounts     141

and board, tuition, fees, books, supplies, and equipment—for any individual under 18 years of age.

### What are some of its features?

You may contribute up to $500 per year to an education IRA for any person under 18 years of age, regardless of whether the beneficiary of the IRA has any gross income that year. The total amount of all contributions from all contributors for a beneficiary is limited to $500 per year. This contribution is not deductible, and it does not count against your own $2000 annual IRA contribution limitation. The contributions can continue until the education IRA beneficiary reaches age 18.

Income limitations for an education IRA contribution are the same as those for the Roth IRA (starting at $95,000 for single taxpayers and $150,000 for joint taxpayers).

When the beneficiary takes a distribution for payment of higher-education costs, he or she receives the money without realizing any income for tax purposes. However, to the extent that distributions exceed the higher-education costs, they are reported as ordinary income to the beneficiary and subject to a 10 percent penalty.

All the education IRA funds must be distributed to the beneficiary no later than age 30 or the money must be withdrawn and distributed to the beneficiary as ordinary income. Before reaching age 30, however, the beneficiary can roll the balance to another qualified family member and avoid the tax. Furthermore, if the beneficiary dies before all the funds are distributed, another qualified family member may be named as beneficiary.

# chapter 4

## Investing
## for Retirement

This chapter provides an overview of investment principles, vehicles, and strategies. Our contributors, despite their varied professional backgrounds, submitted very consistent material in terms of the types of risk you'll face as you put together your investment portfolio for retirement, as well as the techniques that can be used to address these risks.

Given that countless textbooks are devoted to the subject of investments, we were truly impressed by the effectiveness of the messages delivered by our contributors. In fact, you may well benefit more from this summary of investment concerns and how to address them than you would from much longer discussions of the subject.

The questions and answers in this chapter provide you with the information you'll need to begin (or continue) your investment plan for retirement. The discussion on risks and how to address them should help you proceed with more confidence and less anxiety toward your investment goals.

Throughout this chapter, you'll be reminded of the long-term nature of the risks and rewards of retirement investing. During the research period for this book, the stock market continued its record upward march. The first signs of a slowing of the record bull market began to show just as we prepared for final printing. Read in this context, the wisdom of our contributors' calm and steady advice should leap off the pages.

The need for professional advice from trained, experienced, and compassionate advisors has never been greater. We hope you'll be motivated to seek professional assistance to help ensure that you reach your individual goals and objectives.

## INVESTMENT PRINCIPLES

### Risk

*What are some of the risks that can affect the value of my investment assets?*

There are many, but the four primary risks you should be aware of are financial/credit, market, interest rate, and inflation.

*What is financial risk?*

*Financial risk* arises when issuers of investments run into difficulty or are unable to live up to investor expectations. For example, a buyer of uninsured bonds runs a financial risk of the company's defaulting on interest or principal payments or going bankrupt. Additionally, financial risk could occur when a company reports lower-than-expected earnings, as this very often causes the price of the company's stock to drop significantly.

# Chap. 4: Investing for Retirement                    145

### ⋈ *What is market risk?*

*Market risk* arises as a result of price fluctuations in the entire securities market or in a specific industry group, as opposed to one company.

You probably remember the stock market crash on October 19, 1987. During the 8 months before the crash, the stock market had experienced a 30 percent increase—a fantastic marketwide gain. Investors were nervous, though, and wanted to lock their profits into alternative investments, like government bonds, that were trading at an attractive 10 percent interest rate.

What occurred was a massive shift of money from the stock market into government bonds, dropping the price of nearly all the stocks traded in the market and causing the market to drop 22 to 30 percent during a short period of time. The drop in the prices of individual stocks had nothing to do with those companies' individual financial conditions but, rather, had to do with the condition of the market as a whole.

### ⋈ *What is interest rate risk?*

The best way to illustrate interest rate risk is to think of a seesaw, with interest rates on one side and the market value of debt and income securities, such as bonds, on the other side. As interest rates rise, the market value of your bonds decreases; as interest rates fall, the value of your bonds increases. In regard to the stock market, you normally see the market prices of securities move in the opposite direction from interest rates.

### ⋈ *What is inflation risk?*

A very real risk to everyone, especially retired individuals, is inflation. Inflation, of course, is the rate at which prices for goods in our economy rise from year to year. At a 4 percent inflation rate, a dollar today will have the purchasing power of only 82 cents 5 years from now and only 66 cents 10 years from now.

This is a very real risk, especially to people who will be retiring soon and very likely living on a fixed income. The money you are saving today for your retirement years must be increasing at a rate greater than taxes and inflation. If it is not, when the time comes that you need the funds, they may be able to purchase dramatically less than when you first stashed them away.

*One risk you haven't mentioned is taxes. What is tax risk?*

We can never completely anticipate the tax laws that Congress will pass in the future, and some of them may have a negative impact on our retirement dollars. What advisors can do, however, is help you achieve a growth rate greater than taxes and suggest every proven tax-saving technique available to you today that helps meet your retirement goals.

*Why is it important for a financial advisor to measure my risk tolerance or aversion?*

*Risk tolerance* is a subjective measure of a person's willingness to accept lower-than-expected returns on an investment. Risk is often associated with the degree of volatility (ups and downs) of an investment. If you and your advisor do not determine your risk tolerance at the outset, it will be difficult to develop a strategy and structure an investment portfolio that fits your situation.

Financial advisors have an obligation to set up mutual expectations with their clients—what clients expect from them and what they expect from their clients. If expectations are not established, one or the other party may be dissatisfied. Your satisfaction often depends on your planner's ability to guide you toward a rate of return sufficiently high to meet your expectations while keeping your investments within your risk-taking tolerance.

*How can I determine my risk tolerance so that I can construct a retirement portfolio that is right for me?*

This is a critical point where a financial advisor can add objectiv-

Chap. 4: Investing for Retirement        147

ity. Most advisors utilize a risk questionnaire, which consists of a series of questions designed to help you define your personal investment objectives. Some of the questions on a risk questionnaire might be similar to these:

1. What is your primary financial goal?
   a. Preserving my assets
   b. Saving for a major purchase
   c. Saving for a child's education
   d. Planning for retirement
   e. Accumulating wealth

2. What is your expected time horizon?
   a. Less than 1 year
   b. 1 to 5 years
   c. 6 to 10 years
   d. More than 10 years

3. What does the word "risk," in an investment context, mean to you?
   a. Danger
   b. Uncertainty
   c. Opportunity
   d. Thrill

4. For you personally, is it more important to be protected from inflation or to be assured of the safety of your principal?
   a. Much more important to protect my principal
   b. Somewhat more important to protect my principal
   c. Somewhat more important to be protected from inflation
   d. Much more important to be protected from inflation

5. If your portfolio declined in value by 10 percent, what would your reaction be?
   a. Sell
   b. Be concerned and very anxious
   c. Do nothing
   d. Buy more

**6.** Of the following statements, which most closely reflects your attitude?

    *a.* Of greatest importance to me when investing is never to lose any money. I am willing to accept a lower rate of return in exchange for greater safety.

    *b.* The safety of my investments is of greater importance to me than the return on those investments.

    *c.* The safety of my investments and the return are equally important to me.

    *d.* The return on my investments is of somewhat greater importance to me than the safety of those investments.

    *e.* The return on my investments is most important to me. I can accept greater volatility for the potential of receiving higher returns.

### *Why is the time horizon important when investing?*

A difficulty with investing is that there are short-term periods of market volatility during which your portfolio declines in value. It is never fun to watch your portfolio decline, and the fear of decline or loss prevents many people from investing, especially in stocks and stock mutual funds (equities).

Ibbotson Associates, a market research firm, has compiled statistics on the stock market dating back to 1926. When the time between 1926 and 1996 is divided into 5-year holding periods, only 7 of the 60 periods had declines, while 53 showed positive performance. If you take a longer view and look at 10- or 15-year holding periods, there are no declining periods. Thus, the longer you stay invested—the longer your time horizon—the greater the chance that your investments will obtain the average stock market returns. With people living longer today, even retirees need to have a long-term investment horizon.

### *How does my age affect my ability to take risk?*

Age alone is not a determinant of risk tolerance. An 18-year-old can have a higher aversion to risk than an 80-year-old.

# CHAP. 4: INVESTING FOR RETIREMENT 149

It is widely assumed that risk tolerance decreases as one ages. Although this may be true, it cannot be assumed, because each individual is different. It is not unusual for a shift in risk tolerance to be brought about by factors unrelated to age, such as a change in health, the death of a spouse, or other similar events.

### *How much risk should I assume with my investments?*

Risk and reward are usually related to one another. As assumed risk increases, so should one's expected rate of return. The ratio of risk to reward, however, is not 1:1 in all cases. The ratio can actually be massaged through various investment techniques to maximize return for a given amount of risk. A portfolio can be designed to minimize risk by selecting diversified investments. With the vast array of securities available for investments, a competent financial advisor can assist you in selecting the investment mix that will help you meet your goals within your risk tolerance.

### *How much risk should I have in my portfolio?*

It is said that risk can be more intestinal than intellectual. Your ability to live with the market's ups and downs is extremely important in deciding which investment mix is right for you. It's possible that you can overcompensate on safety and fail to achieve your personal income goals at retirement. If you do not need the funds for at least 10 years or more, you may wish to consider accepting higher risks in order to gain better long-term returns. Historically, equities (i.e., stocks and real estate) have offered greater rates of return over time.

### *What are the most serious long-term risks associated with retirement planning?*

There are two: not starting soon enough and not earning a high-enough return on your investments.

Let's say, for example, that between ages 25 and 65 (a 40-year period) you put $2000 in a money market account each year. Compounding the funds monthly at 5 percent, you will have $241,600 for retirement.

On the other hand, if you wait 10 years and make the same annual investment between ages 35 and 65 (a 30-year period), you will accumulate only $132,878. Even though the difference in the amounts invested is $20,000 ($2000 per year for 10 years), the difference in the total amount accumulated will be over $108,722.

Using this same example but from the perspective of return versus length of time, let's assume your funds are invested in a balanced account of equities and bond-type investments potentially earning 8.5 percent instead of the 5 percent money market account. If, when 25 years old, you invest $2000 per year for 40 years, you will accumulate $591,365—more than twice the investment for the same period in the money market. And if, when 35 years old, you invest in an 8.5 percent portfolio for 30 years, it will be worth $248,430, still higher than the 5 percent investment for the 40-year period.

Table 4-1 demonstrates that you should start your investment savings as soon as possible and invest for the highest returns within your acceptable risk tolerance.

*What is the greatest risk to my investment portfolio during retirement?*

Most people, especially those approaching retirement, feel that volatility, with the risk of a decline in the value of their investments, is their greatest risk. As a result, they are inclined to avoid or minimize stocks in their retirement portfolio. Historically, stocks have exhibited volatility over short periods. However, over longer time frames they have been more predictable and have rewarded investors with the best returns. With many people living longer today, we find the greatest risk comes not from market volatility but from inflation and the eroding effect it can have on your retirement income and purchasing power. Equities such as

CHAP. 4: INVESTING FOR RETIREMENT                    151

**TABLE 4-1    Effects of Time and Interest Rates on $2000
Annual Investment**

| Total years | Interest rate, % | Total accumulation |
|---|---|---|
| 30 | 5 | $132,878 |
| | 8.5 | 248,430 |
| 40 | 5 | 241,600 |
| | 8.5 | 591,365 |

stocks and stock mutual funds have historically been one of the
best ways to provide an inflation hedge.

⊷ *Many financial advisors I have interviewed use an investment
risk pyramid. Can you explain what that is?*

An *investment risk pyramid* is a diagram that indicates the relative
levels of risk associated with specific types of assets. Although
many investment counselors use such diagrams, they apply different criteria for assigning assets to the levels and their allocations
are sometimes subjective and arbitrary. One way to eliminate sub-
jectivity is to group assets into four levels of risk on the basis of
the number of primary risks each asset significantly reduces. This
system is shown in Figure 4-1, where the least risky assets—those
that reduce three primary risks—are at the base of the pyramid
(level 1) and the most risky—those that reduce no primary
risks—are at the apex (level 4). Each level represents a broad
category of investments:

*Level 1:* Assets in the *foundation investments* category work to
significantly reduce three of the primary risks: market, interest
rate, and financial. This means that they are primarily fixed-income securities, or securities whose principal and interest are
either ensured or guaranteed.

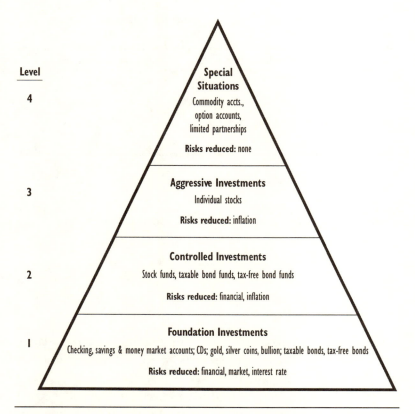

**Figure 4-1** Investment risk pyramid. There are more than four risks to investment assets. However, an understanding and proper allocation of the four primary risks should enhance the consistency of your returns. To be considered as such, foundation investments have to be rated at least AA by Standard and Poor's or Aa by Moody's and owned in a laddered maturity format. (*Source:* Adapted with permission from *MoneyTools.*)

*Level 2:* The second level is often called the "controlled" or "professionally managed" category. *Controlled investments* are investments for which professional money managers with documented track records (usually 5 to 10 years) make the decisions about which stock or bond to buy. Good examples are mutual funds and professionally managed stock accounts. Investments in this

CHAP. 4: INVESTING FOR RETIREMENT                    153

category are exposed to both market risk and interest rate risk. Generally, however, they do not have significant exposure to financial risk, and they tend to return a higher yield than foundation investments do, thus reducing inflation risk.

*Level 3:* The *aggressive investments* category usually consists of small-cap and micro-cap types of stocks. These assets are perhaps more exposed to financial, market, and interest rate risks, but hopefully they will outperform inflation and thus minimize inflation risk.

*Level 4:* The top level represents the *special situations* category. Stock options, commodity futures, and heavily leveraged limited partnerships are examples of investments at this level. Because these investments are typically subject to all the primary risks, they are appropriate only in special, high-risk, closely watched situations.

## Asset Diversification

⌐ *Why is diversification important?*

We have all been told "Never put all your eggs in one basket." If you do, and something happens to the basket, all your eggs are lost—and so may all your investment be lost. *Diversification* is selecting a mix of asset classes and the right investment vehicles within each asset class. Three reasons for diversifying retirement funds are:

1. To achieve higher after-tax returns consistent with asset growth and income needs
2. To acquire the right balance of liquidity
3. To better match the investments with one's risk-taking propensity and temperament

⌐ *How much difference can diversification make?*

Here's an example that demonstrates just how important diversification is: Compare two different ways you could invest $100,000. First, you might put all the money into one investment at a rate of 8 percent. After 25 years, that investment will have grown to about $684,847, a pretty significant increase.

Alternatively, you might divide the money into five different investments of $20,000 each:

- You invest the first $20,000 so badly that you lose it all.
- You bury the second $20,000 in a tin can in the backyard— no growth at all, except for the grass above the can.
- You invest the third $20,000 in something that will earn 5 percent.
- You invest the fourth $20,000 in an investment that grows at 10 percent.
- You invest the last $20,000 at 15 percent.

So you have burned a fifth, buried a fifth, and invested a fifth at only 5 percent, another fifth at 10 percent, and the last fifth at 15 percent. Over 25 years, this set of five different investments will give you a total of $942,800. Even after losing one-fifth of your principal, you have a 37.7 percent increase over the amount produced by placing all the money in one investment at 8 percent.

### What are the different asset classes?

There are three main classes of assets:

**Cash equivalents**
- CDs
- Money market accounts
- Savings accounts
- 30-day Treasury bills
- Short-term bonds

## Fixed-income investments

- Corporate intermediate bonds (2- to 15-year bonds)
- Government intermediate bonds (2- to 15-year Treasury bonds)
- Corporate long-term bonds (15- to 30-year bonds)
- Government long-term bonds (15- to 30-year Treasury bonds)
- High-yielding bonds

## Equity investments

- U.S. large-company growth stocks
- U.S. large-company value stocks
- U.S. small-company growth stocks
- U.S. small-company value stocks
- International bonds (developed countries; emerging markets)
- International large-company growth stocks (developed countries; emerging markets)
- International large-company value stocks (developed countries; emerging markets)
- International small-company growth stocks (developed countries; emerging markets)
- International small-company value stocks (developed countries; emerging markets)
- Real estate
- Commodities

## Asset Allocation

*What is asset allocation?*

Very simply, *asset allocation* is the decision of how many eggs to entrust to each basket. Specifically, asset allocation is the balancing of investment dollars among the different types of investments such as cash, bonds, and various classes of stocks (large- and small-capitalization stocks, international stocks, etc.). It can be the decision of what percentage of your total portfolio resides at each level of the investment risk pyramid.

> *How does an individual investor know what percentage of his or her assets to allocate into each asset class or type of investment?*

Imagine the majestic pyramids of Egypt. Some of them are over 4000 years old. Their physical structures have withstood the test of time. If you structure your investment portfolio like a pyramid, an investment risk pyramid, your portfolio should withstand the test of time as well. Using Figure 4-2, let's review our investment risk pyramid in terms of asset allocation.

*Level 1:* The first level serves as the foundation of the investment pyramid and thus constitutes more of the pyramid's total volume than does any of the levels above it. Most advisors recommend that you allocate the greatest percentage of your money to investments that are exposed to the lowest number of the four primary risks. Conservative investors view this level as the "no-pain, steady-gain" area. Aggressive investors see it as their "war chest." Whatever you call it, many advisors recommend that you keep at least 50 percent of your money in this category, at least until you start to accumulate some assets.

While the foundation investments can significantly reduce three of the four primary risks, there remains one risk that cannot always be reduced at this level: inflation. Investments in this category tend to be lower-yielding because of their low degree of risk, and sometimes the yields don't cover inflation. For this reason, advisors recommend that even the most conservative investors allocate part of their investment assets to levels 2 and 3 of the pyramid.

# CHAP. 4: INVESTING FOR RETIREMENT

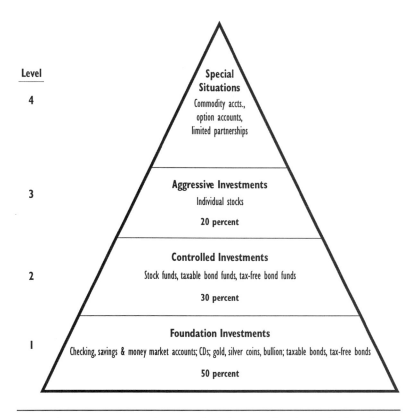

**Figure 4-2** Investment risk pyramid. To be considered as such, foundation investments have to be rated at least AA by Standard and Poor's or Aa by Moody's and owned in a laddered maturity format. (*Source:* Adapted with permission from *MoneyTools.*)

*Level 2:* A smaller percentage of your money, say, 30 percent, should be invested at this level. Although controlled investments are subject to marketwide price swings and the effects of interest rates, adequate diversification should reduce exposure to financial risk. When you buy into a mutual fund, your money is pooled with the money of other investors and used to purchase many different stocks, thus spreading the risk. Controlled investments tend to minimize inflation risk by returning higher yields than foundation investments.

*Level 3:* Although aggressive investments can reduce your inflation risk, they are exposed to financial, market, and interest rate risks. For this reason, you would generally have an even smaller percentage of your money, say, up to 20 percent, invested at this level than at the lower two levels.

*Level 4:* Because investments at this level are typically subject to all the primary risks, you would probably do the smallest amount of investing—or perhaps none at all—in this category.

Constructing an investment risk pyramid will help you determine how much to invest at each level in accordance with your ability to take risk.

### ⤳ *How do you coordinate the concept of diversification with the asset allocation concept?*

The diversification concept can be applied at each level of the investment pyramid. For example, in your foundation investments, you might purchase many different types of bonds from various regions of the country. At the controlled- investment level, you might diversify among several different money managers, among growth and value funds, or across international borders. And at the aggressive-investment level, you would likely diversify your individual stock selections among many industries, capitalization levels, and international stocks.

### ⤳ *Why is asset allocation so important?*

Asset allocation addresses both risk and return and is a focal point in personal financial planning and investment management. Studies have shown that asset allocation accounts for 91.5 percent of investment success over time, while market timing, security selec-

CHAP. 4: INVESTING FOR RETIREMENT                              159

tion, and other factors account for less than 10 percent of investment performance (*Financial Analyst Journal,* May–June 1991).

Picking the "hottest" fund or attempting to buy at the "optimum time" rarely works consistently. If you focus on your entire portfolio's performance instead of individual holdings, you will be focused on overall results, and that is what counts.

It is expected that a mix of assets will allow for some asset classes to be down in value when others appreciate in value. Each asset class will eventually have its turn being the top performer over short time periods. Effective allocation entails having funds that zig when others zag, which, theoretically, should reduce the bumps (volatility) and therefore the risk. For this reason, you will want to focus on total portfolio performance in relation to your time horizon.

### ⅍ When should I reallocate funds among investments?

You should periodically review your portfolio. If you discover that gains or losses have caused changes in the percentage allocations since your initial allocation or last review, you simply reallocate assets to achieve your originally determined percentages. This process of reviewing and reallocating is referred to as *money management.*

Using the investment risk pyramid as an example, let's say it is January 1987, and you decide to allocate 50 percent of your investments to the foundation level, 30 percent to the controlled level, and 20 percent to the aggressive level. When you review your account 6 months later, in July, you discover that your controlled- and aggressive-investment levels have grown significantly since the last review because the stock market rose 30 percent in that period. If you follow a disciplined money management routine, you will reallocate money from the controlled and aggressive levels into foundation-level investments to reestablish your original percentages. In this way, you move your money into safer areas and take profits during good times.

## Return

*❧ If I want high returns, must I bear correspondingly high risks?*

If you define "risk" as being the deviation from, or the volatility of, an expected or average return for a given class of investments, that risk can be minimized by the planning horizon or expected holding period. As your holding period increases, risk (as measured by the range of worst-possible outcomes) decreases. Thus, over longer holding periods, the so-called riskier investments, like common stocks, have historically had higher or even better "worst" performances than "less risky" investments, such as T-bills and bonds.

*❧ What is a reasonable rate of return to assume on my retirement nest egg?*

It depends upon how you have your assets invested. There are long-term statistics for stocks, bonds, and Treasury bills going all the way back to 1926. According to Ibbotson Associates, a portfolio of the 500 largest companies in America—now represented by the S&P 500 index—has averaged a 10.33 percent compounded rate of return per year. The stocks of small companies have averaged 12.68 percent; U.S. Treasury bonds with a 20-year maturity, 5.25 percent; and Treasury bills, 3.89 percent over the same time frame. These figures are all preinflation and pretax.

Keep in mind that these are averages over a long period of time. Rarely has the return in any single year been the average number—and it wouldn't be prudent to have your portfolio in just one asset class. A 7 percent–return assumption might be appropriate for a balanced portfolio. A 5 percent assumption may be more appropriate if your portfolio is allocated to cash and bonds, and a 10 percent assumption might be more appropriate for a portfolio of equities (stocks).

Investment results in stocks in recent years have exceeded the long-term averages, thus making a 10 percent return seem unreasonably low. However, when—not if—the financial markets return to their historical norms, your retirement could be negatively

## CHAP. 4: INVESTING FOR RETIREMENT

161

affected. Just ask anyone who retired in the early 1980s assuming that he or she would always earn a 14 percent return on certificates of deposit!

Most financial advisors agree that the most important lesson you can learn about investment rates of return is not to base your retirement on what is happening now or on what happened in the immediate past. You will likely be better served to use historic, long-term averages as a guide.

### ⅍ *How can I determine how fast my money will grow?*

The easiest way to understand how fast money will grow is to understand the *Rule of 72*, which is simply a formula for determining the approximate time it takes for money to double:

72 ÷ rate of return = approximate number of years to double

If your investment earns 6 percent, it will take approximately 12 years to double (72 ÷ 6 = 12).

Obviously, the Rule of 72 can also help you determine the rate of return you need to earn for money to double in a predetermined time period:

72 ÷ number of years = approximate rate of return

For example, if you are 50 years old, have $300,000 in an IRA, and want it to double by age 59 to cover income needs, the rate you must earn to double the funds in 9 years is approximately 8 percent (72 ÷ 9 = 8).

A similar rule, the *Rule of 116,* when applied in the same manner as above, tells you approximately how long it takes for money to triple.

### ⅍ *What is total return?*

*Total return* is the full amount your mutual fund investment earns

162 WAYS AND MEANS

from all sources: interest, dividends, and capital gains, as well as unrealized capital gains (appreciation).

Total return is usually reported in either of two ways: (1) as net asset value (NAV), that is, without any adjustments for the sales charge, or (2) with adjustments for sales charges (commissions). When total return is listed at the public offering price (POP), the maximum up-front sales charge is included.

The Securities and Exchange Commission (SEC) has guidelines for reporting total returns. Average annual total returns are adjusted to include the maximum applicable sales charges over 1-, 5-, and 10-year periods—or since inception if the mutual fund is less than 10 years old. Because a fund must earn at least as much as the maximum sales charge before it can report positive SEC returns, it is possible to see negative SEC returns in the short term, even when returns at net asset value are positive.

### How important is it to know my total return?

Total return cannot tell you where the stock market is heading or how a particular mutual fund will perform in the future. Neither can it tell you how a manager achieved the returns or what risks the manager assumed. Most importantly, it cannot tell you whether a fund is right for you and your individual objectives. It will, however, give you an indication of how the fund has performed over various time periods. It will also show you the effects of any sales charge on the returns over those time periods.

### How do I properly use this concept?

When comparing funds on a total return basis, be sure that you are comparing growth funds to growth funds; large cap to large cap; small cap to small cap, and so on, to get an "apples-to-apples" comparison. For example, comparing a small-capitalization or technology fund to a balanced fund would not be appropriate given the difference in the degree of risk.

For an added check, you should compare a fund's total return

CHAP. 4: INVESTING FOR RETIREMENT                    163

to the corresponding index for that particular fund (e.g., S&P 500, Wilshire 2000). This should let you know whether the fund's manager is leading, lagging, or in the middle of the pack for his or her particular fund's peer group.

Since most performance records include 1-, 3-, 5-, and 10-year results, you should keep in mind that this leaves out the effects of the October 1987 market crash. To better ascertain how your fund's manager has fared in the tougher markets, compare his or her results from 1991 and 1994 to those of his or her peers for the same years. Finally, you should ascertain how long the current manager has been with the fund. Star managers come and go. Some planners believe a management team philosophy is something to consider.

## Inflation

*Does inflation affect my assumed rate of return on investments?*

To determine the "true" rate of return on your investments, you should consider the effects of inflation and income taxes. By including these two factors in a retirement analysis, it is possible to better assess the actual increase in buying power provided by the investments. For instance, let's say a person has funds in a money market account earning 5 percent. If this is a taxable account and the income tax rate is 28 percent, the investment has a net rate of return of 3.6 percent. Now, if inflation averages 3 percent per year, the money market investment's real rate of return is only .6 percent. The longer the money is in this investment, the more purchasing power is lost.

*How does inflation affect the returns of my retirement investments?*

To determine the effects of inflation on an investment, you have to consider the actual growth rate of the investment on an inflation-adjusted or "real-return" basis. It is important to calculate real rates of return in order to see how your retirement accounts are growing in relation to inflation so that you can assess the purchasing power of your account over time. In other words, by the time your account grows from $100,000 to $500,000, the $500,000 amount will not have the same purchasing effect as $500,000 did when you originally invested the $100,000. The inflationary rate used in calculating the real rate of return is normally equated to the annual increase or decrease in the consumer price index, and the formula for calculating the inflation-adjusted return is:

$$\text{Inflation-adjusted total return} = \frac{1 + \text{total return}}{1 + \text{rate of inflation}} - 1$$

Although this formula helps in determining the real return per year, you need a financial calculation to determine the compound effect over time.

*Inflation doesn't seem to be the concern that it was in the past. How important should inflation be in my investment decisions?*

After 5 years of 3 percent inflation, $1 is worth 86¢; after 10 years, 74¢; after 20 years, 55¢—a reduction of almost one-half of your purchasing power. You feel the effects of inflation when you go to the grocery store, buy a new car, or compare what you pay for something today to what you paid for it last year. Your personal inflation rate may be higher or lower depending on what you are buying and the effect inflation has had on the prices of those particular items. Inflation will always be around, and it should always be considered in the determination of your future retirement income.

Placing money in CDs and money market accounts earning only 2 or 3 percent will give you slim to possibly negative real or

# Chap. 4: Investing for Retirement

165

true returns after you subtract inflation and income taxes. In order to get ahead, your investments must exceed inflation and taxes. You must include the effects of inflation when considering the possible growth outcomes of investing for retirement. Without properly evaluating the influences of inflation, you may be creating only a fraction of the real return that you expect or need for your retirement plan investments.

## Liquidity

⋆ *What is liquidity?*

*Liquidity* is a measure of the speed with which you can convert assets into cash. Liquid investments are those that are very short term in nature, such as checking accounts, money market accounts, and possibly 30-day Treasury bills.

⋆ *I'm ready to start investing for retirement. Are there guidelines for the amount of liquidity I should maintain?*

First, most advisors recommend that you maintain approximately 1 month of living expenses in a checking account that earns interest. Second, maintain a cash reserve as a quick fund for emergencies and opportunities. If you receive a constant amount of pay, maintain at least 3 months of expenses in this fund; if you are in sales, on commission, or the like, keep up to 6 months of expenses.

Now that you have your cash reserves earmarked, take a moment and list every retirement and savings opportunity available to you today. Obviously, you'll want to maximize the one that gives you the greatest opportunity. For example, if you have an opportunity to participate in any formal retirement plan with your company, especially a 401(k) plan, most financial professionals would agree that taking full advantage of the 401(k) plan is your best start. This is because your savings are going into your investment account pretax; more importantly, because many employers actually match a portion of the employee's contribution, you may receive a handsome incentive even before your investment earns a return.

Now that you've listed and taken advantage of all your retirement planning opportunities, you are ready to develop your investment philosophy.

## Market Timing

> *What is the difference between market timing and money management?*

*Market timing* is deciding when to buy and when to sell. In essence, you are attempting to buy when the market is at a low point and to sell when it is at a high.

*Money management* is maintaining a balanced preallocated percentage in each of your pyramid levels by reallocating your assets as necessary. Reallocation forces you to take profits off the table in good times and invest in the market during down times. You have the ability to take your profits when the market is good, but you still have your "war chest" of funds at your risk pyramid's foundation level to take advantage of bargains in the marketplace after a sell-off.

## Other Investment Principles

> *What is dollar cost averaging?*

*Dollar cost averaging* is formal, systematic investing—weekly, monthly, quarterly. It is most often done when investing in common stocks or mutual funds to take advantage of the price fluctuations in an ever-changing equity market. This approach has historically proved to be one of the simplest yet most successful methods of investing in any type of market.

CHAP. 4: INVESTING FOR RETIREMENT                    167

≫ *What is positive correlation and negative correlation, and what is the importance of each in a investment or retirement portfolio?*

*Correlation* is the way in which two or more assets move in relation to one another. For instance, an individual automotive stock may move in tandem with other automotive stocks. This would be considered a *positive correlation*. A *negative correlation* would usually if that same automotive stock were tracked against the price of gold.

Stocks and gold prices usually move independently of each other. Most advisors believe that by examining the correlation between different assets and asset classes, an investor can construct a portfolio with less volatility while staying in harmony with his or her time horizon, risk tolerance, and expected returns.

≫ *What is a "model" portfolio?*

A *model portfolio* is a combination of investments arrived at in relation to your expected return and willingness to take risk. It proposes quantitative asset allocation percentages and suggests a specific portfolio design based on your answers to an investment questionnaire.

## INVESTMENT VEHICLES

### Bonds

≫ *What exactly is a bond?*

Don't be confused by the fact that we talk of someone buying (and owning) a bond. A *bond* is an IOU. It represents a loan from you—the investor—to the borrower—the bond issuer—in return for an IOU—the bond. The bond document states the terms of

168                                          Ways and Means

the loan, the rate of interest to be paid, the maturity date, and so
on.

The many types and variations of bonds only reflect different
loan details, for example, whether the borrower is a corporation,
municipality, or the U.S. Treasury. And don't get too caught up
in whether it is called a "bond," a "note," or a "bill." Those are
only names denoting the initial time frame, or *term,* of the loan.
A bond is generally for 10 years or more; a note, 2 to 9 years;
and a bill, usually 2 years or less.

### ⚜ *What are bond premiums and discounts?*

Bonds are typically issued at *par*—also known as *face* or *maturity*
value—which is the amount that will be paid back at maturity.
If you pay anything more than par, you are said to pay a *premium;*
anything less than par is a *discount.* Bond prices indicate a percentage of par. For instance, a $10,000 bond selling at a price of
97—a discount—would cost $9700, or 97 percent of par. A bond
selling at a premium price of 103 would cost $10,300, or 103
percent of par.

### ⚜ *What are callable bonds?*

Many bonds are redeemable, or *callable,* at some prestipulated
point in time before their maturity. This means the issuer of the
bond has the right to return your money before maturity. The
key point is that call provisions permit the issuer to buy back
(redeem) your bond, usually at a price between par (100) and
103, without your approval. Most municipal bonds, for example,
are callable by the issuers within 10 years of their issuance. Brokers who sell bonds are legally required to disclose call provisions,
but you should always ask about and know exactly how a bond's
call feature works before buying it.

Most call provisions are fairly straightforward. However, always ask if a bond has special, or extraordinary, call features. For
example, housing bonds can be redeemed at any time if enough

Chap. 4: Investing for Retirement                        169

mortgages are prepaid, and they can be called within the first year or two if the issuer simply hasn't used all the bond proceeds as planned. Some industrial development bonds and pollution control bonds can be redeemed if the planned project is later determined to be uneconomical or if the facility burns down—a "calamity call." Certain hospital bonds allow redemption of the issue if the hospital is ever acquired by a group that allows abortions.

The bottom line is that you should always look at a bond's yield to the earliest possible call date *(yield to call,* or *YTC),* not just the often-quoted *yield to maturity (YTM).* When a broker tells you a bond is selling at a certain price, he or she should also tell you its YTM and YTC. These rates take into account both the bond's interest income and the change in value it will experience between your purchase and the maturity or call date.

#### ⚒ *What are the main risks of investing in bonds?*

The two primary risks are credit risk and market risk. Both stem from the fact that a bond is an IOU representing a loan.

*Credit risk* measures the likelihood that the borrower won't keep up its end of the agreement by paying back your principal at maturity and paying the stated interest until then. *Market risk* refers to fluctuation in a bond's price, or market value, before the maturity date. Market value reflects other people's potential willingness to buy your IOU when you want to sell a bond before it matures.

#### ⚒ *How does market risk pertain to bonds?*

Market risk refers to fluctuation in a bond's price—market value—before the maturity date. If you decide to sell a bond before it matures, you can't go to the issuer and get your money back. The issuer's only obligation is to pay you interest and return your principal on the maturity date. To cash out early, you will be forced to sell your bond in the bond market. Unlike the issuer, who is obligated to pay you a certain amount at maturity, the bond market will pay you whatever it sees fit. That amount will be determined by several factors, but essentially it has to do with how attractive the remaining term of your bond looks on that particular day.

### ≥ How does interest rate risk affect bonds?

Perhaps the most important concept for bond investors to understand is the "seesaw" relationship of bonds and interest rates. As Figure 4-3 shows, when interest rates rise, the value of existing bonds falls. The fixed stream of income a bond will pay (until maturity) has been made slightly less attractive if higher rates are now available elsewhere. To persuade other investors to buy an existing bond, you have to offer them a good deal—a lower price! The opposite is true when interest rates fall. Existing bonds, with their higher locked-in rates, become more attractive, and people are now willing to pay more for them.

Figure 4-3 also illustrates that the longer the term of a bond, the wider is its price fluctuation. This means long-term bonds—even U.S. Treasury bonds—entail more price volatility, or market

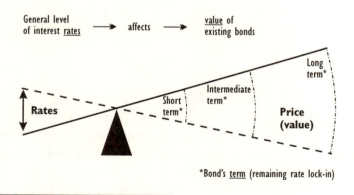

**Figure 4-3**  How bonds fluctuate.

## CHAP. 4: INVESTING FOR RETIREMENT

**TABLE 4-2   Bond Ratings**

| S&P* | Moody's† | |
|------|----------|---|
| **Investment-grade bonds** | | |
| AAA | Aaa | Highest quality |
| AA | Aa | Very high quality |
| A | A | Good quality |
| BBB | Baa | Warrants caution, monitor closely |
| **Lower-grade (or "junk") bonds** | | |
| BB | Ba | Speculative aspects |
| B | B | Very risky |
| CCC | Caa | Having problems |
| CC | Ca | In serious jeopardy |
| C | C | Interest stopped |
| D | C | Defaulted |

*S&P may add a plus or minus to indicate that a bond is relatively strong or weak for that category.
†Moody's adds numeral "1" to denote a strong bond within a category.

risk. The risk isn't that you might not get all your money back when the bond matures; it is the possibility that you will suffer a loss if you sell the bond before maturity.

### ⤴ *How can I tell how much credit risk a bond has?*

Credit risk is reflected in a bond's rating. Several rating companies, most notably Standard & Poor's (S&P) and Moody's, evaluate bond issuers' financial strength. They assign bond ratings to indicate the likelihood of each borrower's being able to live up to the obligation the bonds represent. That obligation usually includes the timely payment of interest at a specified rate and the repayment of the principal amount at the maturity date. The range of ratings assigned by these agencies is shown in Table 4-2.

As you can see, the highest rating assigned by both S&P and Moody's is triple A. Very few corporations or municipalities are in sterling-enough financial condition to garner this rating. However, many issuers, especially municipalities, pay banks or large bond insurers to guaranty their bonds. This double backing generally qualifies for a triple-A rating.

U.S. Treasury securities, together with securities issued by federal agencies which are full-faith and credit obligations of the U.S. government, are deemed to have triple-A status.

⊿ *What types of municipal bonds are there, and can I use the same rating criteria for all of them?*

Municipal bonds generally come in two types. With *general-obligation bonds,* the issuing municipalities typically can use multiple sources of income to make the payments, even raising taxes if necessary. In contrast, *revenue bonds* are backed only by revenues from specific sources, such as hospitals, toll bridges, and colleges. Because revenue bonds have more limited backing, they are usually considered less desirable than general-obligation bonds.

A good guideline is to require a rating of single-A or better when you are buying a general-obligation bond but a half-notch higher when buying a revenue bond (i.e., A+ from S&P or A1 from Moody's). Alternatively, you might buy a bond that is insured; it will probably have a triple-A rating, regardless of whether it is a general-obligation or revenue bond.

## Stocks

⊿ *I'm afraid of the stock market. Isn't there a chance I can lose all my money?*

In terms of investing in the market in general, the main risk you face is market fluctuation, not a total loss. Many controls and margin requirements have been implemented to prevent another 1929-style crash. In terms of your particular investments, it is

## Chap. 4: Investing for Retirement                173

possible to have a total loss. However, if you balance your time horizon and ability to accept risk and diversify efficiently over a number of asset classes, you can significantly reduce the chance of losing all your money.

### *What are preferred stocks?*

Although *preferreds* are technically stocks, unlike common stockholders, preferred stockholders are not entitled to a company's growth in earnings or assets. Instead, preferred stocks pay a fixed (and usually high) income.

### *What is the S&P 500 index?*

"S&P" stands for Standard and Poor's, which is the firm that determines which companies are included in the index. Many people erroneously think of the S&P 500 index as simply an equal weighting of the 500 largest corporations. Actually, S&P bases its index on financial strength and on which companies it determines to be industry leaders. This tilts the index in favor of some companies regardless of how sound they may be. The S&P index is commonly used as a benchmark in comparing returns on portfolios. It may be suggested that if you assume less risk than this index, you will most likely have lower returns. However, if you accept greater risk and receive the same or lower return than the index, you may want to review how your portfolio is being run.

Lower volatility and comparable returns are obviously most desirable. It is important, however, not to jump to conclusions. The index is merely a basis for comparison. Instead of focusing on "beating the S&P," focus first on aligning your portfolio with your needs and risk tolerance.

### *What is the EAFE index?*

This is the Europe, Australia, and Far East index, which is the common benchmark for international investments, just as the

S&P 500 index is for U.S. stock investments. EAFE reflects all major stock markets outside the United States.

### ⋊ What does "dogs of the Dow" mean?

"Dogs of the Dow" is an important strategy involving stocks from the Dow Jones 30. In this strategy, you select Dow stocks with the highest dividend yield (a low price with high dividends). Since Dow stock dividends are relatively stable, you are essentially looking for depressed, or "dog," stock prices, hoping that the price will eventually go up. The dividend yield is calculated by dividing the dividends received by the market price of the stock. Using this strategy is similar to investing in value stocks rather than growth stocks.

### ⋊ What are penny stocks?

*Penny stocks* are stocks in companies with very little capitalization and are priced under $5 per share. Advisors agree that the high risk associated with buying this kind of stock is generally unwarranted for the average investor. With the multitude of high-quality common stocks available, the average investor would be better served by establishing a solid base of quality stocks and only thereafter speculating with small amounts of money.

### ⋊ I've heard the terms "value" and "growth" used to describe different investment styles, but I'm not sure what they mean. Can you explain them?

A *growth* manager invests in growing companies whose sales or market share is expanding. A *value* manager looks for companies which are experiencing a turnaround and whose stocks are currently selling for a low price. For example, a growth manager may invest in a company worth $1 in the expectation that it will soon be worth $1.25. A value manager may pay 60 or 70 cents for a company worth $1 because he or she is looking for companies

# Chap. 4: Investing for Retirement                    175

whose stock appears undervalued. Note that, if the markets were to experience a steep decline, value stocks and mutual funds would tend to decline less than growth stocks and funds because they are already selling at relatively low or undervalued prices.

### ◆ *How often does the stock market decline?*

You should expect 5 to 10 percent declines fairly frequently (a 10 percent "correction" tends to happen every year), and don't be surprised by greater declines every few years. The recent U.S. bull market is very unusual, with far fewer declines than would normally be expected.

### ◆ *What is a dividend reinvestment plan?*

A *dividend reinvestment plan* provides for the automatic reinvestment of cash dividends to be used to purchase additional shares of stock or mutual fund shares. By taking advantage of automatic reinvestment, shareholders can obtain the advantages of dollar cost averaging. The same dollars buy more shares when the price is low, so the average cost per share is lower than the average price paid per share at each purchase date.

## Convertibles

### ◆ *What are convertibles?*

A *convertible* is really a hybrid security, containing some of the advantages of a bond but also some of the growth potential of a stock. Convertibles can thus offer the best of both worlds and can be an excellent addition to a retirement portfolio.

Convertibles come in two forms, bonds and preferred stocks. Both share several common characteristics. They pay a fixed income that is higher than the yield of the company's common stock dividend. Both types of convertibles are also generally callable, or redeemable, by the issuing company on a certain date and at a certain price. Further, in the case of bankruptcy, holders of either type of convertibles have prior claim on assets over holders of common stock.

Convertible bonds do have certain advantages over convertible preferreds. Bonds have prior claim on assets in case of bankruptcy. Bonds also have maturity dates. This means there is a specific point at which their value is predictable. Preferreds have no such date. As a result, bonds are generally the more desirable type of convertible.

### ⚜ *What is the advantage of convertibles?*

The most attractive feature of either type of convertible is its conversion feature. Convertibles can, at the holder's option, be exchanged (converted) into a certain number of shares of the common stock of the issuing company. Holders of common stock are the ones who benefit from a company's good fortunes and growth, but a convertible provides a back door to that growth for income-oriented investors. Retirees, who need the consistent income that a bond or preferred stock can provide, are therefore able to also have the potential for some stock market growth.

### ⚜ *What are the disadvantages of convertibles?*

Growth participation is not without cost. If higher returns were easily available with little risk and high income, the markets would have already gobbled them up. Several drawbacks are generally present with convertibles. First, the stock price at which it makes sense to exercise the conversion option is usually significantly higher than the current price. For example, a $10,000 bond may be convertible into 100 shares of XYZ stock, but the stock might be trading at only $50, so the "conversion value" of the bond is only $5000. In that case, the conversion feature would be of no current value because the stock would need to double to make conversion worthwhile.

Another drawback is that a convertible's yield, although

CHAP. 4: INVESTING FOR RETIREMENT                    177

higher than that of the company's common stock, is likely to be
lower than the current yield available on nonconvertible bonds
and preferreds of similar quality and maturity. In other words,
investors give up some yield in return for the potential that the
conversion feature might someday produce gains.

## Mutual Funds

*When did mutual funds begin?*

Mutual Funds began in the 1920s. If you wanted a fund in 1933,
you could have chosen from thirty-two funds. Today, however,
there are more different mutual funds (nearing 10,000) than there
are stocks listed on the New York Stock Exchange! In general,
investments in the funds are neither insured nor guaranteed by
the U.S. government, any financial institution, the Federal Deposit Insurance Corporation, the Federal Reserve Board, or any
other agency, entity, or person.

Mutual fund assets reached the $1 billion mark in 1945 and
crossed the $1 trillion mark in 1990. Today there is over $3
trillion in mutual funds. Mutual funds truly seem to be the investment choice for millions of individual investors.

*What exactly is a mutual fund?*

A *mutual fund* is a company that makes investments on behalf
of its shareholders—individuals like you and I, who have a common investment objective. The fund company pools our money
and its professional money managers select the underlying investments (various combinations of stocks, bonds, or cash instruments). The fund managers attempt to achieve the highest possible return, consistent with an acceptable amount of risk, to
obtain the investment objective. The concept has worked well for
over 60 years.

As a shareholder, you own a proportionate share of the fund.
Each share represents ownership in all the fund's underlying se-

curities. Funds may pay dividends and capital gains in proportion to the number of fund shares owned. Thus, whether you invested $1000 or $10,000, you'll still receive the same rate of return.

> *There are so many different categories of mutual funds. Can you tell me something about them?*

A mutual fund invests in securities that fit its specific objective. Because not everyone shares the same goals, there are mutual funds to fit just about any investment need, style, and risk tolerance. Depending upon who is reporting the information, there are as many as thirty categories of mutual funds listed. Categories which you may be familiar with include the following:

AGGRESSIVE GROWTH FUNDS These funds seek maximum capital gains as their investment objective. Current income in the form of dividends should not be expected from these funds. Typically, aggressive growth funds invest in smaller, less known companies that the managers believe possess great potential for growth. These funds may also be called small-cap or micro-cap company funds due to the small market capitalization of the companies.

GROWTH FUNDS Typically, growth funds invest in stocks and seek capital growth through the price appreciation of the underlying securities. Once again, the primary objective is to produce an increase in the value of the portfolio holdings rather than to receive income in the form of dividends. Funds may be further subdivided into large-cap or midcap growth funds.

GROWTH AND INCOME FUNDS These funds invest in companies expected to show average or better earnings growth and pay steady or rising dividends. They are more conservative than growth funds and typically invest in the large-cap or blue-chip stock companies.

BALANCED AND ASSET ALLOCATION FUNDS These invest in stocks, bonds, and money market instruments on the basis of the manager's opinion of the direction of the market. These funds are

# Chap. 4: Investing for Retirement    179

more conservative in that they attempt to reduce market volatility through investments in bonds and money markets which add stability, through interest income, to the portfolio.

**Income, equity income, and high-yield income funds**    As their names suggest, dividends and interest are the primary objectives of these funds. The high level of current income is often achieved by investing in companies with good dividend-paying records, such as blue-chip companies and utilities, or fixed-income securities such as corporate and government bonds. Equity income funds are the most conservative stock funds. High-yield income funds are the most aggressive of the bond funds.

**Convertible security funds**    These are funds that invest primarily in convertible bonds and convertible preferred stocks, which can be exchanged for common stock.

**Government and municipal bond funds**    These funds emphasize income through a portfolio of bonds issued by federal and local governments. Income earned is usually federal tax–exempt for most shareholders. There are many triple-tax-exempt state municipal bond funds whose income is exempt from state and ad valorem taxation in addition to federal taxation.

**Emerging-markets funds**    As the name indicates, emerging-markets funds focus on stocks of companies that are based in countries whose economies are small but growing quickly.

**Global and international funds**    Global funds may invest anywhere in the world, including the United States. International funds invest everywhere except the United States. Each fund's prospectus will tell you the percentage of the fund that may be invested in foreign countries as well as percentages that may be invested in certain areas of the world.

**Sector, or specialty, funds**    As the name implies, sector funds concentrate on securities in specific industries, such as utilities, technology, banking, health care, gold, natural resources, and real estate. Because they are concentrated in a specific market sector rather than investing in a variety of sectors, these funds may have greater risk than other mutual funds. When used as part of an asset allocation model, sector funds can be very effective investment vehicles.

### Aren't stock mutual funds risky?

They can be. You can limit your risk, however, by buying the type of fund that matches your investment objectives. Fund families usually have a variety of mutual funds available—aggressive growth funds, growth funds, large-cap growth funds, growth and income funds, balanced funds, and bond funds. These same fund families have a variety of funds within each category which have different investment objectives and risk tolerances. It's up to your investment professional to help you through the maze of mutual fund choices to select the fund or funds that's right for you.

### What are the advantages of mutual funds?

Mutual funds have five main advantages.

**1.** Mutual funds offer the general public what used to be afforded only by the wealthy: access to the investment markets and professional money management. Whether you have $500 or $500,000, you can purchase shares in mutual funds and know that professional managers are handling the trading activity in the fund. Researching and setting up buy-sell disciplines is the portfolio manager's primary function. All investors are rewarded by this expertise. To retain your own professional money manager to manage your individual portfolio, you may need $50,000, $500,000, or even $1 million or more, depending on the individual advisor.

**2.** An added safety feature of most funds (excluding sector, or specialty, funds) is built-in diversification. It would take you

CHAP. 4: INVESTING FOR RETIREMENT 181

several thousand dollars and a great deal of time to diversify properly with individual stocks. The larger pool of money in funds allows managers the luxury of splitting the portfolio. Volatility can be reduced and the potential for gain can be enhanced. Mutual funds offer low cost and immediate diversification across numerous market sectors and industries. Thus, if the oil or retailing companies are currently out of favor, the other companies in the portfolio, such as banking or pharmaceutical firms, may be performing well.

**3.** Mutual funds are easy to add to should you desire. The fund can automatically reinvest your dividends and/or capital gains into new shares. Also, any time you have an extra $25, $50, or $100 (whatever the fund minimum is), you can forward it to the company to purchase additional shares for your account. Many companies provide for automatic deductions from your checking or savings accounts to purchase shares. Mutual funds truly are convenient to use.

**4.** Mutual funds also give you daily calculations of your share values. You need only consult almost any daily paper or call your fund directly. Likewise, if you need to redeem all or a portion of your shares, you normally will receive your money within 5 business days.

**5.** Every time you receive a dividend or capital gain distribution or make a new contribution, you will receive a confirmation of the number of shares purchased, current net asset value, total number of shares now owned, and sometimes the account value. Also, at year-end you will receive a 1099 form for tax preparation purposes.

&gt;&gt; *What are some of the disadvantages of mutual funds?*

Mutual fund directors decide when to declare dividends, short-term gains, and long-term gains, and mutual fund managers may have to sell to meet their funds' cash needs when other investors

182 WAYS AND MEANS

redeem shares for cash. For these reasons, investors in mutual funds do not have control over taxable gains. With individually managed portfolios, investors can offset taxable gains with losses or, even better, can simply hold and not realize gains.

Another disadvantage of mutual funds is investors' lack of control over which securities are purchased. For example, if there are particular companies or segments of the market in which investors do not want to invest, they may not be able to exclude these from their mutual fund investments without limiting their mutual fund investment choices. Individually managed portfolios allow investors to choose the companies or market segments they prefer.

To avoid these concerns, you may wish to explore using professional money managers who work with individuals with your portfolio size and investment objectives.

### ⋇ *What is a load fund, and how does it differ from a no-load fund?*

A *load* is a commission paid to the person who sold you the fund. Normally, loads range from 3 to 6 percent and are either up-front charges, as is the case with Class A shares, or deferred fees charged if you redeem during a certain time period (normally the first through sixth year), for Class B shares. Some funds have Class C shares, which entail a levelized load, usually 1 percent per year. Check the fund's prospectus to find out the length of the contingent deferred-sales-charge period. Many funds also charge *12b-1 fees*. These are "trailing" service fees paid to the advisor selling the fund or kept by the fund itself. The 12b-1 fee can be thought of as a retainer for continued good service of your account over the years.

A *no-load* fund does not have sales commissions. Investors typically select no-loads after reading about them in investment magazines or newspapers, by talking with their families or friends, or by calling the funds directly. No-loads are generally purchased

CHAP. 4: INVESTING FOR RETIREMENT                    183

directly from the fund organization. No-load funds can also be purchased without sales charges from some fee-based financial advisors. These advisors typically charge a fee as a percentage of the assets they are managing. The marketing and selling expenses of no-load funds, including magazine and newspaper ads, are charged to the investor through the fund's operating expenses. Therefore, the operating expenses of some no-loads may be higher than those of many load funds.

Investors can compare the expense ratios of the particular fund under consideration to the average operating expense for that particular fund category (growth, growth and income, etc.). The lower the expense ratio, the more money distributed to the investor. This is one way to measure a fund's efficiency.

Both types of mutual funds charge ongoing management fees for their services. Numerous studies have shown that the longer the investor's time horizon, or the longer you can stay with your investment, the less significant a sales commission will be to the overall return.

### ⊰ *My no-load fund charges a load! What's going on?*

A poll of 1000 U.S. investors, conducted by Princeton Survey Research Associates for the Investor Protection Trust in January 1996, found that 36 percent of investors thought no-load funds had no sales charges or other fees. Clearly, they are mistaken. Many individuals are astonished to find out that some "no-load" funds have high built-in expenses.

Some so-called no-load funds charge distribution fees when you redeem shares. So, while you may not have paid to invest in the fund, you might pay to get your investment out of the fund. The fund prospectus will outline all applicable charges and fees. As stated in *Registered Representative* (July 1996), if more people knew the facts about no-load funds, it is possible more would seek out advisors to ascertain whether a fund fits their investment objective, tolerance for risk, and management style.

### What are the annual costs of a mutual fund?

Mutual funds have annual expenses, whether they are load or no-load. The industry average for equity mutual funds is approximately 1.4 percent. The expense ratio is composed of a management fee and administrative fees, and some funds have additional 12b-1 fees. The expense ratio, however, does not include commission charges the fund may incur when securities are bought and sold. Many investors are unaware of the total cost affiliated with mutual funds. Because the trading costs are not usually disclosed, it may be difficult to know what the exact cost of your fund really is unless you write to your mutual fund company and request a "statement of additional information" or Part B of the prospectus, which will include this information.

### What's the difference between Class A, Class B, and other classes of mutual fund shares?

As mentioned earlier, mutual fund Class A shares carry an up-front load. If the load is 5 percent and you invested $1000, $950 is working for you in the fund. A portion of the remaining $50 went toward your advisor's compensation for recommending the fund for your specific needs. Class A shares have lower internal charges for their other operating expenses. Additional contributions (excluding reinvested dividends or capital gain distributions) to your fund will also be subject to the up-front fee. When you redeem Class A shares, there are no exit fees or penalties. You will receive the full net asset value (NAV) of your account, valued at the close of business on the redemption date.

Mutual fund Class B shares carry no up-front charges. One hundred percent of your initial investment goes to work for you immediately. Class B shares have a *contingent deferred-sales-charge (CDSC) period,* which normally lasts from 1 to 6 years. If you redeem your shares during this period, you will be assessed a fee. The fee decreases the longer you have been with the fund. For example, if you redeem your shares in year 4, your fee will prob-

CHAP. 4: INVESTING FOR RETIREMENT 185

ably be around 2 to 3 percent of the amount that exceeds your earnings. The prospectus contains this information. New contributions into Class B shares usually start a new CDSC period. If the CDSC period has expired at the time of redemption, there are no exit fees.

Class B shares have higher internal operating expenses. For this reason, it is important to ascertain whether your Class B shares will convert to Class A shares at the end of the CDSC period. It is to your advantage if the shares do convert because they will then be assessed the lower internal-operating-expense rate for the remainder of the time you are in the fund. The fund prospectus also provides this information.

Class C or other letter-designated shares usually carry no or very low loads. They have higher internal operating expenses than do Class A shares and usually will not convert to Class A shares. Consult your prospectus for help with determining the share class you should purchase.

Almost all mutual funds automatically reinvest investors' dividends and capital gains into additional fund share purchases without a load or fee.

### ⌇ *What is the difference between open-end and closed-end funds?*

*Open-end funds* are generally the funds we see advertised. They continuously accept new money for investment through the sale of additional shares. Also, open-end funds continuously redeem, or repurchase, shares at the net asset value of the shares. In other words, open-end funds are always open for business.

*Closed-end mutual funds* are similar to open-end mutual funds in that they are professionally managed pools of funds. Closed-end funds differ in that they have a limited number of shares and are usually sold like stock on a stock exchange, such as the NYSE. You pay a commission to buy or sell a closed-end fund just as you do in any stock transaction. According to the June 1997 issue of *Mutual Funds,* there were, at that time, 69 popularly traded closed-end domestic stock funds, 92 closed-end international stock funds, and 347 closed-end bond funds.

### How are mutual fund share prices determined?

Mutual fund share prices are determined at the end of each business day by adding up the value of all the securities in the fund's portfolio after expenses and dividing the sum by the total number of shares outstanding. The final result is the fund's net asset value for that day. This is before sales charges are taken into account. Thus, almost all funds' net asset values will fluctuate daily.

### What are the short-term and long-term risks of a money market fund?

Short-term risk is low, since money market funds tend to invest in securities with very low risk, such as U.S. Treasury bills and CDs of top-rated banks that mature in 1 year or less. The chances of losing money are slim to none. Keep in mind, however, that there are different types of risk. The long-term risk of money market funds tends to be high because they usually produce lower returns than stocks and bonds over the same period of time and thus provide very little protection from inflation. Treat money market funds like the liquid assets they are, not as investments.

### What are the short-term risks and long-term risks of bond funds?

Bond funds have relatively moderate short-term risk. Interest rate changes, more than any other single factor, affect bond fund values. Remember our seesaw. Bonds and interest rates have an inverse relationship: as interest rates rise, the value of the bonds held in the fund falls, and vice versa. Bonds with longer maturities are more sensitive to interest rate changes than bonds with short maturities. In the long term, during a period of rising interest rates, bond funds may decline in value. Fund managers

CHAP. 4: INVESTING FOR RETIREMENT                    187

reduce this risk by investing in bonds with various—laddered—maturities.

The long-term risk of bond funds is also moderate. Changes in interest rates will cause bond values to fluctuate. However, if an investor needs to sell a bond while interest rates are rising, even after holding the fund for several years, he or she may find that the proceeds are less than expected. Periodic interest rates earned by bonds generally serve as a source of stable income, rather than a long-term investment. Historically, long-term returns from bonds have been inferior to those of stocks. For this reason, bonds provide only moderate protection against inflation.

*What are the short-term and long-term risks associated with stock (equity) funds?*

The short-term risk of stock funds is very high. Investing in a broad array of companies and industries will help cushion your return if one company or industry sector falls out of favor. However, even highly diversified stock funds that focus on big, established companies will fluctuate in value and can decline during periods of a general market downturn. Funds with narrower investment focus, such as aggressive growth funds, may be subject to even larger price fluctuations. Many advisors would suggest that you don't invest in stocks unless your time horizon is at least 5 years.

The long-term risk of investing in stocks has been low. History shows that, over an extended time frame, the wide day-to-day and year-to-year fluctuations in the stock market tend to smooth out, resulting in a relatively consistent long-term return. Compared to bond funds or money market accounts, stock funds offer greater potential for long-term growth and inflation protection. Over the years, the stock market, as measured by the S&P 500, has reflected to a greater extent the growth in the overall economy. Stocks plus time have equaled returns greater than those of most other investments. An adequate amount of time is crucial, and

## Unit Investment Trust

⚥ *What is a unit investment trust?*

A *unit investment trust (UIT)* is simply a portfolio of predetermined securities (i.e., you know the holdings) that have been professionally selected. This type of security is also referred to as a *defined asset fund,* since the portfolio has a defined selection of securities. Usually, the strategy is one of "buy and hold." Although UITs are usually invested in tax-exempt bonds, they can also be invested in stocks, bonds, or a combination of both. Unlike mutual funds, UITs are unmanaged portfolios. Because of this, they usually do not have ongoing management fees but, rather, have a low annual administrative cost that is assessed on the portfolio. They have an up-front load, or commission; and like mutual funds, they are sold by prospectus.

## INVESTMENT STRATEGIES

## Establishing an Investment Philosophy

⚥ *Is there a "best" investment that I can make?*

Unequivocally, yes! It's called *education.* Do not rely solely on your advisors. You should read the business and financial reports in the newspapers and keep up with the effects that politics and world economic and social events can have on your financial security. The difference between financial dignity and financial despair may be merely an awareness of what has been happening, what is currently happening, and what is coming.

# CHAP. 4: INVESTING FOR RETIREMENT                                                189

≥ *I'm afraid to invest because I don't know anything about it.*

Many people are reluctant to invest because they don't understand the basic rules of investing: the time power of money, how money doubles (Rule of 72), the effect of taxes and inflation on investments, and so on. Over and over again, individuals tell us they have never had the basics explained to them.

As a nation we are financially illiterate. We do not have classes in high school or even in many colleges that explain financial principles. Most often, it's not until we're in our late twenties or thirties, or beyond, that we realize we need to learn something about finances; and, unfortunately, many of us seem to learn only after making mistakes.

Informed clients make wise decisions. They understand why they need a particular investment and how it works. Make sure you are one of them.

≥ *Before I develop an investment strategy, how much do I need to invest?*

It is possible to purchase a single share of stock; however, that would not be the most economical use of your money. Most firms have minimum commission amounts, so it is necessary to determine those costs in advance. A round lot—100 shares—of stock trading at $20 per share will cost $2000 plus commission.

Taxable bonds often come with $1000 minimums, while municipal bonds have minimums of $5000. Many mutual funds are available with minimums ranging from $250 to $1000 to open an account. After you open an account, you may make additional contributions of $25, $50, or $100 depending upon the fund requirements. Many mutual funds lower their account minimums for IRAs.

≥ *What should I keep in mind as I develop my investment goals and philosophy?*

In the real world, most people who retire in a comfortable lifestyle started building their fortunes early, slowly, and with steady care. Deciding to *save* for retirement is the most critical first step. Sticking with a savings plan is, unfortunately, a difficult task for many Americans. The more you save and invest on a regular basis, the faster your money grows. There are many books, magazines, and words of wisdom from experts. Here are a few important concepts that planners use:

*Pay yourself first.* Remember, if you are working, put the maximum amount allowed into your employer-sponsored qualified plan. Most employers will match your contribution, which is a great benefit. After that, you can see if you are eligible for an individual retirement account. The Taxpayer Relief Act of 1997, the December 1997 amendment to the proposed regulation regarding retirement plans, and the IRS Restructuring and Reform Act of 1998 provide for greater opportunities with IRAs. Check with your planner to determine which type of IRA is best for you.

*Start early.* Compound interest is the "eighth wonder of the world" and can work wonders on your retirement investment portfolio. For example, if you save $100 a month starting at age 35, with a compounded monthly investment return of 8 percent, your savings will grow to $149,036 by the time you are 65. Not so bad, right? Especially considering that your original investment was only $36,000. Now look at the numbers that result if you start saving 10 years earlier, at age 25. That same $100 a month earning the same rate will increase to $349,100—more than twice the return, from only one-third more investment money, than that from saving started at age 35. Got it?

*Inflation can kill your nest egg.* The key to investing is to outpace inflation. Cash accounts and money market accounts, after tax and inflation, give you little or no return. The longer your time horizon—the period before you need to retire—the more important that your nest egg generally contain a large percentage of equities—those things that provide ownership, such as stocks and real estate.

## CHAP. 4: INVESTING FOR RETIREMENT                    191

*Diversify, diversify, diversify.* Never put all your eggs in one basket! Most of us have heard that saying since childhood. Diversify among many different kinds of investments–money market for stability, bonds for steady income, and stocks and real estate for long-term growth. Remember the carousel with the little horses alternately going up and down? Your investment portfolio should resemble that carousel—no two assets should be going up and down at the same time. As one goes up, the other goes down. This can average out in the form of steady growth. With proper diversification and asset allocation, you should be covered, no matter what economic cycles you experience.

*Invest dollars according to your time horizon and investment temperament.* The longer your time horizon, the greater should be your allocation to growth investments. There can be a big difference over time if you are able to improve your average rate of return by even a small amount. In the example above, if you started at age 35 to invest $100 per month at an 8 percent growth rate, you would accumulate $149,036 by age 65. If you were able to achieve a 10 percent growth rate, just 2 percent more, your accumulation by age 65 would be $226,049, or $77,013 more than the amount with the 8 percent investment. However, equity investments tend to be more volatile over short periods. As your time horizon narrows, most advisors would recommend that you shift gradually from growth to income investments.

*Don't touch your retirement savings portfolio.* It'll be tempting over the years to tap into your retirement account for that item you really want—a new car or boat, for instance. Don't do it! Not only will your withdrawal be taxable, but there may also be a 10 percent early-withdrawal penalty. Even if you have enough money to pay the penalties, withdrawing funds is a bad move because you will have less money growing in your tax-deferred account for your future years.

*Avoid trying to time the market.* Most Americans are motivated by either a desire for quick return or a fear of the uncertain or unknown. If we fear that the market is going down, we get out and go to cash. If we think that the market is going up, we rush to buy. Unfortunately, most investors do both too late. If you've been tempted to time the stock market with your retirement savings, listen to the advice of most advisors: Don't do it!

Do not shift funds from one account to another because one seems to be showing a higher return on your latest retirement statement. Investment performance in the immediate past is not a reliable indicator of the long-term future. Markets frequently go down suddenly, and they have had dramatic shifts on their long, upward haul. Last year's or last quarter's hottest investment on Wall Street often cools off in the next time period. It is not unusual to have the top-producing funds this year be the bottom-producing funds a few years from now. The rule is this: Don't chase performance. Let the pros help you decide how to invest in the market.

*Retirement planning is long-term, not short-term.* If you're concerned about the market's going up and down and up and down, recognize that that's the history of the market. Expect it. The market will always go up and down in value.

### *How will baby boomers affect my investment strategy?*

When World War II ended in 1945, the soldiers returned home to begin families, and the "baby boom" began. The baby-boom generation peaked between 1955 and 1960, with the population of people under the age of 20 skyrocketing from 62 million in 1955 to 70 million in 1960. In the year 2015, unless there are policy changes, retiring boomers will send Social Security and Medicare balances into a free fall. The 77 million children born between the years of 1946 and 1964 will continue to have a massive effect on the economy.

The heart of the baby-boomer retirement challenge has to do with *demographics, lifestyle,* and *consumption.* People are living longer, they are retiring earlier, and they are starting to save later.

## CHAP. 4: INVESTING FOR RETIREMENT 193

Social Security was created in 1935, with retirees able to start receiving their benefit checks between ages 62 and 65. However, the majority of the population did not live past 62! Today, life expectancy is 14 years longer for men and 15 years longer for women than it was in 1935. Here is an amazing statistic: In 1945, 42 people were paying into Social Security for every 1 taking out; today, the ratio is 3 paying in for every 1 taking out. By the time the baby boomers have retired, in the year 2030, the ratio will be 2 to 1! Maintaining benefits at the current level will require massive tax increases on younger Americans. The bottom line is that people should not rely entirely on Social Security for their retirements: the system will not survive in its present form—we might even dub it "Social Insecurity." This emphasizes the fact that we have a much greater need today to plan for our retirements than our parents did in the past.

Now, let's discuss the good news of the baby boomers. Economies are driven by predictable spending cycles. The baby-boom generation comprises an unusually large number of consumers, and people tend to spend more money between the ages of 45 and 50 than at any other time of their lives. Thus, the baby boomers should continue to drive the stock market, at least until 2008. The next 10 years, plus or minus, may be a boom for the bears. If your time horizon is at least 10 years, you should consider a well-diversified equities portfolio.

### ✍ *How do I develop my investment portfolio?*

There are seven steps in developing a successful investment portfolio.

STEP 1: *Accumulate funds for retirement in the most tax-advantaged environment possible.* This means:

- Receiving a tax-deduction incentive for putting the money aside, such as through a qualified retirement plan or an IRA

- Having the money grow tax-free or tax-deferred

- Receiving distributions at retirement tax-free.

While the perfect retirement vehicle possessing all three tax-free attributes does not exist, there are numerous strategies you can employ to accomplish at least two of these three objectives.

One of the Rockefellers once said, "Never pay taxes on money you do not plan to spend." Borrowing this famous phrase and applying it to retirement planning vehicles, it is important to invest in a tax-advantaged environment if at all possible. Numerous studies have been done over the past 20 years showing the effect of taxes on net rates of return. Given the risk inherent in trying to achieve a particular target return, losing approximately 33 percent of the return to taxes makes it harder to achieve your goals and the desired after-tax rate of return.

STEP 2: *Set goals.* In developing your investment philosophy, you need to establish specific objectives regarding time, income, and risk tolerance.

*Determine how many years you have for investing.* It is essential to have a time horizon, or a retirement target date. The length of time determines how hard your money will have to work and how aggressive you can be with your dollars. Most advisors agree that the longer the time between now and retirement, the more equity-based the retirement portfolio balance can be.

For example, if you're saving for a home that you're planning to purchase in the next year or two, you will probably want to maintain your cash reserves in money market accounts; certificates of deposit; short-term, high-quality bonds; and the like.

If, on the other hand, you're saving for retirement 20 years away, you probably should not worry about the day-to-day fluctuations, as they are not as important as substantially outperforming inflation. To increase your assets, choose a combination of equity (ownership) investments with high potential for appreciation and less emphasis on income.

If you are near retirement age—that is, you have fewer years to invest for retirement—you might consider an investment strategy

CHAP. 4: INVESTING FOR RETIREMENT 195

of fixed-income investments or change your existing strategy from focusing on the equities marketplace to blending in a larger percentage of fixed-income investments. This certainly reduces market volatility; however, it does not allow for inflation indexing.

*Determine how much income will you need during retirement.* Depending on what your income requirements are and how long you have to achieve those requirements, you will need to do either one or both of the following:

- Invest for greater total returns. This suggests allocating larger segments of your retirement plan portfolio to equities.

- Commit larger amounts of current income to your retirement objectives.

If you are already retired and need current income, you might consider a portfolio of bonds, preferred stocks, high-dividend stocks, and income-producing real estate.

*Determine the amount of risk you are willing to accept.* No matter what investment you select, it will have certain associated risks. The level of risk you are comfortable with depends on several factors, including your personality, your perception of market conditions, and your fear of losing purchasing power because of inflation.

If you are unwilling or unable to accept even temporary fluctuations in the value of your portfolio, you must recognize that you have to accept the lower return that comes with guaranteed investments. If you're willing to accept some fluctuations in the value of your investments, you can take a more aggressive position and go for a higher return. Remember, the amount of the total return on your portfolio is directly related to the amount of risk you're willing to accept.

STEP 3: *Select the right mix of investment vehicles for diversification.* The key to managing financial, market, interest rate, inflation, economic, and liquidity risks is diversification. A portfolio of only one asset class, such as fifty municipal bonds, is not a fully diversified portfolio. If everything you have is in one type of investment or sector and is correlated—going up (or down) at the same time—your portfolio is not diversified against unforeseen changes in the economy and investment environment.

Historically, stocks have been one of the best asset classes to invest in—if your horizon is long enough; bonds, however, can be far less volatile. Thus, a combination of both generally gives you less volatility and more predictability. Don't forget that every individual investment carries some degree of risk, but risks can be reduced by selecting asset classes that tend to move in opposite directions (experience negative correlation) under different economic conditions. While asset diversification can't eliminate all risks, a sound program can limit your exposure to risk and increase your growth potential over a long period of time.

STEP 4: *Determine proper asset allocation.* Each individual's personal investment objectives, time horizon for achieving those objectives, and level of risk tolerance are different from everyone else's, so the only appropriate portfolio for you is one that has been custom-tailored for your needs. Thus, the diagrams shown in Figure 4-4 are intended merely as examples of diversified asset allocation portfolio mixes. You should consult your advisor to determine an appropriate asset mix based on your own needs.

STEP 5: *Develop an investment policy statement.* Every successful business has a written business plan. Consider your investment policy statement as your personal "business plan." It's a framework for your investment decisions, a guideline for money managers, and a way to protect yourself. It is a necessary step in the process of setting up an investment plan.

Both you and your money manager must be involved in developing the investment policy statement. It should include the objective of your investment plan, your risk parameters and the corresponding return estimates, your investment time horizon, an outline of the basic allocation of investments among asset categories, a definition of monitoring and control procedures, and the assumptions used to develop the policy. Your investment policy

CHAP. 4: INVESTING FOR RETIREMENT    197

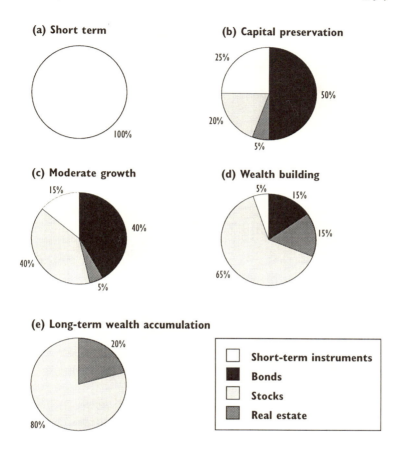

**Figure 4-4** Asset portfolio mixes. (1) Short-term investments include 2 years or less, such as CDs, money markets, high-quality bonds with shorter maturities. (2) Bonds include various government and corporate, with maturities short, intermediate, and long term. (3) Stocks include domestic and overseas; large and small cap with growth and value; and emerging markets. (4) Real estate includes leveraged, REITs, and direct ownership. (*a*) Goal is to keep safe and liquid. (*b*) Goal is income, conservative growth, and preservation of capital. (*c*) Goal is growth and income with moderate risk. (*d*) Goal is higher risk with longer time horizon. (*e*) Goal is highest risk, highest return with long-term time horizon.

statement provides guidelines and standards for the manager to follow in implementing your investment plan and for you to use in evaluating the manager's performance. Specifically, it should include your answers to the following questions:

- What is the purpose of this pool of money?
- What is my time horizon?
- How much liquidity do I need and when?
- What rate of return do I want?
- How much risk (percentage decrease in value) am I willing to accept in any time period?
- What types of investments are acceptable or unacceptable to me?
- What is the target asset allocation (mixture of assets)?
- What assumptions about the economy, inflation, interest rates, and investment performance shall be used?
- When will we review this policy and the investment performance?
- What criteria will be used to evaluate results?
- How will my advisor be compensated?

STEP 6: *Monitor the investment portfolio.* It is critical that you and your advisor monitor your account's performance on a regular basis to make sure that your financial program is following your plan and meeting your goals. Most financial advisors recommend at least two or three formal reviews per year.

STEP 7: *Adjust the allocation to keep the investment portfolio tuned.* If gains or losses caused changes in the percentage allocations since your initial allocation or last review, reallocate assets to achieve your originally determined percentages.

   *I'm getting close to retirement. I have a retirement philosophy, but what else do I need to concern myself with?*

As you get closer to retirement, you should develop a spending

Chap. 4: Investing for Retirement 199

policy. The spending policy, or budget, can be as critical as the asset allocation policy that served you up to this point.

*If I'm already retired, what will investment planning do for me now?*

Looking at one's current investment allocation—income, growth, liquidity, and safety—is always a healthy exercise. Depending on an individual's time horizon, a retiree may want to invest now for use in extreme old age. Or an investor who is also concerned with estate planning may see an opportunity during retirement to focus his or her strategy on turning small discretionary assets into a large amount that could be left as an inheritance. Recommending appropriate investments can depend upon an investor's comparative need for income, capital appreciation, risk avoidance, and, particularly, on his or her need to preserve capital.

*What investment strategy is appropriate for me after retirement?*

After retirement your tolerance for risk will probably go down, and protecting your savings will likely be more important. You may be willing to consider giving up some of your long-term growth in favor of a shorter investment time horizon. However, since retirement seems to be lasting longer than it used to, the philosophy of taking income from growth investments has gained popularity.

## Risk Strategies

*As I approach retirement, I'm becoming very concerned that some unknown event might derail my plans. What can go wrong?*

Most people planning for retirement tend to focus on their retirement savings and the classic investment risks at the expense of other risks often overlooked in retirement planning.

The first category involves mortality and disability. You might live for a long time and run out of money. You might die early without leaving enough assets for your family's care. Or you might become disabled and lose your ability to earn an income. Life and disability insurance can help you transfer the risks of death and disability. Careful financial planning can help you manage the risk of outliving your money.

The next category involves your property—your home, vehicles, possessions, health, and reputation. Caution and adequate insurance can help reduce most of the potential losses in this category.

Relatives and unintended beneficiaries can be worse than exotic investments. You can easily lose more money through bad loans to relatives than through bad investments. Improperly drafted wills, trusts, and beneficiary designations can have disastrous effects on the transfer of wealth.

Taxes are always a risk, especially without strategic planning. Estate taxes can potentially wipe out up to 55 percent of your estate. Fortunately, numerous techniques are available to reduce, if not eliminate, these taxes for those willing to plan ahead.

The bottom line is that we face many kinds of risk. You can't hide from them, nor can you eliminate all of them. You can, however, plan for them and find a level of risk you are willing to accept.

*How can I reduce the risk of loss in my retirement investment accounts?*

Use asset diversification and allocation. There are advantages to investing in a variety of asset classes and investment types. It is important to remember that different assets behave differently under the same economic conditions. For example, a strong economy will likely bring about excellent returns in the stock market, which in turn may bring about rising interest rates, which cause bond funds to decline in value. On the other hand, stocks and stock mutual funds might struggle in a weak economy, which may

## Asset Diversification Strategies

*How many different investments should I own in my portfolio?*

The answer, generally, is the fewer the better, provided you have adequate diversification. Try to diversify your portfolio according to your liquidity needs, risk tolerance, investment time horizon, and expected rate of return. The actual number of investments is irrelevant. Having seven different mutual funds all invested in large-company growth stocks is not efficient diversification. Most advisors use six to twelve different asset classes in an effort to properly diversify a portfolio.

*How many funds should I own in my portfolio?*

This is an area where many investors have difficulty. A common mistake is to assume that if you own ten different funds, you will have a diversified portfolio. However, in many instances, today's popular funds own many of the same holdings and do not produce the diversification you expect. These funds have a high correlation with each other and tend to move in the same direction in response to market forces. If the market declines, therefore, having ten or more large-company growth funds will not help you. They will all decline in price at the same time.

Building a diversified portfolio is the key to achieving superior long-term performance with reduced risk. To achieve diversification, you need to completely understand the investment strategy of each fund as well as what securities each owns. To create proper diversification, you will probably need a minimum of six funds and may need as many as twelve.

*As a retired individual, how should I diversify my investments?*

Although we cannot make specific recommendations for you until we have determined your goals and objectives, in general, we recommend a mix of funds utilizing both growth and value management styles. We use growth, growth and income, and balanced funds, depending on an individual's needs. We recommend some exposure to both large- and small-cap holdings. We like to see investors diversify internationally and have some exposure to real assets. Financial assets have been in favor for several years now, but the cycle will turn, and we are eager for investors to have proper exposure to the asset classes mentioned above for that eventuality.

For fixed-income investments, we will use prime rate trusts or laddered fixed-income securities and a small exposure to high-yield or convertible securities.

*What should I be investing in?*

A professional financial advisor is never "married" to any one strategy. The solutions presented should be dictated by the investor's specific needs and objectives. Variable and fixed annuities, mutual funds, prime rate trusts, long-term-care insurance, and estate planning life insurance trusts that may help pay estate taxes with "discounted dollars" have applications for certain cases. There is never a set answer. Each situation is, and must be treated as, unique.

## Asset Allocation Strategies

*What is a prudent asset allocation strategy for someone approaching retirement?*

At retirement, people have various amounts accumulated, different retirement goals, and different risk tolerances. The asset allo-

# CHAP. 4: INVESTING FOR RETIREMENT                    203

**TABLE 4-3   Sample Asset Allocation Strategy for Moderate-Growth Retirement Portfolio**

| Asset | Percentage of portfolio |
| --- | --- |
| **U.S. equities** | |
| Large-cap stock fund | 10 |
| Income or utility stock fund | 10 |
| Growth and income fund | 8 |
| Small-cap stock fund | 8 |
| **International** | |
| International fund | 18 |
| Emerging-market fund | 3 |
| **Real estate** | |
| Real estate fund | 10 |
| **Bonds** | |
| Treasury bonds or funds (laddered) | 20 |
| High-yield bond fund | 8 |
| Money market | 5 |

cation approach to constructing the retirement portfolio should take these variables into account so that a portfolio can be customized for your individual needs. As you move through your retirement years, your portfolio should be adjusted to reflect your current thinking, as well as to take advantage of the investment opportunities being presented by the markets. Table 4-3 shows a possible starting point for an asset allocation strategy as you approach retirement.

*I am nearing retirement. Sixty percent of my portfolio is in stock mutual funds, and 30 percent is in bonds and bond mutual funds. Should I allocate more to the bonds and bond funds?*

The conventional wisdom says you should. However, this may be

## TABLE 4-4　Bond Yield and Effects of Inflation

| Year | Principal | Annual income | Cost of $1200 of annual goods & services with 3% inflation |
|------|-----------|---------------|-------------------------------------------------------------|
| 1998 | $20,000 | $1200 | $1200 |
| 1999 | 20,000 | 1200 | 1236 |
| 2000 | 20,000 | 1200 | 1273 |
| 2001 | 20,000 | 1200 | 1311 |
| 2002 | 20,000 | 1200 | 1351 |

a serious mistake. Today, we are living longer, and it will not be uncommon for people to spend one-third of their lifetimes in retirement. As a result, inflation is a greater risk for your investment than volatility is.

Here is a good example of the problem with bonds. Suppose that in 1998 you purchase $20,000 of 5-year bonds yielding 6 percent. At a 3 percent inflation rate, the goods and services you can buy with your $1200 income from the bonds in 1998 will cost you $1351 in 2002 (see Table 4-4). After 5 years of receiving an income that does not keep pace with inflation, you get back your principal of $20,000. By that time, you would need to have $23,185 just to keep up with inflation.

When investing completely in bonds, a retiree runs the risk that neither the principal nor the income will keep pace. For retirees, one of the greatest risks is not volatility but the loss of purchasing power. This is why so many financial advisors recommend continuing an equity position during retirement.

## Return Strategies

*I'm afraid to lose money. Does it really matter if my portfolio earns 1 to 2 percent less than one with greater risk?*

This depends on your need for income and capital appreciation

# CHAP. 4: INVESTING FOR RETIREMENT

**TABLE 4-5   Effects of Higher Rates of Return on $10,000 Investment**

| Rate of return, % | Balance after 20 years | Percent increase |
|---|---|---|
| 4 | $21,911 | |
| 6 | 32,071 | 31.7 |
| 8 | 45,610 | 29.7 |
| 10 | 67,275 | 32.2 |

and your investment time horizon. Table 4-5 shows the effects of a 2 percent increase in the rate of return on a $10,000 investment over a 20-year period. Even a 1 or 2 percent higher rate of return, compounded over time, can be very meaningful!

*Is it more important to increase my rate of investing or my rate of return?*

It is easier and safer to find or create small incremental increases of discretionary cash than to uncover or create large amounts of assets or dramatically increase returns. A small increase in regular investments is equal to a dramatic increase in the rate of return on your current investments.

*I've been reviewing the following three investments' 5-year track records. Which investment should I choose based on the returns?*

| | Year 1 | Year 2 | Year 3 | Year 4 | Year 5 |
|---|---|---|---|---|---|
| Investment A | 7% | 7% | 7% | 7% | 7% |
| Investment B | 15 | 15 | 5 | −15 | 3 |
| Investment C | 10 | 20 | 30 | −25 | 8 |

For a $1000 investment in each of the above, the overall returns are:

206                                       WAYS AND MEANS

Investment A     $1402
Investment B     $1331
Investment C     $1389


The steady 7 percent per year of investment A outproduced the
varying, but at times much larger, rates of return of investments
B and C. Most people are surprised to find that consistent positive
returns produce superior long-term results.


✍ *Are there any ways to gain more consistency with my investment results?*

Holding a diversified portfolio among various asset classes has
been shown to reduce the volatility of the portfolio, resulting in
more consistent performance. Let's review an example. In the
August 1998 issue of *Financial Planning*, an article by John
Bowen pointed out a recent study done by Reinhardt Werba &
Bowen, a national asset management firm.

The scenario compared a portfolio that was invested 100 percent in the S&P 500 with one invested in a more conservative
diversified global portfolio. The global portfolio was invested 50
percent in cash/bonds and 50 percent in stocks, as follows: 5
percent, money market; 45 percent, 2-year fixed bonds; 18 percent, U.S. large-cap stocks; 7 percent, U.S. small-cap stocks; 16
percent, international large-cap stocks; 6 percent, international
small-cap stocks; and 3 percent, emerging growth. The analysis
went back to 1972 to include the 1973–1974 recession and the
availability of international data after the Bretton-Woods agreement.

For every dollar invested, the S&P grew to $25.45, while the
global portfolio grew to $25.60. But the real story was the ride
along the way: The global conservative portfolio ended with more
value as a result of the lower volatility.

The results were surprising for most. Let's consider a retired
couple with a $250,000 portfolio who withdrew income of $5000

CHAP. 4: INVESTING FOR RETIREMENT                    207

every quarter from January 1, 1972, to December 31, 1997. If they had invested in Treasury bills, their portfolio would be worth $78,915 at the end of 1997 (26 years later). If they had invested in the S&P 500, their portfolio would have grown to $582,148. Incredibly, the conservative global investment portfolio would be worth $2,229,568.

*How can there be that much difference when the average rates of return were almost identical?*

The answer lies in the volatility. The stock market decline in 1973–1974 caused the S&P 500 portfolio to decline much further than the diversified portfolio. This became more pronounced as withdrawals were made during the downturn. The S&P 500 portfolio subsequently had a more difficult time making a rebound.

There are two important messages here. First, the portfolio with the lesser volatility did better over time, especially when income was being withdrawn. And let's not lose sight of the performance of the fixed-income portfolio that had only $78,915 left after the same time frame. Second, investors who are retiring should not assume that a fixed-income investment portfolio is the only way to achieve a dependable income stream; rather, they should focus on the total return. Diversification among various asset classes provides a viable alternative to the retiree's investment dilemma of inflation and living longer.

## Inflation Strategies

*As a retiree, I'm concerned that I'll be vulnerable if really high inflation returns. Am I right to be concerned?*

High inflation is certainly detrimental to corporations, the economy, and most people—including stock investors. Stocks do well during periods of low to moderate inflation but poorly when inflation rises much above 5 percent.

However, if most of your income comes from your own investments, high inflation sometimes can actually be good for you. Retirees who have built up significant investment assets and know how to manage them may have no reason to fear high inflation, and for many investors it would actually be good news.

Assuming you are living within your means, two factors determine the risk of having your retirement plans derailed by high inflation. The first is the extent to which your income-oriented investments are structured to adjust to higher inflation. The second factor is the extent to which your income comes from your own investments, as opposed to fixed-income sources such as Social Security and/or monthly pensions. At the very times when high inflation is hurting most Americans, it is actually a blessing to retirees who derive most of their income from their own investments rather than from Social Security or fixed pensions.

This apparent paradox arises from the fact that inflation affects two aspects of a retiree's financial situation. First, higher inflation causes living expenses to rise more rapidly. For retirees who must pay those expenses with fixed incomes, this is disastrous. But many people forget that higher inflation also results in higher interest rates. Therefore, retirees with substantial savings and a properly structured investment portfolio are able to take advantage of the higher yields to increase income. What is surprising is that for people with sufficient investments, the increase in income should be more than the increase in living expenses. As a result, their financial situation can actually be made more secure by high inflation.

Let's look at a couple with $70,000 per year in living expenses (including taxes), a $1 million bond portfolio earning 7 percent ($70,000), and $12,000 per year of Social Security income. Their total income of $82,000 is more than enough to cover living expenses of $70,000, so $12,000 can be reinvested to build investment principal. If nothing changes, this should permit them to maintain their lifestyle even with current levels of inflation. (Note: This is a purposely simplistic example; for instance, it excludes stocks entirely.)

CHAP. 4: INVESTING FOR RETIREMENT                    209

Our couple anticipated a 3 percent inflation rate for next year. Living expenses would increase by $2100, so a similar lifestyle next year would theoretically cost $72,100. What if inflation suddenly skyrockets to, say, 7 percent? Living expenses would rise by almost $5000 instead of $2100, nearly $3000 more than they planned.

On the other hand, 7 percent inflation would increase the bond yields to at least 10 percent (versus 6 to 7 percent currently). If even half of the $1 million bond portfolio could be invested to take advantage of those yields, income would increase by $15,000 per year, or five times the unplanned increase in living expenses. In other words, higher inflation could improve the couple's finances by providing a larger increase in income than the increase in expenses.

Note that this principle applies only if your investments are structured properly. Most of your bond holdings need to be short- to intermediate-term—1 to 8 years—so that you can sell some of them or allow them to mature without taking big losses. Most planners consider long-term bonds dangerous retirement vehicles because they reduce the investor's flexibility to adjust income as inflation changes. Keeping maturities shorter, therefore, provides much greater ability to adjust to rising inflation.

*Does that mean I should be worried about deflation?*

Yes. As strange as it sounds, one of the worst things well-to-do retirees could face would be a prolonged period of zero inflation or deflation. With deflation, retirees' living expenses wouldn't rise, but their incomes would decline as investments produced lower yields. In other words, deflation would hurt (through decreased income) more than it would help (through stable or decreased expenses). Therefore, retirees should consider a number of bonds or other securities that are locked in at attractive yields for at least 3 to 7 years.

Even without the deflationary impact of Asia's 1998 economic turmoil, the risk of deflation is increasing as baby boomers approach retirement. The leading edge of the baby-boomer "bulge" will be 60 years old in 2005. As they retire, boomers are likely to save more and consume less, thus slowing the economy. In short, a period of deflation is a very real possibility during the next decade. Make sure your investments are prepared for deflation just as much as you try to be prepared for inflation.

*I've heard that bonds have a higher inflation risk than stocks. Is this true?*

Inflation risk refers to the fact that, when a bond matures years in the future, your principal will not buy as much as those dollars could when you originally bought the bond. Many people conclude that this is evidence that bonds are a poor investment and that only stocks can protect them against inflation. Since stock prices (your principal) increase over time, they can do a good job of keeping your principal ahead of inflation. Stocks also produce higher returns, and gains on stocks get preferential tax treatment—lower tax rates on capital gains, and deferral of the gains until sold.

If the total returns of a stock and a bond were the same, however, stocks would not be a better inflation hedge. For example, if a stock pays 2 percent in taxable dividends and appreciates 4 percent in price, its total return would be 6 percent. Its principal value has increased by 4 percent, but that is because only 2 percent of its return (the dividend) was drawn off and spent. Since all of a bond's return is paid in the form of interest, a 5 percent tax-free municipal bond would theoretically provide about the same inflation protection as this stock, as long as only 1 to 2 percent of its income is spent. If the rest is reinvested, it becomes part of a growing "principal" base that protects against inflation.

Of course, stocks have generally produced returns much higher than 6 percent, and in that respect they are a better long-term inflation hedge. On the other hand, stock returns are much less predictable, and few retirees are comfortable having all their

CHAP. 4: INVESTING FOR RETIREMENT                    211

money in stocks and depending on the high returns to provide stable income every year.

In other words, the inflation risk of bonds might be more accurately called "risk of lower returns" or "risk of failure to reinvest part of the return." Inflation risk must be balanced with each individual investor's overall portfolio planning in retirement. Most retirees still want and need the predictability, safety, and dependable income offered by bonds. As a result, most retirees have a large portion of their money invested in bonds and bond funds.

*Do shorter-term bonds provide better inflation protection than long-term bonds?*

Yes. If you buy a 2-year, 3-year, or even 5-year bond, you probably won't need to worry much about its price fluctuation. You can always hold it to maturity and know you'll get all your money back. The inflation picture is usually reasonably clear for a few years, so you can normally make responsible decisions as to whether you will be comfortable with a bond's yield for 3 to 5 years.

But is it realistic to assume that you know what inflation will be 15, 20, or 30 years from now? If inflation doubles, causing interest rates to skyrocket, investors with long-term bonds locked into today's lower interest rates will face a dilemma. Their bonds might be worth only 60 to 70 cents on the dollar—because of the seesaw effect—so they wouldn't want to sell, even though they would want to buy to take advantage of then-higher yields. Because long-term bonds offer little additional yield over intermediate-term—3- to 8-year—bonds, their additional volatility and inflation risk generally argue for avoiding long-term bonds.

One of the biggest mistakes people make at retirement is putting too much of their savings into long-term bonds, thinking these yields will always be "enough." By keeping most of your money in short- to intermediate-term bonds, you give up a little interest but maintain your flexibility. As inflation rises, your prin-

212                                                    WAYS AND MEANS

cipal is intact, and money from maturing bonds is available to reinvest in higher-yielding bonds. Thus, your income can be "inflation-adjusted." Long-term-bonds—even Treasuries—do not provide inflation flexibility.

As a general rule, financial advisors often recommend keeping no more than 10 to 20 percent of your bond portfolio in long-term bonds (maturities over 10 years) or funds made up of such bonds. However, during periods when you believe both interest rates and inflation are likely to fall for some time, a higher percentage is justified.

Bear in mind that commissions on long-term bonds are typically higher than those on shorter-term bonds. Because long-term yields are easier to sell to investors who only focus on the rate, it is imperative that you be aware of the effects of different bond purchases on your investment goals.

### ⚭  *How can I reduce the inflation risk with bonds?*

For your bond portfolio to be able to adjust for higher inflation and interest rate risks, it is usually recommended that most of your bonds have short or intermediate maturities. A simple way to accomplish this is to "ladder" your bond maturities, with roughly equal amounts maturing each year for the next 8 to 10 years or so. Each year, as the next bonds mature, you simply reinvest the proceeds in new bonds with 8- to 10-year maturities. In this way, you always have some of your money locked in at dependable rates if interest rates fall, yet you have money coming due every year which you can use to take advantage of high yields if interest rates rise.

A *ladder* works as follows: You start by setting a maximum length to maturity for your portfolio, say, 10 years. Then you divide your money into that many parts, and buy bonds with maturity dates in each year. In this way, you have an equal portion of your money maturing each year. As each bond matures, you purchase another bond maturing at the end of the ladder.

CHAP. 4: INVESTING FOR RETIREMENT                    213

*≈ Does laddering the maturities of fixed-income bonds really
significantly reduce interest rate risk?*

With a laddered-maturity bond portfolio, you will still see some
fluctuation of principal on your monthly brokerage statement.
However, remember that your intent is to hold each bond until
it matures, thus ensuring the return of your principal. Also
remember that, because of the laddered maturities, you will have
money maturing on a regular basis. You now have the peace of
mind of knowing that the fluctuation you see on your statement
will matter only if you need to liquidate a bond, or your entire
bond portfolio, at that time.

There are several advantages to this technique. First, the average maturity of your entire portfolio is never more than half
that of the longest bond you purchased. This is important because
the shorter the average maturity, the less you suffer from price
fluctuation in the bond market. Second, as each bond is reinvested, the portfolio will achieve an average yield to maturity
reflecting the longer-term issues (usually a better yield), while
retaining a shorter average life. Finally, you have given yourself
an automatic hedge against interest rate moves. If interest rates
drop, you obtain higher yields with the longer maturities in the
portfolio. If they rise, the portion of bonds that mature each year
can be invested at a higher interest rate.

*≈ Do bond ladders always mature annually?*

The key to structuring a bond ladder is to allow for funds to
mature *periodically* to be reinvested at current rates, which could
be lower or higher than when the bond ladder was originally
structured. Regardless of changing interest rates, investors using
this approach may be less susceptible to wide swings in rates due
to the ability to reinvest some funds periodically. A bond ladder
can be structured with *varying* maturity dates. For example, a
bond ladder for a person with $100,000 to invest in bonds might
be structured as follows:

$20,000 maturing in 1 year
$20,000 maturing in 3 years
$20,000 maturing in 5 years
$20,000 maturing in 7 years
$20,000 maturing in 10 years

## Liquidity Strategies

*How do I structure my investments to meet my liquidity needs for emergencies and large expenditures while still keeping my money hard at work?*

Retirees actually need less liquidity than people still in the work force. The home is usually paid off, and the kids have been educated and are out of the house. Social Security, Medicare, and pensions provide a cushion, and retirees can't be fired or lose income as a result of a disability. Nevertheless, retired persons still need some liquidity.

It is relatively simple to address your liquidity needs while keeping your money invested for the long term. Your *time horizon* is what determines the risk level of most investments, even the so-called safe ones. The risk is having to liquidate at the wrong time. It may be helpful to think of putting all your retirement assets into four conceptual "buckets."

*Bucket 1* is for expenditures you incur on a regular basis for household expenses, insurance, property taxes, trips, and anything else for which you might need access to cash within the next month. A money market fund or interest-bearing checking account may do the job well. Social Security and pension checks are deposited into this account, as well as transfers from bucket 2.

*Bucket 2* is for major short-term expenditures (say, 2 months to 2 years from now). The job of this bucket is to periodically replenish bucket 1 when necessary and to give your assets in buckets 3 and 4 freedom to grow without liquidations during

# CHAP. 4: INVESTING FOR RETIREMENT

215

down financial markets. Treasury bills, short-term bond funds, and certificates of deposit are appropriate here.

*Bucket 3* contains assets appropriate for an intermediate (2- to 5-year) time horizon. It helps generate income for the first two buckets by holding securities such as longer-term bonds, utilities, and dividend-paying blue-chip stocks. Generally speaking, its assets are more volatile than those in bucket 2 but not as volatile as those in bucket 4.

*Bucket 4* is your long-term inflation hedge. Invest its assets in growth vehicles such as real estate, mutual funds that invest internationally, small company stocks, and growth stocks. These investments carry more risk but also more reward. If you need a large sum during a down market, you should completely liquidate the other buckets before touching this one. Even then, with proper diversification, you might often have one fund that is up when others are down.

These buckets don't necessarily have to be in separate accounts. They are simply a way of viewing your various assets and assigning them to different holding periods. Theoretically, you could have all the buckets in one brokerage account with checking attached. The key is to know which ones you will liquidate first.

*Should I maintain some of my assets in liquid investments even though they pay a very low interest rate?*

Yes. The stock market occasionally holds a "clearance sale" (such as on October 19, 1987, and on October 24, 1997). Individuals who have funds available to invest when the market is at a low are the ones who really do well.

Consider these statistics, provided by Wall Street guru Peter Lynch in a 1994 *Modern Maturity* interview:

> There have been 94 years in this century. In that time, 50 [stock market] declines of 10 percent or more have occurred. Of those 50 declines, 15 have dropped 25 percent or more. So on the average, once every two years the market drops 10 percent and once every six years

it goes down a quarter or more. In today's market that means a decline of 800 to 2000 Dow points.

With that type of track record, it makes sense to be following an investment philosophy that can profit from declines.

*As I approach retirement, shouldn't my portfolio be more liquid and less growth-oriented?*

This is perhaps one of the most common questions and biggest myths about investing for retirement. As retirement approaches, people start developing a "circle the wagons" mentality with their various investments.

To answer this question, ask yourself: How long am I likely to live after I retire? Remember, your investment time horizon during retirement could easily be another 20, 30, or 40 years. So you should keep a good part of your portfolio invested for long-term growth as an inflation hedge.

Even if you did circle the wagons, where would you store all this liquid money? After taxes and inflation, liquid assets in money market or cash equivalents can actually lose value. This approach is a good way to risk possibly going broke "safely."

*Should I liquidate some of my existing investments or use what would have gone into monthly savings to pay off the home mortgage by the time I retire?*

Although paying off the home mortgage early brings a sense of security, it is not always the secure thing to do during your peak earning years. Your preretirement goal normally should be to accumulate as much capital as possible. Diverting income-producing assets into a personal asset makes more sense once you are certain that you have enough capital to last you throughout retirement and that you plan to live in your home for a long time.

What if you become disabled, lose your job, or have to relocate? In times of high interest rates or bad housing markets, you

CHAP. 4: INVESTING FOR RETIREMENT                    217

can have too much equity in your home. When the financial markets are doing well, putting your extra cash flow into a mutual fund or a tax-deductible retirement plan makes better economic sense.

Don't trade your youth and health for mortgage payments. Paying off the mortgage during your working years or in the early years of retirement is not a good idea if doing so means having to cut back on travel plans and other activities when you still have your health. Waiting to travel until after you pay down the mortgage is a gamble because you may not have your health.

If your mortgage balance is rather low, and you have sufficient retirement savings, it makes sense to pay down because your interest deduction progressively fades away.

## Investment Vehicle Strategies

*Are popular investment magazines a good place to find the best investments?*

Unfortunately, a common tendency among many investors is to look at current popular investments that have done well over the last quarter or done even average over the last couple of years. Unfortunately, that's risky because yesterday's "hot" investment is unlikely to remain hot over time—past performance is not a reliable indicator of future results. By the time you transfer your funds to that hot fund, you may have missed the benefit you had hoped to reap. It's better to establish a long-term investment strategy and stick with it. A track record of consistent management is really the key determination. Most planners agree: You don't buy the fund; you buy the management.

### Bonds

*Why shouldn't I put all my portfolio into bonds?*

You can if you have enough money. Most people don't. Bonds provide a constant income that doesn't change. What will you do

218 WAYS AND MEANS

to fight rising prices? At 3 percent inflation over 10 years, you'll lose 30 percent of your purchasing power. Can you afford this? Most people can't. Equity or stock investing generally provides more protection against rising prices.

> *It bothers me when I see the value of my bonds dropping on my monthly brokerage statements. How do I know when to really be concerned?*

Although it is unpleasant to watch your account value decline (even temporarily), don't let emotion blind you to what is really going on. Declining bond prices are not necessarily a cause for alarm: they can be a good thing for a properly structured bond portfolio.

Here are several key principles of bond investing:

1. Unless you sell, month-to-month fluctuations do not affect your actual return on a bond. As long as a bond is high-quality and held to maturity, its return (or "yield to maturity") will be exactly as stated on the confirmation slip the day you purchased it. The purchase price, maturity value, and interest received in between are fixed. Changes in price between the purchase date and the maturity date affect your return only if you decide to sell the bond before maturity. As a long-term investor, if you buy only bonds you would be comfortable holding to maturity (or the "call" date, where applicable), month-to-month price fluctuations can generally be ignored.

2. Bond price fluctuations reflect the seesaw principle (Figure 4-3). Remember, there is no mystery to rising and falling bond prices. As interest rates rise, the market price of existing bonds falls, and vice versa. The longer a bond's term, the wider its fluctuation.

3. Bond values on your brokerage statements are more distracting than they are useful. With few exceptions, knowing the price of individual bonds on a given date is of no value whatso-

CHAP. 4: INVESTING FOR RETIREMENT 219

ever. It gives you an idea of what you might have sold the bond for (and of course it's nice when that price is higher than your cost), but since you usually have no intention of selling the bond on that day, principle 1 prevails.

**4.** If your fixed-income portfolio is properly structured, temporary price declines are of little importance as long as you don't plan to sell the bonds before maturity. This is where people who buy long-term (15- to 30-year) bonds get into trouble. They like to think they can hold those bonds to maturity, but in reality they can't predict whether they'll want to sell them before then. For this reason, planners recommend that you diversify but generally buy mostly short- to intermediate-term bonds (8 years or less). Chances are that you can hold them to maturity, but some should be close enough to maturing that you could also sell them early at or near full value if better opportunities arise.

**5.** Rising interest rates create opportunities to buy more bonds and lock in higher yields for years to come. By definition, when interest rates are high, the prices of existing bonds are low. Note that "high" and "low" are not absolute levels but, rather, an assessment of whether interest rates seem relatively high or low compared to expected rates over the next few years. Ironically, the very best time to buy bonds—locking in high yields for years to come—is when the value of your current bonds has been declining.

Note how easy it would be for emotion to make one reach the opposite conclusion. For example, 1994 was a terrible year for bonds (the worst this century). Interest rates rose all year long, causing bond prices to decline. Most people, watching their account values drop month after month, were hardly inclined to buy more of something doing so poorly. Their emotional reaction was to sell (for fear that prices would keep falling) and definitely to avoid buying. The more disciplined and correct response would be to buy bonds to lock in those high yields.

**6.** The ability to take advantage of high interest rates requires liquidity. Therefore, when rates are low, keep maturities shorter. Again, the emotional response is the wrong one. When interest rates are unusually low (e.g., early 1994 and early 1996), many investors feel they must buy bonds or CDs to lock in some money before rates go even lower. Emotion makes us fear that declining interest rates may continue declining and leave us stuck with money market yields. As a result, many investors make exactly the wrong decision, locking money up at low yields.

The better strategy at such times is to keep some extra money short-term in order to (1) protect money against dropping values when interest rates rise again, and (2) have liquid money available to lock in higher rates when they do become available. Instruments such as money markets, CDs, T-bills, and short-term bond funds all serve this purpose. Because they are near (or right on) the fulcrum of the bond seesaw (Figure 4-3), their values fluctuate very little. When interest rates rise again, the money in these instruments will be available to lock in bonds at higher yields because they won't have dropped drastically in value. The money will earn less in the short run but produce higher yields over time.

## Are zero coupon bonds a safe investment?

Only if you are sure you can hold them to maturity. "Zeros," as they are often called, can be very useful, but they can also be very dangerous if you sell them before the maturity date. As Jerry Edgerton of *Money Magazine* (January 1991) pointed out:

> If you choose a [zero coupon] bond that matures when you need a specific amount of money—to pay college tuition, for example—then a zero's return is indeed predictable. But if you buy long-term zero and then decide to sell well before maturity for some reason, you may be in for a shock.

Prices of all bonds rise and fall with changing interest rates. If you sell a regular bond (whether corporate, municipal, or Treasury) before maturity, the amount you receive reflects how "attractive"

CHAP. 4: INVESTING FOR RETIREMENT                    221

the bond is to other investors. For instance, if you own an 8 percent long-term bond, and the "going rate" drops to 7 percent, your bond becomes more attractive to buyers because it continues to pay 8 percent. As a result, buyers will pay more; its price goes up. Conversely, if the going rate rises to 9 percent, your 8 percent bond is relatively unattractive; buyers will only buy it if they can do so at a discounted price. Also, unless your zero is in a tax-deferred retirement account, you will pay taxes on the accrued interest, even though you did not receive any interest.

*Why is the fluctuation more dramatic with zeros?*

The same type of fluctuation in market value occurs with zero coupon bonds as with regular bonds, but the volatility is more dramatic. To understand this concept, you must consider how interest on different bonds is paid and reinvested. A regular bond pays interest, usually every 6 months. Those interest payments can be reinvested at whatever rate of return is available at the future payment dates. A zero, by definition, pays no interest until maturity (your return is the difference between the discounted purchase price and the bond's maturity value). A zero is always purchased at a certain yield to maturity. That yield not only includes the assumed annual return on the bond but also assumes that all future years' returns are intentionally compounded at the same rate. In other words, when you buy a regular bond, you lock in only the annual income (current yield); the reinvestment rate of that income is not locked in. With a zero you lock in both the current yield and the compounding of that yield at the same rate until maturity.

Because of this double lock-in, as interest rates change, buyers find existing zeros either very attractive or very unattractive, and their prices are therefore much more volatile than prices of regular bonds. As is true of all bonds, the longer a zero's maturity, the more extreme its price volatility. Prices of 20- or 30-year zeros can rise or fall more than twice as much as other bonds backed by the same issuers (even issuers like the U.S. government). In other words, the returns on zeros are definitely not predictable unless you are sure you can hold them to maturity.

### ⚜ *Does higher price volatility mean you should never buy zeros?*

Not at all. They can work very well as a way of setting aside money for children's college (although stock funds are generally better for that) or of providing money at specific times. But their increased price risk warrants caution in other circumstances. As with all bonds, you should generally use only those with intermediate (3- to 8-year) maturities. That way, you can hold them to maturity if necessary. Also, buy zeros primarily when you feel interest rates are high—that's when you want to lock in both the current return and the investment rate. At all other times, stick with regular bonds.

Be aware that zero coupon bonds generally pay brokers higher commissions than do regular bonds. Some brokerage firms might push zeros even though yields are frequently lower than those of regular bonds.

One last note: Zeros provide a great way to speculate on sharp declines in interest rates. Because of their wide price swings, buying long-term zeros just before a huge drop in interest rates can produce 20 to 40 percent returns in a year or less! Of course, that's also why you need to be careful; if you're wrong and rates go up instead of down, you can lose just as much.

### ⚜ *I've heard that it's a bad idea to pay a premium price for bonds. Is this always true?*

Many investors refuse to buy bonds at a premium. But if you know the right questions to ask and understand call features, there is absolutely nothing wrong with this premium tactic. In fact, premium bonds often provide better returns and/or reduced risk, so they are certainly worth considering.

People have traditionally been wary of bonds selling at pre-

# CHAP. 4: INVESTING FOR RETIREMENT

223

miums because they can get burned by call provisions. Many investors found that the high-paying bonds they bought in the early 1980s reached call dates in the early 1990s and the issuers redeemed them. Obviously, anyone buying a bond at a premium of 103 or 104 would be rather upset if the bond is suddenly called at 100 (par). But having a bond called unexpectedly can be very frustrating whether you originally paid a premium, a discount, or par. If you are used to a bond's high income, it hardly seems fair that you can be suddenly forced to take your principal back. Nevertheless, callable bonds are perfectly legal. There are all sorts of call features, and they can catch you by surprise without regard to whether you pay a premium.

Bonds sell at premiums because they pay higher interest than the new bonds selling at par. If you buy an old high-coupon bond at a premium but its high semiannual interest more than offsets its extra cost, it can be a good deal. As long as you know when the bond will mature, or be called, its yield to that date (YTM/YTC) can be readily compared to bonds selling at par. Most experienced investors would rather buy a bond at 108 or 109, or more, with a 7 percent YTC than a par bond of the same quality and term yielding 6.75 percent.

Premium municipal bonds that are "prerefunded" or "escrowed to maturity" (ETM) with Treasuries are particularly attractive. Municipalities sometimes refinance their bonds when interest rates fall, much as you might refinance a home mortgage. Even though it may be years before they can actually call old bonds, they may save money by issuing new bonds (at much lower levels). In many cases, they set aside money in U.S. Treasury securities maturing as soon as the old bonds can be redeemed. Because the old high-rate bonds are completely backed by Treasuries, they are arguably the most secure municipals you can buy.

In summary, there is nothing wrong with buying a bond at a premium if (1) you understand the bond's call provisions and earliest call date, and (2) its YTM/YTC compares well with other bonds of similar quality. Because many people have an aversion to paying premiums, demand for premium bonds is often low, so they can provide higher yields with equal or better safety than their alternatives.

### Should I buy only triple-A rated bonds?

Buying triple-A bonds is the surest way to eliminate almost all credit risk, but most investors don't need to be that conservative. In general, individuals should consider only "investment-grade" bonds which have at least a BBB (S&P) or Baa (Moody's) rating. For most investors, bonds at least one notch higher (single-A) are preferable. This is especially true for municipal bonds. Municipal issuers (states, counties, cities, etc.) are more difficult to monitor than corporations. Most corporations issuing bonds also have publicly traded stocks, so you can generally find information on the financial status and outlook for the company. Unfortunately, financial information is not easily accessible for most municipalities. Therefore, it is important to pay special attention to the rating of every municipal bond you buy. Lower-rated bonds can provide a higher return and more risk, but purchasing them through a high-yield mutual fund can reduce your risk because of the fund's diversification and the research and monitoring done by the fund manager.

### Stocks

### I'm young and interested in investing in stocks. What do I need to know about setting up a brokerage account?

To start investing, you need to have reached the age of majority which, depending upon your state of residence, will either be 18 or 21 years of age. To find a broker you will be comfortable with, ask friends or family members whom they would recommend. You might visit with the brokerage branch manager regarding your investment objectives, and he or she should be able to refer you to an appropriate broker. The broker will meet with you to help determine what type of account you need on the basis of

CHAP. 4: INVESTING FOR RETIREMENT                    225

your investment objectives, personal background, and anticipated transactions.

*Can I invest in common stocks if I don't have a lot of money?*

Many New York Stock Exchange brokerage firms have dividend reinvestment programs (DRIPs) that allow small investors to systematically invest as little as $100 per month in common stocks, for a period of 1 year.

*People have said stocks are the best investment for retirement. Is that true?*

Generally, yes. Over a long-enough time period—20 years, for example—stocks have historically outperformed bonds or Treasury bills in over 90 percent of the scenarios evaluated. Compare a $1 million portfolio from 1960 to 1995 invested in three alternative assets: U.S. stocks (the S&P 500), bonds (intermediate-maturity Treasuries), and cash (30-day Treasury bills). An investment of $1 million in stock at 10.1 percent would have grown to $26.6 million; in bonds at 7.4 percent, to $12.2 million; and in T-bills at 6.1 percent, to $8 million. (These figures are from Ibbotson Associates, *Stocks, Bonds, Bills, and Inflation—1996 Yearbook,* which contains market results for 1926 to 1995.)

*Are large company blue-chip stocks the best investment for my IRA?*

They can be excellent investments, but just because they are a household-name stock does not guarantee that they will always do well. Companies such as AT&T, IBM, Merck, Phillip Morris, and Exxon may seem to be low-risk, but many people forget that although they are all "good" companies, they are not always good stocks. Remember the long-distance phone call price wars, company restructuring, the government attempt to impose price controls on the pharmaceutical industry, tobacco class action suits, oil tanker spills?

Never invest in securities for sentimental reasons or just because the name is familiar. Know what you own; and, more importantly, know why you are investing in each holding and how it fits within your allocation of assets. Your financial advisor can help you determine if blue-chip stocks should be part of your investment plan.

### ⚒ *What is a normal return for a stock portfolio?*

Most financial advisors suggest that returns of 10 to 11 percent are reasonable for long-term planning purposes. Since 1982 returns have been 50 percent more than that, but, for planning purposes, expected returns of 15 to 16 percent are considered too aggressive. Investment legend Warren Buffett, and others, claim that although higher returns are wonderful when they occur, returns of 10 percent should be the investor's objective. John Bogle, former chairman of the Vanguard group of funds, reflected the views of many other experts when he said, "We think stock returns will come back down to the 10 percent a year level" during the next decade.

Don't let the projected 10 percent growth rate discourage you, however. Even if it isn't as spectacular as 15 percent, it is still more than three times the recent level of inflation and allows your principal to double every 7 to 8 years.

### ⚒ *The stock market has had an incredible bull run over the past decade or so. Is this likely to continue?*

It is impossible to determine the direction the stock market will take on a short-term basis; however, based on historical information, current economic conditions, market productivity, and specific population demographics, many financial advisors believe the market will continue to appreciate for the foreseeable future.

The first wave of "baby boomers" recently turned age 50, and

## CHAP. 4: INVESTING FOR RETIREMENT

227

subsequent waves of boomers will turn 50 during the next 15 or so years. This is an important happening in American economic history. As baby boomers become "empty nesters" and turn 50, they have higher discretionary income to invest.

In addition, baby boomers will soon experience the largest transfer of wealth in American history through inheritance from their parents. Cornell University economics professors Robert Avery and Michael Rendall calculate that this transfer of wealth will amount to $12.1 trillion between 1990 and 2040 (*Money Management,* June 1994).

With more discretionary income and the transference of so much wealth, there is a picture of prosperous market growth. Any scenario can be dramatically altered in the short term, but over the long term the prospect for continued market appreciation is quite good because there are significant assets chasing limited investment sources.

*I've heard that the stock market is overvalued. Should I postpone making an investment in the market until there is a major correction?*

If you try to time the stock market, you will be disappointed. While you wait to invest, watch how the market continues to climb. Just when you think the market is "cheap" and commit new money, notice how it tends to drop. Unfortunately, one of the biggest mistakes investors make is trying to call the next move that the market will make in the short term. Seeking instant gratification in the stock market only leads to disappointing results.

Focus on long-term results. If you are using stock investments in your investment plan, you should be willing to invest for a bare minimum of 5 years, ideally 10 years. What the market does tomorrow, next week, or over the next 6 months should be irrelevant if you have the proper perspective. More importantly, if you address your liquidity needs on short-, medium-, and long-term bases, you will be able to avoid selling your long-term holdings at an inopportune time when you need funds on short notice. You can accomplish this by using an asset allocation plan that addresses your short- and long-term needs.

### How can I make market fluctuations work for me?

Two time-tested strategies for capitalizing on the ups and downs in the investment markets are diversification and dollar cost averaging. *Diversification* implies putting your retirement eggs into several baskets. If you own several different individual securities or mutual funds, you will reduce the risk associated with owning only one of these investments. The volatility of any security is not necessarily linked to the volatility of other securities.

*Dollar cost averaging* takes advantage of market fluctuations through investing systematically over time. By investing the same amount each week, month, quarter, and so on, you automatically purchase more securities when prices are low and fewer when prices are high. This means that, over time, your average cost per share will be lower.

### When I retire, should I convert the majority of my stock investments to bond investments?

It depends on your needs and personal risk tolerance. When you stop working and no longer receive compensation, you may want to pare back your risk exposure because you will probably reduce the amount you save each year. Focus on what you need, not on what general guidelines suggest. Typically stocks offer growth potential, while bonds produce fixed-interest income. Ask yourself, "Do I need income now or later?" At age 65, your life expectancy may be another 20 or more years. If you do not expect to need investment income to pay your expenses for the next few years, consider investing for growth, since 10 years down the road your cost of living will probably be higher than it is today. Using a combination of stocks for growth and bonds for income will help offset the effects of inflation on your retirement income.

CHAP. 4: INVESTING FOR RETIREMENT                    229

### Convertibles

*When should I invest in convertibles?*

Investment firms do tremendous analysis of convertibles to identify those that offer attractive risk and/or return potential. Numerous books have been published on the subject, and you can spend as much time as you choose becoming an expert on principles like "conversion ratio," "adjusted breakeven," and "parity value." However, a simpler way to begin investing in convertibles is simply to keep an eye out for opportunities to get a free conversion feature.

To get a conversion feature without having to pay for it, you must buy a convertible when at least two of the following three circumstances exist: (1) interest rates seem high and likely to fall, (2) a perfectly good stock is temporarily down on its luck, but the company is sound and you're confident the stock will eventually come back, or (3) the company has a convertible available at a discount to par and with a reasonable yield.

For example, let's say the going interest rate on a 5-year bond is 7 percent and that the stock of XYZ Corp. has dropped from $60 to $30 because it had a few quarters of bad earnings. If the company has a 5-year convertible bond, it will probably be yielding close to 7 percent because few people will be willing to give up much yield to bet on the future prospects of the stock. When stocks are down, few people believe they'll go back up. You can take advantage of that pessimism when buying convertibles.

The advantage of buying a convertible like this (as long as the company really is financially solid) is that you have more ways to win. If the stock doesn't recover, you make 7 percent for 5 years and get the bond's full value at maturity. On the other hand, if the stock recovers 2 or 3 years hence, the bond might appreciate 20 to 30 percent or more. That could more than double your annual return to a 15 to 20 percent per year total return. Do such opportunities come along every day? Certainly not, but you'll find one or two a year if you watch for them, and it's a great way to enhance the overall return of a stodgy old bond portfolio.

## Mutual funds

*There has been an explosion of new mutual funds in the marketplace. Should I avoid them and stick with funds that have 3- to 5-year track records?*

Not necessarily. It may depend on your risk and reward strategy. Current research has shown that a new fund whose manager has a proven track record in a similar type of fund can provide superior performance. The reasoning behind this may involve a small asset base at the new fund, which allows the manager to concentrate and be more nimble. Whatever the reason, with thousands of new funds available, you do not want to ignore these investment opportunities.

*How can I have confidence that my funds will perform?*

There are many methods employed to measure risk and reward, but many planners particularly like valuations that measure against the "riskless rate of return." They believe in measuring downside volatility by concentrating on the months during which a fund underperformed the average return on a 3-month Treasury bill. The amount by which it fell short is divided by the months in the rating period and compared to the average for its investment class. Returns are adjusted for fees and loads and measured over the risk-free rate (Treasury bills) to the average excess return for the investment class. Only funds which survive this first screening should be considered. Negate funds which carry high expense ratios and experience excessive turnover. Performance should then be factored in, with the goal being to purchase only investments that can deliver superior performance and fair pricing.

*How useful is* Morningstar *as an aid in selecting mutual funds?*

*Morningstar* is an excellent third-party resource for selecting mutual funds. However, even its publisher, Don Phillips, has stated

## CHAP. 4: INVESTING FOR RETIREMENT                               231

publicly that *Morningstar* should not be the only source you use. Its data is based upon past performance, which may not have much relevance to the immediate future environment. Use *Morningstar* as one of many resources in selecting funds.

⋙ *Should I use individual stocks or stock mutual funds for my long-term retirement savings?*

Both have appeal for long-term investors, but each has advantages and disadvantages. An advantage offered by individual stocks but not by stock mutual funds, is the ability, with a taxable account, to have greater control over tax implications. Mutual fund owners receive 1099 statements including dividends, short-term gains, and long-term gains at the fund's discretion, while owners of individual stocks can decide when they would like to realize losses or gains. Under the Taxpayer Relief Act of 1997 and the IRS Restructuring and Reform Act of 1998, capital gains on investments held at least 12 months are taxed at 20 percent. Unless the mutual fund is in a tax-deferred retirement account, when the fund declares dividends and short-term gains, they are taxed at the individual's ordinary-income tax rate.

Mutual fund portfolio managers will, on occasion, have to liquidate holdings for purposes of shareholder redemptions from the fund, necessitating the sale of securities that holders of individual stocks would not have to sell. However, mutual funds offer professional management and diversification that may not be available to the average investor.

⋙ *For my retirement plan, should I use single-issue stocks and bonds, or will mutual funds be better?*

Most financial advisors find that average investors are served less well by portfolios of individual stocks and bonds. This is largely because the investment decisions are usually made only from a "bottom-up" perspective, that is, by judging the individual stock or bond rather than the sector or economic situation. History has shown that sector selection has been responsible for 90 percent of performance, with stock-picking being only the final 10 percent of the equation. Also, investors often base their decisions to sell on emotion rather than knowledge.

When you compare the individual investment decisions with the disciplined philosophy of an asset manager, the individual stock picker generally pales by comparison. Particularly in the mutual fund arena, the fund manager is under constant public scrutiny and must demonstrate a defined philosophy. This generally takes emotion out of the equation and results in the commonsense approach of picking sectors through a "top-down" analysis, as well as selecting stocks and bonds from a universe of securities that have been handpicked by a team of analysts. Top management firms earn their fees, many times over.

⋈ *Should I consider load or no-load funds for my portfolio? Are there performance differences?*

Some financial advisors think investors should never purchase a load fund. They believe the compensation structure is flawed and investors receive no help in managing their money.

On the other hand, many financial advisors believe that paying a sales charge does not put long-term investors at a disadvantage. They believe investors are making a big mistake when they opt to put their money in a fund just because it doesn't have a front-end load. Market guru Peter Lynch stated it best when he said, "If you plan to stick with a fund for several years, the 2 to 5 percent you paid to get into it will prove insignificant. You should not buy a fund simply because it does not have a load or refuse to buy one simply because it does."

*Morningstar,* a mutual fund rating and information service, conducted a study of funds which was published in *Registered Representative* (October 1995). The study concluded that annualized 10-year and 5-year returns were virtually identical for both types of funds. Load funds returned 12.64 percent over 10 years and 10.79 percent over 5 years compared to 12.1 percent and

CHAP. 4: INVESTING FOR RETIREMENT                   233

10.78 percent, respectively, for no-loads. The report stated, "The performance differences between these two camps are modest."

*Are there other comparative studies?*

A DALBAR Financial Services study in *Registered Representative* (March 1995) found that, over 10 years, load-fund investors held shares longer and earned better returns than investors in no-load funds. Load investors held funds for 44 months on average as compared to the no-load investors' 19-month holding period. This was not a result of the funds' being load or no-load but, rather, was the result of "help" versus "no help." Many advisors work with no-load funds and charge an asset management fee. The DALBAR study concluded that a financial advisor can help an investor stay on track by not getting into the "hot" fund at the moment and selling out during a period of market decline.

Many investors have both load and no-load funds. The issue is finding the fund that fits your objectives, risk tolerance, and time horizon. If it's not a good fit, chances are you won't stick with the investment and will bail out at a market low.

*Is it important to read the mutual fund prospectus, or can I discard it as junk mail?*

Many fund companies today are changing their prospectuses from the legal language that no one could understand to everyday English. Reading a prospectus is very important because it lists the the manager, the investment philosophy, the administrative fees, conflicts of interest, and what the fund will buy. This information may also be available in other places, but it is all in one convenient location in the prospectus.

If you do not read the prospectus, you will not know what investments are in your fund. If you do not know what investments are in the fund, you should not be buying the fund.

*⚶ I really like a particular fund, but I don't want to pay the load. Is there any way I can get around it?*

Sure. In fact, there are several ways. Most load funds will decrease or discount the commission, usually beginning with contributions of $50,000 or more for their stock funds. The more you contribute, the more the potential fee is discounted, within set limitations.

If you don't currently have that amount but expect to have it within a 13-month time period, many companies allow you to sign a *letter of intent (LOI)*. In this document, you agree to deposit an amount equal to the required amount for the particular discount within the next 13 months. In return, the fund company gives you the discounted fee on your current and future contributions. If you do not fulfill the letter of intent, the company will charge your escrowed account for the applicable sales charge.

You may also receive a discount on the load through what is called *rights of accumulation (ROA)*. Under the ROA method, you add the market value of your current shares to your new contribution to qualify for the discounted fee on the current contribution.

In addition, many fund companies allow you to aggregate your holdings within the fund family to reach the discounted fees or to aggregate your family's accounts (husband, wife, and minor children) to reach the discounted fees.

*⚶ My friends say their investments in stock mutual funds were up 19 percent last year. Should I get out of my 8.5 percent government-guaranteed GNMA and invest in the stock market?*

Before making that change, consider that a 19.5 percent return 3 years in a row followed by a 20 percent loss in year 4 produces a 4-year compound return of 8.1 percent—less than the 8.5 percent that you currently have locked in. Consistent positive returns produce superior long term results without the roller-coaster ride.

CHAP. 4: INVESTING FOR RETIREMENT                    235

※ *I am 55 and expect to retire in 7 years. My entire portfolio is invested in the United States. Should some of it be invested internationally?*

When you go to the supermarket, many of the products you purchase come from overseas. The same is true of products at your pharmacy and department store, of automobile parts, and of many other consumer goods. You are sending some of your money around the globe with your purchases. You should consider doing the same with your investments.

※ *Is an overseas portfolio more risky?*

Which of these two portfolios would you say has *more* risk?

| Portfolio A | Portfolio B |
| --- | --- |
| 50 percent U.S stocks | 50 percent U.S. stocks |
| 50 percent U.S. Treasuries | 50 percent international stocks |

Although most people choose B, the answer, surprisingly, is A. This is because stocks and bonds in the United States are influenced by the same economic events and thus move up or down together. International stocks and U.S. stocks are not linked together closely because they are not influenced by the same economic events. Thus, the diversification in B results in less overall portfolio risk.

※ *What portion of my portfolio should be invested overseas?*

Many advisors feel that 15 to 20 percent should be allocated to overseas investments. Money managers have known for a long time that adding foreign stocks to a portfolio increases the yield and lowers the volatility. The best way to invest overseas is through high-quality mutual funds from companies that actually have analysts in the foreign countries and a history of consistent performance.

☙ *In constructing my retirement portfolio, should I consider real estate or real estate mutual funds?*

Yes, for a number of very good reasons. First, with real estate investment trusts (REITs) or REIT mutual funds, you receive a dividend that is the equivalent of the yield on long-term bonds. Second, unlike bonds, real estate provides the potential for appreciation that will keep up with inflation. Finally, since real estate may respond differently from stocks and bonds to various economic events, it provides real diversification—the ability to zig when the rest of your portfolio zags.

## Life insurance

☙ *I own a closely held business, and I've been advised to establish a nonqualified plan for myself and certain key employees. What is the most effective funding vehicle available?*

Any investment vehicle chosen for the funding of a nonqualified plan requires after-tax contributions. This is because nonqualified plans do not fall under the provisions of ERISA and, therefore, do not receive a pretax-contribution status.

In looking at the universe of investment vehicles for the funding of nonqualified plans, it is important to design funding so that maximum tax efficiency is achieved. The most common and most effective vehicle is an individual variable life policy, as it offers the opportunity for equity appreciation on a tax-deferred basis, with distributions of the accumulated equity being accessible on a tax-free basis as well.

A variable life policy can either use a whole life (scheduled premiums) design or a universal life (flexible premiums) design. Like any life insurance product, a portion of your premiums is used by the insurance company to cover the policy's mortality

Chap. 4: Investing for Retirement    237

charges, sales loads, and internal expense and/or administration charges.

The balance of the premiums is then allocated into separate "mutual fund–like" account choices selected by the insured. Depending upon the selection available, adequate diversification among investment classes to achieve a proper risk tolerance level is possible.

### What is a private pension?

A *private pension* is a strategy, not a pension plan connected to an employer-sponsored qualified plan. A private pension is an investment for channeling personal, after-tax income into mutual funds, annuities, or life insurance to privately fund one's retirement. Life insurance and annuities, for example, can grow without current taxation just as regular qualified employer-sponsored plans can. Keep in mind that a private pension is totally selective as to who will participate. If you are an employer, you can have a private-pension plan done solely for yourself or for select key employees without the participation of all the other employees.

## Tax Planning Strategies

### Is tax deferral a real advantage?

Yes. Your retirement funds grow much faster when you take advantage of tax-deferred growth. The higher your tax bracket, the greater the benefit of tax-deferred growth.

### Are there any special ways to structure my holdings so that they provide tax advantages?

Yes. Consider investing retirement plan assets in income-producing assets where they will be tax-sheltered. Growth assets can be invested with nonqualified money that will primarily be taxed as capital gains when you eventually sell them.

*⚜ Do the recent tax acts affect the way we should invest?*

Before the Taxpayer Relief Act of 1997, the maximum federal capital gain income tax rate was 28 percent for assets held 12 months or longer. Under that act and also under the IRS Restructuring and Reform Act of 1998, the maximum capital gain rate is now 20 percent for assets held 12 months or longer (except art, jewelry, and other collectibles, which can still be subject to tax as high as 28 percent). For assets purchased after the year 2000 and held for 5 years, the maximum capital gain tax rate drops to 18 percent. This is compared to an ordinary-income federal tax rate as high as 39.6 percent.

As a result of these new capital gain rates, you should favor funds run by managers who tend to make long-term bets, rather than those who buy and sell stocks in search of a quick profit. That's because all the short-term gains in a fund will be distributed to you as taxable ordinary income. You can get a rough measure of a fund manager's tendency to trade by asking your broker or checking the fund's turnover ratio.

*⚜ How can I reap the most tax savings from the lowered capital gain rates?*

You can invest more of your savings in investments that tend to appreciate in price, especially stocks and stock funds that pay small or no dividends. Dividends are taxed as ordinary income, at rates that are now more costly than capital gains. Take care, however, not to let taxes rule your investment decisions. Low-yielding growth stocks tend to zigzag in price more than stodgier, higher-dividend-paying blue chips. Make sure the small, potential tax savings is worth the added risk.

*⚜ Under the new tax laws, is there a strategy to beat paying ordinary-income rates on dividend income?*

If you already plan to sell your position, it is possible to capture the dividend as a capital gain, provided you've held it long

CHAP. 4: INVESTING FOR RETIREMENT                    239

enough. The trick is to sell your shares while their price is fat with the expected dividend payment. This lets you avoid the dividend income but receive its value in the form of a capital gain.

With stocks, the time to sell is 1 day before the ex-dividend date, which is the day shares start trading at prices that no longer reflect a stockholder's rights to a declared dividend. Stocks traded on the New York Stock Exchange go ex-dividend 2 business days before the record date—or the day when shareholders must officially own shares to be entitled to the dividend.

Mutual funds have a different schedule. Investors must sell fund shares a day before the record date, which is the day before a fund goes ex-dividend. Be sure your savings from this maneuver exceed any trading costs.

✒ *Which is a better investment for income: a tax-free bond or a taxable bond?*

Obviously, tax free, right? Not necessarily. It depends on your federal and state tax brackets. If you know your combined tax bracket, you can determine whether a tax-free bond or a taxable bond is the better purchase by calculating the *taxable-equivalent yield* on the tax-free bond:

1. Determine the inverse of your combined federal and state tax brackets. The formula for this calculation is:

   $$100 - (\text{federal} + \text{state tax brackets}) = \frac{\text{inverse of}}{\text{combined tax bracket}}$$

   For example, if you are in the 28 percent federal income tax bracket and 5 percent state income tax bracket the inverse would be 100 − (28 percent + 5 percent) = 67.

2. Divide the tax-free yield you are considering by the inverse:

   $$\frac{\text{Tax-free yield}}{\text{Inverse}} = \text{taxable-equivalent yield}$$

   Thus, if you are considering a 5 percent tax-free bond, it

would be equivalent to a 7.46 percent taxable bond (5 ÷ 67 = .0746, or 7.46 percent). Thus, if the yield on your taxable bond exceeds 7.46 percent (with all other characteristics being equal), that bond would be a better investment.

*How do I calculate the taxes owed on my mutual fund investment?*

It is important to keep accurate records or work with a professional investment advisor or fund custodian such as a mutual fund company or trust company that will help determine your actual cost basis in your marketable securities.

The IRS provides several options for calculating your tax. Here are three approaches for your consideration:

AVERAGE COST   With this method, you determine the average price you paid for all shares in a fund. Divide the total dollars invested in the fund by the number of shares you own. Multiply the result by the number of shares you sold. This is your average cost basis. Subtract this number from the value you received in selling the shares. For example, assume you own 200 shares that cost a total of $2000, for an average cost of $10 per share. You sell 100 shares and receive $1500. You must report a gain of $500 ($1500 − $1000).

FIRST IN, FIRST OUT (FIFO)   This method produces the largest gain or smallest loss because stock prices have increased over the long run. When you use this approach, the IRS assumes you are selling the shares you first purchased, which will generally be at the lowest cost. Shares recently purchased will be sold last.

DESIGNATED SHARES   This approach generally provides the most flexibility for mutual fund investors because they can tell their brokers which shares to sell and can control the gain or loss. The drawback to this method is that it requires exact records, and once this approach is implemented, it cannot be changed to another approach until all the shares of that particular fund are sold.

CHAP. 4: INVESTING FOR RETIREMENT                    241

⊀ *In addition to having qualified plans, I invest for retirement on an after-tax basis. I use international funds to diversify my portfolio, so I pay foreign taxes each year. Can I claim a credit for these foreign taxes against the tax I pay to Uncle Sam?*

Yes. The new tax law allows individuals to receive credit for the foreign taxes they've paid and to report those taxes right on their 1040 forms. There is only one limitation: Single persons who need to claim credit for foreign taxes in excess of $299 or married couples who need to claim credit in excess of $599 will have to determine whether they are eligible for amounts greater than the above-mentioned credits by completing Form 1116.

## INVESTING
## WITH EXISTING
## RETIREMENT PLANS

⊀ *How aggressive should the investments in my IRA be?*

Some financial advisors believe investments in an IRA or other retirement plan should generally be the most aggressive in your portfolio. Assets in an IRA are normally held for a very long period of time, because most withdrawals before age 59½ would be subject to the 10 percent penalty tax. The longer the term of the investment, the more it can withstand downturns which come with aggressive growth investing. Growth stock mutual funds are a good means of aggressive investing because diversity is provided through the many stocks these funds hold.

⊀ *What type of investments should I have in my IRA?*

With the lowering of the capital gain tax by the Taxpayer Relief Act of 1997 and the IRS Restructuring and Reform Act of 1998, some financial advisors believe it makes sense to weight toward income-producing investments in an IRA and growth investments outside, since income outside is taxed at a maximum rate of 39.6 percent and capital gains are taxed at a maximum of 20 percent.

> *Doesn't it make sense to invest retirement plan assets in more conservative investments rather than take an additional investment risk to potentially earn extra income that's just going to be taxed and retaxed at very high rates anyway?*

Although on the surface this may sound logical, it's not correct. It's the age-old question: Wouldn't you pay less tax if you earned $50,000 than if you earned $100,000? Of course you would, but you would also end up with less net income, even if your extra income was taxed in a higher marginal tax bracket. Unless the tax were 100 percent, you would always net something additional. More is better—unless making more aggressive investments to achieve higher rates of return will move you out of your investment comfort zone.

Each individual has his or her own comfort zone as to asset allocation and diversification of investments. Some people feel comfortable investing 100 percent of their assets in stock equities (such as stocks and mutual funds), while others prefer 100 percent in fixed-income investments (such as CDs or bonds). For most the comfort zone will probably be somewhere in between.

There is no right or wrong percentage of assets to allocate to certain investments. What is important is that the percentages be within your comfort zone. If it makes sense for your portfolio to be more balanced, with some of your assets allocated to fixed-income or cash-type investments, it could be argued that you should hold fixed-income conservative investments within your retirement plan.

> *Taking tax considerations into account, where should my investments be held?*

If we assume that you invest in capital gain–type growth assets

CHAP. 4: INVESTING FOR RETIREMENT          243

outside a retirement plan, a number of advantages are available to you. Typically, much of the growth within the investments is tax-deferred. If you sell the equities, the long-term capital gain rates would be less than ordinary-income tax rates—20 percent versus as high as 39.6 percent. In addition, if you die without selling the assets, your heirs will receive a stepped-up cost basis at the time they inherit, allowing them to sell the appreciated investments without incurring any capital gain tax.

Fixed-income investments are usually taxed at the ordinary-income tax levels. Similarly, distributions from a retirement plan, no matter what the type of investment, will eventually be taxed to you, your spouse, or your heirs at the same, higher ordinary-income tax levels.

*It sounds like I'm better off having income-oriented assets in my retirement plan and growth assets outside the plan. Is this so?*

It depends on your risk tolerance. If you are comfortable having most of your assets in growth investments, it doesn't make sense to accept potentially (historically) lower yields from fixed-income investments just because they are inside a retirement plan. In addition, if the growth investments are actively managed (e.g., in a stock portfolio) or you are using a money manager who turns over the portfolio on a more regular basis, the tax-shelter and deferral features within the retirement plan would be advantageous.

*How much should I contribute to my company's 401(k)?*

Most planners agree that once adequate cash reserves are established in order to avoid going into debt in emergencies, the best place to save money is in a company-sponsored 401(k) plan. Under most plans, you can defer up to 15 percent of your payroll up to $10,000 (in 1999) into the 401(k) and maintain control over your investment mix. The money that would have been withheld in taxes stays in your account and continues to earn over the years. Most advisors would recommend that you maximize your contributions to your 401(k) plan while you are working.

> *Rather than locking my money up in a qualified plan that's subject to rules by my company and the IRS, can't I just pay my taxes and do my own investments?*

Clearly, you can. It may make you feel better. The problem is that your investment nest egg will most likely suffer. The power of tax deferral is often called the "eighth wonder of the world." Planning and investing for the future can be a whole lot easier if you recognize the importance of tax-deferred investment opportunities. The most popular programs include 401(k), 403(b), and other qualified retirement plans, such as IRAs, Keoghs, and annuities. Most financial advisors would suggest that you first take advantage of every company and personal IRS-qualified retirement program and, after doing so, take advantage of nonqualified plans such as annuities. The more you can put away for the future, the happier your financial future will be.

> *I have most of my 401(k) money invested in my company's stock, which has been spectacular from a performance standpoint. Do you see any problems with my strategy?*

It is very easy to understand your investment in your company's stock within your 401(k) plan. After all, you are quite familiar with the company, the products, and senior management. The problem with this strategy is that you have nearly all your eggs in one basket. AT&T, IBM, and Phillip Morris are three recent examples of great companies that were terrible investments during a transition period. Diversification is a wonderful tool that investors have available to reduce and control risk as well as enhance returns. By transferring some of your company stock to other available investment choices, you may be selling your stock at a high price while obtaining the wonderful advantages of diversification.

CHAP. 4: INVESTING FOR RETIREMENT                    245

*⚑ I keep reading about diversifying my portfolio. Is it better to have one type of investment in a retirement plan and another type outside the plan?*

If you already have a broad variety of investments both within and outside of retirement plans, you can maximize your overall returns by ensuring that investments which are otherwise significantly taxable (corporate bonds, high-yield stocks, REITs) are within the tax-deferred portion of your portfolio (the retirement plan). Investments you hold outside the plan should be the nontaxable (or low-rate-taxable) type, such as long-term growth stocks and real estate.

# chapter 5

# Annuities

In this chapter, our contributors discuss an investment vehicle which has taken the retirement planning world by storm over the last few years—the annuity. Annuities are attractive because of favorable income tax treatment, but they contain provisions that are unfamiliar to many investors.

This chapter covers both the advantages and the disadvantages of annuities, who should purchase them, when they should be purchased, the types of annuities available for purchase, and how annuities compare to other investment opportunities. Our contributors also explain in understandable terms how annuities are taxed for both income and estate tax purposes, as well as how to utilize them to achieve estate planning goals.

We were impressed by the clarity of the explanations in this chapter, as well as the great lengths our contributors went to in order to present an unbiased discussion of an investment vehicle that invokes great emotional response from many investment ad-

248    WAYS AND MEANS

visors. We believe you will benefit greatly from the information contained in this chapter.

## ANNUITIES IN GENERAL

*What is an annuity?*

An *annuity* is a contractual arrangement between an individual and an insurance company or other party. Under the contract, the individual transfers money to the insurance company or other party in exchange for the right to receive the money back, usually in the form of fixed, periodic payments for a term of years or for life.

*Are life insurance and annuities the same thing?*

No. It is important to remember that annuities are not life insurance contracts. In fact, many annuity contracts are almost the reverse of life insurance. With life insurance, you make a series of payments over time—premiums—and an insurance company pays your beneficiary a lump-sum amount when you die. With most annuity contracts, you pay the lump-sum amount up front, or in planned periodic payments, and the insurance company makes a series of payments to you. Typically, life insurance is concerned with how soon you will die, whereas an annuity is concerned with how long you will live. There is also a potential difference in the income tax issues relating to each.

*How much risk is involved in investing in an annuity?*

Investing in an annuity carries no more risk than investing in stocks, bonds, mutual funds, CDs, or any other similar type of investment. Often the investment options inside an annuity are quite similar to those available outside an annuity.

CHAP. 5: ANNUITIES 249

≥\ *Why have tax-deferred annuities become so popular in the last few years?*

Tax advantages and people's need to save more efficiently for retirement are the main reasons the sales of tax-deferred annuity products have skyrocketed as of late. Because of the ceiling on contributions to qualified retirement plans, as well as the red tape associated with most of those plans, many individuals and employers are turning to tax-deferred annuities to supplement their retirement savings and to lower their annual exposure to current income taxes on interest and investment gain.

≥\ *Who are the players in an annuity contract?*

Every annuity contract has an owner, an annuitant, a beneficiary, and an obligor. The *owner* is the person or entity purchasing the annuity. The owner holds the contractual rights, can exercise any and all options under the annuity, and is entitled to all payments from the annuity. The *annuitant* must be a person on whose life all the payment options are calculated. The *beneficiary* is the person or entity that receives any death benefit of the contract after the annuitant or owner dies.

The person or entity that is contractually obligated to pay the annuity benefits to the owner is known as the *obligor.* If the annuity is purchased from an insurance company, the insurance company—the obligor—is usually referred to as the "insurer." The insurer will invest the owner's money either in the insurer's general account or with various select money managers. The insurer's annuity contract will dictate, among other things, whether the owner can substitute parties to the contract, withdraw funds, or add money to the contract.

≥\ *What is a private annuity?*

An annuity contract does not have to be with an insurance company, although this is the most common arrangement. You could contract for a guaranteed stream of payments with a person or an entity other than an insurance company, in which case it would be a *private annuity.*

You, as the annuitant and owner, agree to place a lump sum of money with another party. This other party, the obligor, is usually your child or another highly trusted person or entity. Your child then agrees to pay a set amount to you in regular installments, usually monthly, until your death.

Private annuities are usually used for estate planning purposes. Your child would pay you a stream of payments in return for an asset. At your death, the annuity payments cease, the asset is considered to have been transferred to your child, and the value of the asset is not subject to estate tax.

A legally binding document prepared by an attorney is an absolute necessity in establishing a private annuity.

### ⋙ *How do annuities work?*

An annuity is a mathematical concept that is generally quite simple. You start with a sum of money and pay it out in equal installments over a period of time, until the original amount of money is exhausted. In essence, an annuity is simply a vehicle for liquidating a certain sum of money.

You make contributions to annuities with after-tax dollars, so there is virtually no limit to the amount you can contribute. Another important factor in the annuity is that the interest earned within the annuity is tax-deferred until withdrawn.

Generally the annuity is "annuitized" when the insurance company, or other third party, begins making systematic, periodic payments to you as provided for in the annuity contract. Sometimes this is also known as the "starting," "commencement," or "maturity" date. The amount of each periodic payment will depend upon the payment option selected by the owner from the choices in the contract. One common option is the payment of a fixed periodic amount for the lifetime of the annuitant, regardless of how long the annuitant lives. Under this option, the an-

CHAP. 5: ANNUITIES 251

nuitant can never "outlive" the annuity payments because the insurer has promised to make the payments for the annuitant's actual lifetime.

Once the annuity is annuitized—that is, payments have commenced—each payment to you is partly a return of your original principal contribution and partly earnings on that principal; the proportion is determined by what is called the *exclusion ratio formula.* Only the interest portion of the payments is taxable income to you, and the remainder is a nontaxable return of your principal.

### ⩫ What factors affect the amount of my annuity payments?

There are many factors that go into determining the amount of annuity payments. In general, however, there are certain critical factors that are considered by companies that sell annuities. These are your age and sex, the principal amount you pay into the annuity, the rate of interest the annuity earns, the company's expense of managing the annuity, and the way the annuity will be paid out to you.

### ⩫ As the owner of an annuity, what distribution options do I have before my annuity is annuitized?

Generally you have the following distribution options before annuitization:

1. *Loans:* With many annuities, you can take a loan against the annuity before it is annuitized, subject to possible penalties, charges, or income tax.

2. *Withdrawals:* Withdrawals are usually permitted by contract, subject to penalties, charges, or income tax. It is common for companies to allow yearly withdrawals for 10 percent of the value without penalty.

3. *Surrenders:* Most annuities have decreasing surrender charges associated with termination of the contracts during the early

years. Low-load annuities typically do not have surrender charges.

4.  *Rollovers:* Rollovers—transferring the money from one company to another—are permitted under Internal Revenue Code Section 1035 as tax-free exchanges as long as the amount, annuitant, and owner remain the same. If the annuity is not held in a qualified retirement plan, a full transfer is typically required to avoid triggering a tax on the untransferred amount.


 ᐳ  *What restrictions do annuities have?*

For tax purposes, annuities are treated much like IRAs (IRA taxation is discussed Chapter 6). Withdrawals made before you reach age 59½, with the same exceptions as those for IRAs, are subject to a 10 percent early-withdrawal penalty. With most annuity contracts, however, you may delay withdrawals until as late as age 85 or 90, compared to age 70½ with qualified retirement plans. To the extent that you withdraw any amounts from your contracts, earnings are generally considered to be withdrawn first.

Depending upon the company, there may be a *contingent deferred sales charge (CDSC),* or surrender-charge, period. This period varies but averages about 6 years. During the CDSC period, if you withdraw funds above a stated amount, you will be subject to an insurance company penalty. The penalty generally decreases over the course of the CDSC period. Withdrawals after the CDSC period are not subject to the insurance company's penalty.

There are numerous annuities available with 6-year CDSC periods. However, there are some on the market with 10-year CDSC periods or longer. As a general rule, it is not wise to lock up your money any longer than necessary. Tax laws and investment products change. No one knows when you may wish to change your investment options or, perhaps, when something better may come along.

When considering an annuity, you should consult the annuity

CHAP. 5: ANNUITIES                                                  253

prospectus for particular details on withdrawals, charges, and availability of funds.

⚞ *How can I make sure I'll get my original investment back if I annuitize my annuity?*

In order to ensure that at least the original investment will be paid to you or your family, it is recommended that an annuitization income be specified for 10 years or longer. Ten years of payments will usually reimburse the full investment if the payments begin when you reach normal retirement age.

## Advantages of Annuities

⚞ *What are some of the advantages of an annuity?*

The advantages of an annuity include the following:

- Unless the annuity is owned by a for-profit corporation or a nonnatural entity, all interest or growth is tax-deferred until it is withdrawn.

- By reallocating taxable investments to tax-deferred annuity investments, it is possible to lower your taxable income each year. For example, retirees with large amounts of taxable interest income can reallocate their investments to a tax-deferred annuity and potentially reduce the taxable income used to calculate whether or not their Social Security benefits will be taxed in a given year.

- When the annuity is annuitized(i.e., systematic payments begin), only a portion of each annuity payment is taxable until you have recovered your entire investment in the annuity. This is beneficial because tax on a substantial portion of both the interest earned during the accumulation period and the interest earned after your payments begin continues to be deferred.

- If your spouse is the beneficiary of the annuity, after the

254                                    WAYS AND MEANS

annuitant's death, your spouse can roll the annuity contract over into his or her name and keep the tax-deferred nature of the investment.

- You normally have various withdrawal options to choose from.

- Unlike other investments, an annuity can have as one of its options a payout that you cannot outlive.

- There is no limit on the amount of your annual contribution, as there is with an IRA.

- An annuity is a form of "forced savings" of your investments and may keep you from the temptation of squandering them.

- The beneficiary designation provides that the proceeds or death benefits are paid directly to the beneficiary, thereby avoiding the necessity of probating the annuity, assuming the beneficiary is someone other than the annuity owner's estate.

*What personal or financial situation is best suited for annuities?*

Annuities are usually best suited for you if:

1. You are in a high income tax bracket.
2. You are nearly 59½ years old or older.
3. You have enough income from other sources to allow deferral.
4. You have fully funded your employer retirement plans.
5. You plan to annuitize the contract or to systematically withdraw money from the annuity at a later date.

## Disadvantages of Annuities

*What are some of the disadvantages of annuities?*

Annuities have the following disadvantages:

# CHAP. 5: ANNUITIES

**SURRENDER CHARGES** Annuities are viewed as long-term wealth accumulation vehicles. Insurance companies apply surrender charges in the early years of contracts so that they are guaranteed a return of all expenses incurred in marketing the product. These expenses vary among companies and should be thoroughly reviewed before purchasing an annuity.

**ADMINISTRATION COSTS** Certain types of annuities have higher administration costs than others, and these costs can offset their performance considerably, especially in down markets. However, on average and depending on the time horizon, these expenses can sometimes be partially offset by an account manager's ability to stay more fully invested than mutual fund managers who must keep a cash reserve for redemptions. Annuity investors tend to be more long-sighted, since the investment vehicle they have chosen is more suitable for their retirement needs. It is important for you to review the annuity contract to determine what, if any, administration costs will be charged.

**TAXES** Perhaps of the greatest significance is the tax you will incur upon taking money out of an annuity. All distributions of earnings are taxed at ordinary-income tax rates. Therefore any favorable and lower capital gain tax treatment available through the Taxpayer Relief Act of 1997 and the IRS Restructuring and Reform Act of 1998 is unavailable. If you are in the top federal bracket, this means a tax of 39.6 percent instead of the new capital gain rate of 20 percent, which is potentially available with mutual funds held for 12 months. This income tax will be paid by someone: either by you or your spouse when making withdrawals during your lifetimes or by your heirs after your spouse's and your deaths.

**PENALTIES** Nonsystematic withdrawals of earnings before age 59½ are subject to a 10 percent penalty tax unless you meet with some qualifying event, such as disability or death, or you elect to take substantially equal payments over your lifetime.

**AFTER-DEATH RESTRICTIONS** All nonspouse beneficiaries must elect to annuitize the death benefit or cash value within 1 year of the date of the annuitant's death or take the total amount in one lump sum or in a series of even or uneven distributions within 5 years of the date of death.

BENEFICIARIES' TAXES Your beneficiaries will not receive a step-up in basis—an adjustment in the value of the assets to fair market value at the date of your death. Instead, capital gains will be based on your cost basis—what you paid for the assets—and distributions from your annuity to your beneficiaries after your death will generally continue to be taxed to them as ordinary income. (There is an exception: A variable annuity contract issued before October 21, 1979, may receive this fair market adjustment.)

*Can you explain the 10 percent penalty for early withdrawal?*

To discourage the use of an annuity as a short-term investment, the tax code imposes a penalty on early withdrawals or loans from annuities. Generally, if you withdraw money from your annuity contract before you are 59½, an additional tax of 10 percent of the taxable amount withdrawn is due in the year of the withdrawal.

Lump-sum withdrawals from an annuity are treated as if all the accumulated earnings are distributed first, that is, on a last-in, first-out basis. Therefore, it is likely that most, if not all, of the amount will be subject to the 10 percent tax penalty. If the withdrawal is also subject to early-surrender charges by the insurance company, the affect on the yield can be devastating.

Therefore, it is prudent to invest in an annuity only if you expect to remain in the contract for the long term.

## Annuities in Retirement Planning

*What role does an annuity play in retirement planning?*

Positioning assets to provide sufficient income during retirement

CHAP. 5: ANNUITIES                                                    257

is critical. Annuities offer you the ability to select a payout option for retirement that you cannot outlive. As life expectancies continue to lengthen, it is not unrealistic to predict that you might spend more time in retirement than the time you spent in the work force. Unless carefully managed, other investments, such as CDs or mutual funds, may not last your lifetime. If you are concerned about outliving your assets, an annuit can provide protection and may may generate significantly more after-tax income than mutual funds.

Therefore, an annuity will play an important role in any situation where you need a stream of fixed income for a fixed period of time or even for a lifetime.

*What makes an annuity such a good retirement asset accumulator?*

Annuity contracts have special privileges under the tax code. Any investment in an annuity increases income tax–deferred until a withdrawal is made. The tax benefits continue if you elect to annuitize the contract, that is, receive regular, periodic payments. The annuity payments are reported partially as income, which is income-taxable in the year of payment, and partially as a return of principal, which is nontaxable when paid. Therefore, you are not taxed on the full amount of the cash flow you receive.

## TYPES OF ANNUITIES

*What types of annuities are available?*

There are numerous types of annuities available, all of which are based upon certain options:

- How you purchase the annuity
- When payments from your annuity will commence

258  WAYS AND MEANS

- How you will take those payments
- What the underlying investment structure of your annuity is

Generally, an annuity combines at least two or more of these different options.

## Purchasing Annuities

*How do I purchase or fund an annuity?*

There are essentially two options for purchasing an annuity. One is a lump-sum purchase, in which you immediately deposit the entire principal with the insurance company or other third party. This is known as a *single-premium annuity.*

Under the second method, you make "premium" payments to the insurance company over a period of time. This is known as a *flexible-premium annuity.*

## Starting to Receive Payments

*If I invest in an annuity, when do I start receiving payments?*

Thee answer depends on the type of annuity you wish to purchase. Typically, annuities have two options for the onset of payments: immediate or deferred. If you choose to begin receiving payments immediately, the annuity is known as an *immediate annuity.*

If you choose to defer the commencement of payments until a later date, the annuity is known as a *deferred annuity.* You can set the date on which payments are to begin when you purchase the annuity, or you can turn the payments on and off like a water spigot when you want to receive money from your annuity.

*What is an immediate annuity?*

An *immediate annuity* is a contractual arrangement in which you

CHAP. 5: ANNUITIES                                     259

exchange a lump sum of money for a guaranteed stream of periodic payments which begin immediately upon your purchase of the contract.

### What is a split, or combination, annuity?

A *split,* or *combination, annuity* is actually two annuities in one:

1. An immediate annuity, which begins periodic, usually monthly, payments immediately after you purchase the contract

2. A deferred annuity, which accumulates income tax–deferred until some time in the future.

### Why would I want to purchase a split annuity?

A split annuity is a good investment choice if you want to take advantage of income tax deferral, need an immediate stream of income, and want a guarantee that your original investment will be returned.

### Can you give me an example of how a split annuity works?

Since a split annuity is a combination of an immediate annuity and a deferred annuity, it can be coordinated to give current cash flow while protecting principal. You begin receiving a guaranteed payment for a fixed period of time from the portion invested in the immediate annuity. This will draw down a portion of your original investment, while the tax-deferred portion of your investment grows to replace the amount of principal depleted by the withdrawals. For example, suppose you deposit $100,000 in a split annuity earning 7 percent—$50,835 into the fixed portion and $49,165 into the deferred portion—for 10 years. You will receive $501 per month for 10 years. By the time your period-certain annuity of $50,835 is exhausted, the $49,165 tax-deferred portion will have grown to the original $100,000.

*⊴ Can you summarize the types of annuities in terms of how premiums are paid in and when benefits are paid out?*

There are three main types of annuities based upon how you purchase the annuity and when payments begin:

- *Single-premium, immediate annuity:* You purchase this annuity with a single premium, and you begin receiving payments immediately.
- *Single-premium, deferred annuity:* You purchase this annuity with a single premium, but the payouts to you do not begin until a later date.
- *Flexible-premium, deferred annuity:* You purchase this annuity with periodic premiums over a period of time, and payments to you do not begin until a later date.

## Options for Payments

*⊴ How can annuity payouts be structured?*

Annuity payouts, regardless of the kind or type of annuity, are made under one of the following options:

- *Life-with-no-refund (straight-life) annuity:* A life-with-no-refund, or straight-life, annuity provides you with periodic payments for your life. Upon your death, all payments cease, and no death benefits will be paid to your beneficiary.
- *Life-refund (installment-refund) annuity:* A life-refund, or installment-refund, annuity provides you with periodic payments for life, but if the full purchase price of your annuity has not been returned to you before your death, the balance is paid to your beneficiary.
- *Term-certain annuity:* A term-certain annuity provides you with periodic payments for a set period of time. If you live beyond that period of time, the payments to you stop. If you

## CHAP. 5: ANNUITIES

261

die before the payout period ends, your beneficiary receives the income payments for the balance of the period.

- *Life and term-certain annuity:* A life and term-certain annuity provides you with periodic payments for life, just like a straight-life annuity. However, unlike a straight-life annuity, if you die within a fixed number of years after you begin taking payments, your beneficiary will receive the payments until the end of that period. If you die after the fixed period, your beneficiary will receive nothing.

- *Joint-life annuity:* A joint life annuity provides payments until the death of you or another individual (typically your spouse), whichever occurs *first.*

- *Joint-life and survivorship annuity:* A joint-life and survivorship annuity provides payments until the death of you or another individual (typically your spouse), whichever occurs *last.* You can choose to have the survivor's annuity be a percentage of the original payment (up to 100 percent) or be a specific amount.

## Investment Structure

⚜ *When I purchase an annuity from an insurance company, what are my investment options?*

When you purchase an annuity, you normally have three options regarding how the money will be invested: fixed, variable, or indexed. These options are extremely important because they can ultimately affect the amount of the payments to you.

### Fixed annuity

⚜ *What is a fixed annuity?*

A *fixed annuity* is an annuity that protects both your principal *and* your interest against loss by guaranteeing a fixed rate of return for a certain term.

The investment is held in the insurance company's general account, which is primarily invested in interest income investments such as bonds and mortgages. The insurance company will normally have a 1-year guaranteed rate of return that can increase, decrease, or stay the same at the annual anniversary of the annuity. However, you can also purchase annuities with guaranteed rates for 3-, 5-, or 10- year periods.

### ⋈ *How are earnings determined on a fixed annuity?*

For fixed-rate annuities, earnings are based on the insurer's current declared rate, subject to a minimum guarantee, generally somewhere between 3 and 4 percent. Insurers may also guarantee rates for new contributions for various periods of time. The declared rate issued by the insurance company is dependent on the performance of its own general investment portfolio or general account.

### ⋈ *How does the insurance company invest the money that is in my fixed annuity?*

Your money is invested in the general assets of the insurance company, typically fixed-income investments such as bonds and mortgages. The insurance company makes all the investment decisions, and you cannot alter its decisions.

### Variable annuity

### ⋈ *What is a variable annuity?*

A *variable annuity* is an annuity that gives you—instead of the insurance company—the right to select the underlying investments from stock, bond, and specialty subaccounts. Unlike the case with a fixed annuity, where you have a guaranteed minimum

CHAP. 5: ANNUITIES                                                    263

interest rate, the growth within your variable annuity depends on the performance of your investment. The value of your account will fluctuate with changes in the market value of the underlying securities, and the amount of money available for annuitization or withdrawal could be more or less than your original investment.

Also, there are usually administrative expenses added to a variable annuity that are already built in to the fixed annuity.

### ✵ *What are the advantages of variable annuities?*

In addition to the advantages available with all annuities, variable annuities offer the following advantages over fixed annuities or other direct investments:

- Unlike a fixed annuity, a variable annuity gives you the opportunity to participate in investing in various securities through stock, bond, and specialty subaccounts.

- Variable annuities can give you access to highly rated institutional money managers not normally available to investors in individual stocks.

- Switching from one subaccount to another in a variable annuity will not trigger a taxable event as it would with regular mutual funds held in non-IRA accounts. This permits you to use asset allocation and portfolio rebalancing techniques without the worry of taxation.

- Variable annuities offer expanded death benefit features not available with traditional investments. In general, the annuity can promise to pay your beneficiaries upon your death the greater of the current market value of the account, the amount you contributed, or the amount you contributed plus a guaranteed rate of return. Some variable annuities also offer a step-up feature that guarantees your beneficiaries a death payment that is no lower than your highest account value on any contract anniversary. Thus, the annuity can give you confidence to invest in the market, knowing that if you die while market values are low, the annuity could protect against downward market fluctuations.

- Variable annuity accounts are separate from the general assets of the insurance company and cannot be attached by the company's creditors. This is a degree of protection not available to owners of fixed annuities.

*How do I know if I am a candidate for a variable annuity?*

Variable annuities can be excellent retirement fund accumulation tools. You might consider a variable annuity if these three conditions apply to you:

1. You are investing for long-term needs such as retirement and can invest for at least 5 years—ideally 10 or more years.
2. You are comfortable with market volatility of variable subaccounts within the annuity.
3. You find that you are paying more taxes on your current income and dividends than you need to be paying.

Your financial advisor can assist you in selecting a specific annuity (features and ratings vary widely among insurance carriers), design an asset mix appropriate for your needs and risk tolerance, and help you monitor the annuity's investment performance.

*Are variable annuities guaranteed?*

Generally, no. A variable annuity is invested in many different subaccount alternatives and is subject to the market risk of the investments selected. However, there are some variable annuities that offer a fixed option.

*Are expenses less if more money is put into a variable annuity?*

For the answer to this question, you must read the annuity's pro-

CHAP. 5: ANNUITIES                                                265

spectus thoroughly. The surrender charges are declared and do not change with contributions. You should review all expenses and charges, not just management and mortality fees—the expenses charged by an insurance company for assuming the risk that you will die in a given year.

*I often hear that the expenses in variable annuities make them unattractive compared to mutual funds. Is that true?*

It depends. It is only when the insurance costs for the guaranteed death benefit are added to the normal expenses that the total appears higher. Insurance charges differ from contract to contract, and they may not result in total investment charges as high as you might think. A study done by Lipper Analytical Services revealed that the total average cost difference between variable annuities and mutual funds in 1995 was 67 basis points. This is because many of the underlying funds in variable annuities impose lower fees than those in their publicly offered mutual funds, and these lower expenses offset, to some extent, the additional insurance charges.

You must weigh all these expenses against all the benefits and the options they cover. The fee differential may seem a modest price to pay for the risk management offered, along with the ability to structure a retirement payout plan that meets your individual retirement income needs. The expenses associated with a variable annuity contract are guaranteed not to increase over the life of the contract. Since you might maintain your annuity for 20, 30, or more years, this benefit can be significant. In the past, the expenses for some other types of investments increased over such long periods.

*What is meant by "guaranteed death benefit" in variable annuities?*

The death benefit on the life of the annuitant usually offers the beneficiaries of the contract 100 percent of the annuity premiums contributed less any withdrawals. Some issuers increase the death benefit on the annuity's anniversary date. Note that the cost basis for beneficiaries does not step up at the annuitant's death; as a result, the entire deferred profit is subject to ordinary-income taxation.

If you are purchasing an annuity and are also the annuitant, a variable annuity does not guarantee you a return of your principal, since it is usually invested in stock and bond mutual fund–like accounts. The 100 percent guaranteed death benefit applies for your beneficiaries only if you die.

Variable annuities can be excellent vehicles for deferring and controlling your taxable interest income, and having a guaranteed minimum death benefit, regardless of performance, can be an attractive feature for some investors. Due to the wide variety of different insurance carriers, you should consult your financial advisor for assistance in evaluating annuity contracts.

⋈ *My financial advisor told me my variable annuity could never be less than my contribution at death. Is this true?*

Not exactly. Variable annuities carry an additional expense (which varies by contract) that guarantees a minimum amount at death but only if the contract has not been annuitized.

### Fixed versus variable annuities

⋈ *Can I get a better return if I put my money in a variable annuity instead of a fixed annuity?*

Probably. The opportunity to increase the rate of return on an investment in a variable annuity over that on a fixed annuity does exist. With a fixed annuity, the rate of return is determined by the yield on the insurer's general investment portfolio, but with a variable annuity you determine where to invest your contributions. The array of investment choices include stocks, bonds, or money subaccounts as well as foreign subaccounts, real estate equity and mortgage subaccounts, and asset allocation subaccounts.

CHAP. 5: ANNUITIES                                    267

However, as the owner, you—not the insurer—bear the market risk. Many companies offer "insurance options" at a cost which provide account guarantees in case of death.

≫ *Is my annuity guaranteed by the insurance company's assets?*

It depends on the type of annuity you have. This question brings to light the importance of the financial status of any company selling annuities.

A fixed annuity has investment guarantees backed by the insurance company. A variable annuity is invested in stocks, bonds, money markets, and the like, and has no investment (performance) guarantee.

Under variable contracts, the insurance company may be in financial stress, but your account values could be doing very well. Conversely, the insurance company may have high financial ratings, but your investment selections could reflect poor performance.

≫ *What are the different credit ratings on fixed and variable annuities?*

There are four common agencies that rate insurance companies that issue annuities. Table 5-1 lists the higher rating grades used by each of these agencies. The ratings reflect an insurance carrier's credit and ability to pay benefits.

Your financial advisor can inform you about ratings on your existing annuities and on any you may be considering.

### Indexed annuity

≫ *What is an indexed annuity?*

An *indexed annuity* is a hybrid between a fixed annuity and a variable annuity. It has some of the characteristics of both. Generally an indexed annuity has a guaranteed interest rate, like a

**TABLE 5-1    Fixed and Variable Annuity Credit Ratings**

| AM Best | Moody's | Standard and Poor's | Duff and Phelps |
|---------|---------|---------------------|-----------------|
| A++ | AAA | AAA | AAA |
| A+ | AA1 | AA+ | AA+ |
| A | AA2 | AA | AA |
| A– | AA3 | AA– | AA– |
| B++ | A1 | A+ | A+ |
| B+ | A2 | A | A |
| B | A3 | A– | A– |

fixed annuity; however, it also offers the opportunity of a higher rate of return than that with a fixed annuity.

### ⅍ *What is an index?*

An *index* is a statistical indicator used to measure and report value changes in groups of stocks or bonds. If you follow the stock market, it is a convenient way for you to keep track of movements in the market.

### ⅍ *What are the groups, or indexes, that might be available in an equity- indexed annuity?*

There are several: the Standard and Poor's 500; the Standard and Poor's Mid Cap 400; the Nasdaq 100; and foreign equity indexes, such as the EAFE, DAX, FTSE 100, NIKKEI 225, and CAC 40.

### ⅍ *Of all the indexes, which one seems to be the most popular?*

The S&P 500 index is a widely recognized benchmark of U.S. stock performance. It does not comprise the largest 500 stocks or companies, however, but represents 70 percent of the total U.S.

CHAP. 5: ANNUITIES                                                    269

equity market's capitalization. It is also a price index and does not include dividends. It includes stocks from the New York Stock Exchange, the American Stock Exchange, and the Nasdaq.

### ⋇ *In general, what are the advantages of indexing?*

Purchasing an index-type annuity generally has the following advantages:

- *Results:* Indexing has generally outperformed actively managed mutual funds for the same periods of time. However, your indexed-annuity participation rate may reduce this advantage.
- *Cost:* Indexed funds have lower trading costs.
- *Consistency:* Since 1984, the S&P 500 index has surpassed half of all general equity funds.
- *Tax effectiveness:* Since indexed funds have a buy-and-hold philosophy, there is less turnover and less tax.
- *Diversity:* An indexed fund tends to own many or all of the stocks that make up the index.

### ⋇ *How do indexed annuities differ from indexed mutual funds?*

The indexed mutual fund goes down in a market decline. The indexed annuity provides protection from volatility because the principal is guaranteed when the annuity is held to maturity and surrender fees are not charged.

### ⋇ *What fundamental definitions are used in equity-indexed annuities?*

The *term* is the period of time during which surrender charges are imposed if you terminate the annuity. The annuity may be renewed for another term.

The *participation rate,* also known as the *index rate,* is a percentage of the increase in the index that is credited to your account value. For example, if you have a 100 percent participation rate in an S&P 500 indexed annuity, you will get 100 percent of the growth of the S&P 500 index, less a nominal charge credited to your account. If the participation rate is 70 percent, you will get 70 percent of the growth credited to your account. The lower the U.S. Treasury note interest rates, the lower your participation rate.

The *cap rate* is the maximum increase allowed in the account value each year. Thus, a 100 percent cap rate means the value of your annuity cannot increase by more than 100 percent in a given year.

The *floor* is the minimum guaranteed interest rate credited to the account regardless of the index's market return.

⋈ *When would I need an indexed annuity?*

If you have determined that an annuity meets your needs, an indexed annuity could be beneficial because there is no downside risk with the minimum guaranteed return. Also, you have the opportunity to participate in some of the upside limit of the underlying benchmark, for example, the S&P 500, which may continue to grow. An indexed annuity can give you the advantages of both worlds.

## MULTIPLE ANNUITIES

⋈ *Why would I consider owning two different annuities as opposed to one?*

Compare two investors, both with $100,000 invested in tax-deferred annuities. Investor A puts $100,000 into one annuity policy and investor B puts $100,000 into two $50,000 annuity policies. After 10 years each investor's funds have grown to $200,000.

CHAP. 5: ANNUITIES                                                    271

Investor A withdraws a lump sum of $100,000 and owes tax on the entire withdrawal. Investor B withdraws $100,000 out of one of the policies and owes tax on only half of the withdrawal. Why is this? Remember, income taxes on withdrawals are paid on the growth, not on the return of principal. Investor A is withdrawing only growth dollars (the IRS uses LIFO—last in, first out—on annuity withdrawals), while Investor B is withdrawing $50,000 of growth and $50,000 of original principal. Consult your advisor before using this strategy.

## EXCHANGES OR ROLLOVERS

*I have a fixed annuity that is giving me a low return. How can I change my investment without dire tax consequences?*

You can move from one annuity contract and insurance company to another through an Internal Revenue Code Section 1035 like-kind exchange. Even though the type of annuity contract may change, your money must stay within the protective shelter of the annuity contract, and the annuitant, owner, and beneficiary must be the same on the old and new contracts. The exchange is handled similarly to a trustee-to-trustee transfer for a pension plan or IRA. The transfer of funds is made directly between insurance companies.

An exchange will only defer income taxes and potential tax penalties. The surrender charges of the original contract still apply, and you will be starting a new surrender period with the new contract.

Great care should be exercised when making this exchange. You should have your financial advisor or attorney process the paperwork and retain copies of all documentation, as you would in any other financial dealing. Also, be forewarned that your patience is sometimes required, as many insurance companies go through a conservation process to convince you not to change.

272 WAYS AND MEANS

*Is it possible to do a tax-free exchange of an annuity I purchased before August 14, 1982, and maintain its former tax-free status?*

Yes. The rule is that a replacement contract obtained in a tax-free exchange will maintain the same status as the surrendered contract for purposes of considering when amounts were invested and of determining the taxability of any withdrawals you might take. This allows you to continue to maintain the FIFO tax accounting and to withdraw your entire cost basis in the annuity tax-free before subjecting your earnings to income taxation.

*I inherited an annuity, but I don't feel that the current investment is suitable for my needs. Is there a way to transfer the proceeds to another annuity company without generating an immediate tax liability?*

Because the transfer can be somewhat tricky, you might first check the available investment options within the current annuity before considering a transfer.

If you, as the beneficiary, are not a surviving spouse and have not elected to annuitize the contract within 1 year of the owner's or annuitant's date of death, the proceeds of the inherited annuity must be completely distributed to you within 5 years of the deceased's date of death whether or not you transfer the annuity.

Otherwise, under current law, one tax-deferred annuity may be exchanged for another by following these steps:

1. You will need the executor or personal representative of the deceased to allow the transfer. The current annuity company will explain what it needs from the executor or personal representative to indicate this approval.

2. You must keep the registrations the same. Since the inherited annuity contract is owned by the estate of the deceased owner with you named as the beneficiary, the new annuity contract must be registered in the same way. Further, for tax

CHAP. 5: ANNUITIES                                                273

purposes the new annuity account must use your Social Security number.

3. The exchange of the contracts must be executed as a "direct
   transfer" between annuity companies; otherwise, you may
   find yourself debating the "doctrine of constructive receipt"
   with the IRS, and you would probably lose the debate. Constructive receipt would cause the annuity to be declared immediately taxable in the year of the attempted exchange.

4. Verify that, in the year-end after the transfer, the original
   annuity company will not generate a 1099 to you or the estate
   of the deceased owner for income in respect of a decedent.

Remember, this exchange does not change the requirement that
all the annuity proceeds must be taken and recognized as taxable
income by you within 5 years of the date of death of the deceased
owner of the annuity.

## SURRENDERING ANNUITIES

*What is a bailout clause?*

An annuity *bailout clause* allows you to surrender the contract
without incurring surrender charges under certain circumstances.
The most common provision allows for withdrawal if the rate of
return falls below a specified rate, such as 1 percent below the
original guaranteed rate.

*What is a nursing-home waiver on an annuity?*

Annuities usually have declining surrender charges that disappear
after several years. If your annuity includes a *nursing-home waiver,*
a withdrawal, free of any surrender charges, is allowed if you
require nursing-home care. Note that annuity withdrawal privi-

# TAX ASPECTS OF ANNUITIES

## Exceptions to Withdrawal Penalty

*I need to make withdrawals before I'm 59½. Are there any exceptions to the 10 percent penalty for early withdrawal?*

Yes. You can take pre-59½ distributions without incurring the 10 percent penalty if any of the following apply:

- You are disabled.
- You have an investment in an annuity contract issued before August 14, 1982, including earnings before such date.
- You own an immediate annuity contract that has a start date no later than 1 year from the date of purchase and that provides for a series of substantially equal periodic payments to be made at least annually during the annuity period.
- You were receiving a payment under an annuity contract for benefits due to damages, by lawsuit or by agreement, such as personal injury or accident.
- You begin taking a series of equal and substantial payments at least annually over your life expectancy.

## Income Taxes

### During accumulation

*Do I pay income tax on my annuity?*

When you begin taking withdrawals, you will have to pay in-

# CHAP. 5: ANNUITIES

come tax on the earnings that your annuity generates but not on your principal. For example, if you invest $1000 into an annuity and receive $1600 over ten payments, you would not be taxed on the $1000 but would be taxed on the $600 that your annuity earned.

## *How do deferred annuities affect my Social Security benefits?*

The accumulating funds inside your annuity are not considered part of your "provisional income" under the formula for determining taxation of Social Security benefits.

## *I've been purchasing annuities since 1975. Are all my annuities taxed the same if I make withdrawals before the annuity starting date?*

No. If the withdrawal is part of a series of systematic payments utilizing one of the payment options under the annuity contract, the normal exclusion ratio treats each payment partly as a return of income and partly as a return of principal. However, this ratio does not apply to partial or lump-sum withdrawals.

For lump-sum distributions on any annuity purchased *on or before* August 13, 1982, the distributions are treated as a tax-free recovery on your investment until the entire investment is recovered; after that, the remaining distributions are taxable as ordinary income.

Conversely, lump-sum amounts taken out of an annuity purchased *after* August 13, 1982, are taxed under the interest-first rule. In other words, distributions before the start date are treated entirely as taxable income until all earnings have been taxed, and then the balance is treated as a nontaxable recovery of your investment. For example, you invest $100,000 in an annuity at age 60. The account value grows to $120,000 in 3 years. You then withdraw $10,000. The $10,000 is taxable at your ordinary-income tax rate. It is only after you withdraw more than $20,000—the total accumulated income—that the withdrawals will be considered a nontaxable return of your principal.

These distributions include cash dividends, withdrawals, and even loans. Your investment in the annuities will be increased if you borrowed any of the proceeds and they were included as taxable income for contracts purchased after October 21, 1998.

*⊠ If I need to withdraw my entire annuity to meet an emergency but later put the entire sum back, will there be any penalties?*

The insurer may extend a grace period for withdrawals and subsequent deposits. However, the IRS will require that any taxes due be paid.

### After the start date

*⊠ I will soon begin receiving monthly payments from my deferred annuity. How will these payments be taxed?*

Your payments will be partially taxable and partially nontaxable. Part of each payment is considered a *return of* your invested capital and is therefore nontaxable, and part of each payment is considered a *return on* your capital and is therefore taxable at an ordinary-income tax rate.

*⊠ I have a variable annuity and a fixed annuity. Are they taxed the same?*

Yes. Both are taxed the same.

*⊠ How do I determine the nontaxable portion of each annuity payment?*

You must first calculate the exclusion ratio for your distributions. Take your total investment, or basis, in the contract and divide by the expected return:

$$\text{Exclusion ratio} = \frac{\text{investment in contract}}{\text{expected return}}$$

## Chap. 5: Annuities

Multiplying the payment amount by the exclusion ratio yields the nontaxable portion of each payment.

### After death

⬧ *If I have money in an annuity at my death, what are the estate tax consequences?*

As with any asset you own, the value of your undistributed annuity is taxed in your estate regardless of whether the payments are made to your estate or to a named beneficiary.

⬧ *If I die before receiving the full payout benefits under a fixed-period, refund, or life-certain annuity, is my spouse, as my beneficiary, entitled to receive the remaining money tax-free?*

Yes and no. Your spouse, as the beneficiary, would be entitled to tax-free recovery of only the remaining nontaxable portion of the balance in the contract. Any amounts in excess of your original investment would be taxed as ordinary income.

⬧ *Is it true that the beneficiaries of my annuity will not get a step-up in basis on this asset at my death?*

Most of your property will receive a *step-up in basis* when passed to your beneficiaries at your death; that is, the value of the assets will be increased from your original costs to their fair market values on the date of your death. Annuities, however, do not receive such a benefit. Consequently, when your beneficiaries receive distributions from your annuity, they will pay ordinary-income tax rates on the gains the annuity earned above the value of your original contribution in the annuity.

⬧ *If I die before I am 59½, will my beneficiaries be subject to the 10 percent penalty for early withdrawal?*

No. If you die before 59½, your beneficiaries are not subject to the 10 percent penalty.

278                                    WAYS AND MEANS

*If I die before receiving enough payments to equal my invest-
ment in an annuity, can my heirs report a loss on my final
tax return?*

Yes. Your estate is allowed to report a loss equal to the unrecovered
investment if you selected a payment method which terminates
at your death and you die before recovering all of your investment
in the annuity.

## TAX PLANNING

### Income Tax Planning

*I'm paying an individual income tax rate of 39.6 percent. I
primarily invest in equity-type investments with significant
appreciation potential. If I invest in an annuity using the same
investment philosophy, will I receive the same tax treatment
as I do on my gains at sale?*

No. If your investment in your annuity has a gain due to capital
appreciation, when you begin to take distributions, it will all be
taxed at your 39.6 percent tax rate, regardless of its original character. Under the Taxpayer Relief Act of 1997 and the IRS Restructuring and Reform Act of 1998, the maximum federal rate
on capital gains has been reduced from 28 to 20 percent on most
property held for more than 12 months.

*With the new capital gain tax rates, should I invest my money
in a variable annuity contract?*

At first glance, the lower tax rate on capital gains makes variable
annuities look less attractive because earnings on the annuity will
eventually be taxed as ordinary income.

Remember, annuities are not suited for everyone, but if you
are in a high tax bracket, an annuity can offer considerable tax

CHAP. 5: ANNUITIES                                                           279

benefits. Also, it depends on what type of assets you are investing in within the annuity. If you are investing in ordinary-income-type assets (bonds), you are not going to be affected by the lowering of the capital gain tax bracket because you are earning ordinary income.

If you are investing in capital gain–type assets, you may have to keep the investment inside the annuity a few more years to make up for the lowered tax brackets. Note that this analysis depends on whether or not you are an active trader of the portfolio.

Furthermore, with rising mutual fund trading volume and turnover rates, there are bound to be shorter asset holding periods. In order to receive long-term capital gain treatment, the manager must hold securities for 18 months or more. Realistically, only a small share of mutual fund capital gains will get the new 20 percent rate.

*How much should income tax planning come into play in my investment strategy?*

If you are retired, you should look at every avenue for increasing your retirement income. Having the opportunity to lower tax estimates saves real dollars. Shifting currently taxable assets to investments with tax-deferred status can make a real difference in cash flow. A special benefit can accrue if most of your retirement income comes from Social Security, dividends, and interest. By moving assets to tax-deferred annuities, you can often reduce or exclude the income tax being paid on your Social Security.

*I have my money in CDs that generate taxable income which I don't need now but will need sometime. Will purchasing an annuity give me any current income tax advantages?*

Let's look at an example: Suppose you and your spouse have a $20,000 pension, $30,000 interest income from CDs, and $18,000 of Social Security benefits. Since your taxable income is

$50,000 ($20,000 pension and $30,000 of interest), 85 percent of your Social Security is taxed. Upon maturity, the CDs could be invested in a single-premium deferred annuity. In this way, the $30,000 taxable income becomes tax-deferred income in the annuity, and your taxable income drops to $20,000. The taxes on your Social Security could be reduced or even eliminated. This is one of the most valuable uses of annuities in retirement planning today.

*My spouse and I have money that we don't plan to spend during our lifetimes. Should we use an annuity?*

Probably not. Because of the growth of the annuity, you might create a higher tax bracket for your beneficiaries However, you should consult with your financial advisor.

*Is there an advantage in using annuities from the installment sale of my business?*

Yes! Let's look at an example: We'll assume that you are ready to retire and sell your business for $1 million, to be paid over a 5-year period with 9 percent interest. You do not need the principal and do not want current taxable income. You can use the income-deferral techniques of annuities to defer the money until you need it. This allows you to use the interest, pension plan, and Social Security over the next 5 years and defer all the investment return on the sale of your business.

## Estate Tax Planning

*I have an annuity that has not been annuitized. If I die before my wife, who is the beneficiary of the annuity, must she either take a lump sum or begin immediate periodic payments?*

Your wife does not have to do either. As your surviving spouse, she could elect to treat the entire annuity as her own and make

CHAP. 5: ANNUITIES                                                    281

contributions to it, or she could roll it over. The contract becomes your wife's, and she can make new beneficiary designations if she does so before the first required distribution. In this way, your surviving spouse could name a younger designated beneficiary and the required distributions could be made over the younger person's longer life expectancy.

*I have a large amount of my assets in annuities, and my wife is the beneficiary. I've established a trust under my will in order to save federal estate taxes. Can these assets be used to fund the trust?*

No. Since the proceeds from your annuities will be passed by beneficiary designation rather than through the terms of your will, these assets are not available to fund this trust.

*Are there any pitfalls to owning annuities in my living trust?*

At your death, your trust becomes irrevocable and must be given its own tax ID number. At that time, the trust, as the owner, becomes a "nonnatural person" for purposes of receiving payments from an annuity. Income on the contract (any increase over the year in surrender value, adjusted for contributions and distributions) will be fully taxable in the year earned. Since that is the case, and since annuities are not subject to probate anyway, some professionals advise clients to own annuities outside their living trusts.

## GIFTS OF ANNUITIES

*Can I give my annuity away? If so, what are the income tax consequences?*

You are allowed to make a gift of your annuity. In that circum-

282 WAYS AND MEANS

stance, you are generally taxed for income tax purposes on the difference between your contributions and the cash surrender value of the annuity at the time of the gift. The recipient of your gift will be taxed on any further gain in the contract when he or she begins taking distributions. In contrast, gifts of stocks or other types of appreciated property create no income-taxable event for you. With the annuity, your recipient steps into your shoes in regard to your cost basis in the investment.

*What are the estate tax consequences of making a gift of an annuity?*

If you retain no incidents of ownership in the annuity, the value of the annuity will generally not be included in your gross estate. If you retain the right to be a refund beneficiary, the value of the refund could be taxable in your estate, valued as if the refund took place at your death.

*I purchased an annuity and later gave the contract to my daughter. Is this considered a gift, and if it is, what value do I place on it?*

Giving the annuity to your daughter is considered a gift. The value of the gift is the fair market value of the annuity on the date of the gift. You will owe the income tax on the entire amount of the gain in the annuity.

*I purchased a joint and survivor annuity for my benefit and my brother's benefit. Are there any gift tax consequences?*

Yes. The gift tax value is the cost of the annuity less the cost attributable to a single-life annuity on yourself.

*If I am the annuitant and I name an irrevocable beneficiary*

CHAP. 5: ANNUITIES                                                        283

*under a refund annuity, is this considered a gift? If it is, can
it be used in conjunction with my $10,000 annual exclusions?*

It is considered a gift even though the refund beneficiary gets
nothing unless you die. However, since your gift is contingent
upon your death within a specified period, it is considered a gift
of a future interest, not a gift of a present interest. Only gifts of
a present interest—meaning the recipient has the immediate use
of the property—qualify for the annual exclusion.

*I gave my wife a direct gift of an annuity contract. Does this
gift qualify for the gift tax marital deduction?*

Yes. If your gift was of a direct nature and no one else had an
interest in it, it is similar to a gift of any other kind of property
and thus qualifies for the gift tax marital deduction. (The gift tax
marital deduction is similar in concept to the estate tax marital
deduction, as explained in Chapter 7). Your wife must have a
right to the income from the property for her life and a general
power of appointment over the principal or a "qualified income
interest for life in the qualified terminable interest property." Furthermore, you, as the donor, must make this election in the year
you make the transfer.

The marital deduction cannot be taken if the gift is of a life
estate or some other terminable interest unless it meets certain
statutory requirements for qualification.

*Can I take a charitable income tax deduction if give an an-
nuity to a qualified charitable organization?*

1.  For annuities issued before April 27, 1987, you may take a
    deduction for the full maturity value of the contract, subject
    to limitations for charitable deductions. However, you must
    include as income the amount by which the cash surrender
    value exceeds your basis in the annuity.

2. For annuities issued after April 27, 1987, you may take a charitable deduction for the value of the annuity at the time of transfer, subject to limitations for charitable deductions. However you must include as income in the year of the gift the amount by which the cash surrender value exceeds your basis in the annuity.

## QUALIFIED ANNUITIES

*Does the income tax law make any distinctions among annuities?*

Yes. In general, the tax law classifies an annuity as either a qualified annuity or a nonqualified annuity.

*What is a qualified annuity?*

A *qualified annuity* is used as a holding vehicle for pension or retirement money. In essence, a qualified annuity is a regular annuity which sits inside a qualified retirement plan or IRA. Generally, qualified annuities are those allowed under Internal Revenue Code Section 401 (employer-sponsored plans, discussed in Chapter 2), Section 403 (plans sponsored by nonprofit entities, discussed in Chapter 2), and Section 408 (individual retirement accounts, discussed in Chapter 3). The original investment can be made as an employer contribution, payroll deduction, IRA deposit, or rollover from another retirement plan.

Qualified annuities generally receive the same special income tax advantages that are associated with qualified retirement plans. Contributions are not subject to income taxation at the time of deposit into the annuity. The full amount of withdrawals—principal and interest earned—from a qualified annuity will be taxed as ordinary income.

CHAP. 5: ANNUITIES                                                285

### ⚐ *What is a nonqualified annuity?*

Practically speaking, a *nonqualified annuity* is any annuity that is not a qualified annuity. In this chapter, the discussion up to this point has been about nonqualified annuities.

### ⚐ *Can annuities be in a qualified retirement plan?*

Yes. An annuity may be used to fund many types of qualified retirement plans. If your qualified retirement plan or IRA is invested in an annuity, the annuity is often referred to as a qualified annuity.

### ⚐ *My pension plan is an annuity. What does this mean?*

Your pension is a defined-benefit plan. It is a promise by your employer to pay you a monthly amount for the rest of your life (and sometimes to pay your spouse if you die).

### ⚐ *Are annuities a bad vehicle for investment in a qualified plan but good outside one?*

Annuities, whether in a qualified plan or not, grow on a tax-deferred basis during the accumulation years. They can then be annuitized to guarantee a lifetime of income—an attractive feature for many retirees. In a qualified retirement plan, however, the growth is sheltered by both the annuity and the retirement plan. Some experts say there is no need to pay for this "double shelter." The administrative costs within an annuity contract are usually higher than the administrative costs of a retirement account custodian.

However, an annuity contract will sometimes include features important to the goals of certain individuals, such as the ability to receive a guaranteed income you cannot outlive or a guarantee (through life insurance built into the contract) that your beneficiaries will receive at least the amount of your original investment.

Thus, depending upon your goals, an annuity may be a smart choice inside or outside a qualified plan.

*A variable annuity has been recommended to me for half my IRA. Since IRAs are already tax-deferred, should I reject this recommendation?*

It depends upon your goals. Variable annuities offer a number of significant benefits, apart from tax advantages, which can prove to be of tremendous importance to owners.

Most variable annuities offer fixed investment accounts, in addition to a wide variety of stock and bond portfolio choices. This means that your IRA can be managed through a single provider, which makes it easier to change asset allocations when necessary and reduces record keeping and paperwork.

Also, variable annuities provide protection through the death benefit, which many investors regard as vitally important. No one can predict if he or she will die when the market is up. Even though we have experienced a prolonged period of rising stock prices, it is important to remember that prices can decline. The death benefit guarantees that if you die with assets in an annuity, your beneficiaries will receive at least the amount you invested.

Many contracts go a step further and offer "stepped-up" benefits that lock in investment gains for your beneficiaries. This allows you to consider more aggressive strategies without risk that the market might be in a low cycle at the time of your death. This is a very real comfort to more conservative individuals, and it is covered by the charges variable annuities impose.

If these features appear beneficial, you might want to use an annuity for at least a portion of your IRA proceeds.

*What are the major tax differences between a nonqualified deferred annuity and a nondeductible IRA?*

Your deferred annuity has (1) no limits to annual contributions,

CHAP. 5: ANNUITIES                                    287

(2) no minimum distribution rules before your death, and (3) no required distributions at age 70½.

⚔ *I'm planning to take an annuity from my qualified pension when I retire. What part of this annuity payment will be taxable?*

Annuity payments are fully taxable as ordinary income if you did not contribute any after-tax dollars to your pension or if you have previously received all your after-tax contributions.

⚔ *Is there ever a situation where qualified retirement plan payments would not be taxable?*

Certainly. After-tax contributions that you have made to your employer's pension or qualified plan will be returned as nontaxable payments; however, beginning in 1997, you must follow a new rule in order to determine how much of each payment is a return of cost basis—an after-tax contribution. Further, the recovery factors used to determine the tax-free portion of an annuity payment from a qualified plan have been changed. IRS Publication 575, *Pension and Annuity Income,* provides the factors for the computation.

# chapter 6

## Distributions from Retirement Plans

In the last couple of years, Congress and the IRS have been extremely active in reviewing the rules for distributions from retirement plans. Two recent tax laws, the Taxpayer Relief Act of 1997 and the IRS Restructuring and Reform Act of 1998, as well as recent amendments to IRS regulations, have greatly changed and clarified how taxpayers take distributions.

In this chapter, our contributors lead us through concerns and opportunities for early (before retirement) distributions, review minimum distribution requirements and options, and discuss how your charitable goals affect your distributions.

Recent enactments have made the coordination of your retirement plan distributions and your estate planning goals more predictable. Professionals have become more aware that attention must be paid to distributions both during your lifetime and after your death. One of the greatest turnarounds in advisors' "com-

290                                    WAYS AND MEANS

mon knowledge" is that, properly handled, your retirement plan can be one of the best assets to pass to your heirs, rather than one of the worst, as was frequently thought just a few short years ago. The concept of the stretch-out IRA, reviewed in detail in this chapter, has revolutionized distribution planning.

### ᴬ *Why should I review the distributions from my IRA?*

Your IRA may be your most important asset. It can be one of the most complicated assets and often requires the most sophisticated planning for income tax and estate planning purposes. Yet it is also one of the most underplanned assets.

IRA assets are not taxed by federal or state governments until distributed to you during your life or to your estate or beneficiaries at your death. There are rules for taking early distributions which, if not planned, can trigger penalties and income taxes.

Rules regarding required distributions and various distribution "elections," or choices, are available to you but only if you make those elections before your *required beginning date*—the date you are required to begin taking distributions.

IRA agreements vary by institution but are generally designed to suit the small IRA owner. Most institutions disclaim any responsibility for the required elections and tax consequences. These are solely your responsibilities, but if you are unaware of your deadlines and options, you and your beneficiaries may be irrevocably stuck with the default provisions of the institution's agreement once the deadline passes.

It may come as no surprise, but for the typical IRA agreement, the underlying law and IRS regulations are not designed to save taxes for you and your beneficiaries. In fact, the regulations for distributions are geared primarily for average retirees with modest IRA or qualified retirement plan assets (i.e., $250,000 or less).

If you have an IRA, you should seek competent advice and properly structure your payout election and beneficiary designation or deadlines for planning opportunities may expire before you take action to properly plan your income tax and estate plan-

CHAP. 6: DISTRIBUTIONS FROM RETIREMENT PLANS  291

ning affairs. Also, it is important to plan your IRA withdrawals in conjunction with your estate plan as your payout is affected by your choice of beneficiary.

🔖 *Why should I review my qualified retirement plan distributions?*

You should review your qualified retirement plans for many of the same reasons you should review your IRAs. If you have a qualified plan, you will one day have to deal with an early, lump-sum, or required plan distribution. You should review your plan's early-distribution rules, minimum distribution requirements, lump-sum distribution options, rollover options, and forward-averaging opportunities before electing plan distributions. You may also qualify for special capital gain treatment on any pre-1974 contribution.

While IRA documents might offer similar planning options, this is not the case with qualified retirement plans. You must become knowledgeable about your qualified plan and the options available. Many times you will find that not all options available under the law will be available under your plan. This could conflict with your income, estate, and personal planning goals. Many times the only solution will be to roll over your qualified retirement plan money to an IRA to achieve the flexibility to meet your goals.

## EARLY-DISTRIBUTION RULES

### Penalties and Exceptions for Early Distributions

#### Deductible IRAs

🔖 *What does "early distribution" mean with regard to my deductible IRAs?*

You can take money out of a deductible IRA at any time; however, if you take the distributions before age 59½, they are considered *early,* or too soon, *distributions* and, with some exceptions, are subject to a 10 percent penalty. This penalty applies to all distributions taken before you are 59½ whether or not you are "retired."

In addition, because you received an income tax deduction for the contribution when you made it, you will have to pay income tax on the contribution when you withdraw it.

Once you reach the age of 59½, the 10 percent penalty no longer applies; however, the amounts you withdraw are still taxable income to you in the year of withdrawal.

⚑ *What are the exceptions to the 10 percent early-distribution penalty for my deductible IRA?*

Some of the most useful exceptions to the 10 percent penalty are:

DEATH    The penalty tax disappears if you die. Your beneficiary will not be subject to the 10 percent penalty tax, even if your beneficiary is under the age of 59½.

DISABILITY    If certain requirements are met, the penalty tax is not imposed on distributions due to your disability.

QUALIFYING FIRST-TIME HOME BUYING EXPENSES    The Taxpayer Relief Act of 1997 created the first-time home buyer exception. You can withdraw up to $10,000 during your lifetime from your IRA before age 59½ without penalty if you use those funds (within 120 days from the date of distribution) for expenses of buying the first home for you, your spouse, or the child, grandchild, or ancestors of you or your spouse. A first-time home buyer is one who has not owned a principal residence within the last 2 years.

HIGHER-EDUCATION EXPENSES    The Taxpayer Relief Act of 1997 also created the exception for unlimited withdrawals for higher-education expenses for you, your spouse, your children, and your grandchildren. This is true regardless of whether you are claiming your children or grandchildren as dependents. These expenses include tuition, fees, books, supplies, equipment, and room and board if it is required in order to attend. If your college or university has a prepaid tuition program, those payments would also escape the 10 percent penalty.

UNEMPLOYMENT   With certain qualifications, you may make withdrawals if you are unemployed.

SUBSTANTIALLY EQUAL PAYMENTS   You can avoid the 10 percent penalty tax if you begin taking distributions in substantially equal payments under Internal Revenue Code Section 72(t).

QUALIFIED ROLLOVER   A rollover to another IRA will not trigger the 10 percent tax.

> *I understand that as a first-time home buyer, I may take early withdrawal of up to $10,000 from my IRA for "qualified acquisition costs" with respect to my new home. Is there any reason why I might not want to do this?*

Although early withdrawal for this purpose seems attractive, there are at least three reasons why you might not want to do this:

First, if your state protects your IRA from your creditors more than it protects your residence from creditors, you would lose some creditor protection by making a first-time home buyer withdrawal.

Second, the discipline in allowing your IRA assets to compound tax-deferred year after year is broken to the extent of an early withdrawal. However, you might conclude that the anticipated return on your home will be just as good as the tax-deferred compounding inside an IRA.

Third, you will probably still have to pay current ordinary income tax on the IRA withdrawal.

> *I am currently unemployed. Can I withdraw from my IRA without penalty?*

You may be eligible to withdraw funds from your IRA if you meet the following requirements for unemployed individuals:

1.  The total amount of the withdrawals does not exceed the total amount of payments you have to make for qualifying insurance premiums. *Qualifying premiums* are deductible premiums for your medical care and that of your spouse and dependents. To be excluded, the distributions must be received in the tax year during which unemployment compensation is received or in the following year, and you must still be unemployed when the distribution from the IRA is received.

2.  You have received federal or state unemployment compensation for 12 consecutive weeks. If you are self-employed, you will be treated as having received unemployment compensation for 12 consecutive weeks if, under federal or state law, you would have received that unemployment compensation but for being self-employed.

*If I make an early withdrawal from my IRA to make a direct payment for health care, will I still face both an income tax on the withdrawal and a 10 percent early-distribution penalty?*

Yes, you will be subject to the 10 percent penalty. As for income tax, you should consult your income tax advisor about whether you may deduct health care expenses if you itemize deductions.

*I am 58 years old and want a regular income from my IRA. I have heard that I can avoid the 10 percent penalty by taking "substantially equal payments." Could you explain this to me?*

Understanding the basic rules set forth by Internal Revenue Code Section 72(t) is important. In order to avoid the 10 percent penalty tax, you must choose from one of three different methods to receive the distributions, and you, as the account owner, must take the distributions monthly, quarterly, or annually. Once you begin taking the payments, you must continue taking them throughout the *required payment period,* which is until you either

CHAP. 6: DISTRIBUTIONS FROM RETIREMENT PLANS  295

reach 59½ or have taken them for 5 years, whichever is later. You cannot change the distributions before the end of this required payment period unless you die or become disabled.

Violation of any of these rules might result in the 10 percent penalty (plus interest) being assessed on all previous withdrawals from the IRA.

*How are substantially equal payments determined?*

There are three available methods for taking substantially equal payments, all of which are initially calculated on *life expectancy.* Simply stated, life expectancy is the number of years you are expected to live given your current age. Life expectancy is taken from tables published by the Internal Revenue Service and can be found in IRS Publications 590 and 939. These tables provide single life expectancy and joint life expectancy. Joint life expectancy is the number of expected years until the death of the survivor of two individuals, given their current ages.

Under any of the three methods, you can use your single life expectancy or the joint life expectancy of you and another person. Choosing joint life expectancy will always result in a smaller payment than single life expectancy does. The three methods for taking substantially equal payments include life expectancy, amortization, and annuitization:

LIFE EXPECTANCY  Under this method, the retirement account balance is divided by the number of years in the life expectancy option you choose. You can elect to make this calculation once when you begin taking the distributions, or you can elect to recalculate your life expectancy each year, which results in a lower payment.

Of the three methods, the life expectancy method tends to yield the smallest payment amount. However, under the life expectancy method, the required payment will increase each year.

AMORTIZATION  Again, the initial calculation is made on life expectancy. However, with amortization, the retirement account balance is also projected to grow at an assumed rate of return each year.

Although *rate of return* is defined by the Internal Revenue Code, the definition is subject to various interpretations. Many experts agree that the safest position is to utilize a rate of return not to exceed 120 percent of the 2-year treasury instrument at the time you begin the substantial and equal payment distributions. Conversations with the IRS indicate that a rate of return commensurate with the expected return of a particular investment can be suitable as well. In an effort to remain compliant with the government's requirements, some investment companies limit the interest rate that they will accept for use in exempt distributions. In light of the tremendous growth of equity investments in recent years, investment companies, or mutual fund companies, have been known to accept rates that do not exceed 12 percent.

The amortization method produces a larger annual payment than the life expectancy method. However, unlike the life expectancy method, under the amortization method the payment will remain the same each year.

ANNUITIZATION    Under annuitization, the account balance is divided by an annuity factor which represents the present value of an annuity of $1 per year through life expectancy. This method can give you the highest amount, but it also depletes your balance faster. Like the amortization method, under the annuitization method, the annual payment remains the same each year.

For example, assume that you and your wife are both 50 years old and your IRA is currently worth $300,000. Table 6-1 shows the required monthly withdrawal for the *first* year under the three methods outlined above whether you choose a single life or a joint life expectancy calculation. The example assumes that 7.5 percent is a reasonable rate of return.

The choice of the payment method will depend upon your goals and desires and should only be done after consultation with your professional advisor.

CHAP. 6: DISTRIBUTIONS FROM RETIREMENT PLANS **297**

**TABLE 6-1 Comparison of Substantially Equal Payments Methods**

| Method | Life expectancy calculation | |
|---|---|---|
| | Single | Joint |
| Life expectancy | $ 756 | $ 639 |
| Amortization | 2064 | 1992 |
| Annuitization | 2250 | 2250 |

*⋏ Does my substantially equal payment plan have to be in monthly payments?*

Substantially equal payments could be taken weekly, monthly, quarterly, or annually. It is up to you within the parameters of your IRA agreement.

Your trustee or custodian will issue an IRS Form 1099 for the total distributions made to you in the course of the year, whether you withdrew $12,000 once during the year or $233 per week.

*⋏ What if I don't need as much as the Section 72(t) calculations say I should take?*

You must still take the required payments, or the 10 percent penalty tax will be imposed.

*⋏ What if I get 3 years into the substantially equal payment plan on this IRA and I need to increase the distributions. Can I take extra money from the IRA?*

The requirements of the plan would be "violated," and the 10 percent penalty would be imposed.

However, there is a possible way to avoid this problem. Before beginning distributions, you could split the IRA into two IRAs. You could then begin the payments from the first IRA and not modify them until age 59½ or after 5 years, whichever is longer. If, after a few years, you need additional income and you are still younger than 59½, you can begin a separate substantially equal payment plan from the second IRA.

*How is the 10 percent penalty tax calculated if I make a change to an exempt distribution under 72(t) within the 5-year period or before I reach age 59½?*

Unless there is a qualifying event—disability or death—if the payment amount of a substantial and equal distribution is changed within the required payment period, all the penalty taxes that would have been due if the exemption were never taken would then become due. In other words, all taxable amounts from the start of the substantially equal payment distributions would then become subject to the 10 percent early withdrawal penalty tax. Furthermore, the IRS will assess interest on the penalty tax since the inception of the substantially equal payment distribution.

*I am younger than 59½ and just invested money in an IRA that I would rather have in an accessible nonretirement account. Can I get my money out without paying the IRS the 10 percent early withdrawal penalty?*

If you withdraw the contribution in the same year, that is, by the due date of that year's tax return, and do not take a deduction for the contribution, the withdrawal of the contribution does not have tax ramifications. You will, however, have to pay income tax on the IRA's earnings, and because you are not yet 59½, you will have to pay the 10 percent penalty on those earnings.

*Will I pay a penalty for rolling over my traditional IRA to another traditional IRA?*

No. After taking receipt of your IRA money, you have 60 days to

CHAP. 6: DISTRIBUTIONS FROM RETIREMENT PLANS **299**

roll those funds into another IRA of your choice. However, if you do not deposit the funds into a rollover IRA within those 60 days, you will not only pay the penalty but also have to pay the income tax on those funds.

Note that you do not have to transfer the same funds to the IRA rollover, only the *same* amount of money.

Furthermore, if you receive the funds directly from the trustee or custodian of your old IRA, the trustee is required to withhold and forward 10 percent, which will be applied to your income tax return, to the Internal Revenue Service. (You can, however, consent not to have the 10 percent withholding apply.) If, instead, you have the trustee transfer the funds directly from your old IRA account to the new IRA rollover account (known as a direct transfer), no withholding is required.

### Roth IRAs

🔖 *What are the rules for early withdrawals for my new nondeductible Roth IRA?*

Like a deductible IRA, you can take money out of your Roth IRA at any time. Unlike the deductible IRA, however, you will *not* pay income tax on withdrawals of contributions. Also, you will not pay income tax on the distribution of your accumulated earnings if they are a *qualified* distribution. If the distribution of your accumulated earnings is not a qualified distribution, then you will pay income tax on the earnings you withdraw. However, the code gives you a break because any amounts withdrawn from a Roth IRA are first deemed to be your contributions up to the aggregate total of all contributions from all Roth IRAs, and only thereafter are they considered to be your earnings.

🔖 *What is a qualified distribution of earnings from a Roth IRA?*

A distribution of accumulated earnings from your Roth IRA is considered qualified if it is made after a 5-year tax period (beginning generally with the first tax year in which contributions were

300  WAYS AND MEANS

made to the Roth IRA) *and* it meets one of following four requirements:

1. It is made on or after you reach age 59½.
2. It is given after your death to your beneficiary.
3. It is made because you are disabled.
4. It is made to pay for expenses directly incurred for the purchase of a principal residence, as a first-time home buyer, for you, your spouse, your children, your grandchildren, or the ancestors of you or your spouse. The maximum distribution to cover these acquisition expenses cannot exceed the lifetime limit of $10,000, and the distribution must be used within 120 days.

✒ *Does the 10 percent penalty tax apply to my Roth IRA?*

Yes. The 10 percent penalty tax generally applies to all IRAs, including the Roth IRA. However, the penalty tax is a tax equal to 10 percent of the withdrawals from the IRA which are included in gross income. Since contributions withdrawn from a Roth IRA are never included in gross income, the 10 percent penalty tax does not apply to withdrawals of contributions.

If you withdraw the earnings from a Roth IRA before age 59½, the 10 percent penalty tax will be imposed unless an exception applies. The exceptions for the Roth IRA are the same as a deductible IRA. Some of the exceptions are:

- Death
- Disability
- Qualifying expenses for first-time home buyers
- Higher-education expenses
- Unemployment
- Substantially equal payments
- Qualified rollover

# Chap. 6: Distributions from Retirement Plans · 301

## *Qualified retirement plans*

### 401(k) plans

⋈ *When am I allowed to take money out of my 401(k) without any penalty?*

You have several opportunities for withdrawing funds from your 401(k) plan:

- At age 59½
- On death, disability, retirement, or termination of employment
- If the company cancels the 401(k) and does not replace it with another type of plan
- If you can show a hardship that requires the distribution of funds from the plan
- If you take substantially equal payments under Internal Revenue Code Section 72(t)
- On a qualified rollover to another qualified retirement plan or IRA
- If the company sells all or substantially all its assets to a corporation or sells or disposes of a subsidiary

*Note:* If you as the employee continue to work for the company that was sold, you may take monies out of the 401(k) plan on the date of sale. For this method of withdrawal to work, the purchasing entity must not be a partnership.

⋈ *What is a "hardship" with regard to my taking distributions from my 401(k) plan?*

You may take money from your 401(k) plan without penalty by meeting both of the following conditions:

1. You must have an immediate and heavy financial need.
2. It must be necessary to use 401(k) monies to meet this need; that is, you have no other resources or ways of satisfying the need.

The hardship may be determined by looking at the facts and circumstances of your individual situation, or the 401(k) plan may set forth certain situations that conclusively satisfy the "immediate and heavy financial need" part of the test. Some examples of needs that qualify for hardship are funeral expenses, college tuition for your child or yourself, medical expenses for you and your immediate family, purchase of a home, or prevention of eviction from or foreclosure of your home.

*I am 50 and just took an early retirement offer from my company. I rolled over my 401(k) to an IRA and am looking for a job but haven't found one yet. I need income now. What do I do?*

You might consider starting a substantially equal payment plan now. If, after several months, you find the job of your dreams, you can make the decision to terminate the payment plan and pay the 10 percent penalty on the money you have already withdrawn. It may be more advantageous to pay this relatively small penalty now and keep the remainder of the payments in the tax-deferred IRA where they will continue to grow until you are 59½.

*I'm younger than 55. Can I withdraw my 401(k) funds, use part of the money to pay bills, and roll over the balance into my IRA?*

Provided that the terms of the 401(k) plan would allow a withdrawal (e.g., on separation of service), the money is yours, and you can do what you want with it. However, this may not be exactly the way you want to do it.

First, let's assume your account balance is $20,000. The

401(k) trustee will withhold 20 percent, or $4000, for taxes as he or she is required to do if the distribution is going anywhere other than to another qualified plan or IRA account. You will receive 80 percent, or $16,000. From that money you pay bills of $2000 leaving you with a balance of $14,000 to roll over into an IRA. To avoid paying a penalty on all but the $2000, you need $18,000 to roll over, but you don't have it. You are short by $4000 because it was withheld to pay taxes. In this scenario, to pay $2000 worth of bills, you will have to pay a penalty of $600: 10 percent on the $2000 plus 10 percent on the $4000 withheld for taxes. To avoid the extra $400 penalty, you would have to come up with $4000 from other sources for the rollover. Of course, next year when you file your tax return, you should receive a refund of the $4000, but, in the meantime, you are still out of pocket $4000.

The better way to do this is to have your trustee roll the $20,000 over to the IRA account and then withdraw what you need from the IRA to pay the bills.

### Other qualified retirement plans

*When can I take money out of my qualified retirement plan?*

You can generally take money out of your qualified retirement plan at any time as long as the withdrawal is permitted under the terms of the plan; however, with some exceptions, the 10 percent early-withdrawal penalty may apply.

*If I die before I turn 59½, is my qualified retirement plan subject to 10 percent penalty?*

No. Distributions made after your death from your qualified retirement plan are not subject to the 10 percent penalty.

*If I become disabled, do I have access to my qualified retirement plan money?*

As a participant in a qualified retirement plan, normally you cannot have access to your funds in the event of a disability unless the plan document includes a such a provision. Generally speaking, your employer will have decided whether or not to include this option when the plan was established. Normally, there is no disadvantage to your employer if a disability provision is included, except in the case of a defined-benefit plan. Defined-benefit plans typically guarantee a stated benefit amount at retirement. In order for your employer to ensure that there are enough funds in the plan to make your guaranteed payments at retirement, preretirement distributions will be minimized. Because the company is at risk, it is not desirable to release funds for disability. Conversely, defined contribution plans are more prevalent, and with the advent and evolution of 401(k) profit-sharing plans since the mid-1980s, it is common to include a disability provision to give you greater access to your money.

Essentially, a qualified plan with a disability provision will set forth the guidelines to meet eligibility for payment. There is no 10 percent penalty on these distributions if you are under age 59½; however, all the distributions are subject to federal income tax and any applicable state income tax. Typically under a plan, you qualify for the disability benefit if an independent attending physician certifies that you are disabled. It generally cannot be your personal physician.

*I am 56 years of age. I want to retire and withdraw all my money from my qualified retirement plan. Do I have to wait until 59½ in order to avoid the 10 percent penalty tax?*

No. You have several options. First, if you are at least 55 years of age and you are no longer working for the employer that provided the qualified retirement plan, you can take a distribution from that plan, and it will not be subject to the 10 percent early distribution penalty.

Second, you can receive a pro rata return of any nondeductible contributions that you made into your qualified plan.

CHAP. 6: DISTRIBUTIONS FROM RETIREMENT PLANS  305

Third, you can roll your qualified plan money over into an IRA. You have 60 days to complete the rollover before the 10 percent early-withdrawal penalty applies.

*What are my options if I retire with the company retirement plan before 59½?*

Your options will depend on the company itself. Some companies offer several options for distribution of a retirement plan; others only offer one or two distribution options. The following are a list of the general options available from most companies upon retirement:

- Leave the money in the company's retirement plan.
- Receive an annuity for the rest of your life and your spouse's life.
- Take all the money out of the company plan in one lump sum.
- Roll the money over to an IRA rollover account.

*What happens if I choose to take my qualified retirement funds and transfer them to an IRA rollover account?*

There are two options with regard to transferring funds from a qualified retirement plan into an IRA rollover account.

First, you can have your company issue a check to you in the amount you are transferring, less 20 percent that all companies must take out and send directly to the IRS for an income tax deposit. However, within 60 days of your receipt of the remaining 80 percent, you must deposit an amount equal to 100 percent of the withdrawn funds into an IRA rollover account. Thus you will have to come up with the additional 20 percent from your own resources. You can get back the 20 percent that the company took out when you file your income taxes for that year, but it will obviously be several months before you are able to do so.

Second, you can have the company transfer the retirement funds to an IRA rollover account for you. This method avoids the 20 percent withholding for tax deposit purposes.

With an IRA rollover account, you are not obligated to pay any income tax when you make the transfer, and the IRA rollover account continues the tax-deferred status of your retirement funds. If, however, you take any monies out of the IRA rollover account before you are 59½, you will be subject to the early-withdrawal rules of IRAs, which will require you to pay income taxes and perhaps the 10 percent early-withdrawal penalty.

*My employer will allow me to leave my retirement plan assets in the company-sponsored plan after I retire. What advantages are there to rolling the funds to my own IRA?*

Most employer plans are written with the cost of administering the plan in mind. The result is that most company-sponsored plans are far more restrictive for your beneficiaries than IRAs are. For example, your employer will handle your plan as part of the company's plan because of your value as an employee and the benefits to other employees, officers, and directors of the company. They have little incentive to carry that benefit on for your spouse after your death and no incentive or desire to carry it on for your children. This means that many employer-qualified retirement plan documents severely restrict much, if not all, of your ability to integrate your retirement plan with your estate plan.

Your spouse has certain rights to your qualified plan under the Retirement Equity Act of 1985. Your spouse does not have those rights under an IRA. In some situations you may not want your spouse to have those rights, and this may be a reason to roll over your qualified plan to an IRA.

Greater planning flexibility, in addition to greater investment flexibility, generally make IRAs superior tools. Retirees with all but modest accounts should probably consider an IRA rollover rather than keeping their funds in their former employer's plan.

# CHAP. 6: DISTRIBUTIONS FROM RETIREMENT PLANS    307

⋬ *Why would I consider leaving my money in my former employer's retirement plan instead of rolling it to an IRA?*

If the provisions of your qualified retirement account allow, there are many advantages in keeping plan funds within a qualified plan rather that rolling them into an IRA:

- Qualified plans are better-protected against the plan participant's creditors than those held within an IRA (although current law on this issue is complex and not totally resolved).

- It is possible to obtain loans of up to $50,000 from a qualified plan. An IRA owner cannot borrow from his or her IRA.

- While IRAs cannot own life insurance, a qualified retirement plan can invest in life insurance.

- Favorable 5- or 10-year averaging provisions are available only for distributions from qualified plans. Neither is allowed for a distribution from a rollover IRA.

- A spouse's right to IRA assets might be cut off once the spouse consents to the rollover. Spousal rights might be better protected in a qualified plan.

⋬ *I want to retire before age 59½. Can I elect to take substantially equal payments from my qualified retirement plan and avoid the 10 percent penalty?*

Yes. Just like IRAs, under Section 72(t), you can take equal installments without penalty from your qualified retirement plan, including a profit-sharing plan, money purchase pension plan, or 403(b)(7) plan. These distributions can begin at any time, except for the 403(b) plan in which you must also be separated from service.

The requirements are basically the same as those for IRAs. Distributions must be made using one of three different methods, and once distributions begin, they must continue until you reach 59½ or for 5 years, whichever is later. The distributions cannot be changed before the end of the required payment period unless you die or become disabled. Violation of any of these rules may result in the 10 percent penalty (plus accrued interest) being assessed on all prior withdrawals from the qualified retirement plan.

*I am a health care professional, and although I have ample liability insurance to cover professional negligence, I want to be sure that under federal law my qualified pension plan remains protected from someone who might unexpectedly sue me. Will the transfer or rollover of my pension plan into an IRA weaken this protection?*

State law might or might not give your IRA protection equal to the protection given to your qualified pension plan. You should consult a knowledgeable lawyer in each state in which you expect to live and maintain your IRA.

*Can I roll my simplified employee pension plan money into my savings incentive match plan for employees IRA?*

Savings incentive match plan for employees (SIMPLE) IRA accounts can only house SIMPLE IRA money. Personal IRA and rollovers from other employer-sponsored plans are not allowed.

*Can I roll over my SIMPLE IRA to another IRA in a tax-free, trustee-to-trustee transfer?*

Yes, if you do it after the 2-year period beginning on the first day which your employer deposited contributions in your SIMPLE IRA. If, during this 2-year period, an amount is paid from a SIMPLE IRA directly to the trustee of an IRA that is not a SIM-PLE IRA, the payment is neither a tax-free, trustee-to-trustee transfer nor a rollover contribution. The payment is a distribution from the SIMPLE IRA and a contribution to the other IRA that

Chap. 6: Distributions from Retirement Plans  309

does not qualify as a rollover contribution. After the expiration of the 2-year period, an amount in a SIMPLE IRA can be transferred in a tax-free, trustee-to-trustee transfer to an IRA that is not a SIMPLE IRA.

*Can I transfer a distribution from my tax-sheltered annuity to an IRA?*

If distributions from a tax-sheltered annuity (TSA) are received in the form of an annuity, the distribution cannot be rolled over into an IRA. You must also be aware that any distribution equal to less than half of the value of the TSA cannot be rolled into an IRA.

## Early Distributions and Income Tax

*Is there a circumstance when it could be prudent to make a premature distribution from a qualified plan, IRA, 403(b,) or other retirement vehicle even in the face of incurring the 10 percent early-distribution penalty?*

It would depend upon your reasons for the distribution. If for personal reasons you needed the money, if you had large deductible losses in a given year that would offset the 10 percent penalty tax, or if your overall tax bracket (including the 10 percent penalty tax) is relatively low, it might make sense.

In addition, if you have an adjusted gross income below $100,000 and are considering a rollover of qualified retirement accounts to the new Roth IRA, it may be acceptable to take the 10 percent early-withdrawal penalty. This strategy would clearly depend on the time horizon and projected rate of return, as well as your income and estate tax brackets. *Projections should be made cautiously.*

## Lump-Sum Distributions
## and Income Tax

*What are the pros and cons with regard to my taking all my money from my retirement plan?*

Taking a lump-sum distribution from your retirement plan means that you simply take all the money out of the plan. At such time you have total control of the funds and can do whatever you like with them. However, all the previously deferred income tax comes due upon such a distribution as ordinary income for the year of such distribution. Depending on the size of your retirement plan funds, this income tax could be substantial.

The biggest disadvantage to taking a lump-sum distribution is that you no longer enjoy any tax deferral. If you invest your retirement funds in any other investment, you will probably have to pay taxes on the income from those investments.

*Are there any special income tax rules that apply to lump-sum distributions from qualified pension plans?*

Yes, there is special federal income tax treatment for lump-sum distributions. Congress has changed these rules so often that it has almost become a full-time job just to keep current.

Simply stated, lump-sum tax treatment is available only to qualified plans, such as pension, profit sharing, 401(k) plans, and Keogh plans. IRAs and 403(b) plans do not qualify.

To qualify for lump-sum tax treatment, the distribution from the qualified plan must be made because of the employee's death, the employee's having reached age 59½ or separation of service, or the employee has been a participant in the plan for at least five years.

Lump-sum averaging is available only once for a participant for a particular plan. Distribution of the amount must be made in the same taxable year as it receives the lump-sum treatment. If a wrong move is made, the income taxes can be substantial. Depending on your years of employment, the distribution is taxed

CHAP. 6: DISTRIBUTIONS FROM RETIREMENT PLANS    311

separately under 10-year forward averaging, 5-year forward averaging, or the 20 percent capital gain tax method (available only for the pre-1974 portion of the plan assets). Also, you should make note that not all states allow favorable lump-sum averaging for state income tax purposes.

### ⋈ How does income tax averaging work?

If you qualify for averaging, it can be on a 5-year basis or a 10-year basis. The 5-year averaging calculation is as follows: Divide the lump-sum amount by 5. Calculate the income tax that would be due on that amount. Then multiply the tax by 5. This calculation treats the lump sum as if it were distributed over 5 years, and not added to any other income you may have had for any of those years.

The 10-year averaging uses the same formula as the 5-year averaging, but you divide by 10 instead of 5 and you use 1986 single tax rates instead of current tax rates. You must also have been born before January 1, 1936.

If you select a lump-sum distribution from your retirement plan, you can get a substantial tax savings by using these methods.

### ⋈ What is the difference between an IRA rollover and a lump-sum distribution?

There are many differences between these two methods of distribution. They are the most popular options with regard to retirement plan distributions. However, if you actually calculate how much will be paid to you, for instance, under the same time frame, the same growth rate, and the same income tax rate, the annual income amounts tend to be relatively close.

Keep in mind that with an IRA rollover, even though you get continued tax deferral on the assets, you are much more restricted with regard to access to your funds. There are strict requirements on when you have to take distributions and how much the distribution has to be. Also, you cannot borrow against an IRA or

312 WAYS AND MEANS

put it up for any type of collateral. The federal government dictates all the requirements for you and your retirement funds to come together. Furthermore, if the income tax rates continue to go up, not down, many retirees will pay more tax on the distributions from their IRA rollovers than from the money as a lump-sum distribution.

An advisor practicing in this area should easily be able to do the analysis as to whether a lump-sum distribution is better than doing an IRA rollover.

*Can I buy my own annuity with my retirement funds if I take a lump-sum distribution?*

Yes. Actually, you can purchase a tax-deferred annuity from the company of your choice. You can also purchase an annuity out of your IRA rollover account if that is the option you have chosen for your retirement accounts. Take time to investigate the companies issuing the annuities. The company offering the highest return may not always be the most secure and financially stable company. Unlike an IRA account, an annuity guarantees an income for your life. It will not run out before you die. On the other hand, it is a fixed amount, and you cannot take loans against it if such a need should arise.

## MINIMUM DISTRIBUTION RULES

*What are the minimum distribution rules?*

Congress determined that the principal purpose of qualified retirement plans and IRAs is to provide income during your lifetime, not to provide a vehicle for the transmission of wealth between generations. For this reason, the Internal Revenue Code contains rules which require that distributions—*required minimum distributions*—from a qualified retirement plan or IRA must

# Chap. 6: Distributions from Retirement Plans   313

begin by a certain age—*required beginning date*—and must be distributed each year thereafter in a manner which promotes a distribution over your lifetime. Furthermore, at your death, these rules also determine how quickly any remaining funds must be distributed to your beneficiaries.

## Required Beginning Date and Required Minimum Distributions

*When do I have to start taking distributions from my qualified retirement plan?*

You must begin taking minimum distributions from your qualified retirement plan, as well as your traditional IRAs, by your required beginning date (RBD).

*What is the required beginning date for my traditional IRA?*

Distributions from your traditional (deductible and nondeductible) IRA must *begin* no later than April 1 of the year following the year in which you reach age 70½.

*My seventieth birthday will be this year. What is my required beginning date for distributions from my IRA?*

That depends. If your birthday falls between January 1 and June 30 of this year, the rule says that you turn 70½ this year. Therefore, your RBD will be April 1 of next year.

On the other hand, if your birthday falls between July 1 and December 31 of this year, the rules says that you turn 70½ next year; therefore, your RBD will be April 1 of the year after next.

*Is my required beginning date determined the same way for my qualified retirement plan as it is for the IRA?*

Up until a few years ago the answer was yes. However, under the

314 WAYS AND MEANS

Small Business Job Protection Act of 1996, the required beginning date for qualified retirement plans is the *later* of April 1 of the year following either the year in which you turn 70½ or the year you retire.

Thus, if you continue to work well into your seventies, your requirement beginning date can be postponed. This change only applies to plans sponsored by your current employer and only if you are not a 5 percent owner of the employer.

Furthermore, certain plans that were established under former law have been "grandfathered" and have different rules for the required beginning date.

### *What is my required beginning date for my Roth IRA?*

There is no required beginning date for your Roth IRA. There is *no* requirement that you withdraw any money from your Roth IRA during your lifetime. In fact, you can leave all the money in your Roth IRA and distribute those assets at your death to your spouse, children, other family members, or any other individual or charity.

### *What happens if I fail to take money out of my IRA or qualified retirement plan after my required beginning date?*

Failure to take the required minimum distribution each year will subject you to an excise tax equal to 50 percent of the undistributed amount. For example, if the minimum distribution rules require you to take $20,000 this year and you only withdraw $5000, then you failed to withdraw $15,000, and the penalty tax would be 50 percent, or $7500.

### *Can I withdraw more than my required minimum distribution?*

Before December 31, 1996, under certain circumstances you might have incurred a 15 percent distribution penalty if you with-

# CHAP. 6: DISTRIBUTIONS FROM RETIREMENT PLANS  315

drew too much in a given year. The Taxpayer Relief Act of 1997 removed this 15 percent penalty tax.

The minimum distribution rules only determine the *minimum* amount which you must withdraw each year. *You are always free to withdraw more, without tax penalty.* However, keep in mind that the amount withdrawn will normally be taxable income to you, and you will lose the future income tax deferral on that money.

### ⋠ *Is there any other significance to my required beginning date?*

Yes, by this date you must decide irrevocably—permanently—the payout option under which you will take withdrawals. In general, there are several options from which you can choose. The option you select will determine the required amount to be distributed to you each year—*required minimum distribution (RMD)*—during your lifetime and to your beneficiaries after your death.

These decisions are critical and must be made *before* your required beginning date. You must carefully review your financial needs before reaching age 70½ in order to ensure that you make the proper decisions to accomplish your objectives. The decisions you make cannot be reversed, and to change them after the required beginning date will only result in a form of damage control. You should make your decisions early and with the assistance of your professional advisors.

### ⋠ *How is my required minimum distribution determined each year?*

Generally, it is based upon the value of your IRA or qualified retirement plan as of December 31 of the previous year. The payout option you voluntarily elected (or involuntarily selected by default) as of your required beginning date will usually determine a number of years that you are to receive your distributions. By dividing the account balance by that number of years, you obtain the RMD. For example, if the balance of your IRA was

$150,000 on December 31 of last year, and the payout option calculated a number of years equal to 15, your RMD for this year would be $10,000 (150,000 ÷ 15 = 10,000).

*I turn 70½ this year. Based on what you've told me, my required beginning date is April 1 of next year. When do I actually take the first distribution and on which December 31 is my first RMD determined?*

You *may* take your first RMD this year; but you *must* take it no later than April 1 of next year. However, the RMD for each year thereafter *must* be distributed to you by December 31 of that year.

Your first required minimum distribution is based upon the account balance on December 31 of the year before you turn 70½. Therefore, you will use the value of your qualified retirement plan or IRA as of December 31 of last year and divide it by the number of years under your payout option to determine the amount of your RMD.

*I became 70 on February 12 of this year. If I do not have to make a withdrawal from my IRA until April 1 of next year, why did my accountant tell me to make a withdrawal this year?*

While you are not required to take your *first* RMD until April 1 of next year, you will be required to take your second and subsequent payments by December 31 of each year thereafter.

If you elect to postpone the first withdrawal until next year, then you will be making two withdrawals next year. This could push you into a higher income tax bracket, costing you more total income taxes than would be owing if you spread those withdrawals over this year and next year. Your accountant probably advised you to make a voluntary withdrawal this year in order to save taxes.

CHAP. 6: DISTRIBUTIONS FROM RETIREMENT PLANS **317**

*I turn 70½ this year. Under what circumstances would I elect to take my first IRA withdrawal next year instead of this year?*

There are certain advantages of deferring the payment of taxes as long as possible:

- If you wait until April 1 of next year to take the first withdrawal, the amount of that withdrawal will have at least an extra 3 months to grow tax-free.

- It would give you additional time to liquidate sufficient assets to cover the withdrawal, which might be advantageous from an investment standpoint.

- If you have substantially more income this year than you will next year, you may actually reduce your overall income tax liability for this year by lumping both payments into next year.

- If you expect to have unusually high deductions or offsetting losses, such as a loss from the operation of a business next year, then you might also reduce your overall income tax liability by making two withdrawals next year.

The object is to quantify the advantages of when to take your first RMD and determine whether they outweigh the disadvantages.

## Life Expectancy and Required Minimum Distributions

*Which payout options can I choose from to determine my required minimum distribution?*

There are four accepted payout options available to calculate your RMD. Each payout option is based upon a certain length of time. They are as follows:

- *Your actual lifetime:* Normally this payment would be in the form of an annuity for your lifetime.

- *Your life expectancy:* The number of years you are expected to live based upon your current age.

- *The actual joint lifetime of you and another person:* Again, this payment would normally be in the form of a joint and survivor annuity.

- *The life expectancy of you and another person:* The number of years you and another person are expected to live based upon your current ages.

### ✍ *How is my life expectancy initially determined?*

As mentioned earlier in this chapter, the Internal Revenue Service publishes single life and joint life expectancy tables.

Two of the four payout options available to calculate your yearly RMD are based upon life expectancy. You can choose to take your distributions either over your own life expectancy or use the joint life expectancy of you and another person. By your using life expectancy, the IRS is usually assured that your qualified retirement plans and IRAs are "put back into circulation," that is, made taxable, at least by the end of your life.

### ✍ *What about an example of single and joint life expectancy?*

Yes. If you are 70, your life expectancy according to the IRS tables is 16.0 years. In other words, the IRS expects you to live to age 86. (Of course, in reality, one of three things will happen: you will die before 86, you will die at 86, or you will die after 86.)

If you and your spouse are both 70, your joint life expectancy according to the IRS tables is 20.6 years. This means that the survivor of the two of you is expected to live to age 90.6.

### ✍ *How do I calculate my first required minimum distribution if I use the life expectancy payout option?*

Your first RMD is calculated by dividing the total fair market

CHAP. 6: DISTRIBUTIONS FROM RETIREMENT PLANS  319

value (FMV) of your qualified retirement plan or IRA as of December 31 of the preceding year by the applicable life expectancy (LE):

$$RMD = FMV \div LE$$

For example, assume you and your spouse are both 70, and the fair market value of your IRA is $600,000. With a single life expectancy method, the IRS tables have you living 16.0 years, and your RMD is $37,500:

$$\$600,000 \div 16.0 = \$37,500$$

With the joint life expectancy method, the IRS tables have one of you living 20.6 years, and your RMD is $29,126:

$$\$600,000 \div 20.6 = \$29,126$$

The example illustrates that the greater the life expectancy, the lower the RMD.

⚖ *What guidelines could I use in making the decision between single life and joint life expectancy to determine the RMD?*

Since the joint life expectancy of any two persons will always be longer than the single life expectancy for either of them, joint life expectancy will always produce a lower RMD.

This is important to understand. If you wish to maximize the continued tax-deferral benefit of your qualified retirement plan or IRA, the smaller the amount of money you should take out in RMDs, so more remains in the retirement account growing tax-free for a longer period of time. The power of tax deferral on an investment is incredible.

Since you can always take out more than the required minimum amount in any year, but not less than the RMD, joint life expectancy offers the most flexibility because you can use it to establish the lower RMD and then take out more if you need it.

*My ancestors all lived into their 90s. I know that my life expectancy is longer than the IRS table says it is. To whom do I turn for acceptable proof that my longer life expectancy will permit me to take out smaller minimum distributions than would be required under the IRS table?*

There is no relief from your life expectancy determined by the IRS. If you don't take out the minimum distribution according to IRS life expectancy, you will pay a 50 percent tax on insufficiency of distribution.

*If I withdraw money from my qualified retirement plan or IRA before my required beginning date, do I get a credit against future required minimum distributions once I reach my required beginning date?*

No, at least not directly. Any withdrawals made before your required beginning date do not count against your required minimum distributions. However, to the extent that you have withdrawn money before your required beginning date, the balance in your plan account or IRA will be less. Therefore, the required minimum distribution will indirectly be lower than if you had never withdrawn the money.

*I have several IRAs, and I have reached my required beginning date. Do I calculate my required minimum distribution for each IRA?*

Yes. You must determine the required minimum distribution for each IRA. The amount of the required minimum distribution for each will depend upon the value of the IRA and the payout option which you selected (or the default payout option if you failed to select).

## CHAP. 6: DISTRIBUTIONS FROM RETIREMENT PLANS 321

≈ *Must I take a distribution from* each *of the IRAs in order to avoid the 50 percent penalty?*

No. Once you have determined the required minimum distribution amount for each of your IRAs, you are allowed to total all the required minimum distribution amounts for all your IRAs and withdraw this total amount each year from *one or all* of your IRAs in equal or unequal amounts.

≈ *How do I calculate the required minimum distributions if I have more than one qualified retirement plan?*

Just like the IRAs, the required minimum distribution must be determined separately for *each* qualified retirement plan. For each qualified retirement plan, the amount of the required minimum distribution will depend upon the value of the plan account and payout option which you selected (or the default payout option if you failed to select one).

Unlike IRAs, however, you must usually withdraw the yearly required minimum distribution for each plan from that account in order to avoid the 50 percent penalty tax. Thus you do not have the freedom to pick and choose from which plan accounts to take your minimum withdrawals.

≈ *I have $100,000 in a 401(k) plan, $150,000 in a profit-sharing plan, $75,000 in one IRA, and $50,000 in another IRA. My required minimum distributions are $5000 from the 401(k), $7500 from my profit-sharing plan, $3750 from one IRA, and $2500 from the other IRA. Can I choose where I take these funds from?*

Yes and no. The law treats IRAs differently from qualified retirement plans. You must withdraw $5000 from your 401(k), and must withdraw $7500 from your profit-sharing plan.

With regard to your IRAs, however, the total required distribution is $6250 ($3750 + $2500), which you can withdraw entirely from one IRA, equally from both IRAs, or any other combination you choose as long as the total of the withdrawals adds up to $6250.

## Beneficiaries

### *Primary death beneficiary*

*How are qualified retirement plan and IRA proceeds distributed after my death?*

Qualified retirement plans and IRAs are contractual agreements that usually allow you to name a person who will receive the remaining proceeds (if any) at your death. You accomplish this by filling out a beneficiary designation form at the time you establish your plan account or IRA.

If you fail to name a beneficiary—or if all your named beneficiaries predecease you—there are provisions in the document that will dictate who receives the proceeds. In many documents this default beneficiary is your estate.

Drafting the beneficiary designation is extremely important, especially as it relates to your estate plan. A mistake in drafting can cause serious estate tax problems, including the loss of the marital deduction for assets in the qualified plan or IRA at your death.

Be careful when using standard forms for naming your beneficiary. It is wise to have these forms reviewed by your attorney, accountant, and other estate planning professionals.

*Can I name anyone I want as the death beneficiary of my IRA?*

Unless the IRA document has otherwise, you may name any person or entity you wish as beneficiary. The most common beneficiaries are spouses, children, grandchildren, trusts, or charities.

# CHAP. 6: DISTRIBUTIONS FROM RETIREMENT PLANS 323

The consequences of your beneficiary choice vary greatly, and you should decide on a beneficiary only after careful analysis.

*Can I name anyone I want as the death beneficiary of my qualified retirement plan?*

Probably not. There are a number of plan provisions and statutory requirements that may interfere with your right to select your qualified plan beneficiary.

Some plans limit your right to name beneficiaries, while others control whom you can name as beneficiary.

If the retirement plan is a pension plan or a profit-sharing plan, the Retirement Equity Act of 1984 (REA84) requires (1) the consent of your spouse if you are choosing any RMD payout method other than a qualified joint-and-survivor annuity or (2) to make the death benefits payable to someone other than your surviving spouse.

If you plan to name a beneficiary of your qualified plan other than your spouse, he or she must sign a consent to the new beneficiary designation and sign a waiver of his or her rights to the funds in the plan. The consent and waiver must be complete and unequivocal. It cannot be a general waiver and consent; it must address the benefits of the plan directly. IRS Notice 97-10 gives sample language that can be helpful. The alternative language choices in the notice can help you to understand the purpose and mechanics of the waiver and consent. Before signing the waiver and consent, be sure that you and your spouse understand the projections of future benefits and how they work into the mosaic of your overall retirement planning.

REA84 does not apply to IRAs or to annuity plans under Internal Revenue Code Section 403(b).

Again, the consequences of your beneficiary choice on your retirement, financial, and estate plans vary greatly, and the decision of naming a beneficiary should be made only after careful analysis. Before naming or changing any beneficiary, you should consult your advisors to ensure avoiding any negative impact on you or on your ability to accomplish your ultimate planning goals.

*Is there a limit to the number of death beneficiaries that I can name?*

The law does not impose a limit, but a trustee, an administrator, a custodian, or an institution involved in a qualified retirement plan or an IRA might refuse to stay involved if you name more than a certain number of beneficiaries.

*Once I name a beneficiary of my qualified retirement plan or IRA, can I change that beneficiary?*

Unless your plan or IRA provides otherwise, you can always change a beneficiary designation. However, if this occurs after your required beginning date, the change will either have no effect on your required minimum distributions or increase the amount. It cannot have the effect of lowering your required minimum distributions.

*If I become disabled, can someone else change the beneficiary designation of my retirement plan or IRA?*

It depends. Generally speaking, no one can change your retirement plan beneficiary designation except you. However, if you have appointed an agent to act for you through a power of attorney, and that power of attorney provides the agent with the authority to change your beneficiary designation, then, yes, the agent can change it.

This assumes that the plan administrator or custodian will honor the power of attorney. The safest course of action would be to contact the plan administrator or custodian today in order to determine whether he or she would honor a power of attorney.

Another possibility would be if you are declared incompetent and the court appoints a guardian to act on your behalf. With

CHAP. 6: DISTRIBUTIONS FROM RETIREMENT PLANS **325**

court permission, your guardian may be able to change your beneficiary.

*⅍ My wife is deceased and my children are wealthy in their own right. Is there any problem in naming my grandchildren as beneficiaries of my IRA?*

There are no RMD rules restricting this action; however, it is of utmost importance for you to understand that if you name your grandchildren as your beneficiaries, you are skipping your children's generation to pass your wealth to your grandchildren. Assets dispensed in this nature are also skipping a generation of tax. In addition to the possible estate tax already imposed, the government will impose a *generation-skipping transfer (GST)* tax of 55 percent on all assets in excess of $1 million that you leave to your children's descendants. You should be careful not to exceed this amount if you name your grandchildren as beneficiaries or work with your financial advisors and estate planning attorney to implement some of the techniques available to reduce or eliminate the GST taxes..

### Contingent beneficiaries

*⅍ At present, I do not have a contingent beneficiary listed on my qualified retirement plans and IRAs. Is it important for me to do this?*

Yes. It is very important that you have a contingent beneficiary. If your primary beneficiary predeceases you, the default provisions in the document will dictate who receives the proceeds. In many documents the default beneficiary is your estate. If this occurs, the balance of your qualified retirement plan or IRA could be subject to immediate income taxation in the year following your death.

A contingent beneficiary also adds flexibility once you have

326                                    WAYS AND MEANS

died. If the primary beneficiary does not need the money, it can
go to the contingent beneficiary if you have named one.

### Designated beneficiary

*Does my beneficiary selection affect the minimum distribution rules?*

Yes. The beneficiary you name will affect your required minimum
distributions. You can only use the joint life expectancy payout
method with certain beneficiaries. Remember, joint life expectancy (as opposed to single life expectancy) reduces your required
minimum distribution amount each year. This allows more
money to remain in your qualified retirement plan or IRA which
continues to grow, tax-free, for a longer period of time.

*When can I use joint life expectancy to determine my mini-mum distribution amount?*

You can only use joint life expectancy if you have a designated
beneficiary as of your required beginning date.

*Is the beneficiary named on my qualified retirement plan or IRA a designated beneficiary?*

That depends. A *designated beneficiary* is a term defined by the
Internal Revenue Code and has a particular meaning for required
minimum distributions. The beneficiary you have selected to receive your retirement proceeds may or may not meet the definition of designated beneficiary under the code.

*Who is a designated beneficiary?*

Any natural person you have named as the primary beneficiary
of your qualified retirement plan or IRA is your designated beneficiary under the code. Generally, only a natural person will meet

# CHAP. 6: DISTRIBUTIONS FROM RETIREMENT PLANS    327

the definition of a designated beneficiary. Any entity, such as a corporation or charity or your estate, does not meet the definition of a designated beneficiary. There is, however, an exception for naming certain types of trusts.

### ⅍ *Can I have more than one designated beneficiary?*

No. Subject to the terms of the plan, you can always name more than one beneficiary to receive the proceeds from your qualified retirement plan or IRA upon your death; however, for purposes of the minimum distribution rules, you can have only *one* designated beneficiary.

### ⅍ *If I name my two children (ages 40 and 30) as equal beneficiaries of my qualified retirement plan or IRA, do I have a designated beneficiary, and if so, who is it?*

If more than one person is named as beneficiary, then the oldest person (with the shortest life expectancy) will be deemed the designated beneficiary for calculating the required minimum distribution. Since your beneficiary designation was 50 percent to child 1 (age 40) and 50 percent to child 2 (age 30), the required minimum distribution would be calculated based upon the joint life expectancy of you and your 40-year-old child (subject to the MDIB rule, discussed later in this chapter).

### ⅍ *If I name my child and my favorite charity as equal beneficiaries of my qualified retirement plan or IRA, do I have a designated beneficiary?*

No. If you name multiple primary beneficiaries, the rules require that each named beneficiary qualifies as a designated beneficiary even though for purposes of the code only one will be deemed your designated beneficiary. (Remember from the previous answer that if you name more than one person as beneficiary, the oldest person is deemed to be your designated beneficiary.)

If any portion of the benefit is to be distributed to a beneficiary who would not qualify as a designated beneficiary, then you will be treated as if you don't have any designated beneficiary for the entire plan or IRA. Since your beneficiary designation was 50 percent to your child and 50 percent to your charity, you will be deemed to have no designated beneficiary because a charity cannot qualify as a designated beneficiary.

*I'm only 60. Is it important that I name a designated beneficiary and select a life expectancy option and calculation method now?*

It is important that you follow the steps to ensure that you have a designated beneficiary even before your required beginning date. Before your required beginning date, failure to have a designated beneficiary of your retirement plan means that all the retirement plan proceeds will be distributed to your beneficiaries no later than December 31 of the fifth-year anniversary of your date of death. If you have a designated beneficiary before your required beginning date, your beneficiary will usually have the option of stretching the plan proceeds over his or her life expectancy, allowing for increased income tax deferral.

It is not as important to select your calculation method and life expectancy now. However, it is important that you make these elections as of your required beginning date. Failure to make these elections by your required beginning date will result in the plan's default elections being used. The default provisions are usually the provisions that generate the greatest amount of tax.

*What happens for purposes of calculating my RMD if I don't name a designated beneficiary by my required beginning date?*

You are deemed to have no designated beneficiary for required minimum distributions; therefore, distributions are calculated over your single life expectancy.

If single life expectancy and larger required minimum distri-

Chap. 6: Distributions from Retirement Plans  **329**

butions each year are your goal, there is no problem. If your goal, however, is to withdraw the smallest amount each year, you need to name a designated beneficiary by your required beginning date.

### Can a trust ever be a designated beneficiary?

On December 29, 1997, the IRS issued new proposed regulations that a trust named as a primary beneficiary can be the designated beneficiary if it meets certain requirements:

1. The trust must be valid under state law.
2. All beneficiaries of the trust must be individuals—not estates, corporations, or charities.
3. The beneficiaries must be "identifiable from the trust instrument."
4. A copy of the trust instrument (or certain selected information about the trust) must be provided to the plan administrator on whichever is earlier: (a) 9 months from the date of your death or (b) your required beginning date.
5. The trust must become irrevocable on your death.

If all five requirements are met, then under the proposed regulations, the trust qualifies as a designated beneficiary.

Under the old regulations, requirements 4 and 5 read respectively:

- A copy of the trust instrument must be provided to the plan administrator.
- The trust must be irrevocable as of the earlier of your death or your required beginning date.

Such requirements proved troublesome. A literal reading of the old regulations required a copy of the trust instrument to be delivered to the plan administrator immediately, even if the required beginning date was years away. Furthermore, if your revocable living trust was named as your beneficiary at your required beginning date, then you failed the fifth requirement because you were still alive—your revocable living trust was not irrevocable as of your required beginning date.

*Are the new rules for a trust becoming a designated beneficiary advantageous?*

Yes! If you named your revocable living trust as the primary beneficiary of your qualified retirement plan or IRA and have not yet reached your required beginning date, then you are not required to provide a copy of the trust to the plan administrator or custodian. With proper drafting by your attorney, you should easily meet the other four requirements.

At your required beginning date, your revocable living trust can remain your primary beneficiary and still be considered your designated beneficiary. You will need to provide a copy of the trust (or certain selected information) to the plan administrator or custodian and continue to meet the other requirements.

*If a trust qualifies as my designated beneficiary, whose life expectancy do I use?*

In order for a trust to be a designated beneficiary, generally, all beneficiaries of the trust must be individuals. Thus, the same rule applies as if you had named multiple individuals as beneficiaries: The oldest beneficiary of the trust—the one with the shortest life expectancy—will be the designated beneficiary for purposes of the joint life expectancy calculations.

### MDIB rule

*Can I name my grandson as the beneficiary of my IRA and*

# Chap. 6: Distributions from Retirement Plans   331

*use our combined life expectancy for taking required distributions?*

Nice try. There is a limit on how young the designated beneficiary can be for minimum distribution purposes. This is known as the *minimum distribution incidental benefit (MDIB) rule*. The purpose of the MDIB rule is to ensure that funds you accumulate under a qualified retirement plan or IRA are, in fact, for your benefit and that payments to your beneficiaries after your death are merely incidental.

For purposes of calculating your required minimum distribution under the joint life expectancy payout method, a nonspouse designated beneficiary is treated as being no more than 10 years younger than you.

For example, you are 70 and your designated beneficiary, your brother, is age 65. The joint life expectancy will be based on the actual ages of you and your brother, 70 and 65, respectively, which is 23.1 years.

On the other hand, if the designated beneficiary were your 35-year-old grandson, the MDIB rule would require the joint life expectancy to be based on your age of 70 and your grandson's *deemed age* of 60—10 years younger than you. The MDIB joint life expectancy results in 26.2 years instead of the *actual* joint life expectancy of you and your grandson, which would have been 47.5 years.

*Are there any exceptions to the MDIB rule?*

Yes. As stated earlier, this rule does not apply to your spouse, regardless of his or her age. Furthermore, the MDIB rule does not apply after your death. At your death, your beneficiary can commence receiving the balance of the qualified retirement plan or IRA benefits under the required minimum distributions based upon that beneficiary's actual life expectancy. This is known as the "flip" and occurs in the year following your death. It is also

332 WAYS AND MEANS

the basis for the planning option known as the *IRA stretch-out,* which we will discuss later.

## Changing the beneficiary

*Once I name a beneficiary of my qualified retirement plan or IRA, can I change that beneficiary?*

Unless your plan or IRA provides otherwise, you can always change the beneficiary both before and after the required beginning date.

If you are married and have a qualified retirement plan, this change might require the consent of your spouse.

*What happens to my joint life expectancy calculation if I change my beneficiary after my required beginning date?*

That depends. Remember, in order to use the joint life expectancy calculation, you must have a designated beneficiary as of your required beginning date. The beneficiary whom you select to receive the retirement proceeds at your death is a designated beneficiary if he or she is an individual or a trust that meets certain requirements.

The payout method which you select at your required beginning date is usually irrevocable. The law allows, however, for two exceptions. Unfortunately, both work against you and in favor of the IRS. The general rules for the effect of a changed beneficiary can be stated as follows:

1.  If the new beneficiary, who also meets the definition of a designated beneficiary, is younger than the earlier designated beneficiary, the change will not affect the calculation of the life expectancies for determining the required minimum distribution.

2.  If the new beneficiary, who also meets the definition of a designated beneficiary, is older than the earlier designated

# CHAP. 6: DISTRIBUTIONS FROM RETIREMENT PLANS 333

beneficiary, then the required minimum distributions will be changed to reflect the new, shorter joint life expectancy, and the required minimum distributions will be increased.

3. If the new beneficiary does *not* meet the definition of a designated beneficiary, such as a charity, then the required minimum distributions will be changed. You will have to revert to single life expectancy (effective as of the year in which the beneficiary change occurs) because you no longer have a designated beneficiary, and the required minimum distributions will be increased even more.

In other words, the change of a beneficiary cannot increase the life expectancy and thereby reduce the size of your required minimum distribution; it must decrease the life expectancy and thereby increase the size of your required minimum distribution.

As you can see, the only change that the IRS will permit following the required beginning date is to shorten life expectancy and accelerate the distributions.

*My wife just died and my child, who is 45, is the alternate beneficiary of my retirement plan assets. I am 80. Can I now redetermine my required minimum withdrawal amount on the basis of a joint life expectancy with my child?*

No. As we discussed in the previous question, once you passed your required beginning date, there are no changes you can make to reduce the amount of your required minimum distribution amount.

## Spousal Consent Rules

*How do spousal consent rules work in regard to a qualified retirement plan?*

If you are a participant in a qualified retirement plan (as opposed to an IRA), federal law gives your spouse certain rights in your plan.

Any form of distribution from your qualified retirement plan—that is, distributions at termination or retirement, upon disability, for hardship, or as loans, etc.—requires your spouse's consent. Spousal consent to the form of distribution is necessary when the distribution amount exceeds $3500 or, when added to previous distributions, exceeds $3500. This $3500 figure has been in the law since 1985, and it is expected that future legislation will increase the amount, perhaps to $5000. In essence, for distributions in excess of $3500, your spouse is being protected under the law since distributions can be made only with his or her consent.

If you plan to name a beneficiary of your qualified plan other than your spouse, he or she must sign a consent to the new beneficiary designation and sign a waiver of his or her rights to the funds in the plan.

The method of gaining your spouse's consent for a distribution or a change of beneficiary requires that your spouse sign the proper forms waiving the right to any benefit currently in effect and consenting to the form of distribution. These rules only apply if you are married. If you are separated, that is, still legally married in most states, then the rules are still binding. This consent must be in writing and witnessed by a plan trustee or notary.

As a participant in a qualified retirement plan, the law requires that you be given a summary description of the plan within 90 days of being eligible to participate. This summary plan description discusses in detail its spousal consent rules.

*If I am married, can I withdraw benefits from my retirement plan without the consent of my spouse?*

Under federal law, you may withdraw funds from your IRA without the consent of you spouse. However, spousal consent is required for all pension plans and certain employer profit-sharing plans.

CHAP. 6: DISTRIBUTIONS FROM RETIREMENT PLANS **335**

Additionally, your spouse may have rights under the laws of the state of your residence, including rights under community property law.

## DEATH BEFORE THE REQUIRED BEGINNING DATE

*What is the general rule for distribution of retirement plan assets if I die before my required beginning date?*

The general rule is that if you die before your required beginning date, all benefits must be distributed by December 31 of the fifth anniversary year of your death. For example, if you die on February 26, 1999, all benefits must be distributed by December 31, 2004. This is known as the *5-year rule.*

The distribution of all the benefits need not commence at any particular time and need not be made in any particular installment amounts, so long as all the plan benefits have been fully distributed within the 5-year period.

*Are there any exceptions to this 5-year rule?*

Yes, the law provides two exceptions depending upon the beneficiary. One exception applies if your spouse is the beneficiary, and the other exception applies if someone other than your spouse is a designated beneficiary. These exceptions generally allow the beneficiary to reduce or postpone required minimum distributions after your death.

Subject to the terms of the qualified retirement plan or IRA, your beneficiary will normally have the freedom to take more than the required minimum amount at any time after your death.

# 336

*WAYS AND MEANS*

### ⚜ *What is the exception to the 5-year rule for my spouse?*

Your spouse has two options. The first is to leaving the balance of the benefits in your plan account or IRA. Under this option, your spouse must take the first required minimum distribution by December 31 of the year following your death or by December 31 of the year in which you would have been 70½, whichever is the later date.

For example, suppose you die on June 1, 1999, on your sixty-fifth birthday, and your spouse is 60. Your seventieth birthday would have been on June 1, 2004, so you would have been 70½ in 2004. Based upon these facts, your spouse does not have to begin distributions until December 31, 2004, the year you would have been 70½, at which time required minimum distributions can be based on your spouse's life expectancy.

The second option is to do a spousal IRA rollover. In the event your spouse rolls over the money into a new IRA, your spouse will now be treated as the owner of the IRA for purposes of the minimum distribution rules. Your spouse now has the ability to name designated beneficiaries and can postpone distributions until reaching his or her required beginning date, which, in our example, might not be until 2009 or 2010.

### ⚜ *What happens if my surviving spouse chooses the option to delay receipt of benefits until I would have reached 70½ but dies before benefits commence?*

Under current regulations, your surviving spouse is allowed to name a beneficiary or beneficiaries, and if your spouse dies before receiving any distributions from your plan, your spouse shall be treated as if he or she were the participant. If the beneficiary your spouse names is a designated beneficiary, then required minimum distributions after your spouse's death will be based on the life expectancy of the designated beneficiary, and must begin by December 31 of the year following your spouse's death.

If your surviving spouse fails to name a designated benefici-

CHAP. 6: DISTRIBUTIONS FROM RETIREMENT PLANS  337

ary, then the entire balance must be distributed under the 5-year rule.

> ⤦ *What is the exception to the 5-year rule for a designated beneficiary who is not my spouse?*

If a nonspouse is the designated beneficiary, he or she could, of course, take the entire amount at your death if paying income taxes on the full amount is not an issue. On the other hand, if the qualified plan or IRA allows, your beneficiary could elect to spread the distributions out over his or her single life expectancy. The first distribution must begin no later than December 31 of the calendar year following your death.

For example, suppose you die on June 1, 1999, at the age of 65 with your 60-year-old brother as your beneficiary. Since your designated beneficiary is not your spouse, your brother's required minimum distributions must be calculated on his single life expectancy of 24.2 years and would have to commence no later than December 31, 2000.

His required minimum distribution amount for the first year will be $\frac{1}{24.2}$ of the fund balance; $\frac{1}{23.2}$ for the second year (a reduction of 1 year), $\frac{1}{22.2}$ for the third year, and so on.

If your brother survives this 24.2-year term, then all your retirement benefits will have been distributed to him during his lifetime. If your brother does not survive this 24.2-year term, then whoever is entitled to the balance of the proceeds at his death may continue to take required minimum distributions for the remaining number of years.

If there are several nonspouse beneficiaries named, such as all children who share equally, then a single life expectancy for the oldest beneficiary will be used to calculate the required minimum distributions for all the beneficiaries, thereby requiring the fastest distribution.

The plan assets could be divided into separate accounts, and each child named the designated beneficiary of one of the accounts. In this event, each beneficiary uses his or her own single life expectancy factor.

It is important to note that if you were to include a nonindividual, such as a charity, as a beneficiary even for $1, it could cause the plan to have no designated beneficiary. This seemingly innocent charitable beneficiary designation would subsequently require the plan assets to be paid under the 5-year rule.

## CALCULATING RMD

### Recalculation and Nonrecalculation Methods

*I understand how to calculate my first required minimum distribution amount under the life expectancy payout option. Does the amount stay the same each year?*

No. Your required minimum distribution amount must be redetermined each year after your required beginning date.

*Under the life expectancy payout option, how do I calculate my required minimum distribution for each year after the first year of mandatory distribution?*

There are two methods for calculating your required minimum distribution amount for each subsequent year: the *recalculation* method and the *nonrecalculation* method.

#### Recalculation method

Your life expectancy is redetermined every year. Each year you must ascertain your remaining number of years of life expectancy by using the tables published by the Internal Revenue Service.

## Chap. 6: Distributions from Retirement Plans   339

- *For single life expectancy:* You find your remaining life expectancy number based upon your current age.

- *For joint life expectancy:* You find your remaining number of years of combined life expectancy based upon your current age and the current age of your designated beneficiary.

It is important to understand two facts about the recalculation method. First, for each subsequent year, your life expectancy does *not* decrease by one full year. For example, if you are 70, your single life expectancy for the first year is 16 years; for the second year, 15.3 years; for the third, 14.6 years; and so on. Recalculation assumes that as long as you are alive, you always have a life expectancy. Thus, even a 105-year-old has a life expectancy of 1.8 years. Second, recalculation also assumes the corollary: When you die, your life expectancy goes to zero. These two facts are important in determining required minimum distributions under this method.

### Nonrecalculation, or term-certain, method

The calculation begins with the original single or joint life expectancy, and for each subsequent year, life expectancy is reduced by 1 year.

For example, if you are 70, your single life expectancy for the first year is 16 years; for the second year, 15 years; for the third, 14 years, and so on. Thus, if you are still alive 16 years later at age 86, for purposes of the nonrecalculation method, you have no remaining life expectancy.

Unlike the recalculation method, the nonrecalculation method assumes that if you die before age 86—or before the end of the 16 years—you still have a remaining life expectancy, even though you are dead. Under certain circumstances, that remaining life expectancy can be "passed on" to your beneficiaries.

It is important to note that under both methods, your life expectancy is always the same for the first year. Also, as long as you are still living, the recalculation method will always produce a longer life expectancy.

*What are the advantages and disadvantages of the recalculation and nonrecalculation methods?*

The advantage of the recalculation method is that it produces a smaller required distribution in every year after the first, for as long as you—or your joint measuring life—live. This is because as long as you are alive, you have some life expectancy. Smaller annual minimum distributions leave a larger balance in the account to continue to grow on a tax-deferred basis and generate lower income taxes to you.

The disadvantage of the recalculation method, as trite as it sounds, is that life expectancy at death is zero. Therefore, at your death under the single life expectancy, or at the death of both parties under joint life expectancy, all the remaining funds *must* be paid out and be subject to taxation by December 31 of the year following the year of death.

The advantage of the nonrecalculation method is that you have the possibility of continuing the tax deferral of your retirement plan for your beneficiaries. Thus, if you under single life expectancy, or you and your spouse under joint life expectancy, live for fewer years than your fixed-term calculation, you can "pass on" the remaining fixed term to allow the qualified plan or IRA to continue for as long as you were expected to live.

The nonrecalculation method has two disadvantages:

- If you live longer than your life expectancy, all the proceeds from your qualified retirement plan or IRA will have been distributed to you before your death and you lose the tax-deferred status.

- All your retirement savings will have been subjected to income taxation before your death.

The decision of whether to use the recalculation or nonrecalculation method would be an easy one if only we knew how long you and your beneficiary were going to live. Since we obviously don't, you will want to consider choices that offer maximum flexibility.

# CHAP. 6: DISTRIBUTIONS FROM RETIREMENT PLANS   341

⚖ *What happens under each of these methods if my spouse is the designated beneficiary?*

There will be different results, based not only on the calculation method but also on which of you dies first. Let's look at several scenarios.

### Joint life expectancy payout option and recalculation method

YOUR SPOUSE DIES FIRST   Your spouse's life expectancy goes to 0 years. You move to a *single life* expectancy, instead of joint life expectancy, on a recalculation basis to determine your annual RMD. When you die, your life expectancy goes to zero, and the entire account balance in the retirement plan must be distributed (and therefore taxed) by December 31 of the year following the year of your death.

YOU DIE FIRST   Your life expectancy goes to zero, and your spouse moves to the single life expectancy table on a recalculation basis. When your spouse dies, your spouse's life expectancy goes to zero, and the entire account balance in the retirement plan must be distributed (and therefore taxed) by December 31 of the year following the year of your spouse's death.

At your death, your surviving spouse does have the option of doing a spousal rollover. If your spouse dies before the rollover is completed, the final distribution will take place by December 31 of the year following the year of your spouse's death. Therefore, if a rollover is desired, your spouse should do this shortly after your death.

### Joint life expectancy option and nonrecalculation method

YOUR SPOUSE DIES FIRST   You will continue to receive your RMD under the remaining joint life expectancy fixed term. If you die before the end of the fixed term, your beneficiaries can continue taking RMDs until the fixed term expires. This is the main advantage of the nonrecalculation method.

YOU DIE FIRST  Your surviving spouse can continue with the remaining joint life expectancy fixed term. If your surviving spouse dies before the end of the fixed term, the beneficiaries can continue taking RMDs until the fixed term expires. This is the main advantage of the nonrecalculation method.

*Can you show me numerical comparisons of the recalculation and nonrecalculation methods?*

The number of variations of these methods is mind-boggling, so we included two simple examples of the recalculation method on both husband's life and wife's life and of the nonrecalculation method on both lives.

In Table 6-2, the husband is age 71 and the plan owner; his wife is age 69. The husband's retirement plan balance today is $100,000. The husband dies first at age 77, and his wife dies later at age 85.

In the second part of Table 6-2, we used a different age for the wife to demonstrate the overall effect. Her age is 66, and she dies later at age 73. For illustrative purposes, figures in the table assume 0 percent growth on the IRA assets.

*Remind me again why I am going through the brain damage of trying to decipher life expectancies and calculation methods and which one is better than the next. All I know is that I have a retirement plan, and I'm just trying to figure out if it's going to be enough for me to live on after I retire at 65.*

Once you reach your required beginning date, the life expectancy and calculation method you choose will affect the amount of your retirement plan that you will be forced to take out each year.

# CHAP. 6: DISTRIBUTIONS FROM RETIREMENT PLANS 343

Your life expectancy and calculation methods will also affect how your plan is distributed to your beneficiaries on your death.

*⅍ Okay, you've convinced me that I need to be aware of these issues. Can you please summarize some of the general principles you've explained so far?*

Once you reach your required beginning date, the government mandates that you must begin withdrawing minimum amounts from your qualified retirement plan or non-Roth IRA each year. These are known as required minimum distributions (RMDs). RMDs must continue during your lifetime and after your death until all amounts have been withdrawn.

After your required beginning date, you, as the plan participant or account owner, or your beneficiary can always withdraw more than the RMDs at any time based on needs, wants, income tax situation, or any other considerations.

If you wish to maximize the continued tax-deferral benefit of your qualified retirement plan or non-Roth IRA, the smaller the amount of money you take out in RMDs, the more that remains in the retirement account growing, tax-free, for a longer period of time for you or your beneficiaries.

The amount of the RMD is determined by the payout option which you have selected (either voluntarily or by the default provisions of the plan) as of your RBD.

- You cannot change the payout option after your RBD.

- Joint life expectancy of any two persons will always be longer than the single life expectancy of either of them.

- The joint life expectancy payout option will always produce a lower RMD.

In order to utilize the joint life expectancy payout option, you must have a designated beneficiary as of your RBD. Individuals

344 WAYS AND MEANS

**TABLE 6-2 Comparison of Recalculation and Nonrecalculation Methods**

The husband is age 71 and the plan owner; his wife is age 69. Husband's retirement plan balance today is $100,000. The husband dies first at age 77, and his wife dies later at age 85. For illustration purposes, figures assume 0 percent growth on the IRA assets.

| | Age | | Distribution | | | |
| | | | Recalculation | | Nonrecalculation | |
| Year | Husband | Wife | Fraction | Amount | Fraction | Amount |
|---|---|---|---|---|---|---|
| 1 | 71 | 69 | $1/20.7$ | $ 4,831 | $1/20.7$ | $4831 |
| 2 | 72 | 70 | $1/19.8$ | 4,807 | $1/19.7$ | 4831 |
| 3 | 73 | 71 | $1/19.0$ | 4,756 | $1/18.7$ | 4831 |
| 4 | 74 | 72 | $1/18.2$ | 4,704 | $1/17.7$ | 4831 |
| 5 | 75 | 73 | $1/17.3$ | 4,676 | $1/16.7$ | 4831 |
| 6 | 76 | 74 | $1/16.5$ | 4,620 | $1/15.7$ | 4831 |
| 7 | 77 | 75 | $1/15.8$ | 4,532 | $1/14.7$ | 4831 |
| 8 | dec. | 76 | $1/15.0$* | 4,780 | $1/13.7$† | 4831 |
| 9 | | 77 | $1/11.2$ | 5,975 | $1/12.7$ | 4831 |
| 10 | | 78 | $1/10.6$ | 5,749 | $1/11.7$ | 4831 |
| 11 | | 79 | $1/10$ | 5,519 | $1/10.7$ | 4831 |
| 12 | | 80 | $1/9.5$ | 5,229 | $1/9.7$ | 4831 |
| 13 | | 81 | $1/8.9$ | 4,994 | $1/8.7$ | 4831 |
| 14 | | 82 | $1/8.4$ | 4,696 | $1/7.7$ | 4831 |
| 15 | | 83 | $1/7.9$ | 5,031 | $1/6.7$ | 4831 |
| 16 | | 84 | $1/7.4$ | 4,691 | $1/5.7$ | 4831 |
| 17 | | 85 | $1/6.9$ | 4,351 | $1/4.7$ | 4831 |
| 18 | | dec. | $1/1$‡ | 25,673 | $1/3.7$§ | 4831 |
| 19 | | | | | $1/2.7$ | 4831 |
| 20 | | | | | $1/1.7$ | 4831 |
| 21 | | | | | $1/1$ | 3380 |

# Chap. 6: Distributions from Retirement Plans  345

## TABLE 6-2  *Continued*

All the facts are the same except the wife is age 66 and dies at age 73.

| | Age | | Distribution | | | |
| | | | Recalculation | | Nonrecalculation | |
| Year | Husband | Wife | Fraction | Amount | Fraction | Amount |
|---|---|---|---|---|---|---|
| 1 | 71 | 66 | $1/22.2$ | $ 4,504 | $1/22.2$ | $4348 |
| 2 | 72 | 67 | $1/21.3$ | 4,483 | $1/21.2$ | 4348 |
| 3 | 73 | 68 | $1/20.5$ | 4,440 | $1/20.2$ | 4348 |
| 4 | 74 | 69 | $1/19.6$ | 4,417 | $1/19.2$ | 4348 |
| 5 | 75 | 70 | $1/18.8$ | 4,370 | $1/18.2$ | 4348 |
| 6 | 76 | 71 | $1/18.0$ | 4,321 | $1/17.2$ | 4348 |
| 7 | 77 | 72 | $1/17.2$ | 4,271 | $1/16.2$ | 4348 |
| 8 | dec. | 73 | $1/13.9$* | 4,978 | $1/15.2$† | 4348 |
| 9 | | dec. | $1/1$‡ | 60,001 | $1/14.2$§ | 4348 |
| 10 | | | | | $1/13.2$ | 4348 |
| 11 | | | | | $1/12.2$ | 4348 |
| 12 | | | | | $1/11.2$ | 4348 |
| 13 | | | | | $1/10.2$ | 4348 |
| 14 | | | | | $1/9.2$ | 4348 |
| 15 | | | | | $1/8.2$ | 4348 |
| 16 | | | | | $1/7.2$ | 4348 |
| 17 | | | | | $1/6.2$ | 4348 |
| 18 | | | | | $1/5.2$ | 4348 |
| 19 | | | | | $1/4.2$ | 4348 |
| 20 | | | | | $1/3.2$ | 4348 |
| 21 | | | | | $1/2.2$ | 4348 |
| 22 | | | | | $1/1.2$ | 4348 |
| 23 | | | | | $1/1$ | 4344 |

*Wife continues taking her required minimum distributions based on her single life expectancy and recalculation method.

†Wife continues taking her required minimum distributions under husband's original fixed term.

‡Under the recalculation method, at wife's subsequent death, her life expectancy goes to zero, and entire balance must be distributed to beneficiaries by December 31 of the year following the year of her death.

§Under nonrecalculation method, at wife's subsequent death, the beneficiaries can continue taking their required minimum distributions under the husband's original fixed term.

and certain trusts are your choices for designated beneficiaries under the law.

The amount of the RMD is also determined by the calculation method which you have selected (either voluntarily or by the default provisions of the plan). During your lifetime, the recalculation method and the nonrecalculation method always produce the same RMD in the first year, but the recalculation method always produces a lower RMD than the nonrecalculation method does from the second year on. After your death, the recalculation method will generally require larger RMDs than the nonrecalculation method does.

Generally, you can change the beneficiary (who gets the money) of your qualified retirement plan or non-Roth IRA, both before and after your RBD. If the new beneficiary is younger, the amount of your RMDs is not affected, but if the new beneficiary is older, the amount of your RMDs will be increased to reflect his or her lower life expectancy.

## Split-Calculation Method

*What is the split-calculation method?*

The *split-calculation method* is a combination of both the recalculation and the nonrecalculation methods for the participant and the designated beneficiary. Under the split method, recalculation is selected for one life and nonrecalculation is selected for the other life. The participant can select either the recalculation or nonrecalculation method for himself or herself and can select either method for his or her spouse. The participant must select the nonrecalculation method for any nonspouse designated beneficiary. Thus the choices available are as follows:

| Method | Participant | Spouse as DB | Nonspouse as DB |
|---|---|---|---|
| Recalculation | Yes | Yes | No |
| Nonrecalculation | Yes | Yes | Yes |

# CHAP. 6: DISTRIBUTIONS FROM RETIREMENT PLANS    347

≫ *My spouse is my designated beneficiary. If I use the split-calculation method, which combination should I use?*

The best combination depends upon various factors, including the age and health of each of you.

The method most commonly used is recalculation on your life and nonrecalculation on your spouse's life. If you elect to recalculate your life expectancy, this method ensures that if you survive your spouse, the amount of the minimum distributions will be reduced and the proceeds will be distributed over your actual lifetime. On the other hand, if you and your spouse both die shortly after your required beginning date, your children (or other beneficiaries) are guaranteed a fixed term (your spouse's remaining life expectancy) over which to take the remaining proceeds.

Here is how it works: If your spouse predeceases you, you continue with the same joint life recalculation originally established. Upon your own death, your beneficiaries can elect to stretch out the income taxes over the balance of the period remaining of your spouse's original single life expectancy.

If you die first, your spouse would more likely do a rollover even though the distribution would then be on nonrecalculation based on his or her single life. The rollover enables your spouse to start fresh and establish a new option (for example, selecting your children as designated beneficiaries using the MDIB table). At your spouse's subsequent death, this gives the children (or other beneficiaries) the ability to stretch out the distributions and the income tax due on the distributions over their life expectancies. This can be a significant tax advantage compared to being forced to pay all the income tax in the year after the second spouse's death.

≫ *Are there any drawbacks to the split-calculation method?*

Yes. After the first year, the minimum distribution is always a little larger than if both spouses used the nonrecalculation method. But most practitioners feel this disadvantage is offset by the potential planning flexibility the split method offers.

348 WAYS AND MEANS

The split method is often selected upon the assumption that one spouse will die first. If in reality the opposite occurs, another method might have produced more favorable results.

Also, a surprisingly large number of plan administrators and custodians don't offer a split option. Some will allow you to select the split option, but they may not be able to provide you with the calculations. But in those cases, calculation factors can be easily obtained from an advisor who specializes in distribution planning. On the other hand, it is sometimes easier just to move your account to another custodian that does offer these options. The fees may be nominal but are usually based on how many different accounts and sometimes the types of assets you have. There are also a few trust companies that wrap their trust umbrella around your current investments for a nominal annual fee. This way you can keep your account with your favorite broker yet still avail yourself of all the options.

*If my spouse is my designated beneficiary at my required beginning date and dies before me, how will distributions be made to my beneficiaries after my death?*

That will depend on the payout option and calculation method you select at your required beginning date. More than likely you will select the joint life expectancy payout option because your spouse is your designated beneficiary at your required beginning date. The main issue is the calculation method you selected at your required beginning date. There are four possible choices under the law, although your plan or IRA might not offer all these choices.

| Method | Participant-owner | Spouse |
|---|:---:|:---:|
| Recalculation | ✓ | ✓ |
| Nonrecalculation | | |

CHAP. 6: DISTRIBUTIONS FROM RETIREMENT PLANS   349

FIRST CHOICE   Under this first method, you begin with a joint life expectancy. Because both lives are being recalculated, you return to the IRS tables each year to redetermine your joint life expectancy. Upon the death of your spouse, his or her life expectancy reduces to zero. From that point forward, you are required to take your required minimum distributions over your single life expectancy, and you have to redetermine your life expectancy each year. Upon your death, your life expectancy reduces to zero. Your beneficiaries will be forced to withdraw all account balances by December 31 of the year following your death.

| Method | Participant-owner | Spouse |
| --- | --- | --- |
| Recalculation | ✓ | |
| Nonrecalculation | | ✓ |

SECOND CHOICE   Under this second approach, you still begin with a joint life expectancy. Because one of your lives is being recalculated, you use the IRS tables each year to redetermine life expectancy. Under the proposed regulations, it appears that your spouse's death has no impact on the joint expectancy calculation. In other words, you are allowed to continue to redetermine the joint life expectancy as if your spouse were still alive. Upon your death, your life expectancy reduces to zero. However, if the original single life expectancy of your spouse (as of your required beginning date) exceeds the number of years of distributions from your required beginning date to your date of death, then your beneficiaries can continue to take required minimum distributions for your spouse's remaining fixed term. For example, assume your spouse is 60 at your required beginning date. The single life expectancy of your spouse is 24.2 years. If you receive required minimum distributions for 10 years and then you die, your beneficiaries could receive the balance of your funds over your spouse's remaining term of 14.2 years (24.2 minus 10). If you die after this 24.2-year fixed term, then your beneficiaries will be forced

350

WAYS AND MEANS

to withdraw all account balances by December 31 of the year following your death.

| Method | Participant-owner | Spouse |
| --- | --- | --- |
| Recalculation | | ✓ |
| Nonrecalculation | ✓ | |

THIRD CHOICE   With the third choice, you still begin with a joint life expectancy. Because one of your lives is being recalculated, you use the IRS tables each year to redetermine life expectancy. Upon your spouse's death, her life expectancy reduces to zero. From that point forward, you are required to take your required minimum distributions over the remaining term of your original single life expectancy (as of your required beginning date). If you die before the expiration of your fixed term, your beneficiaries can receive the balance of your funds over the remaining term. Of course if you die after this fixed term, then all the money would have been distributed to you during your lifetime, and there are no account balances to leave to your beneficiaries.

| Method | Participant-owner | Spouse |
| --- | --- | --- |
| Recalculation | | |
| Nonrecalculation | ✓ | ✓ |

FOURTH CHOICE   Under this fourth method, you again begin with a joint life expectancy. However this method produces a fixed term of years, and you do not have to refer to the IRS tables in the future. Required minimum distributions are made over this fixed number of years, regardless of death. Your spouse's death has no impact on your distributions which will continue to be made over this fixed term. If you die before the expiration of this fixed term, your beneficiaries can receive the balance of your funds over the remaining term. Of course if you die after this fixed term, then all of the money would have been distributed to you during

CHAP. 6: DISTRIBUTIONS FROM RETIREMENT PLANS    351

your lifetime, and there are no account balances to leave to your beneficiaries.

*What happens if I don't choose a calculation method for my qualified plan or IRA account?*

Election of the calculation method must be made by the required beginning date and is irrevocable.

In most plan documents and custodian agreements, the default provision is joint life expectancy with recalculation for both you and your spouse. Generally you must affirmatively elect otherwise by your required beginning date, or the default provision will control. The default is generally not the best choice for you.

If, for some reason, a plan agreement does not have a default method, it then falls back on the IRS's default provision, which is joint life expectancy with recalculation if married and single life expectancy with recalculation if not married.

*What planning recommendations are generally given about the calculation method to select if I am married?*

Assuming your spouse is the designated beneficiary, it is generally recommended that at required beginning date, you elect to recalculate one life and not recalculate the other. Choosing which life to recalculate is generally based upon the facts known at the time. If either of you is significantly younger than the other, it is usually recommended to recalculate the younger spouse's life expectancy. However, if the younger spouse has a medical condition which makes his or her life expectancy shorter than the other spouse, then the reverse should be chosen.

*What planning recommendations are generally given about the calculation method to select if I am not married?*

When a nonspouse is the designated beneficiary, the decision on recalculation is generally easier to make. Since only your life expectancy can be recalculated, if the beneficiary is a "designated beneficiary," then recalculation should be elected unless you are in ill health or there are reasons to expect that you will not survive to your normal life expectancy.

*It would seem that if a person lives to or beyond his or her life expectancy, the recalculation method would be better.*

The short answer is yes. However, when you use the joint life expectancy payment option, it's a pretty good rule of thumb that if either person dies several years short of his or her life expectancy, the nonrecalculation method will be the better distribution plan and create smaller minimum distributions.

If you and your spouse are both in really good health, do not engage in hazardous activity, drive carefully, and keep a working carbon monoxide detector in your home, it might not be a bad bet to take the recalculation method with your spouse as the joint measuring life.

*On the other hand, if I elect the nonrecalculation method and I'm in really good health, could I outlive my retirement account?*

The idea of "outliving" your retirement account is misleading. The biggest risk with the nonrecalculation method is that the entire account will have been distributed to you during your lifetime and been subjected to income tax. You still have money; it has just been pulled out of your retirement plan and redeposited into an investment that is no longer tax-deferred.

*What if my IRA document does not permit me to use a nonrecalculation method?*

Ask your custodian to add a custom clause allowing you the election (which you must make by your required beginning date) to avoid having to recalculate life expectancies for purposes of mini-

CHAP. 6: DISTRIBUTIONS FROM RETIREMENT PLANS  353

mum distribution rules. Alternatively, you could consider rolling your plan into an IRA at an institution which allows the election.

## DEATH AFTER
## THE REQUIRED BEGINNING DATE

*How must distributions be made if I die after my required beginning date?*

Once you have reached your required beginning date and begun receiving required minimum distributions, the benefits must continue to be distributed after your death *at least as rapidly* as under the same payout method being used at your death. This is known as the *at-least-as-rapidly* rule. The determination of what is to be distributed and to whom is controlled by a combination of the following factors:

1. The designated beneficiary, or the absence of one, on the required beginning date
2. The life expectancy option used and the life expectancy
3. The calculation method elected (or mandated by the retirement plan provisions)
4. The beneficiary at the date of death

*How is the RMD calculated for my death beneficiaries if I had no designated beneficiary as of my required beginning date?*

In general, if you did not name a designated beneficiary at your required beginning date, you would have to calculate your RMD using single life expectancy.

Upon your death, how fast the money must be distributed to your beneficiaries will depend upon whether you were using the recalculation or the nonrecalculation method. If you die after your required beginning date, the money remaining in your plan account or IRA must be distributed to your beneficiaries at least as rapidly as if you were alive.

If you were using the recalculation method, then upon your death your life expectancy became zero. Therefore, the entire balance in your plan account or IRA must be distributed to your beneficiary by December 31 of the year following the year of your death. More than likely, all the money would be taxable income to your beneficiary. Depending upon the size of the account, this could present a significant income tax problem to your beneficiary.

However, if you were using the nonrecalculation method, upon your death, your beneficiary could continue taking required minimum distributions for the remainder of your original fixed-term period. If you had outlived your fixed term, then all of the money was distributed to you during your lifetime, and there is no remaining account balance at your death.

*How are required minimum distributions calculated for my nonspouse designated beneficiary if I die after my required beginning date?*

That will depend on the payout option and calculation method that you selected at your required beginning date. More than likely, you selected the joint life expectancy payout option because you had a designated beneficiary at your required beginning date. Since the designated beneficiary was not your spouse, the nonrecalculation method had to be used for the designated beneficiary.

If you elected to *recalculate* your life expectancy, then upon your death, your life expectancy reduces to zero. After your death, the required minimum distributions for the beneficiary will be based upon your designated beneficiary's original single life expectancy (as of your required beginning date) reduced by the number of years of distributions from your required beginning date to the date of your death.

CHAP. 6: DISTRIBUTIONS FROM RETIREMENT PLANS **355**

If you elected *not* to recalculate your life expectancy, then you received a joint fixed number of years to take distributions at your required beginning date. Your death has no impact on this calculation method. After your death, the beneficiary's required minimum distributions will be based upon the original joint life expectancy (as of your required beginning date) reduced by the number of years of distributions from your required beginning date to the date of your death.

However, if your designated beneficiary was more than 10 years younger than you, then during your lifetime the MDIB rule requires using an artificial joint life expectancy based upon your age and a person exactly 10 years younger than you. Upon your death, the MDIB rule vanishes. That is why, under either of the above scenarios, after your death your beneficiary will always refer back to the original life expectancy calculation as of your required beginning date.

For example, let's assume the following facts:

- You are a widower age 71 at your required beginning date.

- Your 45-year-old daughter is your designated beneficiary.

- The actual joint life expectancy of you and your daughter is 38.2 years.

- Because your daughter is more than 10 years younger than you, your MDIB joint life expectancy is 25.3 years.

- Your daughter's actual single life expectancy at your RBD is 37.7 years.

- You begin your distributions and die 12 years later at age 83.

During your life your RMD is recalculated each year beginning with the artificial joint life expectancy of 25.3 years. At your death we have the following two scenarios.

ELECTED RECALCULATION   Your life expectancy goes to zero, but your daughter's life expectancy must become a fixed term. After your death, the MDIB rule is ignored, so to calculate her fixed term, we start with your daughter's single life expectancy at your RBD which was 37.7 years and subtract the 12 years for which you received distributions before your death. Your daughter now has the remaining 25.7 years (37.7 minus 12) to calculate her required minimum distributions.

She would receive $\frac{1}{25.7}$, or 3.89 percent, of the value of the retirement plan account the first year, $\frac{1}{24.7}$, the second year, $\frac{1}{23.7}$ the third year, and so on, thereby stretching out the future required minimum distributions, and the income taxes on those distributions, over 25.7 years.

ELECTED NONRECALCULATION   Your daughter must use the non-recalculation method, and at your death the MDIB rule is ignored. To calculate your daughter's fixed term, we begin with your actual joint life expectancy at your RBD of 38.2 years and subtract the 12 years that you received distributions. Your daughter's term is 36.2 years (38.2 minus the 12 years).

In either scenario, your daughter can always withdraw more than the RMD in any year, even up to 100 percent of the account. Furthermore, even if she is not yet 59½ at the time of your death, she can make pre-59½ distributions without the 10 percent penalty, as the plan is technically still in your name. She can also roll over the entire account into her own IRA plan, although if she were to do so, the entire amount would become taxable in that year, as only spouses are permitted to do a tax-free rollover.

## Rollovers

### Spousal rollovers

*After my death, can my spouse roll over my qualified retirement plan or IRA into his or her own IRA?*

Yes, your spouse can roll over your qualified retirement plan or IRA into his or her own IRA. The slate is wiped clean as far as

# Chap. 6: Distributions from Retirement Plans  357

any elections you may have made at your required beginning date. Your spouse gets a fresh start.

### ⚶ *What are the advantages of a spousal rollover?*

A surviving spouse has the ability to defer income taxes by rolling over inherited benefits into another IRA plan. All minimum distribution choices that were in effect before this rollover are gone. The spouse, as owner of the new IRA, starts distributions at his or her required beginning date and can make his or her own choices of designated beneficiary, life expectancy option, and calculation method.

### ⚶ *I am a 50-year-old widow. My husband, who was 62, named me as the beneficiary of his IRA. Should I exercise my right to roll this over into an IRA of my own?*

It is generally a good idea to roll over your deceased husband's IRA into your own IRA. By doing this, you extend by 12 years the date by which you must begin to make withdrawals.

The real answer to your question, however, depends greatly upon whether you think you will need to make any withdrawals from his IRA before you reach 59½. As you make withdrawals from your deceased husband's IRA, you are not subject to the 10 percent early-withdrawal penalty. However, if you roll his IRA over into your own IRA, then you will be subject to the 10 percent early-withdrawal penalty for most withdrawals you make before age 59½.

### ⚶ *I am about to receive IRA proceeds from my deceased spouse's trust. Can I roll the proceeds into my own IRA?*

No. If your deceased spouse's IRA proceeds pass through a third party, such as a trustee or executor, and the proceeds are then distributed to you, generally you will be treated as acquiring them from a third party and not from your deceased spouse.

*Are there any circumstances in which I will not be treated as acquiring my deceased spouse's IRA proceeds from a third party?*

Yes. You would not be considered a third party if the trustee has no *discretion* with respect to either allocation of the IRA proceeds to the trust or subtrust for your benefit or payment of the proceeds from the trust to you as trust beneficiary. The IRS has indicated that you could roll over the proceeds in the following example. If, under the terms of the trust, the trustee was required to allocate the IRA proceeds to a subtrust for your benefit and you had the right as beneficiary to demand the proceeds at any time and you did in fact withdraw the proceeds, then you would be able to roll the proceeds over to your own IRA. However, the rollover must generally take place within 60 days of your receipt of the IRA proceeds.

*Can I, as a surviving spouse who is under age 59½, withdraw death benefits from my deceased spouse's IRA?*

As a surviving spouse beneficiary, you may before age 59½ withdraw death benefits from your deceased spouse's IRA with no 10 percent early-withdrawal penalty. However, if you make withdrawals penalty-free before age 70½, you are making an irreversible election not to treat your spouse's IRA as your own. Therefore, no spousal rollover can occur.

*If I am the designated beneficiary of my spouse's retirement plan, do I have any options beyond receiving benefits from my spouse's plan over my life expectancy?*

Yes. In addition to the right to receive distributions over your life expectancy (commencing either December 31 of the year following the date of death or the year your spouse would have turned 70½), you may roll over the retirement plan benefits into your own IRA. If you elect to roll over the benefits, you then become

# Chap. 6: Distributions from Retirement Plans    359

the participant with respect to those assets, can name your own designated beneficiary, and can commence receiving distributions at your required beginning date.

Distributions from your deceased spouse's plan can be rolled over except (1) *any* distribution which is one of a series of substantially equal periodic payments made annually, or more often, over the life expectancy of your deceased spouse and (2) nontaxable distributions (i.e., return of after-tax contributions or the pure death benefit portion of life insurance proceeds within the retirement plan).

### ✒ *Are there any disadvantages if I roll over the benefits of my deceased spouse's qualified retirement plan or IRA to my own IRA?*

In general, a spousal rollover of benefits from your deceased spouse's qualified retirement plan or IRA will provide you with the greatest degree of flexibility and deferral of income taxes. There are some drawbacks.

If you are under age 59½, distributions from your deceased spouse's plan or IRA would not be subject to the 10 percent excise tax on early distributions. If you elect to roll over the benefits into your own IRA, those benefits will be subject to the early-withdrawal penalty. If you desire to ensure some ability to make early distributions and yet maximize the deferral possibilities from a rollover, you can make a partial rollover and leave a portion of the benefits in your deceased spouse's plan or IRA. This will ensure that a portion of the benefits can be distributed, without penalty, before you reach 59½.

The other potential drawback is that once the rollover is made from your deceased spouse's qualified retirement plan, the benefits are not eligible for treatment as a qualified lump-sum distribution. Although difficult to obtain, there are significant income tax benefits from a qualified lump-sum distribution, which would have to be evaluated before making the rollover decision.

360 WAYS AND MEANS

### Rollovers by other beneficiaries

*Can any of my beneficiaries roll over the funds to their own IRAs after my death?*

Yes, any beneficiary can roll over funds to a new IRA of which he or she is the new owner and start with a clean slate as far as a new required beginning date, naming beneficiaries, electing payout options, etc.

Your spouse, however, is the only beneficiary who can do a "spousal rollover," which means that the transfer of your retirement account balances to your spouse's new IRA does not trigger any income tax at the time of the transfer. Nonspouse beneficiaries who do a rollover trigger income tax on the entire rollover amount in the year in which the rollover was done.

## Stretch-Out IRA

*What is a stretch-out IRA?*

The *stretch-out IRA*, also known as a *multigenerational IRA, ghost IRA*, or *perpetual IRA*, is not a particular type of IRA. It is a planning strategy that involves creating a distribution plan to enable your beneficiaries (after your death) to keep the money in your IRA for as long as possible.

*Why would I use the stretch-out strategy?*

If the plan assets remain in the tax-deferred account for a longer period of time, the value of tax-free accumulation increases dramatically. Combined with the deferral in the payment of the income taxes, this can allow an account to multiply in value to children or grandchildren.

*How does this strategy work?*

The strategy begins by naming a much younger person (usually a child or grandchild) as the designated beneficiary of your IRA.

# Chap. 6: Distributions from Retirement Plans   361

If you die before your required beginning date, your designated beneficiary will be able distribute the balance of your retirement plan proceeds over his or her remaining life expectancy.

In order for the stretch-out strategy to continue working, you must also select the appropriate payout option and calculation method as of your required beginning date. During your lifetime, required minimum distributions will be determined by the MDIB rule; however, after your death, the balance will be distributed over the remaining life expectancy of the young beneficiary. A young person as the designated beneficiary would have a very long life expectancy, which would defer the payment of income taxes for many years after your death.

*When using the stretch-out strategy, how should my beneficiary handle my IRA account after my death?*

After your death, your beneficiary must follow certain steps in order to continue the stretch-out strategy. First, the money must remain in the IRA account after your death. Any distribution to your beneficiary would be taxable income. No beneficiary (except your spouse) is entitled to roll over an inherited IRA and postpone the income tax.

Second, your name must remain on the IRA account; for example, it should be titled "John Doe, deceased, for the benefit of Jim Doe." If the funds in the IRA account are transferred to a new IRA account, the new account must be titled in the same way. If the original account (or any subsequent account) is put in the name of your beneficiary, the entire amount would become taxable income in that year.

Third, your beneficiary must take the first required minimum distribution no later than December 31 of the year following your death.

Finally, in order to maximize the value of the account and stretch-out strategy, your beneficiary should only withdraw the required minimum distribution each year.

*I am a single person with no immediate family and have a large IRA. I want to leave my IRA to several nieces and nephews. How can I best use the stretch-out strategy?*

The goal, after your death, is to allow each beneficiary to take required minimum distributions based on his or her own remaining life expectancy. If you named all your nieces and nephews as beneficiaries of your IRA, then after your death, each one will be forced to take required minimum distributions based on the life expectancy of the oldest niece or nephew. This is known as the *multiple beneficiary rule.*

However, as long as you have not reached your required beginning date, you could split your large IRA into multiple IRAs and name each niece or nephew as the beneficiary of one IRA.

If you die before your required beginning date, each niece and nephew could withdraw his or her required minimum distribution based on his or her own remaining life expectancy.

Should you die after your required beginning date, each niece and nephew could withdraw his or her required minimum distribution based on the remaining fixed term. The fixed term would depend upon whether you were recalculating your life expectancy. If you were recalculating your life expectancy, the fixed term would be the niece or nephew's single life expectancy as of your required beginning date less the number of years of distributions made to you. If you were not recalculating your life expectancy, the fixed term would be the joint life expectancy of you and your niece or nephew as of your required beginning date less the number of years of distributions made to you.

This design can be extremely valuable to a younger beneficiary when there is a wide spread between your ages. For example, a beneficiary who is 10 years younger can receive almost an additional 10 years of income tax deferral if he or she is the sole beneficiary of the IRA.

Furthermore, each beneficiary can make his or her own decisions on how to handle an inherited IRA. It is impossible to predict each niece or nephew might want to take distributions.

# CHAP. 6: DISTRIBUTIONS FROM RETIREMENT PLANS 363

In order to maximize the stretch-out strategy, any time you want to leave your IRA account to multiple beneficiaries, you should consider splitting your IRA into multiple accounts. The additional benefit to your beneficiaries could be substantial.

*Can you give me some examples of how the stretch-out strategy works?*

Following are two scenarios that highlight the stretch-out strategy.

SCENARIO 1  You are 75, recently widowed, and roll over your spouse's IRA into your own name. This allows you the opportunity to reestablish your designated beneficiary even though you are past 70½.

You name your two sons as equal beneficiaries. At the time of the rollover, the total plan account is worth $650,000. You then split the account into two $325,000 accounts and name each son as the designated beneficiary of his own account. This permits each child's own life expectancy to be used, rather than just the older son's had the account not been divided.

You continue to make your required minimum distributions but withdraw the money in such a way as to keep the accounts equal. We'll use the older son's age to illustrate this example, although the projections would be even better using the age of your younger son.

Your older son is age 50 with an individual life expectancy of 33.1 years. Being more than 10 years younger than you, the MDIB table is applied. Using recalculation on your life and non-recalculation on your son's life results in an artificial joint life expectancy of 21.8 years during your lifetime.

Assume you die 13 years later. Even though the assumed growth rate was 8 percent, the growth on the IRA account is greater than your minimum required distributions, leaving you with a larger IRA account size than when you first started. Your plan accounts are worth approximately $800,000, or $400,000 in each account.

After your death, the MDIB rule disappears, so each son has a required minimum distribution based on his own life expectancy as of your required beginning date. If you recall, your older son's original life expectancy was 33.1 years. This gives him 20.1 years as his life-expectancy factor, (33.1 minus the 13 years of your distributions). Under the nonrecalculation method, this results in an RMD as follows:

Year 1:  $1/20.1$ (about 5 percent of the account balance)
Year 2:  $1/19.1$
Year 3:  $1/18.1$

And so forth. It should be kept in mind that the required minimum distribution is just that: a minimum. Each child can always withdraw more than the required minimum.

By your doing this stretch-out planning and your sons following the plan, the following is achieved:

- Your sons are given an additional option to continue to defer the taxation on the bulk of the retirement plan assets for over 20 years.

- Each one will have over $200,000 of additional income produced from the $400,000 IRA balance you left.

- There would be close to $2 million in distributions ($1 million to each son).

Remember, this all stemmed from your $650,000 spousal rollover IRA.

SCENARIO 2  Let's change the scenario and assume you name your grandchildren as designated beneficiaries. Perhaps you feel your sons will inherit enough from the other assets in the estate, or perhaps you plan to leave some assets outright to your grandchildren anyway, and it is just a matter of identifying which specific assets.

CHAP. 6: DISTRIBUTIONS FROM RETIREMENT PLANS   365

You establish separate accounts equal to the number of your grandchildren and designate each grandchild as a beneficiary of his or her own account. If we assume the oldest grandchild is age 38 at the time of your death, he or she would be able to stretch out the distributions and income taxes over 44 years. (This would obviously be longer for the younger grandchildren.)

If all the grandchildren choose to stretch out the IRA income over the 44-year time frame, this would generate an additional $2 million of income. The total income stream provided over 44 years would be over $7 million with the stretch-out versus $5 million without the stretch-out strategy.

The impact of compound interest can be staggering, especially over time. This example assumes a growth rate of 8 percent. If the growth rate is 10 percent, the difference would be almost $4 million ($13 million with stretch-out versus $9.1 million without the stretch-out strategy).

It should be emphasized that it is only the income tax that is being stretched out. If your estate is large enough, your children will still have to come up with the estate tax within 9 months after your death.

*Is it really worth jumping through all these hoops, trying to figure out all the various options to take advantage of stretching out the income taxes on my IRA?*

The answer to this depends on a couple of factors. Certainly the size of the IRA account is one factor. If the IRA account is small, it might not be practical to go through the process. Another consideration would be your tolerance threshold for dealing with the complexity of the process. Even if you are the type who enjoys researching all the angles, you may reach a level beyond your tolerance. Fortunately this can be minimized by seeking qualified professional advice.

If you take the time and effort to plan in this area, you will probably find it very worthwhile. The longer you can defer the taxation on your IRA distributions, the better. The potential

366                                    WAYS AND MEANS

benefits for you, your spouse, and your heirs can be quite substantial.

## BENEFICIARIES

### Trust as Designated Beneficiary

*I've been told that if I have a spouse, I cannot have a trust as the beneficiary of my qualified retirement plan. Is that true?*

That depends. As long as the trust meets the requirements we discussed earlier in this chapter, it can be a designated beneficiary under the law. However, the plan itself may limit who can be named as a beneficiary and specifically prohibit a trust. Furthermore, most qualified retirement plans will require the consent and waiver of your spouse before you can name a trust as the beneficiary.

*Do I name a trust as the beneficiary in order to avoid probate?*

There is no need to name a trust as the retirement plan beneficiary in order to avoid probate. Unless you or the terms of your plan have designated your estate as the beneficiary, retirement plan assets already pass outside probate.

*Do I name a trust as the beneficiary in order to save taxes?*

While there are exceptions, naming the trust as beneficiary is generally not done for purposes of saving taxes. The single most important exception is if the retirement plan assets are needed as a source of funds to fully utilize the available estate tax credits and deductions as discussed in Chapter 7.

*If naming a trust is not necessary to avoid probate or to reduce*

Chap. 6: Distributions from Retirement Plans   367

*taxes, then why would I name a trust as a beneficiary of retirement plan assets?*

There are excellent reasons other than probate avoidance and tax reduction for naming a trust as your beneficiary. If you name individuals as beneficiaries, there is no way to adequately cover all the contingencies without drafting a beneficiary designation form which looks just like a trust. For example, we all assume that our children will outlive us. Unfortunately, exceptions can occur, and when that child dies, retirement plan assets may go to the wrong person or to the right person but under undesirable circumstances.

A properly drafted trust anticipates each of these contingencies.

⚑ *I read where you should never name a trust as the primary beneficiary of any retirement plan. Is this correct?*

There is no reason why a properly drafted trust cannot be named as the primary beneficiary of a retirement plan and also qualify as the designated beneficiary for minimum distribution purposes. There are certain rules for naming a trust as beneficiary to avoid adverse tax consequences, but if you follow those rules, a trust as the beneficiary of your retirement accounts can be a highly effective strategy in planning your estate.

⚑ *What disadvantage is there to naming a trust the beneficiary of retirement plan assets?*

A trust does not have the option of rolling over the plan assets to a new IRA account. This can be especially restricting if the deceased spouse had not chosen properly and that choice had become irrevocable after passing the required beginning date.

Furthermore, unless carefully planned, distributions to a trust may cause an acceleration of distributions with the resulting loss of extended deferral of income taxes.

## Spouse as Designated Beneficiary

*Can you summarize the advantages of naming my spouse as the designated beneficiary?*

The Internal Revenue Code and the regulations provide a number of special rules for distributions to your surviving spouse.

If you die *before* your required beginning date, your spouse can elect to defer distributions until after you would otherwise have reached your required beginning date. Any *designated beneficiary* other than your spouse would have to begin receiving distributions by December 31 of the year following the year of your death. Your surviving spouse is entitled to roll over your retirement proceeds to his or her own IRA, name new designated beneficiaries, and postpone distributions (and therefore income taxation) until reaching his or her required beginning date.

When calculating your required minimum distributions, if your spouse is the designated beneficiary at your required beginning date, you can elect to have both your life expectancies recalculated annually or to have one life expectancy recalculated and one not recalculated. In certain circumstances, this allows an extended payout over the joint life expectancies of you and your spouse. You can also use your actual joint life expectancy, regardless of the age of your spouse. This can be useful if your spouse is much younger than you are. Remember, if you name someone other than your spouse as the designated beneficiary and that other person is more than 10 years younger than you, under the MDIB rule, you must use an artificial joint life expectancy calculation for determining your required minimum distributions. This artificial joint life expectancy will require larger distributions during your lifetime.

If you die *after* your required beginning date:

- Your surviving spouse is entitled to roll over your retirement proceeds to his or her own IRA, name new designated beneficiaries, and postpone distributions (and therefore income taxation) until reaching his or her required beginning date.

Chap. 6: Distributions from Retirement Plans    369

- Assets left to your spouse receive a special marital deduction for federal estate tax purposes. Although remaining assets may be subsequently taxed in your spouse's estate, this deferral of estate taxes could be beneficial.

- Distributions to a spouse will generally be deferred for a longer period of time than if the distributions are made to a trust.

## Charities as Beneficiaries

*What happens if a charity is named as a beneficiary?*

If a charity is named as the beneficiary of all or any portion of a retirement plan, then you will be deemed to have no designated beneficiary.

If you die before your required beginning date, then all proceeds must be distributed by December 31 of the fifth-year anniversary of your death.

At the required beginning date, your required minimum distributions will be based upon your single life expectancy.

If you die after your required beginning date, the entire balance of the retirement plan would have to be distributed over either (1) your remaining single life expectancy if life expectancy was not being recalculated or (2) by December 31 of the year following your death if your life expectancy was being recalculated.

*Can I avoid the "charitable disqualification" if I want to name a charity to receive a portion of the benefits under my qualified retirement plan?*

Dividing qualified retirement plan benefits into multiple shares can avoid the treatment of the entire plan as not having any designated beneficiary.

If a charity is to be named to take a portion of the qualified retirement plan benefits on your death, you should divide your plan so that the charity is the only beneficiary named to take benefits.

*≫ I heard that giving my IRA to charity can make sense. How could that possibly be?*

While you cannot, during your life, give the IRA itself to a charity, it can make sense for you to make a charity the beneficiary of your IRA, especially a non-Roth IRA. Careful analysis is required. Often the combination of an irrevocable life insurance trust with a charitable remainder trust as a beneficiary results in reducing or eliminating estate tax on life insurance proceeds and an IRA while benefiting both your family members and a charity.

It is not unusual for individuals wishing to make charitable contributions to use retirement plan assets. By leaving retirement plan assets to the charity, you avoid the income tax as well as receive an estate tax deduction. It might make sense if you are charitably inclined since your beneficiaries (in the absence of further planning), may receive as little as 25 cents on the dollar after taxes, while, depending on the estate tax deduction generated, the charity could possibly receive 100 percent.

## Estate as Beneficiary

*≫ Can I name my estate as the beneficiary of my qualified retirement plans and IRAs?*

While you can name your estate as the beneficiary of your qualified retirement plans and IRAs, it is not recommended. If your estate is named as the beneficiary of all or any portion of a qualified retirement plan or IRA, then you will be deemed to have no designated beneficiary.

If you die before your required beginning date, then all proceeds must be distributed by December 31 of the fifth-year anniversary of your death.

# CHAP. 6: DISTRIBUTIONS FROM RETIREMENT PLANS   371

At your RBD, your required minimum distributions will be based upon your single life expectancy.

If you die after your RBD, the entire balance of the retirement proceeds will have to be distributed either over your remaining single life expectancy if you were not recalculating life expectancy or by December 31 of the year following your death if you were recalculating your life expectancy. This shortchanges the growth potential available through properly structured retirement planning, and it forfeits the increase in value which would have occurred tax-deferred.

The loss of these enormous benefits normally mandates not naming your estate as a beneficiary of your qualified retirement plans or IRAs.

# chapter 7

## Estate Planning and Retirement Plans

For people who have significant retirement plan balances, proper coordination with estate planning goals can be the difference between a plan that effectively transfers wealth and one that causes a tax debacle. Because the beneficiary you name for your retirement plans determines both your minimum distribution requirements for income tax purposes and who inherits the funds upon your death, estate planning and retirement plan distribution planning are inextricably tied together.

Careful integration of your retirement plan with your estate plan is necessary to ensure taking advantage of the estate tax avoidance techniques available to you. Our contributors review the pitfalls to avoid and opportunities available through proper integration. These issues can literally mean a difference of hundreds of thousands of dollars.

The basics of the federal estate tax system are reviewed in this chapter, as well as the income tax rules regarding distribution of income after your death. Additionally, the concept of a disclaimer, a valuable tool that allows you to achieve optimal integration of estate (or death) and income tax planning, is introduced.

Finally, the contributors review how to coordinate your non-tax estate planning goals with your retirement distributions. Planning for spouses, charities, and other beneficiaries is also discussed.

For readers who wish to have more detail on tax and estate planning, we recommend *Loving Trust,* (Viking Penguin, 1994) and *Protect Your Estate,* (McGraw-Hill, 1993), both by Robert A. Esperti and Renno L. Peterson, and two books from the Esperti Peterson Institute, *Wealth Enhancement and Preservation* (1996) and *Generations: Planning Your Legacy* (1999).

## COORDINATING RETIREMENT PLANNING AND ESTATE PLANNING

*What is the difference between retirement planning and estate planning?*

Retirement planning is a process determining your financial goals and needs after retirement and developing a strategy today to achieve those desires. It is generally accomplished with your financial advisor.

Estate planning is defined as controlling what you own during your lifetime, providing for your possible disability, and then leaving what you have to whom you want, when you want, and the way that you want, all at the lowest overall cost to your loved ones. Estate planning is usually accomplished with an attorney.

Often these two professional disciplines interact, and that is why it is so important to work with a team of professionals.

CHAP. 7: ESTATE PLANNING / RETIREMENT PLANS    375

### Should I consider doing my estate plan at the time I retire?

No, you should consider planning your estate now. Retirement is just another phase of your life. There are as many important decisions that you need to make today as there are at retirement. There is no guarantee that you will live to retirement. As with any estate plan, you should develop a strategy for continuously updating your plan. If you are getting close to retirement, it would be a good time to review your estate plan with your attorney.

### Why does my estate planning lawyer need to know how much money is in my retirement plan?

Every piece of property you own or dollar you have invested comprises your estate. How you hold the property and what you want done with the property are crucial elements to your estate plan. Your attorney must know all your finances, so he or she can plan your estate in accordance with your goals.

### Do retirement plan assets have to be handled differently from other kinds of assets for estate planning?

Yes. Retirement plan assets must be handled differently because they are unique. First, every qualified retirement plan asset includes a deferred income tax component that must be considered. Second, retirement plan assets are subject to very complex rules regarding distribution which must be considered when developing an estate plan. Third, the provisions for distribution of all retirement plans are controlled by the terms of the respective retirement plan, and, therefore, each one is different.

### How do the rules on distributions from retirement plans affect estate planning?

The manner in which benefits under a retirement plan are to be distributed following your death are controlled by a combination of (1) the terms of the retirement plan and (2) the "minimum distribution rules" of Section 401(a)(9) of the Internal Revenue Code. The effect of the minimum distribution rules, in turn, differs depending on whether you die before or after reaching the date when you must begin taking distributions from your retirement plan—which is known as the *required beginning date.* Your estate planner must review the terms of the retirement plan(s), understand the minimum distribution rules, and take all these rules and plan provisions into account when developing an estate plan that meets your individual needs, goals, and aspirations. Evaluating the impact of estate, income, and excise taxes based upon the distribution scheme adopted in the estate plan generally requires a balancing of many factors.

## Federal Estate Tax

### ⚜ *What is the federal estate tax?*

The *federal estate tax* is a tax applied at the time of your death and involves your right to transfer property. In general, every asset that you *own* or *control* at the time of your death is subject to this tax. These assets include personal property, real estate, cash, stock, bonds, business interests, life insurance, and, most importantly for purposes of this book, qualified retirement plans and IRA proceeds.

### ⚜ *How are my assets valued for purposes of this tax?*

The fair market value of each asset must be determined as of the date of your death. If there is estate tax due, then your legal representative can choose an alternate time to value your assets (six months from the date of your death) provided that the total amount of tax decreases. For cash accounts, brokerage accounts, publicly traded stock and bonds, the fair market value is normally easy to obtain. For hard-to-value assets, such as business interests

CHAP. 7: ESTATE PLANNING / RETIREMENT PLANS 377

and real estate, the fair market value must be determined by a qualified appraiser.

### ⅍ Does a tax return need to be filed after my death?

After your death, your legal representative is responsible for filing a federal death tax return (Form 706, U.S. Estate Tax Return), which is similar to your federal income tax return. This return must list the fair market value of all your assets. This is known as your *gross taxable estate* or *gross estate*. Generally, your legal representative must file the return if your gross estate exceeds your applicable exclusion amount.

### ⅍ What is the applicable exclusion amount?

The *applicable exclusion amount* is the amount of property which can be excluded from your taxable estate. For 1999, the applicable exclusion amount is $650,000.

### ⅍ Is my estate allowed any tax deductions?

Yes. Just like your income tax return, your estate is allowed certain tax deductions. Typical deductions would include your outstanding debts, claims against your estate, and funeral and administration expenses. Under certain circumstances additional deductions are allowed for property which you have left to charity and property which you have left to your spouse. Subtracting all these deductions from your gross estate results in your net taxable estate. Your legal representative must then determine the amount of federal estate tax due.

### ⅍ How is the amount of federal estate tax determined?

The amount of tax depends upon the size of your taxable estate. The federal estate tax rates increase as the size of your taxable

378          WAYS AND MEANS

estate increases. The rates start at 37 percent and top out at 55 percent for estates over $3 million.

### ⚜ *Is my estate allowed any credits against the federal estate tax?*

Yes. Again, similar to your income tax return, your estate is allowed *tax credits.* A tax credit is a dollar-for-dollar reduction in the amount of tax due. Every U.S. citizen or resident is allowed a tax credit called the *unified tax credit.* Before 1998, this tax credit was $192,800. For deaths before 1998, this tax credit resulted in no tax being due on the first $600,000 of your taxable estate. For example, if before 1998 you died with a taxable estate worth $600,000, the calculation of the tax due was $192,800. From this tax bill, your legal representative would have subtracted your tax credit of $192,800, resulting in no federal estate tax due. Thus your unified tax credit of $192,800 resulted in $600,000 of your property escaping taxation. Instead of referring to the unified tax credit most people preferred to think in terms of the corresponding dollar amount of tax-free property. This $600,000 amount came to be known at the *exemption equivalent* or *exemption.*

The Taxpayer Relief Act of 1997 included a systematic increase in the $600,000 exemption through the year 2006. Table 7-1 shows the increases.

The new tax law refers to this increased exemption as the *applicable exclusion amount.* Thus for 1999, the applicable exclusion amount is $650,000, which resulted from a unified tax credit of $211,300.

### ⚜ *Is my estate allowed any other tax credits aside from the unified credit?*

Yes. Under certain circumstances, there are other limited tax credits available. These include state death tax credits, foreign tax credits, and credits for previously taxed property.

CHAP. 7: ESTATE PLANNING / RETIREMENT PLANS **379**

**TABLE 7-1    Annual Increases of the Applicable Exclusion**

| Year | Amount | Tax credit |
|---|---|---|
| 1998 | $ 625,000 | $202,050 |
| 1999 | 650,000 | 211,300 |
| 2000 | 675,000 | 220,550 |
| 2001 | 675,000 | 220,550 |
| 2002 | 700,000 | 229,800 |
| 2003 | 700,000 | 229,800 |
| 2004 | 850,000 | 287,300 |
| 2005 | 950,000 | 326,300 |
| 2006 & thereafter | 1,000,000 | 345,800 |

### ⚜ *How can my spouse and I save on federal estate tax?*

You must first take advantage of two estate tax laws: the unlimited marital deduction and the applicable exclusion amount. In addition, there are many other estate tax–saving tools and techniques which are outside the scope of this book. You should consult with your estate planning attorney, financial advisors, and accountant to assist you in planning your estate.

### ⚜ *What is the unlimited marital deduction?*

If your spouse is a U.S. citizen, then upon your death you can leave all your property to your spouse without incurring federal estate tax. This is known as the *unlimited marital deduction.* For example if you die owning $10 million of property and leave it all to your spouse, then your estate will get a $10 million marital deduction and your taxable estate will be zero. In order to get this full deduction, you must generally leave this property outright to your spouse with no strings attached. Therefore, if you leave property in a trust for the benefit of your spouse, your estate would normally not get this full deduction since you have placed limitations, or strings, on your spouse: he or she does not have full control over these assets.

However, the tax law will allow this full deduction for a trust that meets certain requirements. Such a trust is known as a *marital trust,* which can be created as a subtrust within a revocable living trust or a will. A marital trust defers, but does not avoid, federal estate tax. In order to get the full marital deduction at your death, the property must be included in your surviving spouse's estate upon his or her subsequent death.

### ⚔ *So how do I combine the exclusion amount and unlimited marital deduction to avoid federal estate tax?*

The challenge for a married couple is for each spouse to use his or her applicable exclusion amount ($650,000 for 1999) at death. Using both of your exclusions would allow you to pass $1.3 million (for 1999) to your family without federal estate tax.

Assume you and your husband each own $650,000 of assets in 1999. You die and leave all of your property outright to your husband. Your husband now owns $1.3 million of assets and dies the next day. His taxable estate is $1.3 million but his estate gets a tax credit of $211,300, thus shielding the first $650,000 of his taxable estate. His estate owes federal estate tax on the remaining $650,000 which amounts to approximately $258,500 of federal estate tax.

The easiest way for you to avoid this tax would be for you to leave your $650,000 to someone other than your husband, perhaps your children. However, this often conflicts with your and your husband's goals of providing for each other. Instead, you could create a trust for the benefit of your husband to shelter your $650,000 applicable exclusion amount. This is commonly known as a *family trust* (also known as a *by-pass trust, B trust,* or *unified credit trust*), which can be created as a subtrust within a revocable living trust or a will. The terms of the family trust normally

# CHAP. 7: ESTATE PLANNING / RETIREMENT PLANS    381

provide that your husband has the use of the money for his life-time, but not so much control as to be taxed in his estate when he dies. Therefore, using the above example, if your husband dies the next day, he has only his own assets of $650,000 which are covered by his applicable exclusion of $650,000, resulting in no federal estate tax due.

Alternatively, if you die, $650,000 would be left to your family trust. Since your husband did not have too much control over the family trust, none of the $650,000 is included in his estate when he dies. Therefore, with proper planning $1.3 million of your combined assets (in 1999) would be protected from federal estate tax.

### ❧ *How do I create a family trust for the benefit of my spouse?*

A family trust is created at your death. Your will can be designed to create a family trust. Alternatively, your revocable living trust could be divided into one or more subtrusts at your death, one of which would be a family trust.

### ❧ *What is the maximum control my spouse can have in the family trust?*

The maximum rights which your spouse can be given in the family trust—without the assets of the trust being included in your spouse's estate when he or she dies—are:

- All of the income

- Any or all of the principal in the trustee's discretion for your spouse's health, education, maintenance, and support

- The absolute right to demand the greater of $5000 or 5 percent of the value of the principal each year

- A limited right to determine (normally among your descendants) where the remaining trust property should go at your spouse's death (This limited right is known as a *limited testamentary power of appointment.*)

⚜ *What are the minimum rights my spouse can have in the family trust?*

The family trust does not have to provide for your spouse. However, at your death, your spouse may have certain rights under state law. These laws determine the minimum amount of your property which must be left to your spouse. If you do not leave your spouse this minimum amount of property, your spouse may be able to "elect" to take this minimum amount.

⚜ *I understand that if I die before my spouse, the family trust will shelter my applicable exclusion amount. How do I avoid federal estate tax on the balance of my property?*

If you die owning more assets than your applicable exclusion amount, in order to avoid federal estate tax on your estate, you must leave the balance of your property in such a way that it qualifies for the unlimited marital deduction. This can be accomplished by leaving the balance of your property outright to your spouse or in a certain type of trust, called a marital trust, for the benefit of your spouse. If the balance of your property qualifies for the marital deduction, then all federal estate tax will be deferred until your spouse's death. In order to get the full marital deduction at your death, this property must be included in your surviving spouse's estate upon his or her subsequent death.

⚜ *How do I create a marital trust for the benefit of my spouse?*

A marital trust is created at your death. Your will can be designed to create a marital trust. Alternatively, your revocable living trust could be divided into one or more subtrusts at your death, one of which would be a marital trust.

## CHAP. 7: ESTATE PLANNING / RETIREMENT PLANS    383

∌ *What are the maximum rights my spouse can have in the marital trust?*

Unlike the assets of the family trust, the assets of the marital trust will be included in your spouse's estate; therefore, there are no tax reasons for limiting your spouse's rights under the marital trust. However, in order to accomplish your personal planning goals, you may want to limit your spouse's rights. For example, you may wish to restrict your spouse's access to the principal of the marital trust to ensure that these assets will ultimately be distributed to your children at your spouse's subsequent death.

∌ *What are the minimum rights my spouse can have in the marital trust?*

In order to qualify for the unlimited marital deduction, your spouse *must* have the following rights in the marital trust:

- All of the income (payable at least annually) for his or her lifetime
- The right to compel the trustee to convert non-income-producing assets into income-producing assets.

Furthermore, distributions of principal from the marital trust can be made to no one other than to your spouse during his or her lifetime. Finally, your executor must elect on your federal estate tax return to qualify the marital trust for the marital deduction.

A marital trust that provides these minimum rights is known as a *qualified terminable interest property (QTIP)* trust.

∌ *Could you please summarize how my spouse and I can save federal estate tax?*

If you are married, your estate is in excess of the applicable exclusion amount, and you desire to save federal estate taxes, you cannot leave all your property outright to your spouse. Your will or living trust should establish a family trust and a marital trust if you die first. The family trust will be funded with your assets, up to your applicable exclusion amount. This will shelter your applicable exclusion amount from federal estate tax in either your or your spouse's estate. The balance of your assets, if any, will be distributed to the marital trust. Drafted properly, the marital trust will qualify for the full marital deduction and postpone any federal estate tax until your spouse dies. Upon your spouse's death, your spouse will be able to shelter his or her applicable exclusion amount from federal estate tax. Thus, if you both died in 1999, $1.3 million will have been sheltered from federal estate tax.

## Revocable Living Trusts

⊀ *What is a revocable living trust?*

A *revocable living trust* is a written document, which an estate planning lawyer can draft for you, wherein you, or you and your spouse, as the *trust maker* of the trust appoint yourself as your own *trustee* (the manager of the trust) and name yourself as the life *beneficiary* (the person who enjoys the use of the properties of the trust). Thus you, or you and your spouse, are the three essential parties to the trust:

1. The trust maker (or *grantor, trustor, settlor,* or *creator*)
2. The trustee
3. The life beneficiary

Most of your assets will be retitled in the name of the living trust. As trustee of your own trust, you have 100 percent control over your assets: you can sell assets, buy assets, add assets to the trust, and remove assets from the trust. Since the trust is revocable, you

CHAP. 7: ESTATE PLANNING / RETIREMENT PLANS    385

can amend, alter, or revoke your trust and your estate plan at any time.

In the document, you usually name one or more individuals to serve as successor, or backup, trustees should you die or become unable to serve as the trustee. A successor trustee can be one of your adult children or a close friend, a relative, or a trust company or bank trust department.

Most often, the trust includes instructions specifying that upon your death or upon the death of the surviving spouse your children or other loved ones will become the *remainder beneficiaries,* the persons who enjoy the remaining property of the trust. Your trust agreement can also include your instructions on how to distribute the remaining property to those beneficiaries. For example, you can designate that your remainder beneficiaries must attain a certain age or level of maturity before receiving the property, and you can instruct the trustee to distribute that property to them outright or in increments.

If your children are both successor trustees and remainder beneficiaries, they will, as trustees and with the assistance of a lawyer, transfer the property to themselves.

If any of your children are too young to receive their distribution, the successor trustee will manage their shares for their health, support, maintenance, and education until they attain the age you designated. At that time, the trustee can distribute their shares.

⚜ *Can I put my qualified retirement plan or IRA into my revocable living trust?*

No. You cannot put your qualified retirement plan or IRA directly into your revocable living trust. A transfer of ownership of your qualified retirement plan or IRA is a legal change in ownership. If you did this, the full balance of your plan or account would be subject to income tax. If the change of ownership occurred before age 59½ you might also be subjected to the 10 percent penalty for early withdrawal.

## 386    WAYS AND MEANS

> ✍ *If I cannot transfer my qualified retirement plan or IRA into my living trust, how do I control it?*

It is controlled by the beneficiary designation of the qualified retirement plan or IRA; however, although this answer sounds simple, it is actually quite complex. You should consult with a professional advisor who is well-versed in this area. A careless use of the beneficiary designation could result in additional taxation, not only from an income tax perspective but from an estate tax perspective as well. Not only could you be faced with additional taxation, but your retirement plan could go to unintended heirs. This is a particularly critical issue in second marriages. If you do not analyze the designation properly, it could ultimately conflict with your estate planning goals.

> ✍ *If my largest asset is my retirement plan, why should I name my living trust as the beneficiary? Doesn't my retirement plan avoid probate anyway?*

Your living trust has the ability to stretch out your retirement plan distributions to defer additional taxes, as well as provide creditor and divorce protection, and protect your retirement plan from estate taxes. These are just some of the added benefits that your living trust can provide you. For this reason, you should discuss with your attorney the need to protect your retirement plan by coordinating it with your living trust.

> ✍ *Why doesn't my will control where my assets go at my death?*

A will only controls probate assets. Not all assets go through the probate process. Assets that are jointly owned, contractual in nature, or have beneficiary designations bypass probate. Such assets go straight to the joint owner or the person named in the beneficiary designation. Insurance policies are a good example. If a policy names a beneficiary, the proceeds pass outside probate and go directly to the beneficiary.

CHAP. 7: ESTATE PLANNING / RETIREMENT PLANS   387

*If my will controls how my assets go, should I leave my retirement plan payable to my estate?*

No. If you want to maintain the best control for your estate, you want your assets to pass into your revocable living trust. Through proper planning, you can create some very powerful options for your surviving spouse and family members that will not be available through probate court.

## Trust as Beneficiary of a Retirement Plan

*Why would I want to name a trust as the beneficiary of a qualified retirement plan or IRA benefits?*

Using a revocable living trust—the primary estate planning tool for many individuals—to receive retirement plan benefits is often the best way to retain control over the ultimate distribution of retirement plan assets. By utilizing a trust as the beneficiary, you guarantee that the benefits will be distributed to whom you want, when you want, and the way you want. If the distribution is made to an individual directly, you lose control over the distribution and cannot protect those assets from the creditors (including ex-spouses) and predators of the beneficiary.

It is not unusual to use a trust to manage the distribution of retirement plan assets for the benefit of your beneficiaries. Perhaps you feel your spouse may not have the necessary investment expertise or doesn't want to manage the portfolio, or perhaps it is your desire that your assets remain in your bloodline after your death.

If the beneficiaries are your children or grandchildren, you might use a trust to alleviate some of your "value" concerns as to how much money and the timing of when your money is distributed to them. Furthermore, you can provide that the assets remain available to successive generations without further estate taxation.

388                                    WAYS AND MEANS

Another alternative is that you are in a second marriage and want to eventually pass your assets to your children of your first marriage yet desire your new spouse to have all the income for his or her lifetime.

*I am in my forties and have a living trust–centered estate plan. I also have a 401(k) plan and an IRA. Should my living trust be named as the primary beneficiary of my retirement plans?*

Structured properly, your living trust can be named as the primary beneficiary and can accomplish your goals and objectives. However, please bear in mind that for us to answer this question best, we need to know the size of your estate and the nature of your assets. Further, our knowing your goals, objectives, needs, and concerns are critical. There are many variables, such as whether your combined gross estate is under $1.3 million in 1999, whether you have children from a previous marriage whom you want to protect, and whether there is liquidity in your estate other than the retirement accounts.

## Spouse as Beneficiary of a Retirement Plan

*What are the possible disadvantages of making my spouse the beneficiary of my IRA or qualified retirement plan?*

First, to take advantage of certain techniques, such as utilizing your applicable exclusion amount or your $1 million generation-skipping exemption effectively, you may prefer naming a trust as a beneficiary of your qualified retirement plan or IRA. This is especially true if your retirement assets make up the bulk of your estate.

Second, if your spouse already has sufficient funds to live on, paying the retirement assets to your spouse could expose the assets to greater taxation than if you left them to a child, for example.

CHAP. 7: ESTATE PLANNING / RETIREMENT PLANS   389

While this might involve a tax at the first death, it is sometimes wise to incur the early tax.

Third, leaving the retirement plan assets to a trust enables the owner of the assets to control their ultimate distribution, which is advantageous if you are in a second marriage or have concerns about your spouse's remarriage and loss of control of the IRA or qualified plan funds to a new spouse.

In the final analysis, it is always your estate planning goals that govern a choice such as this.

*What is the possible advantage of making my spouse the beneficiary of my IRA or qualified retirement plan?*

Although it is generally advisable to name your spouse as the beneficiary of the retirement plan for income tax reasons, taxes should not control your estate planning decisions. Under the definition of proper estate planning, saving taxes is the last item to be considered in making a viable estate plan. Using a trust to receive retirement plan benefits is often a better option, even with the adverse tax consequences, if your goals are to be satisfied.

## THE FAMILY TRUST

*Are there any income tax disadvantages to using qualified retirement plan or IRA assets to fund the family trust?*

Yes. If income tax deferral is the most important goal, it is not recommended that you use qualified retirement plan or IRA assets to fund the family trust. For every dollar of plan benefit value which is allocated to the family trust, the trustee will be required to pay income tax on that dollar when the benefits are actually received by the trust. In this way, less than the full value of your applicable exclusion amount will be available for distribution to the beneficiaries since your applicable exclusion amount will be

390                                    WAYS AND MEANS

reduced by the amount of income taxes paid. The greater the amount of retirement benefits allocated to the family trust, the less actual value available to your ultimate beneficiaries.

> *What is the estate tax advantage to leaving my qualified retirement plans or IRAs to the family trust rather than directly to my spouse?*

One of the best ways to avoid estate tax is to leave assets *up to* your applicable exclusion amount to someone other than your spouse, typically in a family trust, of which your spouse is a limited beneficiary. The applicable exclusion amount of $650,000 in 1999 will gradually increase, until it reaches $1 million in 2006. Whatever the applicable exclusion amount is for the year in which the death occurs will be the relevant number.

Let's assume the 1999 figure of $650,000 for illustration. If you do not have $650,000 in other assets to allocate to the family trust at your death, you are not maximizing the amount that you can pass estate tax–free to the next generation, unless you also leave part of your qualified retirement plan or IRA to the family trust.

SCENARIO 1 Assume that your estate consists of $300,000 in other assets and $400,000 in an IRA; your wife has $700,000 of assets; and you both die in 1999. At your death, your estate plan leaves the $300,000 in other assets to a family trust for your family and leaves your wife the $400,000 IRA. Your wife rolls over your IRA to her own IRA. When your wife dies, her taxable estate will be her $700,000 plus the $400,000 rollover IRA you left her, or $1,100,000. Your wife will pay estate tax on $450,000, which is everything over her own $650,000 applicable exclusion amount.

SCENARIO 2 If you left $300,000 in nonretirement assets plus $350,000 of your IRA to the family trust and only left the extra $50,000 to your wife, then at her death, she would pay estate tax on $100,000: her own $700,000 plus the $50,000 you left to her directly from your IRA, less her applicable exclusion of $650,000.

# CHAP. 7: ESTATE PLANNING / RETIREMENT PLANS    391

By putting $350,000 of your IRA into the family trust instead of leaving it outright to your spouse, this saves your children approximately 40 percent in federal estate taxes on the $350,000 of your IRA.

The same estate tax result would occur if you left $350,000 of your IRA to your children or grandchildren outright. The important point is *not* to leave it to your spouse directly, to be added to his or her taxable estate.

Therefore, in order to avoid any unnecessary estate tax, it is normally best to leave as much of your qualified retirement plan or IRA in a family trust (of which your spouse can be the primary lifetime beneficiary) as necessary to take advantage of your applicable exclusion amount or, as an alternative, to your children or grandchildren.

 

≤ *There are estate tax advantages if I leave my qualified retirement plans or IRAs to the family trust. However, this results in less income tax deferral. What should I do?*

The answer to this question depends upon your estate planning goals. If saving federal estate tax is your primary goal, then leaving the qualified retirement plan or IRA to the family trust makes sense. In addition, the family trust can provide your beneficiaries with creditor and divorce protection and ensure that your assets stay in your bloodline.

However, if maximum deferral of income taxes after your death is your primary goal, then leaving your qualified retirement plan or IRA to your spouse generally results in the longest income tax deferral.

After reviewing their estate planning goals, many married couples might use the following strategy:

1.  Direct that assets other than qualified retirement plans and IRAs be placed in the family trust.

392                                    WAYS AND MEANS

2. If the value of all other assets are less than the applicable exclusion amount, then leave to the family trust only an amount of the qualified retirement plans and IRAs necessary to fully utilize the remaining applicable exclusion amount.

3. Leave the balance of qualified retirement plans and IRAs to the surviving spouse.

*If my living trust or will creates a family trust at my death, what benefits can be provided to my surviving spouse?*

With proper drafting, your spouse can have all the following benefits in the family trust:

- All the income
- As much of the principal necessary for his or her health, education, maintenance, or support
- The unilateral right to withdraw up to the greater of 5 percent of the principal or $5000 each year, without any showing of "need"
- A limited right to direct the distribution of the balance at his or her death (limited in that it cannot be given to your spouse's own estate or his or her creditors)

As discussed earlier in this chapter, the family trust could limit the benefits provided above but cannot give the spouse any greater benefits.

The key is to allow your spouse enough access to the family trust to live on without giving too much control which will cause your spouse to be treated as owning the assets of the family trust and therefore taxed in your spouse's estate when he or she dies.

Your planning goals, within the minimum and maximum limits, will dictate the benefits of the family trust, which is certainly well within settled estate tax law and can be included in your estate plan by an experienced estate planning attorney.

## CHAP. 7: ESTATE PLANNING / RETIREMENT PLANS    393

## PLANNING FOR SPOUSES

## Marital Trust Planning

*How much property can I leave to my surviving spouse without federal death tax?*

There is no limit on the amount of property which you can leave outright to your spouse and hence the term *unlimited marital deduction*. In order for your estate to receive the marital deduction, your surviving spouse must normally receive the property outright, with no strings attached. However, the law has made a few exceptions, including the type of marital trust called the qualified terminable interest property (QTIP) trust, which you create for the benefit of your spouse within your revocable living trust or will. Property left in a QTIP trust will receive the full marital deduction, even though the property has not passed outright to your surviving spouse.

*What is a qualified terminable interest property trust?*

A *qualified terminable interest property (QTIP)* trust is a special kind of trust created for the benefit of your spouse and can be a useful estate planning tool. It can be created during your lifetime or after your death through your will or revocable living trust. The QTIP must contain certain provisions required by law in order to receive the full marital deduction.

*What are the requirements of a QTIP trust?*

Four basic requirements must be met in order for the QTIP trust to qualify for the unlimited marital deduction:

1. The trust must give your surviving spouse the right to all the income produced by the trust for his or her lifetime, and the income must be paid at least annually.

394

2. If the assets placed in the trust do not generate income, your spouse must have the right to compel the trustee to "exchange" these assets for those that do produce income.

3. During the lifetime of your spouse, no other person or entity can have any power to transfer any part of the trust property to any person other than to your spouse.

4. Your executor must elect the QTIP marital deduction on your federal estate tax return, and the election must be irrevocable.

⇘ *Why would I want to create a QTIP trust instead of leaving my assets outright to my surviving spouse?*

What might be perceived as the biggest advantage of leaving assets outright to your surviving spouse—total control of the assets—could also be perceived as the biggest disadvantage. For a variety of reasons, you might not want to give your surviving spouse total control of your assets. These reasons could include:

- The fear of your spouse's remarriage and later divorce resulting in your assets going outside your bloodline
- Providing for your spouse but ensuring that your and your spouse's children (or your children from a previous marriage) receive property after both of your deaths
- Your spouse's lack of investment experience
- Your spouse's potential to squander money
- Your spouse's potential to be influenced by others, including family members
- Protection from your spouse's creditors

⇘ *Can an IRA or qualified plan balance be left to QTIP trust?*

Yes, but certain provisions need to be included in the trust to coordinate with the minimum distribution rules.

## CHAP. 7: ESTATE PLANNING / RETIREMENT PLANS — 395

*⧖ You have explained previously some estate planning advantages of the QTIP trust. Under the minimum distribution rules are there any advantages of leaving retirement plan proceeds to a QTIP trust instead of to my spouse?*

No. Distributions to a spouse will generally be deferred for a longer period of time than if the distribution is made to a QTIP trust. Under the QTIP rules, a QTIP trust must distribute to the spouse all income earned each year. If retirement plan benefits are payable to a QTIP trust, regulations require that all the retirement plan income be distributed annually to the trust (and from the trust to the spouse) even if the income so distributed is more than the required minimum distribution. Depending on the life expectancy of the spouse, it is likely that, at least in the early years, the income will exceed the required minimum distribution. This will have the effect, therefore, of accelerating the distribution of taxable income from the retirement plan. If the amount distributed by the retirement plan to the QTIP trust is deemed to be principal under trust accounting rules and not income and if the distribution is not transferred to the spouse, there could be significant additional income taxes paid on the plan distribution due to the high trust income tax bracket.

There are also substantial problems if the trust agreement utilizes a "pecuniary formula" for determining the marital trust share, since this would have the effect of requiring the immediate payment of all deferred income taxes. Retirement plan distributions are *income in respect of a decedent (IRD),* and distribution to a trust using a pecuniary formula will result in immediate acceleration of all IRD. You should consult your attorney to ascertain whether your will or living trust contains a pecuniary formula.

## Planning for Second Marriages

*⧖ Is it important for me to name my children from my first*

*marriage as beneficiaries of my qualified plan if I have a valid
will and a prenuptial agreement with my new wife?*

First, the beneficiary designation at the plan level—that is, a written designation on file kept by the plan administrator of the company retirement plan—is the governing designation for purposes of determining who has the rights to receive benefits under a qualified retirement plan after the participant's death. Thus, your beneficiary designation, rather than your will, controls the disposition of these assets.

Second, it is a common mistake to assume that a prenuptial agreement can legally waive a spouse's rights in a qualified plan. With most qualified plans, the law provides that a spouse has to waive, in writing, his or her rights under the plan in order for the participant to leave those assets to someone else. Many prenuptial agreements have each spouse waiving his or her rights in the other spouse's qualified plans. However, these prenuptial agreements are based on state law. Qualified plans are governed by federal law. If the laws conflict, then federal law controls. Some cases have held that, under federal law, a spouse's rights in a qualified plan do not arise until after the marriage and therefore he or she cannot waive these rights before marriage. In order for the waiver to be valid, the spouse must execute a written waiver and deliver it to the plan administrator after the marriage.

There have been numerous court cases involving disputes over beneficiary designations. In second marriages, it is common for new spouses to waive their rights to the participants' retirement benefits in order for the participants to leave these benefits to their children from previous marriages. However, upon a participant's death, the children from the previous marriage may soon discover that a valid waiver was not executed at the plan level. Even though a prenuptial agreement or valid will under state law acknowledges the waiver of the new spouse's rights, the new spouse will be entitled to the benefits under the plan because no valid waiver existed.

It is therefore critical to have qualified retirement plans with

CHAP. 7: ESTATE PLANNING / RETIREMENT PLANS **397**

properly executed paperwork and to keep valid copies with your personal records.

🔖 *My husband and I both have children from prior marriages. We both have substantial retirement plans which constitute the majority of our combined assets. We each want the security of having access to all the funds should we need them. We have been happily married for many years and want to care for each other, but we each want to guarantee that what remains of each estate will take care of the children from each of our previous marriages. What should we do?*

The first issue is to determine to what extent you will need these funds upon retirement to maintain your desired lifestyle. Second, it is important to assess what extent your husband will need the retirement funds to maintain his lifestyle in the event you predecease him. In making determinations about the need for funds, it is important that the primary issues of health care and long-term care have been adequately addressed in order to make proper assessments. Upon analysis of your anticipated needs, if you plan to rely on systematic withdrawals from your retirement funds, above the minimum-required distribution, then your retirement funds may be depleted over time leaving very little for your children.

Therefore, the best way to meet your objective of providing a definite inheritance for your children may be through a wealth-replacement trust funded with life insurance. Through such a trust, you can guarantee the amount your children will inherit, and these funds will be estate tax–free. Then you or your husband can utilize the remaining funds held in the retirement accounts.

Furthermore, when making this assessment of lifestyle assurance, you should determine if you need life insurance to meet the needs of the surviving spouse. Life insurance could provide the funds for your husband to live on in the event he survives you, and you could then leave your retirement plan assets directly to your children.

> ✒ *I have heard that it is important to equalize our estates for estate tax planning. Our combined estates are valued at $1.4 million, which consists of my family home and my $1 million retirement plan. First and foremost, I want to guarantee that my children from a prior marriage receive what I have worked many years to accumulate. I am unwilling to take chances on their inheritance. What should I do?*

Based on the nature and ownership of your assets and your desire to retain full control of them, common estate tax planning is not an option. By holding all the assets in your name, if your spouse predeceases you, you would forfeit the opportunity to utilize your spouse's applicable exclusion amount. If your spouse died in 1999 and your combined gross estate exceeded $1.3 million, this would result in over $258,000 of additional estate taxes being due to the IRS at your subsequent death.

Even if your primary goal were to transfer assets to your children rather than to your spouse, you might find it difficult to forgo utilizing your spouse's applicable exclusion amount which would save $258,000 in estate taxes. Since estate taxes begin at 37 percent and quickly increase to 55 percent, it is important to utilize every means available to shelter hard-earned dollars from the IRS's grasp while keeping your goals and objectives.

There is a way to take advantage of your spouse's applicable exclusion amount without forfeiting control of who ultimately inherits your assets. You can establish an irrevocable *inter vivos* QTIP trust. In establishing such a trust, you can utilize your spouse's applicable exclusion amount, and the trustee whom you name can control the assets according to the terms you have designated during your life and upon your death. Through a properly structured trust, you can designate who ultimately receives the assets. The trust must provide that (1) during your spouse's lifetime, your spouse is entitled to receive all income from the property and (2) if the property is nonproductive, your spouse can demand that it be made productive to allow your spouse the opportunity to collect any income earned. You cannot diminish

Chap. 7: Estate Planning / Retirement Plans   399

those two rights of your spouse even in the event you and your spouse divorce.

This planning opportunity is ideal for a long-term second marriage with a taxable estate, in which one of you holds title to the majority of the assets and also has children from a prior marriage that you want to protect.

Also, this plan can be effectively used in combination with other planning techniques, such as wealth replacement trusts, dynasty trusts, and a stretch-out plan for the retirement funds.

*I'm in a second marriage, and although I love my spouse, I want to know that my children from a previous marriage will inherit my retirement funds. What can I do?*

Planning for your spouse can be accomplished through the use of a QTIP trust. Such a trust allows your spouse's lifetime needs to be met according to the terms you establish, but you govern the distribution of assets remaining in the trust at the death of your spouse.

## Planning for Noncitizen Spouses

*Do I need to make special retirement and estate plans for my noncitizen spouse?*

Yes. The Technical and Miscellaneous Revenue Act (TAMRA) of 1988 has quietly but effectively eliminated the estate and gift tax marital deduction on property passing to a surviving spouse who is *not* a U.S. citizen. TAMRA closed a loophole in the 1981 tax act which gave the unlimited marital deduction to noncitizen spouses. Apparently, numerous noncitizen spouses returned to their homelands following the death of their citizen spouses, taking the marital property with them without paying any U.S. estate tax.

Unfortunately, property held jointly with a noncitizen spouse does not fall under the "qualified joint interest" provisions of IRS Code Section 2040. Joint property is included in the estate of the first spouse to die except to the extent the surviving spouse can prove contribution (i.e., helped pay for the property).

This makes jointly owned property with rights of survivorship particularly disastrous to a citizen spouse who paid for the property and dies before his or her noncitizen spouse. The entire value of the property is included in the estate of the citizen spouse, and no marital deduction is available as the property passes to the surviving noncitizen spouse. Therefore, any amounts left to the noncitizen spouse above the deceased citizen spouse's applicable exclusion amount will be subject to federal estate tax at the citizen spouse's death.

*If my noncitizen spouse dies first, what are the estate tax consequences?*

A person who is a resident of the United States at the time of his or her death but who is not a citizen (i.e., a resident alien) does receive the usual unified credit and estate tax charitable deduction. Thus, the resident alien may leave up to his or her applicable exclusion amount to heirs estate tax–free and may bequeath an unlimited amount to charity.

However, there is no unlimited marital deduction if your noncitizen spouse leaves property to you and you are also a noncitizen. In that circumstance, if your spouse dies with more than $650,000 (in 1999), federal estate tax will be due at your spouse's death, even though the excess property was left to you.

*Is the unlimited marital deduction available to a noncitizen spouse?*

No, but the gift tax annual exclusion has been increased from $10,000 to $100,000 per year for gifts to a noncitizen spouse, if such transfer would otherwise qualify for the marital deduction.

CHAP. 7: ESTATE PLANNING / RETIREMENT PLANS **401**

❧ *If a noncitizen is married to a U.S. citizen and the U.S. citizen dies, may the noncitizen receive Social Security payments as a surviving spouse?*

Yes, if the surviving spouse is lawfully present in the United States at the time of the U.S. citizen's death.

❧ *Is the estate tax marital deduction available in my estate for transfers to my surviving spouse, even though she is not a U.S. citizen?*

No, transfers to your surviving spouse who is not a U.S. citizen are not eligible for the marital deduction unless the transfer is to a qualified domestic trust.

❧ *What is a qualified domestic trust?*

A *qualified domestic trust (QDOT)* allows the deceased spouse's estate to postpone paying federal estate tax.

❧ *What are the requirements for a qualified domestic trust?*

The general requirements for a QDOT are:

- The trustee of the QDOT must be either a U.S. citizen or a U.S. domestic corporation.
- No distribution of principal, only income, can be made from the trust unless the U.S. trustee has the right to withhold from that distribution the deferred estate tax payable under Internal Revenue Code Section 2056(A).
- The trust must be administered and maintained under the laws of a particular state or the District of Columbia.
- The decedent's personal representatives must treat the trust as a QDOT.

402 WAYS AND MEANS

- The trust must be either a marital deduction, power of appointment trust or a QTIP trust.

## INCOME TAXES

### Income in Respect of a Decedent

*What is income in respect of a decedent?*

*Income in respect of a decedent (IRD)* is any income which you earned before your death but was not paid until after your death. An example would be a paycheck issued after an employee's death: The employee earned the income but did not receive it before his or her death. Therefore, no income tax has been paid on this income, and whoever receives these funds will have to pay the income tax.

Generally, all qualified retirement plan and IRA proceeds received by your beneficiaries after your death are IRD. Your beneficiaries will be responsible for paying the income tax as they receive the proceeds.

*I have named my daughter as beneficiary of my retirement plan assets, and she is in a 39.6 percent federal income tax bracket. Does my daughter have to pay 39.6 cents in federal income taxes on each dollar she withdraws from my retirement plan account?*

Your understanding would be correct if there were no estate taxes paid on these retirement plan assets at the time of your death. However, in the usual situation when estate taxes are paid, there is an income tax deduction for any estate taxes paid with respect to retirement plan assets. The calculation is complicated by having to determine the amount of the income tax on each withdrawal. In general terms, however, retirement plan assets are as-

# Chap. 7: Estate Planning / Retirement Plans 403

sumed to be the most heavily taxed assets in an estate. Therefore, the deduction is somewhat greater than it would be if the retirement plan assets only received a pro rata share of the estate taxes paid.

It should also be noted that your daughter would receive this deduction only if she itemized her deductions on her federal income tax return. Otherwise, she would not get the deduction, which would result in a double tax. In the highest income and estate tax brackets, the combined tax hit to your retirement plan assets could be as high as 95 percent.

## Retirement Plan Beneficiaries

*My father left an estate of $1 million to my brother and me. My brother received $500,000 of nonretirement assets, and I received $500,000 of retirement fund assets. My brother and I paid the estate tax on the estate equally. When I make withdrawals from the retirement plan accounts, do I get a deduction on my income tax return only for the half of the estate taxes that I actually paid?*

No. On these facts, assuming your father made no taxable gifts during his lifetime, the entire estate tax is attributable to the retirement plan account, and therefore, under the law, you are entitled to 100 percent of the deduction, assuming you itemize.

*Is there any way that my family can eventually avoid paying income taxes on my IRA?*

Generally, when funds are distributed from an IRA, income taxes are due. If you leave your IRA proceeds to your spouse, the taxes can be deferred, but income taxes will eventually have to be paid. If you leave the proceeds to your children, heirs, or your estate, income taxes will likewise eventually have to be paid. However, there is one exception. If you leave the proceeds to a qualified

# 404

charity, the charity will not have to pay income taxes as distributions are made.

Therefore, for most people, the tax planning goal is not to eliminate income taxes but instead to defer these taxes as long as possible. Only with proper planning can this goal be accomplished.

## ESTATE TAXES

### Paying Federal Estate Tax

*How can my family pay my federal estate tax?*

Your federal estate tax is due within 9 months from your date of death, and your family has basically four ways to pay it:

1. Use your remaining cash or other liquid assets.
2. Liquidate your assets to cash.
3. Borrow money (under certain circumstances, even from the federal government). or
4. Use prearranged assets, such as life insurance proceeds.

### Estate Tax Planning

*I am concerned about the amount of estate taxes that will be due at my death, but I have a substantial amount of assets in my IRA, all of which can be readily turned into cash. Is my IRA account a good source from which to pay estate taxes at my death?*

Your IRA is probably the worst place to look for cash with which to pay these taxes, since any withdrawal made to get cash to pay estate taxes triggers IRD taxes. Assets held in retirement plans lost the last of their exemptions from estate taxes in 1985. With rela-

CHAP. 7: ESTATE PLANNING / RETIREMENT PLANS    405

tively few exceptions, taxes on all estate assets are due in full, and in cash, within 9 months of death, at rates up to 55 percent.

IRD taxes, the income tax paid by the beneficiary of an IRA or other qualified retirement plan, is due as distributions are made. Since this is considered income to the recipient, it is added to all of his or her other income for the year and is, therefore, usually taxed at high rates. Even though the estate tax attributable to the IRA is deductible when calculating the IRD tax, the result is often an effective IRD tax rate of 21 percent.

*I really like the idea of turning my IRA into a stretch-out IRA for the benefit of my children and postponing the income taxes. But I also understand that the estate taxes have to be paid. Is there a better way to pay them?*

Absolutely! The key is for the estate to have liquid assets outside the IRA which are sufficient to pay the estate tax at death. For many people, the best way to create that pool of liquid assets is through an *irrevocable life insurance trust (ILIT)*.

Here's how the strategy works. Preferably you use non-IRA assets or, if necessary, distributions from the IRA each year (usually just a portion of the IRA's expected earnings) to make gifts to the ILIT. The trustee of the ILIT uses the gifts you make to the ILIT to pay the premiums on a second-to-die life insurance policy covering your life and your spouse's life, or an individual policy if you are single.

These gifts help slow the rate of growth of the estate and thus reduce the amount of estate taxes ultimately due. More importantly, at the death of you and your spouse, the life insurance proceeds are received income tax–free and estate tax–free by the ILIT.

If desirable, the ILIT can also include generation-skipping provisions. These will provide your children, and eventually your grandchildren, access to the funds without the assets being included—and taxed—in your children's and grandchildren's estates.

### How can using IRA distributions to fund an ILIT be an effective way to fund my estate tax liability?

Let's look at the case of Doris and Les. Doris is 65, and Les is 68. Their total estate is valued at $2 million, of which $750,000 is in a rollover IRA from Les's 401(k) plan. Their heirs are their two sons, ages 42 and 39, to whom they would like their wealth to pass with maximum tax efficiency.

Doris's and Les's wills direct $650,000 to pass to a family trust (assuming death in 1999), with the balance to the surviving spouse. At the survivor's death, their assets pass to their sons. Figure 7-1 shows their estate plan and assumes Les dies first (the actuarial probable event).

The required minimum distributions are shown in Table 7-2. As an alternative, Table 7-3 has Les begin taking distributions of $19,356 from his IRA, even though his required beginning date is almost 3 years away. Even if we assume that Doris and Les have to pay taxes at a 36 percent rate on the distributions, a higher tax bracket than most people ever have to face, the balance of $12,388 is available to Les and Doris. This amount is then given to their sons each year through an irrevocable life insurance trust. These gifts are used by the trustee to pay the annual premiums on a second-to-die policy with a death benefit of $500,000, the proceeds of which will be received income tax–free and estate tax–free after the deaths of both Doris and Les.

Table 7-4 shows the effect of the recommended plan to the heirs. Their net inheritance jumps from $3,099,500 under the current plan to $3,522,744 under the recommended plan. Even after accounting for the cost of the insurance purchased through the trust, the heirs are substantially better off with the recommended plan.

### My heirs will receive an income tax deduction for the estate taxes that have to be paid on my IRA. Does this present any unique problems in my estate planning?

Typical language found in wills and living trusts stipulates that

CHAP. 7: ESTATE PLANNING / RETIREMENT PLANS 407

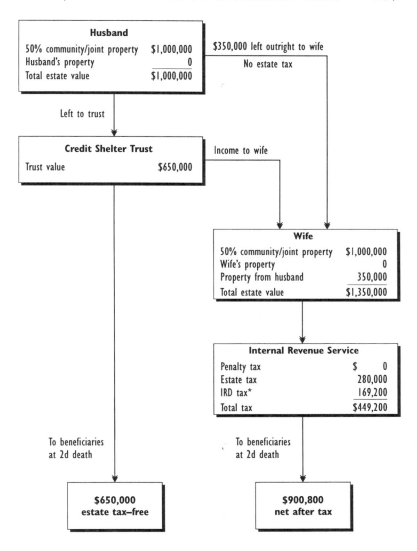

*Assumes income tax is due within 1 year of wife's death.

**Figure 7-1** Estate plan of Doris and Les.

## TABLE 7-2  Minimum Required Distribution Schedule

| Age | | Year | Retirement plan value | Distr. | Income tax, 36% | Net distr. |
|---|---|---|---|---|---|---|
| 68 | 65 | 1999 | $750,000 | | | |
| 69 | 66 | 2000 | 795,000 | | | |
| 70 | 67 | 2001 | 842,700 | $38,304 | $13,789 | $24,515 |
| 71 | 68 | 2002 | 854,958 | 40,328 | 14,518 | 25,810 |
| 72 | 69 | 2003 | 865,927 | 42,656 | 15,356 | 27,300 |
| 73 | 70 | 2004 | 875,226 | 45,114 | 16,241 | 28,873 |
| 74 | 71 | 2005 | 882,625 | 47,452 | 17,082 | 30,370 |
| 75 | 72 | 2006 | 888,130 | 49,894 | 17,961 | 31,933 |
| 76 | 73 | 2007 | 891,523 | 52,442 | 18,879 | 33,563 |
| 77 | 74 | 2008 | 892,572 | 55,097 | 19,834 | 35,263 |
| 78 | 75 | 2009 | 891,029 | 57,859 | 20,829 | 37,030 |
| 79 | 76 | 2010 | 886,631 | 60,315 | 21,713 | 38,602 |
| 80 | 77 | 2011 | 879,513 | 62,822 | 22,615 | 40,207 |
| 81 | 78 | 2012 | 869,461 | 65,868 | 23,712 | 42,156 |
| 82 | 79 | 2013 | 855,760 | 68,460 | 24,645 | 43,815 |
| 83 | 80 | 2014 | 838,645 | 70,474 | 25,370 | 45,104 |
| 84 | 81 | 2015 | 818,489 | 73,079 | 26,308 | 46,771 |
| 85 | 82 | 2016 | 794,519 | 74,954 | 26,983 | 47,971 |
| 86 | 83 | 2017 | 767,236 | 76,723 | 27,620 | 49,103 |
| 87 | 84 | 2018 | 736,547 | 78,356 | 28,208 | 50,148 |

after certain specific bequests, any estate taxes are to be paid out of the "residual estate." IRA assets are passed by beneficiary designation, outside of the will or living trust, and often the heir to the residual estate is different from the beneficiary of the IRA.

Consider this scenario, and imagine the family feud. Sarah leaves an estate of $2 million consisting of a $1 million IRA and $1 million of other assets. She names her children from her first marriage beneficiaries of her IRA and names her second husband

## CHAP. 7: ESTATE PLANNING / RETIREMENT PLANS    409

**TABLE 7-3  Recommended Retirement Plan Distribution**

| Age | | Year | Retirement plan value | Distr. | Income tax, 36% | Net ins. trust | Net distr. |
|---|---|---|---|---|---|---|---|
| 68 | 65 | 1999 | $750,000 | $19,356 | $ 6,968 | $12,388 | |
| 69 | 66 | 2000 | 775,644 | 19,356 | 6,968 | 12,388 | |
| 70 | 67 | 2001 | 802,826 | 36,492 | 13,137 | 12,388 | $10,967 |
| 71 | 68 | 2002 | 814,503 | 38,419 | 13,830 | 12,388 | 12,201 |
| 72 | 69 | 2003 | 833,813 | 40,638 | 14,629 | 12,388 | 13,621 |
| 73 | 70 | 2004 | 824,954 | 42,980 | 15,472 | 12,388 | 15,120 |
| 74 | 71 | 2005 | 840,861 | 45,207 | 16,274 | 12,388 | 16,545 |
| 75 | 72 | 2006 | 846,105 | 47,533 | 17,111 | 12,388 | 18,034 |
| 76 | 73 | 2007 | 849,338 | 49,961 | 17,985 | 12,388 | 19,588 |
| 77 | 74 | 2008 | 850,337 | 52,489 | 18,896 | 12,388 | 21,205 |
| 78 | 75 | 2009 | 848,868 | 55,121 | 19,843 | 12,388 | 22,890 |
| 79 | 76 | 2010 | 844,679 | 57,461 | 20,685 | 11,031 | 25,745 |
| 80 | 77 | 2011 | 837,898 | 59,849 | 21,545 | – | 38,304 |
| 81 | 78 | 2012 | 828,322 | 62,751 | 22,590 | – | 40,161 |
| 82 | 79 | 2013 | 815,270 | 65,221 | 23,479 | – | 41,742 |
| 83 | 80 | 2014 | 798,965 | 67,139 | 14,170 | – | 72,969 |
| 84 | 81 | 2015 | 779,763 | 69,621 | 25,063 | – | 44,558 |
| 85 | 82 | 2016 | 756,927 | 71,408 | 25,706 | – | 45,702 |
| 86 | 83 | 2017 | 730,934 | 73,093 | 26,313 | – | 46,780 |
| 87 | 84 | 2018 | 701,697 | 74,648 | 26,873 | – | 47,775 |

heir to the rest of her estate under her will, which contains the typical language referred to in the preceding paragraph.

The result is that Sarah's residual estate, which goes to her second husband, will pay the estate taxes on the IRA proceeds that she left to her children from her first marriage. To add insult to injury, the children not only receive Sarah's IRA proceeds but also receive an income tax deduction for the estate taxes that Sarah's second husband has to pay.

# 410

## TABLE 7-4 Summary of Values in 10 Years (2009)

| | Plan distributions | |
|---|---|---|
| | Current | Recommended |
| **Projected estate value** | | |
| Retirement plan value | $ 891,029 | $ 848,868 |
| Plan distributions, reinvested at 5% tax-free | 293,877 | 155,766 |
| Other assets (includes 10% growth) | 3,242,175 | 3,242,175 |
| Total estate value | $4,427,081 | $4,246,809 |
| **Projected estate taxes** | | |
| Retirement plan estate penalty tax | $ 0 | $ 0 |
| Federal estate tax (on total estate) | 1,179,894 | 1,080,744 |
| IRD | 147,687 | 143,321 |
| Total tax | $1,327,581 | $1,224,065 |
| **Projected value to heirs** | | |
| Net estate value, after tax | $3,099,500 | $3,022,744 |
| *plus* Insurance trust | 0 | 500,000 |
| Net estate to heirs | $3,099,500 | $3,522,744 |
| **Percent of estate transferred** | 70 | 83 |

> ⚜ *Is it a good strategy to name my children as beneficiaries of my IRA, even though my spouse is still living, and consider that amount as all or part of the assets that can be passed estate tax–free at my death?*

This can be a very effective strategy, especially as it can facilitate a stretch-out IRA. One possible disadvantage is that when the IRD taxes are paid on amounts withdrawn from your IRA, there is an income tax deduction for any estate taxes attributable to that asset. If the IRA assets left to your children were considered part

CHAP. 7: ESTATE PLANNING / RETIREMENT PLANS    411

of your applicable exclusion amount and, therefore, free from estate taxes, no such income tax deduction would be available.

*Why should I designate a trust for the benefit of my children as the beneficiary of my IRA instead of my children?*

The quick answer is your ability to plan and control the distributions. If you name your children as beneficiaries, they will have total control over your proceeds at your death. For many, there are advantages to not leaving an inheritance outright to children:

- The ability to leave the funds to your children in a creditor-proof form
- The ability to give your children assets they cannot lose in a divorce
- The option of appointing someone else as trustee for the benefit of your children in the event a child is immature, disabled, or a minor who needs someone else to manage his or her money
- The ability to create a supplemental needs trust for a child who is eligible for governmental assistance, and, therefore, provide that the funds be used to supplement and not replace governmental benefits
- The ability to keep the asset out of your children's probate estates

*My spouse and I have a combined gross estate of just under $1.3 million (1999), which consists of real estate and bank accounts but is predominantly composed of our 401(k) accounts and IRAs. We have basic estate tax planning in place. Is this sufficient?*

First, it is critical to determine your goals, objectives, needs, and concerns. Your goals and objectives will determine what planning is appropriate to accomplish those desired results. Addressing tax issues is the last piece of the puzzle to put into place. Since income and estate taxes are at issue in regard to retirement plans, it is important that the tax planning, which if implemented accurately, allocates the taxes to the appropriate persons and accomplishes the long-term objectives of the participant and the participant's loved ones. The provisions in your will or trust would determine who pays the taxes. But even more importantly, it must be determined how the taxes are to be paid. If the only liquidity in the estate is in the retirement plans, this is a problem because the more that is withdrawn from the plan means that more income taxes must be paid. It can become a vicious cycle of withdrawals and taxes if proper planning is not designed in advance.

## Generation-Skipping Tax Planning

*⅍ What are the advantages of generation-skipping trusts?*

Under the current law, up to $1 million of assets can be held in a trust for the benefit of your children and ultimately distributed to your grandchildren without being subject to estate tax in your children's estates. If you are married, each spouse can utilize the $1 million tax exemption. Such a trust is called a *generation-skipping trust.* If you have sufficient assets, it makes sense to have your trust arrangements for your children structured to include generation-skipping transfer (GST) provisions for the following reasons:

REDUCED ESTATE TAX   The assets in a properly structured generation-skipping trust, including accumulated earnings and appreciation from the date the trust is created until the your child's death, are exempt from death taxes in your child's estate.

POSSIBILITY OF REDUCED INCOME TAX   If the trust includes the power to distribute income to your grandchildren and great-

# Chap. 7: Estate Planning / Retirement Plans    413

grandchildren, the income may be taxed at a much lower income tax rate than if it were taxed at your child's income tax bracket.

**FLEXIBILITY**   Your child can act as a trustee of the trust and, in that capacity, can manage the investment of the trust assets and determine to whom the income and principal will be distributed. Through the use of a special power of appointment, your child can make provisions for a spouse to receive income or change the distribution among grandchildren or great-grandchildren following his or her death.

**ASSET PROTECTION**   The trust can contain "spendthrift" provisions which can help protect the assets in the trust from your child's creditors or a divorcing spouse.

As with any estate planning tool, GST provisions should be tailored to your family's circumstances.

## Disclaimers

*What is a disclaimer?*

A *disclaimer* is your legal refusal to accept property, either as the result of a gift or an inheritance. It is a legal "no thank you." If you disclaim property, then you will be treated as having predeceased the person from whom you received the gift or inheritance, and the property would automatically pass to the next named entity or person legally entitled to the property or would pass under the appropriate state law. Because you never accepted the gift or inheritance, your disclaimer is not a gift from you to the person who ultimately receives the property.

*Can anyone disclaim any asset?*

Yes—if certain requirements are met under IRS Code Section 2518. The requirements are:

1. The disclaimer must be made within 9 months of a person becoming entitled to the property.

2. The person must not have received *any* benefits from the property disclaimed.

3. The person must not have any authority to direct who receives the property.

4. The disclaimer must comply with local state law.

*Can a surviving spouse named as beneficiary disclaim any benefits from a qualified retirement plan or IRA?*

Yes. In the event of a disclaimer, the proceeds would go to the contingent beneficiary you named or to the default beneficiary under the plan document in the event you did not name a contingent beneficiary.

*How can disclaimers be used in planning distributions from qualified retirement plans and IRAs?*

Disclaimers are a very important part of estate planning. They give your family the flexibility to determine who will ultimately receive your retirement benefits. For example, if you are married, you could name your revocable living trust as primary beneficiary and your spouse as contingent beneficiary. After your death, your trustee could keep as much of the retirement benefits as necessary to fully fund the family trust. The balance could be disclaimed by the trustee. As contingent beneficiary, your spouse would be entitled to the balance. Your spouse would have the flexibility of rolling over the balance to her own IRA, naming a designated beneficiary, and extending the deferral of income taxes.

Thus, after your death, your trustee is able to evaluate all the factors associated with the transfer of the plan benefits, including the estate and income tax ramifications, and decide whether to

CHAP. 7: ESTATE PLANNING / RETIREMENT PLANS **415**

accept the benefits or disclaim and allow the benefits to be paid to your spouse.

*Are there any reasons not to use disclaimers in coordinating retirement plan benefits with estate planning?*

The principal problem with using disclaimers is the requirement that the disclaimant must not accept any benefits of the disclaimed property before filing the disclaimer. Retirement plans, particularly where payments have commenced before death, often have provisions for automatic payments to be made. If the primary beneficiary receives *any* payments from the plan, then he or she will be unable to make a disclaimer.

Disclaimers also must be made within a limited period of time (9 months from the date of death). If your estate plan depends primarily on disclaimers, your family must act quickly after your death.

There is also a potential problem with plan administrators who may be unfamiliar with the use of disclaimers and may be unwilling to recognize them before making distributions.

*How can I control who will be my beneficiary if the primary beneficiary rejects the benefit?*

You can name a contingent, or alternative, beneficiary if the primary beneficiary disclaims. The trustee, administrator, custodian, or institution involved in your IRA might resist your taking up a lot of space on a designation form to make clear who is the contingent beneficiary. Consult your lawyer or retirement professional about wording the designation.

If your beneficiary is your revocable living trust, you should also consider stating in the trust instrument who will take the IRA benefit passing through the trust if a trust beneficiary disclaims any part of it. This should be coordinated with the contingent beneficiaries you have named on the IRA beneficiary designation form.

*After my death, I want my wife to have all my retirement funds if she needs them. But if she has enough, I am concerned about the estate taxes due at her death. How can I plan now for these conflicting goals?*

There are several ways to plan around such unknowns. Although it appears to be a quandary—not knowing what your wife's needs will be in the future—you can accomplish this type of planning if you and your wife take the time to understand what rights she actually has to the death benefits from your qualified funds.

If your wife knows she will not need all or a portion of your retirement funds when the benefits would be paid over, she could execute a disclaimer, a legal "no thank you," to the portion of the benefits she feels are not required for her future support. The balance of the retirement funds not taken by her will then be available to the next listed beneficiary.

One very important point must be remembered, however. If your wife accepts *any* portion of the retirement benefits—even cashing a retirement distribution check—before executing the disclaimer, she will have waived any right to disclaim and will then have to take all the benefits for herself, which might cause her taxable estate to pay more in federal or state death taxes than might otherwise be necessary.

*If a revocable trust is named as primary beneficiary of an IRA and the owner of the IRA dies, is there any way to have the proceeds distributed to the spouse rather than the trust?*

The answer to this question depends on how the trust was drafted. Some practitioners word the trust so that if the trustee disclaims under state law, the benefits of the IRA are to be paid to the spouse.

A word of caution is necessary because some companies have construed a disclaimer by the trustee of a trust to be a complete and total disclaimer of both the trust's interest and the spouse's interest pursuant to the trust. They have, therefore, concluded that the next successor beneficiary named in the IRA becomes the beneficiary entitled to distributions and not the spouse. Care must be taken to make it clear that the trustee is only partially disclaiming so as to implement the provision of the trust that the IRA beneficiary becomes the spouse. Sometimes a problem with this occurs because the custodian requires the disclaimer to be on forms that it provides—which are not easily modified—to show the intent of the trustee to disclaim in such a manner that the spouse becomes the beneficiary.

Another method of planning when using the trust as primary beneficiary is to name the spouse as the contingent beneficiary. Then it is not a problem if the custodian construes the first disclaimer by the trustee as a complete and total disclaimer because the spouse is the beneficiary either way.

Whether the spouse becomes the beneficiary by means of trust language in the primary beneficial trust or by means of the disclaimer to a contingent beneficiary makes no difference as to the ability of the spouse to roll over the benefits to the spouse's pre-existing IRA or to a new IRA established for the purpose of receiving the benefits. In both situations, the planning must have been done before the owner's death.

## CHARITABLE PLANNING WITH RETIREMENT FUNDS

### Lifetime Gifts to Charity

⋈ *What is the easiest way to make a gift from my retirement plan to charity?*

The simplest way to make a gift to charity is through an outright gift, meaning you would take a distribution from your plan and give that money to the charity of your choice.

418                                    WAYS AND MEANS

### *How do I make an outright gift to a charity?*

After receiving a distribution from your plan, you should deposit the proceeds in your personal account and then contribute the proceeds directly to the charity. If you have used the proceeds to buy an investment, you would have the investment re-registered in the name of the charity and deliver the original investment paperwork to your charity.

### *Is there a limit on the amount I can give as an outright distribution to charity?*

There is currently no limit on the amount you can give to charity other than the total sum of all your assets. You are, however, limited in the amount of the charitable income tax deduction you can claim for the gift. The amount of the deduction depends upon your adjusted gross income and the total amount of your gifts for the year.

### *How many times can I make an outright distribution to a charity?*

There are no limits on the number of times during a year you can make a distribution to charity. You receive a charitable income tax deduction for the amount given, subject to the percentage limitation based on your adjusted gross income.

### *What is the drawback of giving an immediate outright distribution to a charity?*

By making an outright gift, you are relying upon the charity to choose how you would like your money to be used. If you give the money to a community foundation, you can retain slightly more control by establishing a donor-advised account. In this format, you may consult with and leave instructions with the

# CHAP. 7: ESTATE PLANNING / RETIREMENT PLANS 419

community foundation as to the purposes you want your funds to support.

The best method to control your proceeds is to pass them in trust. In this manner, the income can be used for your charitable purposes and the principal can be preserved so that the gifts can continue over a specified term—or even indefinitely if you choose. You may also leave detailed instructions with your successor trustees as to how your funds should be used.

*≫ I do not need the money in my qualified retirement account. If I just donate the entire account to a charitable organization while I am living, won't I avoid having to pay income taxes on the distributions?*

In some cases, yes. But it can be trickier than it seems and will require some advance planning. This is because when assets are transferred during your lifetime from your qualified retirement account directly to a charity of your choice, the IRS will tax the transaction as if the distribution were first made to you, then followed by the donation. As a result, whatever amount is donated must be included on your income tax return for that year as ordinary income and fully taxable to you. This will be offset by a charitable deduction equal to the amount of income reported. Remember, because of the percentage of adjusted gross income limitations and the phaseout of itemized deductions, you may not be able to use all of the deduction in the year of the donation, which means that you could have an income tax liability.

*≫ Why might I have to pay income taxes if I donate my entire qualified retirement account to charity?*

Charitable deductions are always limited to no more than 50 percent of your adjusted gross income and in some cases even less. As an example, suppose your adjusted gross income is $50,000 this year, before any distributions from your qualified retirement account. If you donate $100,000 from your retirement account to

420 WAYS AND MEANS

charity this year, your adjusted gross income instantly increases to $150,000. However, your charitable deduction for the year is limited to $75,000 (50 percent of your adjusted gross income). While this may be offset somewhat by the fact that you can carry forward the remaining $25,000 deduction for up to 5 years, the immediate effect of your generosity is that you will have to pay income tax this year on $25,000.

*It doesn't seem fair that I have to pay thousands of dollars in taxes just to donate my qualified retirement account to my favorite charity. Is there a way to get around this problem?*

Yes. Let's assume the same facts as in the example described above, but instead of donating the entire account in one calendar year, you donate half the value of the account this year and half next year. Your adjusted gross income increases both years to $100,000. Your charitable deduction each year is limited to $50,000, which is the amount that you withdrew from the retirement account. Thus, by planning the timing of the distributions, you are able to completely offset the income attributed to you with a corresponding charitable deduction.

*If I would like to make an outright donation of my qualified retirement account to charity, can I do so now or do I have to wait until I reach 59½ years of age?*

You can always make withdrawals from your IRA and from most qualified retirement accounts. But with limited exceptions, for anyone under age 59½, the 10 percent premature distribution penalty will apply. Distributions for charitable purposes are *not* included in the list of exceptions.

## After-Death Gifts to Charity

*Why do individuals who do not appear to be especially phil-*

CHAP. 7: ESTATE PLANNING / RETIREMENT PLANS 421

*anthropic name a charity as the beneficiary of some of their retirement plan assets?*

Once a decision to make a charitable bequest has been made, using retirement plan assets can, in some circumstances, be an advantageous source of funds. This is especially true if improper beneficiary designation planning and/or improper selection of minimum distribution calculation methods occurred and the retirement plan assets will have to be withdrawn immediately or within a few years after the death of the participant.

While retirement plan assets are subject to income taxation at the time of withdrawal by most recipients, withdrawals made by a qualified charity are exempt from income taxation. It is, therefore, sometimes a better strategy to leave assets to the family which are not subject to income taxation while leaving the retirement plan assets to your charity so that no income tax is due.

Unless the plan proceeds have to be distributed during a short period of time, it will usually be more advantageous to leave your retirement assets to family through a stretch-out IRA strategy. Before choosing to use retirement plan assets for the purpose of funding charitable bequests, careful calculations should be made on all available options. Your retirement team of advisors can help you with this analysis.

*Are there any pitfalls to using my retirement plan assets to fulfill a charitable bequest?*

Yes. If you name a charity as sole or partial beneficiary of you qualified retirement plan or IRA, you would be considered as not having a "designated beneficiary" according to the minimum distribution rules. It appears that the result is the same if you name a trust as the beneficiary of your qualified retirement plan or IRA if the trust contains one or more charities as beneficiaries.

The lack of a designated beneficiary can have negative income tax consequences both during your lifetime and after your death.

When you begin taking your minimum distributions at age

70½, you must base your distributions on your single life expectancy. You will not have the option of spreading the distributions over the joint life expectancy of you and your beneficiaries, as is possible with "named" individuals. Taking distributions under a single life expectancy means that your required annual distributions will be larger each year. That means you report more taxable income each year, which results in less tax deferral.

If you die before your required beginning date and you don't have a designated beneficiary, all the plan proceeds must be distributed by December 31 of the fifth anniversary of your date of death. If you die after your required beginning date and you had elected to recalculate your life expectancy, then all plan proceeds must be distributed by December 31 following the year of your death. In either circumstance, your beneficiaries will lose the benefit of long-term tax deferral.

*I do not want to donate my qualified retirement to charity now because I may need it in the future. However, I do plan to leave my entire estate to charity at my death. Can I designate charities as the beneficiaries of my retirement accounts?*

Yes. For individuals who want to leave their entire estate to charity, it is perfectly acceptable to designate one or more charities as beneficiaries of their retirement accounts by naming the charities under the beneficiary designation form. At your death, the proceeds of your account will go to the charities you have designated, free of estate and income taxes and without being subject to probate. Care should be taken so that the charity properly qualifies under the IRS rules as a charitable organization and that the proper name of the charity is used.

*Are there any disadvantages of naming a charity as the beneficiary of my qualified retirement account upon my death?*

Yes. First, anything left to charity is obviously not going to your family or friends. This is a personal choice and is not a problem

Chap. 7: Estate Planning / Retirement Plans     **423**

if you truly intend that a portion of your estate be set aside for charitable purposes. Second, by designating charities rather than individuals as your beneficiaries, you may be subject to more income tax during your lifetime due to higher required minimum distributions.

*Would it be better to designate my revocable living trust as the beneficiary of my qualified retirement accounts and to direct the trust to distribute the proceeds to my charities?*

Yes. We believe that it is wise to have the complete distribution of an estate controlled by one concise master document, which can only be done with a will or a trust. Of the two, only trusts avoid subjecting the entire estate to probate. Trusts may also prove to be much more convenient.

For example, suppose you have numerous retirement accounts (not to mention life insurance policies and annuities), and you want to change beneficiaries from time to time. Without a trust, you will have to go through the inconvenience of contacting all the companies your accounts are with and completing their change of beneficiary forms every time you want to adjust your beneficiaries. With a trust that has already been named as the sole beneficiary of every account, you simply prepare an amendment to the trust to change the beneficiaries of the trust. This will enable you to use the proceeds should you need them and to pass them to charity if you don't.

*Is there an estate tax advantage to giving my retirement account to charity or individuals?*

There may be, depending upon your situation. For most single, divorced, or widowed people with estates large enough to incur an estate tax, it really does not matter (for estate tax purposes) which assets go to charity and which go to individuals. Many married couples, however, include in the design of their estate plans a family (or credit shelter) trust. This strategy allows the couple to permanently set aside for the benefit of the surviving spouse a trust valued up to the amount that is exempt from federal estate tax in the year the deceased spouse dies. When the surviving spouse later dies, the entire balance in the family trust at that time is distributed to the beneficiaries free of federal estate tax.

Quite often we see wills or trust agreements that specifically state that a portion of the family trust is to go to charity. If the surviving spouse's estate is small enough that it is not subject to the estate tax, this is not a problem. For larger estates, it makes no sense to distribute family trust assets, exempt from estate taxes, to charity and have the surviving spouse leave equivalent assets that are subject to estate taxes (in the 37 to 55 percent range) to the individual beneficiaries.

*I want to make a charitable contribution with some of my retirement plan assets, but I want to make certain that my spouse will have enough to live on after my death. What should I do?*

If you have no intended beneficiaries besides each other, your IRAs and other tax-deferred retirement plans make excellent sources for charitable bequests because the full amount distributed from these plans is taxable as ordinary income, called income in respect of a decedent (IRD), when you die. These IRD assets given to tax-exempt charitable organizations escape the IRD tax and also lower the size of your taxable estate.

The easiest way to implement this strategy is for you and your spouse to name each other as primary beneficiary of each other's IRA and your intended charity as the contingent beneficiary. Upon your death, your account can be rolled over tax-free to your spouse's account, who then changes the primary beneficiary to your charity. Upon the subsequent death of your spouse, the proceeds pass tax free to the charity.

Be careful! Many advisors present the IRD tax as immediate and automatic. This is not the case. If you want children to

CHAP. 7: ESTATE PLANNING / RETIREMENT PLANS    425

receive any part of your IRA, you should divide your IRA into separate accounts—one for the charity and one for each child. If you don't, your children will not be able to continue deferring your IRA over their life expectancies after your death. Also, keep in mind that this strategy depends upon your spouse following your wishes and changing his or her primary beneficiary designation after you die.

*What if we are both charitably inclined, but we are not certain if the surviving spouse will need to have full access to the retirement plan and IRA accounts?*

You would use the same strategy as discussed above. Name each other as the primary beneficiary of each other's IRA and retirement plans, and name your charity as the contingent beneficiary. Upon the first death, the surviving spouse can either roll the accounts into his or her IRA or disclaim the proceeds in favor of the charity. The surviving spouse can name charities as the primary beneficiaries on any account not disclaimed. This wait-and-see approach allows maximum flexibility.

*I want to leave a portion of my estate to charity and a portion to my family and/or friends. Does it make any difference whether I use my qualified retirement accounts or my other assets to satisfy the charitable bequests?*

For people who want to divide their estates between charitable and noncharitable beneficiaries, it is generally better to satisfy the charitable bequest as much as possible out of the retirement assets. For estate tax purposes, it really does not matter which assets go to charity or the individual. However, retirement accounts are also subject to income tax. It does not make sense to give individuals an asset that they must pay income taxes on instead of to the charity that does not have an income tax liability. So to the extent possible, you want to satisfy your charitable bequests with funds from your qualified retirement accounts and give individuals the assets that have no income tax ramifications.

One major exception to this general rule involves the stretch-out IRA technique. With proper advance planning, an individual may prefer to inherit your tax-deferred assets if continued long-term deferral is possible. To ensure this result, proper beneficiary planning, minimum distribution planning, and legal document drafting is necessary.

## Charitable Remainder Trusts

*I have heard that many people are setting up charitable remainder trusts to be beneficiaries of their retirement accounts. What exactly are they talking about, and how does it work?*

A *charitable remainder trust (CRT)* is a unique arrangement that is specifically authorized under our federal tax laws. Congress recognized that people often have competing priorities, or "split interests," that include charitable giving. For example, you may want to ensure that some or all of your estate goes to a worthwhile charitable organization upon your death yet provide one or more individuals with an income stream in the interim. A charitable remainder trust is designed for that purpose.

Assets are placed in trust for a designated period of time—specified either in years or based on the actual life of the individual beneficiaries. During that period of time, the individuals receive an annual income from the trust at a predetermined rate. When the time period expires, usually at the death of the last surviving individual beneficiary, the trust terminates and the remaining assets are distributed to charitable organizations selected by the creator of the trust.

*How can I avoid the threat of significant losses in my retirement assets at my death due to income and estate taxes?*

A technique that may be used during your life as well as for

Chap. 7: Estate Planning / Retirement Plans    427

testamentary (or after-death) planning involves the use of a charitable remainder trust. For lifetime planning, qualified plan assets may be transferred to a charitable remainder trust.

This will not avoid all income tax for the retiree. There will, however, be a charitable deduction to partially offset the income tax impact. Once the assets are in the charitable trust, income can be payable to you just as it would have been from the retirement plan. Upon your death, the remainder of these assets will not be included in your estate because they pass to the qualified charity.

You may wish instead to name a testamentary charitable remainder trust established under your will or trust as the beneficiary of qualified plan assets. This will eliminate income in respect of a decedent. Further, this transfer to the testamentary charitable trust will produce an estate tax charitable deduction equal to the present value of the remainder interest that will eventually pass to charity.

#### ⁂ Is there more than one type of CRT?

There are two types of charitable remainder trusts. One is a charitable remainder *unitrust*. It allows flexibility through an accumulation option and the ability to add contributions to the trust at any time. The unitrust income payments are based on a percentage of the assets in the trust, which helps protect against inflation.

The second type is a charitable remainder *annuity* trust, which has a fixed payout with a one-time-only contribution.

#### ⁂ Are there any income tax advantages to naming a charitable remainder trust as the beneficiary of my qualified retirement plans?

Yes. Charitable remainder trusts are tax-exempt entities. They can receive distributions from qualified retirement accounts without having to pay the income tax that an individual beneficiary would incur. This allows the full value of the account to be invested in order to create a higher stream of income for the individual than

428                                    WAYS AND MEANS

would be possible from investing only the after-tax portion of the account.

*Are there any estate tax advantages to naming a charitable remainder trust as the beneficiary of my qualified retirement plans?*

Absolutely. Under the federal tax laws, estates are entitled to charitable deductions for the value of assets bequeathed to charities, and charitable remainder trusts are specifically included. However, one dollar contributed to a charitable remainder trust does not translate into a one dollar charitable deduction. Instead, the deduction is discounted to reflect the present value of the gift to the charity because the charity has to wait for many years—often someone's lifetime—before it is free to use the assets for its charitable purposes.

*Are there any nontax reasons for naming a charitable remainder trust as the beneficiary of my qualified retirement plans?*

Charitable remainder trusts allow people to use a limited amount of wealth to meet their dual objectives of contributing to charity and supporting their loved ones. As discussed above, this may result in a higher net income for the individual beneficiary. In addition, because charitable remainder trusts can be structured for the lifetime of the individual, it is possible to ensure that he or she does not outlive the income, does not squander it, and does not lose it to creditors, to lawsuits, in divorce court, or in any of the many other ways people find to separate themselves from their inheritances.

*What is "social capital," and why is it relevant to every retirement and estate plan?*

If you have accumulated a net worth exceeding your applicable

CHAP. 7: ESTATE PLANNING / RETIREMENT PLANS **429**

exclusion amount, you are going to be a philanthropist—whether you know it or not.

According to tax law, 9 months after you die, your estate must "contribute" to society taxes on that portion of your estate that exceeds the applicable exclusion amount. Chances are excellent that this will be the most significant charitable gift you will ever make to social causes—and it will be completely involuntary. *Social capital* is, one might say, the portion of your estate that you earn and you own but do not get to keep.

If you do not actively plan your estate, your social capital will be government-directed throughout the U.S. tax system. In many cases, what it took a lifetime to earn, the government will spend in a matter of seconds.

You essentially have two choices. You can allow your social capital to be spent by the government as it sees fit. Or you can plan your estate to direct where you want the money to go. You can convert from involuntary philanthropy to voluntary philanthropy without disrupting your lifestyle or your children's inheritance.

There are only three possible beneficiaries for your wealth: (1) your intended heirs, (2) the Internal Revenue Service, or (3) the nonprofit sector.

Although the tax code mandates that individuals with taxable estates must make contributions to society upon their deaths, most people do not realize they can have direct control over the portion of their wealth that they must contribute to society through estate planning tools.

If you think this sounds unpatriotic, the government doesn't. The Internal Revenue Code encourages contributing to nonprofit organizations by offering tax deductions and credits.

Laws governing CRTs have been part of the U.S. tax code since 1969 and reflect Congress's intention of motivating taxpayers' charitable giving. With increased charitable giving by the private sector, more government dollars will be available to work in other areas of the economy.

To summarize, with CRTs you can avoid income tax, earn

more income, create a tax deduction, reduce estate taxes, protect your assets from the claims of creditors, and establish a charitable legacy—all with the blessing of the U.S. government.

*What if I want to be certain that the assets in my IRA pass to charity yet still provide my spouse an income if needed?*

Ask your financial planner and attorney to help you set up a testamentary charitable remainder trust. The provisions of the CRT can specify that your spouse is entitled to receive a certain percentage from the trust during his or her lifetime. Upon your death, the remaining IRA assets pass tax-free to the CRT. Your spouse would continue to receive the income.

*Caution:* This strategy may not work if your spouse is young and/or you select a high payout rate on the CRT. The Taxpayer Relief Act of 1997 requires that the value of the remainder in the trust going to charity be at least 10 percent of the net fair market value of the property transferred to the trust on the date of contribution. You can avoid this problem by selecting a lower payout rate or specifying that your spouse receive the income for a term of years, up to 20. This problem will diminish because the tax deduction increases as you get older, so you and your advisor should be able to design your CRT around the problem.

It is prudent to actually fund the trust with $5000 to $10,000 while you are still living, so that it is up and running. It is also a good strategy to fund it if you are over age 70½ and taking the required minimum distributions but don't need the income. Each contribution is partially tax deductible, and you can "store" the income in the CRT until you or your spouse needs it at a later date.

*Can I direct my IRA to my favorite charity and still benefit my family at death?*

Yes, you can accomplish this by naming your charitable remainder

CHAP. 7: ESTATE PLANNING / RETIREMENT PLANS    431

trust as the beneficiary of your retirement plan. Your spouse could be named as beneficiary of the CRT, with your children as contingent beneficiaries. Or your children (or anyone else for that matter) could be named as the primary beneficiaries of the CRT.

The CRT can be an excellent planning strategy, but a few points should be kept in mind. When implementing a CRT, once the retirement plan assets are given to the charity, the assets no longer belong to your heirs. The beneficiaries only have a right to the income being generated. The income would be fully subject to income tax as it is paid out. The principal can never be invaded, as it belongs to the charity, although the charity does not actually receive it until everyone has died or the term of the trust has expired.

It should be noted, when children are named as beneficiaries, even on a contingent basis, there is an estate tax due when the children eventually inherit the income stream. The estate tax is due on the present value of the future income stream they are likely to receive over their life expectancies. We actually don't know what the estate tax will be until death occurs. An IRS table is used to help calculate the beneficiaries' life expectancies. This table and the income payout rate you select will determine the estimated income they are expected to receive. Although it will depend on the age of the beneficiaries at the time of your death, it is not unusual for the estate tax due (on the projected income stream) to be equal to what the estate tax would have been had the beneficiaries actually inherited 60 percent to 90 percent of the plan assets outright.

You will want to be sure that the beneficiaries have other assets from which to pay the estate taxes. Remember, they will not be permitted to invade the principal of the CRT for any purpose, including payment of taxes. In effect, the children will be paying an estate tax on assets they do not have, as the future income stream over their life expectancies is all they receive.

*I have heard that payment of retirement assets at my death*

432  WAYS AND MEANS

*into a charitable remainder trust for the benefit of my children and then to charity reduces my estate taxes and avoids the income tax on withdrawals altogether. If this is true, then why wouldn't I want to do this?*

It is true that a properly established CRT does not pay income taxes on withdrawals and that a testamentary contribution of retirement plan assets to that CRT generally results in a reduction of estate taxes. However, the benefit of this must be weighed against the benefits of leaving the retirement plan assets to one or more individuals who make only the minimum required withdrawals. Since the minimum required withdrawals are generally less than what the retirement plan assets are earning in the early years, the tax-free accumulation in the retirement plan can more than make up for the tax advantages of leaving those retirement plan assets to a CRT. There are situations, however, where it is impossible to defer total withdrawal of the retirement plan assets over a long period of time. If a short-term payout is unavoidable, then making a CRT (or a charity) the beneficiary of the retirement plan assets could produce a highly beneficial result.

*My spouse passed away recently. I am past my required beginning date and had my spouse as my designated beneficiary, with both of our life expectancies being recalculated annually for minimum distribution purposes. Can I still use the stretch-out IRA strategy to maximize the value of my retirement plan for my children?*

Unfortunately, the stretch-out IRA strategy is no longer available to you. Because you are past your required beginning date, your minimum distribution calculation methods are now "set in stone" and cannot be changed. Therefore, when you pass away, the entire balance of the qualified retirement plan must be distributed to your children in a single year.

All is not lost, however. One remaining method you have to prevent the loss due to estate and income taxation of the qualified

# CHAP. 7: ESTATE PLANNING / RETIREMENT PLANS    433

plan is to create a charitable remainder trust for the benefit of each of your children. Each CRT would pay an income amount to one of your children each year after you pass away. When that child dies, the balance of the CRT assets would pass to the charity of your choice.

If you name the CRTs as the beneficiaries of your qualified retirement plan at your death, there would be a substantial estate tax deduction because of the amount eventually passing to charity when your children pass away. The qualified retirement plan assets would still have to be distributed in 1 year, but because the CRT does not pay income taxes, there would be no loss in value from the payout. The proceeds could then be reinvested inside the CRT and grow income tax–free (similar to the growth inside your qualified retirement plan). Only the distributions to your children each year would be subject to income taxation. Although this strategy doesn't have the full power of the stretch-out IRA, it may be an excellent fallback position in your situation.

*In your examples, CRT beneficiaries receive income payments. Who selects the income payout rate, and how much can be paid out?*

You select the payout rate when you establish the CRT. The Taxpayer Relief Act of 1997 made the rules governing the amount of income being paid out each year from a charitable remainder trust more restrictive. Annual payout rates cannot be less than 5 percent and cannot exceed 50 percent of the trust's annual value. More importantly, however, to qualify for the income tax deductions granted to the trust maker, the present value of the remaining assets that go to charity must equal or exceed 10 percent of the value of the assets at the time they were donated. Thus, the maximum annual income received by the noncharitable beneficiary of a CRT will primarily depend on the new 10 percent rule.

*If I name a charitable remainder trust as the beneficiary of my qualified retirement plans, will the income payments to my loved ones be a fixed amount or will they keep up with inflation?*

Actually, you can choose whichever you prefer. If you like the idea of a steady, fixed income, you can create what is known as a charitable remainder annuity trust. At your death, when the trust receives its distribution from your retirement plan, the value of the donation is multiplied by the percentage rate you establish in the trust agreement. Once that calculation has been made, the beneficiary knows exactly what his or her income will be every year for the duration of the trust. While this provides certainty, there is no protection from inflation.

If you would like the income payments to increase over time in order to keep up with inflation, you may prefer to create a charitable remainder unitrust. With a unitrust, every year the value of the trust assets are recalculated and multiplied by the selected percentage rate. While the percentage rate never changes, the value of the trust does. So if the trust has increased in value, the income payments increase accordingly. On the other hand, if the value of the trust has decreased in value, the income will drop.

*Besides the limits imposed by Congress, what other factors should I consider in choosing the distribution rate for my loved ones?*

Your particular circumstances and objectives are really the most important considerations. Is your primary objective to maximize income for the individual beneficiaries or to maximize the ultimate gift to the charity? Do you prefer the security of a fixed income or are you willing to assume some risk to try for an increased income in the future? One of our clients had a situation where she was able to place the charitable trust assets in a long-term, high-yield, fixed-income investment. In that case, an annuity payment set slightly below the investment's rate of return made sense. Those who want the income payments to increase over time

CHAP. 7: ESTATE PLANNING / RETIREMENT PLANS    435

must remember that the income only goes up if the value of the trust goes up. Obviously, that only happens when the total rate of return on trust investments exceeds the payout, so the more modest the payout rate, the more likely the income increase over time.

*What happens if all the income has not been paid to the trust maker before he or she dies?*

Your charity gets a larger gift than expected. The estate of the trust maker is not allowed to collect interest owed. It represents a lost opportunity to get money out of the CRT.

*Is the estate tax deduction on a testamentary gift of retirement plan assets to a charitable remainder trust more or less than on a gift of another type of asset?*

The estate tax deduction is no less favorable for retirement plan assets than for any other type of asset. The only difference is in the income tax consequences between retirement plan and other types of assets. Because a charity and a charitable remainder trust are exempt from income taxation, neither would pay the income tax owing on a withdrawal. Any other noncharitable beneficiary would have to pay the income tax on the entire withdrawal.

*Can a charitable remainder trust be used as a retirement planning funding vehicle?*

The charitable remainder unitrust may provide an opportunity to provide supplemental retirement income. This may be accomplished through a *net income makeup charitable remainder unitrust (NIMCRUT)*.

Under this arrangement contributions are made to the NIMCRUT during your working years. Contributions are partially deductible (based on your age and the payout rate you select) as charitable contributions. This particular type of charitable remainder trust specifies that if the trust does not generate the required amount of income in a year to make the payouts required, it can use excess earnings in future years to make up the deficit. This strategy requires careful investment coordination, so seeking the advice of an advisor experienced in charitable trust planning is crucial.

*What are the advantages of a makeup charitable remainder trust over a qualified retirement plan?*

The donor alone gets the benefits from the trust. No other employees need to be covered, as is the case with qualified pension or profit-sharing plans.

*Are there any disadvantages compared to qualified plans?*

Yes. As mentioned, only a portion of the annual contribution to the trust is deductible (based on IRS tables, the age of the donor, and the specified income which will be paid at retirement). Contributions to qualified plans are fully deductible.

*What is the risk in setting up a charitable remainder trust?*

The tax risk is very small. The law and regulations have been on the books for many years, and the IRS even distributes preapproved sample CRT documents. The only significant downside is that after you (or you and your spouse) die, the property in the trust passes to designated charities, thus "disinheriting" your heirs. If this concerns you, there is usually a fairly straightforward solution.

*What are these solutions if the loss of the property is a concern?*

Many donors set up wealth replacement trusts (irrevocable life insurance trusts), in which the trust uses some or all of the income tax savings from setting up the charitable remainder trust to pur-

## CHAP. 7: ESTATE PLANNING / RETIREMENT PLANS    437

chase life insurance. If the income tax savings is not sufficient, then the balance of the premiums is paid out of the increased income from the charitable remainder trust. Typically, the donor uses the funds to purchase life insurance to replace the wealth represented by the assets given and, in some cases, generate additional wealth.

The insurance is owned by the ILIT, so that it is not taxable in the estate of the donor (or the donor's spouse). If the charitable remainder trust pays income to both the donor and the donor's spouse, the ILIT usually purchases a second-to-die (survivorship) policy.

Thus, a properly structured wealth replacement trust avoids gift and estate taxes, so your heirs will receive the same or *more* benefits than they would have received had the assets not been transferred to your CRT.

*How can I time my gifts to get maximum tax benefits in a CRT?*

The goal of any gift plan is to remove the most value from your estate at the least tax cost. Many estate planning techniques are interest rate–sensitive; that is, the perceived benefits increase or decrease as interest rates change. Charitable remainder annuity trusts (CRATs) are more efficient when interest rates are lower. Charitable remainder unitrusts (CRUTs) are not significantly affected by changes in the interest rates.

*What factors influence the present value of the remaining assets in a charitable remainder trust?*

Present value calculations have several factors that affect the results. A federal government discount rate, the "7520 rate," is one of the factors and is out of anyone's control. How long the charitable organization has to wait to receive its remainder amount also plays a significant role. The charitable organization has to wait until the end of the trust's term, which can be a specified

438                                          WAYS AND MEANS

number of years or until the death of any or all of the noncharitable beneficiaries. After these factors have been included in the calculation, the maximum payout rate can be determined. Because of the 1998 revised regulations governing CRTs, younger people may not be able to use this planning tool and others will likely have to accept a lower payout rate.

## Charitable Gift Annuities

*What is a charitable gift annuity?*

A *charitable gift annuity* is a simple contract between you and a charitable organization. In exchange for your irrevocable gift of cash, securities, or other assets, the charity agrees to pay one or two annuitants, which you name, a fixed sum each year for life. The payments are usually made in annual, semiannual, or quarterly installments. The payments are guaranteed by the general resources of the foundation and are backed by separate reserve accounts in which the original gift amounts are held, less any expenses and income payments.

*How long have charitable gift annuities been available?*

Gift annuities are the oldest charitable giving program, having been in use for over 150 years.

*How is the payout rate determined?*

The payout rate is determined by your age at the time of the gift. The older you are, the more income the foundation can agree to pay.

*Am I, the donor, entitled to a current charitable income tax deduction?*

You can claim an income tax deduction for the portion of the gift

# Chap. 7: Estate Planning / Retirement Plans    439

annuity that represents the charitable gift. The tax deduction is claimed in the year the gift is made; however, if income is insufficient to use the entire deduction in one year, the unused portion can be carried forward for an additional 5 years.

### 🖎 *Are there any other tax benefits?*

In most cases, part of each payment is tax-free, increasing each payment's after-tax value. The tax-free portion is greatest when the annuity is funded with cash. If you give appreciated property, some of the income you receive will be treated as a partial capital gain.

### 🖎 *May I use stock, real estate, and other assets to fund my gift annuity?*

Yes, if you have a long-term appreciated asset, selling that asset would create a large capital gain tax liability for you. If you leave this valuable asset to your heirs, it becomes subject to high federal estate taxes. With a charitable gift annuity this asset can help neutralize those taxes and provide a tax-favored income to you for the rest of your life.

For example, say Mrs. Baker, age 75, bought some stock several years ago for $5000. Today, that stock has grown in value to $50,000, but is only paying a 2 percent dividend, or $1000 a year. Mrs. Baker would like to have additional income. By donating the stock in exchange for a gift annuity, she achieves the following:

- Mrs. Baker receives an annuity payment of $4500 per year (over 4.5 times more income than before!), of which 55.5 percent is a tax-free return of principal.

- The gift provides a charitable tax deduction of $20,029. Presuming she is in the 31 percent tax bracket, the tax savings is $6209. This means the effective rate of return is 11.4 percent.

440

- She receives a partial bypass of capital gains with tax savings of up to $3605.
- Probate costs and federal estate taxes are avoided.

### *Will I save on capital gain tax?*

If your gift was an appreciated asset, the capital gain tax is taxed each year over your projected life expectancy. Since this tax is spread out over your life and you receive some tax-free income, the transfer of highly appreciated property into a charitable gift annuity can generate very favorable financial results for both you and the charity.

### *When will I start receiving income from this gift annuity?*

That's your decision. You can begin receiving it in the following month after the assets you donate are transferred to the foundation, or you can defer it to a later date if you prefer. Deferring the income until the time you reach a lower tax bracket may bring the best results.

### *How much income can I earn with my annuity?*

The amount of your income will be based on guidelines set forth by the American Council of Gift Annuities and the amount and type of asset donated.

### *Can I outlive my funds?*

No. Your payment is guaranteed by the foundation for as long as you live.

### *Will gift annuity payments affect my Social Security?*

No, your annuity payments will not affect your Social Security

# Chap. 7: Estate Planning / Retirement Plans    441

payments. In fact, it may enhance your payments. Discuss this with your financial planner and accountant.

*Can I make additional withdrawals from the gift annuity?*

No, but you can make additional donations to increase your income and tax benefits.

*What happens to my income when I die?*

If you establish a joint-survivor annuity, then your beneficiary would be paid the income for life.

*Why are rates lower for a two-life annuity?*

The combined life expectancies of two annuitants are greater than a single life expectancy. That means payments will be made for a longer period of time in a two-life annuity, so the overall rate of payment for a two-life annuity will usually be slightly lower; however, though the rate is lower, the combined payout may be greater than the original donation.

# appendix A

## The Contributory Book Series and Protocol for *Ways and Means*

*Eileen Sacco, Managing Editor*

### HISTORY OF THE CONTRIBUTORY BOOK SERIES

With the publication of the first edition of *Wealth Enhancement and Preservation*, in 1995, the Institute formally established its Contributory Book Series, for which many highly regarded professionals from all over the United States participated in the creation of a comprehensive book on financial planning. In 1996, the Institute published a second edition of *Wealth Enhancement and Preservation*, which incorporated more research from ten additional contributing authors. It next invited a select group of members from the National Network of Estate Planning Attorneys to participate in a similar research project, which culminated in 1996 with the publication of *Legacy: Plan, Protect, and Preserve Your*

443

*Estate,* with eighty-seven contributors. *Legacy* focused on the most commonly asked questions about estate, business, and tax planning. Next, in December 1998, the Institute published *Generations: Planning Your Legacy,* a reconceptualization of *Legacy*—featuring up-to-date planning and more comprehensive questions and answers—with forty-nine new contributors.

One of the most complex and, thus, misunderstood planning areas for most Americans is that of retirement planning. In 1997, the Institute launched its first cross-discipline endeavor to bring together the expertise and experience of both the estate and financial planning professions to assist the public in understanding how to plan properly for retirement *and* how to coordinate the results of those efforts with their estate planning. *Ways and Means: Maximize the Value of Your Retirement Savings* is the result of that research project.

The objectives of each book in the series are:

- To be the largest research project of its kind that will be recognized as professionally unique in both its focus and scope

- To ascertain the critical planning questions that clients are asking their professional advisors nationwide and the precise answers of those advisors

- To publish a meaningful text that will ensure the readers that they can get immediate assistance from professionals on the basis of the planning concepts and strategies learned from the book

- To heighten the public's understanding of the knowledge and contributions that highly experienced financial advisors and attorneys bring into the planning and investing lives of their clients

- To improve the quality of financial and estate planning services offered by professionals to clients by sharing the ideas and techniques of a number of authorities in a highly condensed and user-friendly form

## APP. A: CONTRIBUTORY SERIES AND PROTOCOL    445

- To be recognized as a major contribution to the estate and financial planning literature

The Institute staff invested many hundreds of hours in establishing the protocol for the original *Wealth Enhancement and Preservation* research project and have diligently adhered to that protocol in all subsequent contributory book projects.

## PROTOCOL

### Definition of "Authority" or "Expert"

The Institute defines an *authority* or *expert* as an outstanding professional who is technically competent, is an effective communicator, and has a proven record of meeting his or her clients' needs.

### Research Protocol

As with all the previous contributory books, the first step in following the protocol was to create the "Research Questionnaire" for *Ways and Means,* which is an outline of potential topics for the final book, organized in a cohesive chapter format. However, every contributing author is encouraged to provide his or her own input outside the parameters of the "Research Questionnaire." Based upon logistical considerations of time, demanding schedules, and the need to eliminate as much repetition as possible, the Institute established a protocol of a minimum of twenty-five and a maximum of thirty questions and answers from each contributing author.

## Prospective Contributors

### *Financial planning professionals*

The Institute began its search for financial planning authorities across the nation as follows:

- The Institute contacted the members of the National Network of Estate Planning Attorneys and asked each of them to recommend a financial planning professional: one whom he or she had worked with and considered to be the best candidate for the project.
- The Institute contacted the expert financial planners who had participated in *Wealth* and asked them whether they would like to participate in a research project focused on the topic of retirement planning.
- The Institute also asked these *Wealth* contributors to recommend other financial advisors whom they considered to be the best candidates for the project.

### *National Network member attorneys*

The National Network has two levels of members, primary and associate. The Institute invited only primary members in good standing of the National Network to participate.

### *Qualifying financial planning professionals*

When originally developing the protocol for *Wealth,* the Institute submitted its definition of authority and the objectives of the research project to trusted financial planning colleagues and asked them to design the criteria that would help the Institute not only identify potential contributors but also judge the level of their expertise and credentials. Based on the input of these colleagues, the Institute established criteria for an authority and developed an extensive "Application and Profile" for the financial planning professionals.

### Qualifying
### National Network member attorneys

Participation by attorneys in the contributory books (*Legacy, Generations,* and *Ways and Means*) has been limited to members of the National Network of Estate Planning Attorneys. The National Network is an affiliated organization of the Institute and was founded by Robert A. Esperti and Renno L. Peterson. Some of the Network attorneys are also Fellows of the Esperti Peterson Institute. When attorneys apply for membership in the Network, their references, credentials, and license status in their respective states are checked. After they become National Network members, the Network and the Institute track their attendance at Network-sponsored continuing legal education programs which are some of the most advanced and technical estate planning seminars available to attorneys in the country.

As such, the "Application and Profile" developed by the Institute for use with the attorney applicants to the research projects confirms their current good standing in their states and in the National Network and updates credentials obtained by the attorney since he or she became a Network member.

## Application Process

After receipt of an applicant's "Application and Profile," a member of the Institute's staff carefully reviews and grades the person on a number of criteria, which were appropriately weighted based on an internal system that Bob Esperti, Renno Peterson, and the Institute staff developed for the original *Wealth* project. The staff member preliminarily accepted or rejected the applicant based on the final score. Before the Institute finally accepted an applicant for the *Ways and Means* project, Rick Randall or Scot Overdorf,

448   App. A: Contributory Series and Protocol

editors of *Ways and Means,* interviewed the applicant by telephone. This interview allowed Rick or Scot to determine the level of knowledge each applicant had with regard to retirement planning and to satisfy Rick or Scot that the applicant was committed to the project and understood all its parameters. The interview also allowed the applicant to ask any additional questions that he or she had of the individuals who would be editing their research.

The Institute then mailed a second letter containing either a nonacceptance or an acceptance. For an acceptance, in addition to the letter, a package contained a "Contributing Authority and Author Agreement"; a "Research Questionnaire"; and specifications for submitting a photograph, a personalized introduction, and biographical information.

The applicants who were ultimately accepted into the *Ways and Means* project submitted a total of 1350 questions and answers amounting to over 800 manuscript pages. The Institute staff combined and organized the research from all the contributing authors by "Research Questionnaire" category and delivered it to Rick and Scot. They read the research questions and answers, combined similar material, eliminated those questions and answers that were *not* common to a majority of the contributors, and edited the remaining questions and answers to provide the most cohesive and understandable questions and answers that appear in this text.

The Institute provided a working manuscript to each contributing author for purposes of review. In this way, the Institute ascertained the validity of the responses and added to the quality of the final text, and contributors were able to increase the level of their participation in the research project. A number of contributing authors provided a series of subsequent edits to the working manuscript.

The logistics of a Contributory Book Series project is daunting, to say the least. To initiate the project; create the materials for the invitees, applicants, and contributing authors; follow up on all of the invitations; collect and track all the necessary informa-

# App. A: Contributory Series and Protocol 449

tion, including the questions and answers; and then turn the material into a book calls for an extraordinary level of organization and commitment from the contributors, editors, the Institute, and its staff. In fact, this brief overview of the process does not do it justice simply because the volume of information and protocol developed for these projects consisted of hundreds of pages of material and thousands of hours of effort. The Institute is proud of the degree of professionalism displayed by all participants in the creation and completion of *Ways and Means.*

# appendix B

## Contributing Authors

**Rock W. Allen, J.D.**
Rock W. Allen & Associates
541 Main Street
Longmont, CO 80501
Phone (303) 774-1976
Fax (303) 682-9633
e-mail: rock.allen.law@internetmci.com


**Lois Anthonisen, CFP**
Anthonisen Financial Services
17450 South Halsted Street, Suite 2SW
Homewood, IL 60430
Phone (708) 957-2121
Fax (708) 957-2154
e-mail: anthonis@theramp.net

### Martin Anthonisen

Anthonisen Financial Services
17450 South Halsted Street, Suite 2SW
Homewood, IL 60430
Phone (708) 957-2121
Fax (708) 957-2154
e-mail: anthonis@theramp.net

### Joel R. Baker, CPhD

FFR Financial & Insurance Services, L.L.C.
P.O. Box 66
560 McMurray Road
Buellton, CA 93427
Phone (805) 688-8562
Fax (805) 688-2985
e-mail: ffrllc@silcom.com

### Autumn Corns Barber, J.D.

Executive Financial Group
305 Ann Street, Suite 405
Frankfort, KY 40601
Phone (502) 875-0037
Fax (502) 227-8957

### Lemuel M. Bargeron, CLU, CFP

First Financial Resources
250 South Tennessee Street
Cartersville, GA 30120
Phone (770) 386-2491
Fax (770) 386-4486

### Michael R. Bascom, J.D.

Coyle, Bascom & Bergman, P.C.
1000 Cambridge Square, Suite C
Alpharetta, GA 30004
Phone (770) 650-9670
Fax (770) 650-6670

## App. B: Contributing Authors

**Norman H. Bevan, MSFS, CLU, ChFC, AEP**
First Financial Resources
2777 Allen Parkway, Suite 1122
Houston, TX 77019
Phone (713) 526-6914
Fax (713) 529-0226
e-mail: norm@normbevan.com

**Gerard T. Breitner, CFP, ChFC, CLU, MSFS**
Excomp Asset Management Ltd.
40 West 57th Street
New York, NY 10019
Phone (212) 245-7200
Fax (212) 245-1155

**Chris L. Brisendine, J.D.**
The Brisendine Law Firm, P.C.
205 Corporate Center Drive, Suite B
Stockbridge, GA 30281
Phone (770) 507-8818
Fax (770)506-6880
*and*
One Live Oak Center
3475 Lenox Road, NE, Suite 400
Atlanta, GA 30326
Phone (404) 238-0567
e-mail: kbrisendine@mindspring.com

**David A. Carpenter, J.D.**
Law Offices of David Carpenter
5555 East 71st Street, Suite 6300
Tulsa, OK 74136-6549
Phone (918) 481-0877
Fax (918) 481-6242
e-mail: dac@webtek.com

### Michael J. Chapman, CFP
NatCity Investments, Inc.
251 North Illinois Street, Suite 500
Indianapolis, IN 46204
Phone (317) 686-3552
Fax (317) 686-3550
e-mail: michael_chapman@natcity.com


### Teresa H. Cherry, CPA, CFP
Cherry & Associates, Inc.
First Bank Plaza, Suite 306
Lake Zurich, IL 60047
Phone (847) 550-0515
Fax (847) 550-1620
e-mail: IFP29@aol.com


### Terry R. Cole, M.B.A, CFP
Senior Financial Advisors, Inc.
11911 NE 1st Street, Suite 312
Bellevue, WA 98005
Phone (425) 635-0600
Fax (425) 635-0056
e-mail: tcole@sfai.net


### Keith A. Colson, RIA
Roundy, Colson & Sivulich, LLC
7090 South Union Park Avenue, Suite 540
Salt Lake City, UT 84093
Phone (801) 561-7500
Fax (801) 561-7577
e-mail: rcs@aros.net

## App. B: Contributing Authors

**Richard F. DeFluri, CIMC, RFC**
Pennsylvania Financial Group
270 Walker Drive
P.O. Box 259
State College, PA 16804
Phone (800) 253-3760
Fax (814) 231-2276
e-mail: defluri-shute@pfginc.com

**Curt W. Ferguson, J.D.**
The Estate Planning Center
401B West Main
P.O. Box 418
Salem, IL 62881
Phone (618) 548-3729
Fax (618) 548-3585
e-mail: flurcal@accessus.net

**Jeffrey A. Forrest, ChFC, CFP, MS, MSFS**
Wealth Enhancement & Preservation, L.L.C.
1177 Marsh Street, Suite 200
San Luis Obispo, CA 93401
Phone (805) 547-1177
Fax (805) 547-1625
e-mail: jeffstar1@aol.com
http://www.Wealth-Enhancement.com

**Frederick H. Goldinov, J.D., LL.M.**
Law Offices of Frederick H. Goldinov
6619 North Scottsdale Road
Scottsdale, AZ 85250
Phone (602) 948-6713
Fax (602) 948-6775
e-mail: FHG111@aol.com

### Joseph M. Gordon, CFP, CLU, ChFC, APM-ASPA
Praxis Consulting, Inc.
3101 Industrial Drive, Suite 204
Raleigh, NC 27609
Phone (919) 832-8311
 (800) 222-8783
Fax (919) 832-2693
e-mail: joegordon@praxisconsultinginc.com


### Steven W. Graber, J.D.
Steven W. Graber, P.A.
3818 East Stroud Road
Hutchinson, KS 67501
Phone (316) 665-0077
Fax (316) 665-0620


### Carl P. Grissom, CLU
Carl P. Grissom Organization
8191 College Parkway, Suite 206
Fort Myers, FL 33919
Phone (941) 437-6800
Fax (941) 437-6228
e-mail: grissomone@aol.com


### Lewis B. Hampton, J.D.
Hagen, Dye, Hirschy & DiLorenzo, P.C.
888 S.W. Fifth Avenue, 10th Floor
Portland, OR 97204-2024
Phone (503) 222-1812
Fax (503) 274-7979
e-mail: lhampton@hagendye.com

## APP. B: CONTRIBUTING AUTHORS

**David P. Herrmann, CFP**
Herrmann Financial Services, Inc.
370 Diablo Road, Suite 201
Danville, CA 94526
Phone (925) 831-0200
Fax (925) 831-8957
e-mail: hfinvest@pacbell.net

**N. Douglas Hostetler, CLU, ChFC, CFP**
Hostetler & Associates, LLC
10400 Little Patuxent Parkway, Suite 200
Columbia, MD 21044
Phone (410) 740-3303
Fax (410) 740-0716
e-mail: dhostetler@pfinancial.com

**Darrel E. Johnson, J.D.**
White & Johnson, L.L.P.
701 Vilymaca
Post Office Drawer 0
Elkhart, KS 67950
Phone (316) 697-2163
Fax (316) 697-2165

**Reid S. Johnson, MSFS, MSM, CIMC, CFP, CEBS, ChFC, CLU, RHU**
The Planning Group, Inc.
8777 North Gainey Center Drive, Suite 265
Scottsdale, AZ 85258
Phone (602) 596-1580
Fax (602) 596-2165
e-mail: reidj@futureone.com

## Stuart B. Kalb, J.D., LL.M., Taxation
Kalb & Peck, P.L.L.C.
5728 LBJ Freeway, Suite 400
Dallas, TX 75240
Phone (972) 490-8383
Fax (972) 490-8390
e-mail: kalbs@airmail.net


## Ronald W. Kelemen, CFP
The H Group, Inc.
960 Liberty Street SE, Suite 210
Salem, OR 97302
Phone (503) 371-3333
Fax (503) 371-1410
e-mail: ron@kelemen.com
http://www.kelemen.com


## Robert L. Keys, CFP
Interwest Financial Group, Inc.
4650 SW Macadam Avenue, Suite 400
Portland, OR 97201
Phone (503) 224-0782
Fax (503) 224-0787
e-mail: bkeys@pcg-ifg.com


## E. Michael Kilbourn, CLU, ChFC, CCIM, CEP
Kilbourn Associates
3033 Riviera Drive, Suite 202
Naples, FL 34103
Phone (941) 261-1888
Fax (941) 643-7017
e-mail: wpn@sprynet.com

## App. B: Contributing Authors

**A. Gary Kovacs**
Harris, Webb & Garrison
5599 San Felipe, Suite 301
Houston, TX 77056
Phone (713) 993-4627
Fax (713) 993-4699

**Paul R. Lang**
Investment Representative Edward Jones
10892 Crabapple Road, Suite 201
Roswell, GA 30075
Phone (770) 998-0202
Fax (770) 998-3024
e-mail: lang3@mindspring.com

**Andrew J. Lewis, AAMS, CMFC**
1300 I Street NW, Suite 1100W
Washington, D.C. 20005
Phone (202) 336-5078
  (703) 719-9126
  (800) 382-9989
Fax (202) 336-5095
e-mail: alewis1@erols.com

**Eugene T. Linkous, Jr., J.D.**
The Linkous Law Offices
P.O. Box 2807
210 Duncan Hill Road
Hendersonville, NC 28793
Phone (828) 693-7681
Fax (828) 692-8555
e-mail: eugene@linkous.net

## App. B: Contributing Authors

**Richard H. Linsday, CLU, ChFc, AEP**
Planned Estate Services
70 South Lake Avenue, Suite 1050
Pasadena, CA 91101
Phone (626) 356-9600
Fax (626) 356-1334
e-mail: richard_linsday@phl.com

**Stephen J. Livens, J.D., CPA, MBA**
The Livens Law Firm
2516 Harwood Road
Bedford, TX 76021
Phone (817) 545-3425
Fax (817) 545-9847
e-mail: trustlwyr@aol.com

**W. Aubrey Morrow, CFP**
Financial Designs Ltd.
5075 Shoreham Place, Suite 230
San Diego, CA 92122-5929
Phone (619) 597-1980
Fax (619) 546-1106
e-mail: morrow@prodigy.net

**Peter S. Myers, J.D.**
Myers Law Firm
260 California Street, Suite 801
San Francisco, CA 94111
Phone (415) 951-8100
Fax (415) 951-8700

## App. B: Contributing Authors

**Ketra A. Mytich, J.D.**
Ketra A. Mytich, Ltd.
Commerce Bank Building
416 Main Street, Suite 815
Peoria, IL 61602-1103
Phone (309) 673-1805
Fax (309) 673-3700
e-mail: kam@est-planning.com
http://www.est-planning.com

**Bret A. Overdorf, CPA, CFP**
Bret A. Overdorf, CPA, PC
5952 Alexandria Pike
Anderson, IN 46012
Phone (765) 642-9997
Fax (765) 642-8966

**Richard L. Overdorf, CLU**
Overdorf Financial Services, Inc.
5952 Alexandria Pike
Anderson, IN 46012
Phone (765) 642-9997
Fax (765) 642-8966

**Scot W. Overdorf, J.D.**
5913 Camelback Court
Indianapolis, IN 46250
Phone (317) 845-5444
Fax (317) 845-5443
e-mail: soverdorf@iquest.net

### David C. Partheymuller, CFP
Normandy Investment Services, Inc.
575 Union Boulveard, Suite 101
Lakewood, CO 80228-1240
Phone (303) 716-2700
Fax (303) 716-2734


### Laurie S. Peck, J.D.
Kalb & Peck, P.L.L.C.
5728 LBJ Freeway, Suite 400
Dallas, TX 75240
Phone (972) 490-8383
Fax (972) 490-8390
e-mail: lspeck@airmail.net


### Carl Peterson, CFP
Money Resources Inc.
Baltej Pavilion, Suite 210
415 Chalan San Antonio Road
Tamuning, Guam 96911
Phone (671) 646-0000
Fax (671) 649-0014
e-mail: invest@moneyresourcesinc.com
http://www.moneyresourcesinc.com


### John S. Pfarr, J.D.
Law Offices of John S. Pfarr
120 Wayland Avenue
Providence, RI 02906
Phone (401) 274-4100
Fax (401) 831-3837
e-mail: jpfarr@idt.net

### Steven Pruiett, CLU, CFP, ChFC

Investment Planners, Inc.
201 North Main Street
Decatur, IL 62523
Phone (217) 425-6340
Fax (217) 425-9581
e-mail: stevep@investmentplanners.com

### Chester M. Przybylo, J.D., MBA

Law Offices of Przybylo and Kubiatowski
5339 North Milwaukee Avenue
Chicago, IL 60630
Phone (773) 631-2525
Fax (773) 631-7101
e-mail: trustnow@mcs.net

### Richard L. Randall, J.D.

Randall & Galbraith, P.C.
10333 North Meridian, Suite 375
Indianapolis, IN 46290
Phone (317) 574-9911
Fax (317) 574-9922
e-mail: randall_law@iquest.net

### Steven P. Riley, J.D.

Law Office of Steven P. Riley, P.A.
3333 Henderson Boulevard, Suite 150
Tampa, FL 33609
Phone (813) 877-4357
Fax (813) 875-2013

### John S. Tuve, CFP
Tuve Investments, Inc.
227 East San Marnan Drive
Waterloo, IA 50702
Phone (319) 235-0075
Fax (319) 235-7419
e-mail: jtuve@aol.com

### Clifford F. Veatch, J.D.
Spear, Holliday & Veatch
201 North Cherry
P.O. Box 1000
Olathe, KS 66051-1000
Phone (913) 782-1000
   (800) 793-6385
Fax (913) 782-0852
e-mail: est8plan@ix.netcom.com

### John C. Watson, III, CLU, ChFC, AEP, RFC
823 North Elm Street, Suite 100
Greensboro, NC 27401
Phone (336) 379-8207
   (800) 822-1086
Fax (336) 379-8349
e-mail: jcw-3@mailexcite.com

### Richard G. Wohltman, J.D.
Law Offices - Richard G. Wohltman, P.C.
908 King Street, Suite 200
Alexandria, VA 22314
Phone (703) 548-4990
Fax (703) 548-3181
e-mail: trustlaw@rgwpc.com

**Bruce M. Yates, CFM**
Appropriate Balance Financial Services, Inc.
12737 Bel-Red Road, Suite 200
Bellevue, WA 98005
Phone (425) 451-0499
Fax (425) 451-1316
e-mail: abfsi@aol.com

# index

accountant, role of, 33
advisors, working with, 31–43
   accountant, 33
   attorney, 38–39
   financial planner, 33–38
   investment counselor, 39–43
AM Best, 268
annuities, 247–287
   charitable gift, 438–441
   credit ratings of, 267, 268
   early withdrawals from, 274
   exchanges of, 271–273
   fixed, 261–262, 266–267
   general facts about, 248–257
   as gifts, 281–284
   indexed, 267–270
   investment options for,
      261–270
   IRA, 124–125
   multiple, 270–271
   payout options for, 260–261

   private, 249–240
   private pension for, 237
   qualified, 284–287
   for retirement income,
      256–257
   rollovers of, 271–273
   surrender of, 273–274
   tax aspects of, 274–278,
      281–284
   tax planning with, 278–281
   tax-sheltered, 112–114
   types of, 257–270
   variable, 262–267
applicable exclusion amount,
   377–379
asset allocation, 155–159
   portfolio mix and, 196–198
   strategies for, 202–204
asset diversification, 153–155
   allocation and, 158
   in portfolio, 195–196

468 INDEX

strategies for, 201–202
asset protection:
 IRAs and, 127–130
 with qualified plans, 90–93
assets:
 classes of, 154–155
 correlation of, 167
 liquidity and, 165–166
 probate and, 386
 valuation of, for estate tax, 376–377
 *See also* investments
attorney, role of, 38–39

bankruptcy:
 IRAs and, 129
 qualified plans and, 91
beneficiaries (retirement plan), 322–334
 changing, 332–333
 charities as, 369–370, 420–423
 children as, 410–411
 contingent, 325–326
 CRT as, 427–428, 430–434
 designated, 326–330
  trust as, 329–330, 366–367
 disclaimers and, 413–417
 estate as, 370–371
 family trust as, 390–392
 income tax and, 402–403
 irrevocable trust as, 129–130
 living trust as, 386–388, 411
 MDIB rule and, 330–332

prenuptial agreements and, 396
primary death, 322–325
QTIP trust as, 394–395
rollovers by, 356–360
spousal consent and, 333–335
spouse as, 368–369, 388–389
stretch-out strategy for, 360–366
bonds, 167–172
 callable, 168–169
 convertible, 175–177, 229
 investment strategies for, 217–224
 municipal, 172
 mutual funds vs., 231–232
 ratings of, 171–172
 risk and, 169–172, 210–214
 stocks vs., 228, 229
 tax-free vs. taxable, 239–240
 zero coupon, 220–222
bonus plan, 97–98

capital gain tax, 102, 440
 dividend income and, 238–239
 home-sale exemption for, 58–59
 new rates of, 238
cash-or-deferred arrangement (CODA), 69, 70
Certified Financial Planner (CFP), 35, 36

# Index 469

charitable planning, 417–441
   after-death gifts, 420–426
   with gift annuity, 438–441
   lifetime gifts in, 417–420
   with CRT, 426–438
charitable remainder trust
   (CRT), 426–438
   types of, 427, 435
CODA (cash-or-deferred
   arrangement), 69, 70
collateral-assignment split
   dollar, 106
consumer price index, 51
convertibles, 175–177
   investment strategies for, 229
corporate/business-entity
   profit-sharing plan,
   66–76
correlation, asset, 167
creditors, *see* asset protection;
   bankruptcy
CRT (charitable remainder
   trust), 426–438
custodial IRA, 120–121

debt, consumer, 54
deferred-compensation plan,
   94–95
defined asset fund, 188
defined-benefit plan, 63–65
defined-contribution plan,
   64–65
deflation, risk of, 209
disclaimers, 413–417

distributions (retirement
   plan), 289–371
   if death after required
    beginning date,
    353–366
   if death before required
    beginning date,
    335–338
   early:
    from deductible IRAs,
     291–299
    income tax and, 309
    from qualified plans,
     301–309
    from Roth IRAs, 299–300
   effect of, on estate planning,
    375–376
   lump-sum, 310
   minimum, 312–322
    calculating, 338–353
    life expectancy and,
     317–322
   spousal consent rules and,
    333–335
dividend reinvestment plan,
   175, 225
"dogs of the Dow," 174
dollar cost averaging, 166
Duff and Phelps, 268

EAFE index, 173–174
early retirement, 24
education IRA, 140–141
employee stock purchase plan,
   99–104

# 470 INDEX

employer-sponsored
retirement plans,
61–114
types of, 62–63
*See also* nonqualified plans;
qualified plans
endorsement split dollar,
107
equity split dollar, 106
estate planning, 373–441
and retirement goals, 18
retirement planning and,
373–376
*See also specific topics, e.g.,*
beneficiaries; charitable
planning
estate tax, *see* federal estate tax
exemption equivalent, 378

family trust, 380–382, 384
retirement plans and,
389–392
federal estate tax, 376–384,
404–417
annuities and, 280–282
applicable exclusion
amount, 377–379
credits for, 378, 379
deductions for, 377, 379
exemption equivalent, 378
minimizing, 379–384,
390–391
noncitizen spouse and, 400
planning for, 404–412
disclaimers, 413–417

fees:
of financial planners, 36–37
of investment counselors,
42–43
mutual fund, 182–184
12b-1, 182
financial goals, 14–21, 26–28
amount needed for, 16–17,
43–46
estate planning and, 18
near-retirement, 26–28
setting, 14–21
*See also* income analysis
financial planner, role of,
33–38
financial risk, 144
401(k), SIMPLE, *see* SIMPLE
plans
401(k) profit-sharing plan,
69–76
advantages of, 70
contributions to, 71–73
creation of, 70–71
features of, 69
investments of, 75–76
loans from, 73
withdrawals from, 73–75
403(b) plan, 113–114

generation-skipping tax planning, 412–413
ghost IRA, 360–365
gift tax:
annuities and, 282–283
noncitizen spouse and, 400

# INDEX

471

gifts:
  annuities as, 281–284
  *See also* charitable planning
goals:
  investment portfolio and,
    192–198
  *See also* planning for
    retirement

ILIT (irrevocable life insur-
    ance trust), 405–406,
    436–437
incentive stock option plan,
    100–104
income, postretirement:
  inflation and, 51–53, 57–58
  investment portfolio and,
    195
  sources of additional, 49–51
  NIMCRUTs as, 435–436
income analysis, 43–59
  before retirement, 43–56
    cash-flow analysis in,
      46–48, 56
    factors in, 44–45
    projections for, 48–56
  during retirement, 56–59
income in respect of decedent,
    402
income tax:
  annuities and, 274–284
  deferred-compensation
    plans and, 94–95
  family trust and, 389–392
  403(b) plans and, 114

IRAs and, 116–118
  qualified plans and, 65–66
  retirement plan beneficiaries
    and, 402–403
  SEPs and, 88
  split dollar plans and, 107
  stock options and, 100–104
individual retirement account,
    *see* IRAs
inflation:
  investment return and,
    163–165
  bond yield, 204
  as investment risk,
    145–146, 150–151
  strategies for reducing,
    207–214
  postretirement income and,
    51–53, 57–58
Institute of Certified Financial
    Planners, 36
interest rate risk, 145
International Association for
    Financial Planning, 36
international investments,
    235–236, 241
investment (process), 143–245
  growth style in, 174–175
  model portfolio for, 167
  philosophy of, 188–199
  principles of, 144–167
    asset allocation, 155–159
    asset diversification,
      153–155
    inflation, 163–165
    liquidity, 165–166

market timing, 166
other, 166–167
return, 160–163
risk, 144–153
strategies of, *see* investment
strategies
value style in, 174–175
*See also* investments
investment counselor, role of,
39–43
investment policy statement,
196–197
investment risk pyramid,
151–153
for asset allocation, 156–158
investment strategies, 188–241
asset allocation, 202–204
asset diversification,
201–202
inflation, 207–214
for IRAs and qualified
plans, 241–245
liquidity, 214–217
return, 204–207
risk, 199–201
for specific assets, 217–237
bonds, 217–224
convertibles, 229
life insurance, 236–237
mutual funds, 230–236
stocks, 224–228
for taxes, 237–241
investments:
developing portfolio of,
193–198
international, 235–236

*See also* investment; *specific
investments, e.g.,* bonds
IRA (qualified plan):
SEP-, 88–90
SIMPLE, *see* SIMPLE plans
IRAs (individual retirement
accounts), 115–141
accounts vs. annuities,
124–125
asset protection and,
127–130
beneficiaries of, *see*
beneficiaries
contributions to, 118–120
custodial, 120–121
deductible, 117–118,
130–134
contributions to, 131–133
features of, 130–131
income limits for, 132,
133
withdrawals from, 134,
291–299
distributions from, *see*
distributions
education, 140–141
investments for, 125–126,
241–245
living trust and, 385–388,
411
loans from, 126–127
nondeductible, 117–118
Roth, 117–118, 134–137
contributions to, 136–137
features of, 134–135
rollovers to, 137–140

## I N D E X     473

withdrawals from, 137
self-directed, 122–124
spousal rollovers and,
356–359
stretch-out strategy for,
360–366
trust, 120–121
types of, 116–118
irrevocable trust, 129–130
irrevocable life insurance trust
(ILIT), 405–406,
436–437

life insurance:
investment strategies for,
236–237
key person, 96, 236
split-dollar plans and,
104–112
*See also* irrevocable life
insurance trust
liquidity, asset, 165–166
strategies for, 214–217
living trust, revocable,
384–388
retirement plans and,
385–388, 411

marital deduction, unlimited,
379–380, 393, 400
marital trust, 380, 382–384,
393
market risk, 145
volatility and, 150–151

market timing, 166, 191–192
Medicare, cutbacks in, 3
money management, 159, 166
money purchase pension plan,
76–79
Moody's:
annuity ratings, 268
bond ratings, 171–172, 224
*Morningstar,* 230–233
mortgage:
reverse, 50
whether to pay down,
54–55, 216–217
multigenerational IRA,
360–365
mutual funds, 177–188
classes of, 184–185
investment strategies for,
230–236
load vs. no-load, 182–183,
232–233
open-end vs. closed-end,
185–186
private pension for, 237
taxes on, 240
types of, 178–180

net income makeup charitable
remainder trust (NIM-
CRUT), 435–436
nonqualified plans, 62–63,
93–112
bonus, 97–98
deferred-compensation,
94–95

474 INDEX

Rabbi trusts as, 98–99
salary continuation, 95–97
split-dollar, 104–112
stock option, 99–104
nonqualified stock option
plan, 100

pension, private, 237
Pension Benefit Guaranty
Corp., 126
pension plans, *see* qualified
plans
perpetual IRA, 360–365
planning:
investment, 188–199
*See also* investment
strategies
for retirement, *see* planning
for retirement
for second marriages,
395–399
for spouse, 393–401
tax, 237–241
*See also specific taxes, e.g.,*
income tax; *specific
topics, e.g.,* annuities
planning for retirement, 1–31
estate planning and,
373–376
financial goals in, 14–21,
26–28
how to begin, 11–23
importance of, 2–4
lack of, reasons for, 7

psychological considerations
in, 21–23, 28–31
starting to save and, 6–10
when near retirement, 24–31
when to start, 4–6
prenuptial agreement, 396
private pension, 237
probate, 386
profit-sharing plan, 66–76
401(k), 69–76
traditional, 66–69
PS-58 cost, 105–106
psychological considerations,
21–23, 28–31
stress, 29–30

QDOT (qualified domestic
trust), 401–402
QTIP (qualified terminable
interest property) trust,
393–395, 398–399
qualified domestic trust
(QDOT), 401–402
qualified plans, 61–93
asset protection with, 90–93
beneficiaries of, *see*
beneficiaries
defined-benefit, 63–65
defined-contribution, 64–65
distributions from, *see*
distributions
income tax incentives with,
65–66
investments for, 241–245
living trust and, 385–388

money purchase pension,
76–79
profit-sharing, 66–76
401(k), 69–76
traditional, 66–69
savings incentive match
(SIMPLE), 79–88
simplified employee pension
(SEP), 88–90
spousal rollovers and,
356–359
vesting and, 66
QTIP (qualified terminable
interest property) trust,
393–395, 398–399

Rabbi trusts, 98–99
Restructuring and Reform Act
(1998):
and investments, 238–239,
241–242
and retirement plan
distributions, 289
and Roth IRAs, 138
retirement:
length of, 3–4
planning for, see planning
for retirement
"practice," 17
split, 30–31
working after, 49–51
*See also specific topics, e.g.,*
income
retirement income account,
114

retirement plans, *see*
employer-sponsored
retirement plans; IRAs
return, investment, 160–163
inflation and, 163–165
normal, on stock, 226
strategies for increasing,
204–207
reverse split-dollar plan,
110–112
risk, investment, 144–153
greatest, 150–151
long-term, 149–151
with specific assets, 151–153
strategies for reducing,
199–201
time horizon and, 148
types of, 144–146, 209–210
*See also specific investments,*
*e.g.,* bonds
risk pyramid, investment,
151–153
risk tolerance, 146–149
investment portfolio and,
195
rollovers:
of annuities, 271–273
of retirement plan funds,
356–360
to Roth IRA, 137–140
Roth IRA, 117–118, 134–137
Rule of 72, 161

salary continuation plan, 95–
97

## INDEX

sale-leaseback, 50
S&P, *see* Standard and Poor's
saving, 6–10
  establishing priorities for,
    9–10
savings incentive match plan,
    *see* SIMPLE plans
second marriages, planning
    for, 395–399
select executive retirement
    plan (SERP), 95–97
self-employed persons:
  planning and, 19
  SEP plan for, 88, 90
  SIMPLE plan and, 85
SEP (simplified employee
    pension) plan, 88–90
SEP-IRA, 88–90
SERP (select executive
    retirement plan), 95–97
SIMPLE (savings incentive
    match) plans, 79–88
  contributions to, 85–86
  creation of, 82–85
  features of, 79–82
    SIMPLE 401(k), 81–82
    SIMPLE IRA, 79–81
  investments of, 87–88
  loans from, 86–87
  withdrawals from, 87
simplified employee pension
    (SEP) plan, 88–90
"social capital," 428–429
Social Security:
  benefit estimate of, 48–49
  noncitizen spouse and, 401

shaky future of, 193
unfunded liability of, 2–3
when to begin taking, 59
Society of Financial Service
    Professionals, 36
split-dollar plan, 104–112
  reverse, 110–112
  types of, 106–107
spousal rollover, 356–359
spouse, planning for, 393–401
  with marital trust, 380,
    382–384, 393
  noncitizen spouse, 399–402
  with QTIP trust, 393–395
  second marriages and,
    395–399
Standard and Poor's (S&P):
  annuity ratings, 268–269
  bond ratings, 171–172, 224
  500 index of, 173
stock option plan, 99–104
stocks, 172–175
  blue-chip, 225–226
  convertible, 175–177
  investment strategies for,
    224–228
  penny, 174
  preferred, 173
  risk and, 210–211
  stock mutual fund vs.,
    231–232, 234
stretch-out IRA, 360–365

tax-sheltered annuity (TSA),
    112–114

# INDEX

477

taxes:
  as investment risk, 146
  investment strategies for,
    237–241
  projecting, for retirement,
    53–54
  sale of home and, 58–59
  *See also specific taxes, e.g.,*
    income tax
Taxpayer Relief Act (1997):
  and capital gain tax, 102,
    238
  and education IRAs, 140
  and investments, 238–239,
    241–241
  and retirement plan
    distributions, 289
  and Roth IRAs, 117, 138
trust, *see specific trust, e.g.,*
  living trust
trust IRA, 120–121

TSA (tax-sheltered annuity),
  112–114

UIT (unit investment trust),
  188
unified tax credit, 378, 379
unit investment trust (UIT),
  188
unlimited marital deduction,
  379–380, 393
  noncitizen spouse and, 400

vested, defined, 66

wealth replacement trust, 436–
  437
wills, 386–387, 392